MENTAL HEALTH LAW

AUSTRALIA AND NEW ZEALAND
The Law Book Company Ltd.
Sydney : Melbourne : Perth

CANADA AND U.S.A.
The Carswell Company Ltd.
Agincourt, Ontario

INDIA
N. M. Tripathi Private Ltd.
Bombay
and
Eastern Law House Private Ltd.
Calcutta and Delhi
M.P.P. House
Bangalore

ISRAEL
Steimatzky's Agency Ltd.
Jerusalem : Tel Aviv : Haifa

MALAYSIA : SINGAPORE : BRUNEI
Malayan Law Journal (Pte.) Ltd.
Singapore

PAKISTAN
Pakistan Law House
Karachi

MENTAL HEALTH LAW

SECOND EDITION

Brenda M. Hoggett M.A.
of Gray's Inn and the Northern Circuit, Barrister
Reader in Law, University of Manchester

LONDON
SWEET & MAXWELL
1984

First Edition   1976
Second Edition   1984

Published by
Sweet & Maxwell Limited of
11, New Fetter Lane, London
Computerset by Promenade Graphics Limited, Cheltenham
Printed in Great Britain by
Robert Hartnoll Limited, Bodmin, Cornwall

British Library Cataloguing in Publication Data

Hoggett, Brenda M.
  Mental health law.—2nd ed.
  1. Great Britain. Mental Health Act 1983
  2. Mental health laws—England
  I. Title
  344.204'44   KD3412.A3/

  ISBN 0–421–30220–8

H6136/3/2

Preface

A very great deal has happened to mental health law since the first edition of this work was written in 1975. The law itself has become much more complex, but it has also become still more essential for all the professionals involved, medical, social work and legal, to have a thorough understanding of what the law says and what it means. Social workers must be trained for their new responsibilities. Doctors, nurses and others in the clinical professions must be quite clear about their powers in the treatment and control of hospital and other patients. Lawyers must know the context in which they represent patients before mental health review tribunals and elsewhere. In catering for all of these, the text has inevitably lengthened and the casualty has been the Appendix on the Scottish law which appeared in the first edition. I am sorry about this and hope to remedy it elsewhere.

It has been impossible to acknowledge the source of every item mentioned in the text, although I have tried to indicate the major contributors. The bibliography gives a more complete list. But I am particularly grateful to the Department of Health and Social Security and to the Welsh Office, who have supplied me with the figures to update the tables contained in the 1981 White Paper on the Reform of Mental Health Legislation and with a great deal of other helpful information. I should also like to acknowledge with thanks the help of the Home Office, the many Mental Health Review Tribunals which I have visited, and a great many colleagues and students in social work, psychiatry and the law. Amongst these, I owe a particular debt to Rosemary Morrison, Martin Wasik, and above all to David Kenny, who undertook the onerous task of reading the typescript for me. Sweet and Maxwell have been as helpful and understanding as ever. None of these, of course, is to be blamed for any errors or deficiencies, or for the views expressed, which are entirely my own.

I have tried to state the law in most respects as it was at September 30, 1983, when the Mental Health Act 1983 came into force. But in relation to mental nursing homes, residential homes, and certain other aspects of community care, account has been taken of the law as it will be once the Health and Social Services and Social Security Adjudications Act 1983 is implemented, although unfortunately the relevant regulations are not yet available. I have also dealt with the position of approved social workers and with the courts' powers to remand to hospital and make interim hospital orders, although these are not yet in force. In this way, I hope that the book is as comprehensive as possible.

This is a law book written by a lawyer. I have not attempted to deal with the purely medical aspects of mental disorder and many non-medical readers may find it useful to consult a simple source on psychiatry. I have found particularly helpful the World Health Organisation's *Glossary and Guide to Mental Disorders,* the *Concise Encyclopedia of Psychiatry*, by Leigh, Pare and Marks, and the *Notes on Psychiatry*, by Ingram, Timbury and Mowbray. Once again, it is not their fault if I have got it wrong.

Brenda Hoggett

December, 1983

Contents

Table of Cases

xi

Table of Statutes

Table of Statutory Instruments

Introduction

Mental health law serves a mass of conflicting interests and ideologies. The general public are no doubt suspicious that mental disorder may too readily be used as an excuse for criminal behaviour. But they forget that (at least since the abolition of the death penalty) the consequences may be just as severe for the patient and sometimes more so. One reason for this is the public outcry which greets any mistaken decision to set a mental patient free. We can all perceive the benefits in keeping mental patients in an institution out of harm's way, especially if this holds out some comforting hope of eventual improvement or cure. This probably explains why the Victorians were prepared to spend more public money on keeping patients in asylums than on keeping paupers in the workhouse. But it also explains why they wanted watertight guarantees against confinement of the wrong people. The fit pauper did not deserve it and the sane man did not want it. The resulting legalism was seen as a disaster for those who genuinely needed treatment.

Given the public attitudes which still surface from time to time, the Mental Health Act 1959 was little short of revolutionary. There had been such advances in treatment and in psychiatry that the medical profession were able to argue that both they and their patients should be set free from the straitjacket of the past. Henceforward, mental patients should be treated no differently from any others. They should be admitted to hospital without special formalities. It should still be possible to compel them to accept treatment if they refused to accept their doctors' advice, but this should be done with the minimum of formality and only when strictly necessary. Mentally disordered people who committed crimes should be able to be admitted to hospital for treatment in just the same circumstances as other patients who needed it. Once there, they should be treated just like those other patients, unless they were so dangerous that special safeguards were needed to protect the public. That apart, the length of time patients would spend in hospital, and the treatment they would receive while there, could safely be left in the hands of the medical profession. The patients undoubtedly benefitted from the new approach of psychiatry. But with hindsight the new law can be seen as just as liberating for the psychiatrists as it was for their patients. Freed from their duty to guard society's misfits and rejects in isolated barracks in the countryside, they could concentrate on their new-found power to cure the sick. Although accompanied by a policy of transferring as many patients as possible out into the community, this was an almost wholly medical and therapeutic approach to hospital admission and treatment.

In the 20 years which followed, it became clear that many of the patients formerly given asylum did not fit the new system. The 1959 Act assimilated the law relating to mental handicap with that relating to mental illness, but was mental handicap a medical problem at all? What was to happen to the chronic or psycho-geriatric patients who took up so many psychiatric beds which might have been filled by more treatable cases? Above all, should hospitals have to take people with inadequate, aggressive or irresponsible personalities whom society did not want but whom the courts were often anxious to send to hospital rather than to prison? As ordinary hospitals became more open, special hospitals filled up with patients who in the past would have easily been managed in an asylum, until eventually there was nowhere prepared to have them.

As the medical model showed itself more and more reluctant to provide for many whom society and the courts wanted it to provide, the model itself was increasingly challenged both in theory and in practice. Some of that challenge came from the "anti-psychiatrists" within the profession itself. They argued that mental illness was not an objective fact, but a label applied to behaviour which the psychiatrist regards as abnormal because of his own ideas about what is appropriate in any given situation. This mythical label, it is said, places the patient in complete subjection to the doctor, ruling out effective communication between them. Instead of helping the patient, it manipulates him for its own ends, by attempting to cure or control behaviour which only the system has defined as abnormal. Other challenges came from other professions who claimed an increasing role in understanding and treating the patient. These added to the distrust of institutional solutions and stressed the importance of social factors in the causation and identification of mental illness.

Despite the much-vaunted concern of the common lawyer for individual freedom, lawyers in this country played little part in all this ferment. On the other side of the Atlantic, however, they had woken up to the possibilities of the Constitution in controlling the activities of the "therapeutic state." A mass of research and litigation attempted to lay down acceptable criteria for the psychiatric deprivation of liberty, the procedural safeguards required, and the right to a minimum standard of treatment in return. The United Kingdom was still mainly concerned with the protection of society from the dangerous offender. This was the impetus for the Butler Committee on Mentally Abnormal Offenders which reported in 1975. But a series of scandals in mental hospitals had revealed that many mental patients were not dangerous at all, but a chronically under-privileged group who were particularly vulnerable to exploitation both in and out of hospital.

The National Association for Mental Health (MIND) began to subject the comfortable assumptions in the 1959 Act to an increasingly uncomfortable scrutiny. This was largely the work of an American lawyer, who produced their two influential studies of the Act in practice, with suggestions for reform largely in line with principles being developed in the United States (Gostin, 1975 and 1977). The DHSS set about reviewing the Act (1976 and 1978) and attempted to reconcile the various approaches of all the different professions and interests involved. The Mental Health Act 1983 has greatly improved procedural safeguards, but changed the underlying substance and purpose very little. The purpose is still to ensure that people suffering from mental disorder of almost any description can be given the care and treatment which the doctors and other professionals think that they need. But does this mean a return to the legalism of the past, in which the only people who benefit are the lawyers and the bureaucrats, while the patients are deprived of treatment and the hospital and community services are starved of resources? Or does it mean that lip-service is paid to procedure, while the substance of the therapeutic state is largely undisturbed? Or does it mean that in our pragmatic and non-doctrinal way, we have achieved the best of both worlds?

What follows is a textbook designed for all who have anything to do with mental patients, for social workers and others who care for them in the community but who may have to use compulsory powers, for doctors, nurses and other professionals concerned with their care in hospital, and for lawyers and advice workers who try to protect their interests. It tries to explain the arguments which lie behind the present state of the law and which may go on in the future. But it is not a work of philosophy committed to any particular point of view, except to the proper recognition of the status and needs of all concerned.

1 Hospital Admission: The Basic Scheme

The present law relating to the care and treatment of mentally disordered people in England and Wales is contained in the Mental Health Act 1983. This consolidated the Mental Health Act 1959 with the substantial amendments made by the Mental Health (Amendment) Act 1982. The 1959 Act followed the deliberations of the Royal Commission on the Law relating to Mental Illness and Mental Deficiency of 1954 to 1957, the Percy Commission. At the time, it constituted a revolutionary break with the traditions of the past. The provision on which that claim is based is now section 131(1) of the 1983 Act:

> "Nothing in this Act shall be construed as preventing a patient who requires treatment for mental disorder from being admitted to any hospital or mental nursing home in pursuance of arrangements made in that behalf and without any application, order or direction rendering him liable to be detained under this Act, or from remaining in any hospital or mental nursing home in pursuance of such arrangements after he has ceased to be so liable to be detained."

To appreciate just how revolutionary were those twin concepts, of informal admission to hospital for mental treatment and of the possibility of treatment in any type of hospital, it is necessary to take a brief look at the earlier attitude of the law.

1. *Out of Mind and Out of Sight*

In the early days, the only forms of mental disorder generally recognised were "lunacy" or "madness" and "idiocy." The common law allowed the confinement of the dangerously insane, those who seemed disposed to do mischief to themselves or others

5

(Lanham, 1974; see also Chapter 4), but not the harmlessly eccentric or weak-witted. The insane might be kept in conditions which are now thought appalling, and often subject to individual "mechanical restraint" (a euphemism for shackles, manacles, cages and the like). By the turn of the eighteenth and nineteenth centuries, a growing body of opinion was inspired by the more humane system of "moral treatment" pioneered by places such as the Retreat, the Quaker institution in York. Reformers pressed for control and supervision over the private madhouses run for profit (beginning with the Act for regulating Madhouses of 1774) and later over the charitable hospitals funded by public subscription then being set up. They also persuaded the county authorities to set up rate-funded asylums (first permitted in the County Asylums Act of 1808). These were started for pauper and criminal lunatics, but were soon allowed to take paying patients. The culmination of all these efforts came in 1845, when the Lunatic Asylums Act obliged all county and borough authorities to set up asylums, and the Lunatics Act established the Lunacy Commissioners. They were an independent body with powers to supervise standards and protect patients in all the hospitals, asylums and licensed houses in the country (apart from the oldest charitable hospital, Bethlem, which escaped control until 1854). Reconstituted as the Board of Control in 1913, this body continued, with some modifications, until the 1959 Act.

But the reformers thought that the answer to the bad institutions of the past lay in the good institutions of the future. Their measures reinforced the assumption that mental patients were to be segregated and imprisoned, whether or not they could be treated or made better. Demand for places in asylums grew and grew, as workhouses and families recognised the opportunity of disposing of some very inconvenient people. In 1807, there were only 2,248 (or 2·26 per 10,000 of the population) officially recognised as insane, both in and out of institutions. By 1890, there were 86,167 (or 29·26 per 10,000). Ninety per cent. of these were paupers and all but a small proportion, particularly in the county and borough asylums, were acknowledged to be incurable (Scull, 1979). Not surprisingly, considerations of economy had turned these huge and isolated "warehouses for the insane" into very different places from those which the early reformers had envisaged.

The other concern of the legislators (often bitterly opposed by the pioneers of reform, such as Lord Shaftesbury) was with the procedures for commitment. Ordinary members of the public could perceive the benefit in removing the disordered out of harm's way but only if there was no risk that they themselves might be confined. This led to demands for much more elaborate commitment procedures, particularly for private patients, culminating in the Lunacy Act of 1890. This provided for formal certification by a judicial order, following a petition by relatives or poor law officials and supported by medical evidence. The same approach was adopted when publicly-financed institutions for the mentally handicapped were established under the Mental Deficiency Act of 1913, following the Report of the Royal Commission on the Care and Control of the Feeble-minded of 1908, the Radnor Commission. The most severely handicapped "idiots" had previously been included in the definition of "lunatics," but this Act extended the concept of segregation to a much wider class of socially inadequate or inconvenient, as well as intellectually deficient people.

These two reform movements had two results which were unpopular with medical opinion from at least the end of the nineteenth century. First, because of the original desire to improve standards in institutions, patients who were certified under the Acts could only be admitted to the specialised institutions controlled under them. Mentally ill patients could only be committed to asylums, mental hospitals and madhouses, although these became known as "designated" public mental hospitals, "registered" hospitals, or "licensed" private nursing homes. Mental "defectives" could only be committed to "directed" public institutions or "certified" private ones. A mental "defective" could not be admitted to a mental illness hospital, although the personality disorders which were included as "defects" are now treated (if at all) as part of psychiatry rather than the care of the mentally handicapped. Nor could a mentally ill patient be admitted to a mental handicap institution. There was a growing number of other hospitals prepared to treat patients outside the ambit of the Acts altogether (some of them in "de-designated" parts of mental hospitals), but these could only take patients informally and could never use the compulsory measures.

Secondly, on the other hand, although private "licensed"

houses had long been allowed to take "voluntary boarders" who could afford to pay, the asylums and institutions maintained at public expense were at first only permitted to take certified patients. The impecunious, who constituted the great majority, could not be treated in hospital on a voluntary basis. Formal certification was attacked because it involved a stigma which many doctors shrank from imposing upon their patients until, it was said, it was too late for treatment to have any chance of success. The medical profession were also finding new forms of mental disorder falling far short of obvious "madness" or "lunacy" and for which certification and confinement were thought neither necessary nor appropriate. The "shell shock" cases of the First World War increased public awareness of these, and the first step towards freely available treatment without certification was taken when the Maudsley Hospital was founded in 1915, with a special statutory dispensation to admit voluntary non-paying patients.

For most mentally ill patients, however, the major change came with the Mental Treatment Act of 1930. This followed the Royal Commission on Lunacy and Mental Disorders of 1924 to 1926, the MacMillan Commission. It converted "asylums" into "mental hospitals" and "lunatics" into "persons of unsound mind." It also introduced a "temporary" status for non-volitional patients who required treatment for no more than a year, and a "voluntary" status for those who were able to make a written application to be treated in hospital. Until the 1959 Act, then, there were three different types of patient in mental illness hospitals—voluntary and temporary patients under the 1930 Act and patients certified under the various procedures in the 1890 Act. For mental "defectives" there was a totally different, if rather less complex, set of procedures under the Mental Deficiency Acts of 1913 and 1927. These did not include a voluntary status, but the institutions were not expressly prohibited from taking patients without formality. After 1952, this was officially encouraged for short stays, and the Percy Commission recommended that it could be extended to long stay patients without waiting for legislation.

Two developments lay behind much of the Commission's thinking. First was the introduction of the National Health Service in 1948. This had led to most hospitals of any type being vested in the then Ministry of Health, and to some rearrangement of the functions of the Board of Control, but nothing had been done to remove the rigid and antiquated categorisation of mental hospitals. The Commission believed that there was no longer any need for strict legal control over public hospitals. Further, as improvements depend upon the availability of resources, full responsibility should rest with the government department which controlled the allocation of resources within the health service as a whole. The Board of Control could safely be abolished, and with it the legal segregation of mental hospitals from the main stream of hospital development.

Secondly, it was a time of great optimism about the advances in medical treatment for the major mental illnesses, through psycho-surgery, electro-convulsive therapy and above all the new breed of psycho-tropic drugs, the major tranquillisers. These made it possible for increasing numbers of seriously disordered patients to be discharged into the community or treated on open wards in ordinary hospital conditions. It no longer seemed necessary for the law to assume that these patients were inevitably different from the physically sick or injured. For the most part, they could be admitted to hospital in just the same way. Compulsory procedures could be kept only for those for whom they were absolutely necessary. Once in hospital, their treatment and care could be left in the hands of the medical profession. As many as possible would be discharged back into the community just like other patients.

Thus, removing the legal controls over mental patients was inextricably linked with removing the legal controls over their doctors. In the years following the 1959 Act, the second half of this equation was increasingly called in question.

2. *Informal Admission*

The basic principle now relegated to section 131 of the 1983 Act (page 5 above) means that patients may enter hospital for treatment for mental disorder in just the same way that they would enter hospital for a physical disorder, without any special formalities. There has been a steady decline in the proportion of compulsory admissions for mental illness, continuing the trend which was well established before the 1959 Act. Even in 1955, they were only 27 per cent.; by 1970, this had fallen to 17·5 per cent., and by 1981 to 9·6 per cent. The decline in compulsory admissions to mental handicap hospitals has been even more dramatic, partly because there was previously no statutory voluntary status, and partly because there are even fewer cases where compulsion is necessary. By 1981, they were only 1·7 per cent. of admissions.

More significant still has been the decline in the proportion of *resident* patients who are liable to be detained. In 1955, 70·4 per cent. of those in mental illness hospitals were certified, because most of the voluntary patients stayed only for a short time and compulsion was still used for the chronically ill long stay patients. By 1971, the proportion had dropped to 6 per cent. (DHSS, 1975). In 1955, all mentally handicapped patients, apart from those admitted for very short stays, were detained. By 1970, this had fallen to 3 per cent. of the severely handicapped and 11 per cent. of the mildly handicapped (DHSS, 1972). During the 1970s, the proportion for all types of hospital fluctuated between 5·1 per cent. and 5·5 per cent. (DHSS and others, 1981).

The numbers of long stay patients, particularly in mental illness hospitals, have been much reduced as a result of the "open door" policy. But this has still not been as successful as was originally hoped. In 1981, there were over 73,000 resident patients in mental illness hospitals in England, and over 43,000 in mental handicap hospitals. Thirty years ago, most of these would have been detained: now fewer than 7,000 of them are. Theoretically, at least, informal patients enjoy two legal rights which the detained patients do not. They may leave hospital whenever they like (see further in Chapter 7) and they may refuse to accept any form of treatment which they do not like (see further in Chapter 6). Their mail is not censored in any way, they may be registered to vote, and they have unimpeded access to the courts. In practice, however, there are several very different types of informal patient. Only those who appreciate the need to be in hospital and are generally content to accept their doctor's advice can be classed as completely "voluntary." There are many others to whom that description cannot be applied and for whom the benefits of being "informal" rather than "compulsory" are harder to assess.

First, there are those who lack any real understanding of their situation, whether because of severe mental handicap, brain damage, senile dementia or similar disability. A major conclusion of the Percy Commission was that such patients need no longer automatically be certified. But that does not mean that the law permits the hospital to restrain or treat them as it sees fit. The precise extent to which it may do so depends upon principles of the common law which are discussed in detail in Chapter 6. But it is clear that whenever it is proposed to exceed the limits of the common law, in particular where the patient has evinced a definite desire to leave the hospital or to refuse a specific form of treatment, the hospital can only proceed if it is both able and willing to invoke the compulsory procedures in the 1983 Act.

In such cases, these procedures should be seen as a protection of, rather than a threat to the patient's integrity. They ensure that active and precise attention is given to the patient's case by medical staff. Thereafter the case must periodically be reconsidered by the consultant. The patient has the right to apply to a Mental Health Review Tribunal for his discharge and to the protection of the Mental Health Act Commission while he remains subject to detention. There are stricter safeguards over the use of electro-convulsive therapy and long-term drug treatments (Carson, 1983, has even suggested that some informal patients would do well to get themselves "sectioned" in order to obtain a second opinion on their treatment). The hospital has a positive duty to ensure that the patient understands his position. At present, there is no English body comparable to the Mental Welfare Commission in Scotland, which has a legal duty to protect *all* people who may, because of mental disorder, be incapable of protecting themselves, whether or not they are detained in hospital. A stricter regard for the legal rights of "incapable" patients might lead to an increased use of compulsory procedures, but this should not be seen as detrimental to their interests (DHSS, 1978).

Secondly, there are those children who are "volunteered" for admission by their parents or child care agencies. Section 131(2) of the 1983 Act provides that a child who has reached the age of 16 "and is capable of expressing his own wishes" may be informally admitted "notwithstanding any right of custody or control vested by law in his parent or guardian." Children who are *not* capable of expressing their own wishes or who are under the age of 16 will usually be admitted by arrangement with their parents. The precise extent of their parents' (or child care agencies') rights in this matter is not entirely clear and is discussed further in Chapter 3. The number of mentally handicapped children resident in hospital has fallen sharply in recent years: there were some 5,800 resident patients in England in 1972, but just under 2,000 in 1981.

There have never been as many mentally ill child residents, but they also fell from over 800 in 1973 to under 600 in 1981. Nevertheless it is a matter of great concern that *any* child should be growing up in hospital unless he needs constant medical and nursing care. There are many short term admissions to mental handicap hospitals "for social reasons," in other words to give the hard-pressed families of severely handicapped children a much-needed break. More troubling are the admissions of mentally ill or "disturbed" children to psychiatric hospitals and units. All constitute another group who do not have the safeguards attached to the compulsory procedures but who cannot be described as genuine volunteers.

Finally, there are those informal patients who are reluctant to accept their doctors' advice and wish either to leave the hospital or to refuse a suggested course of treatment. In theory, it should be possible to divide this group into two: those who do not fall within the criteria for the use of compulsion and those who do. The former have the right to do as they wish, although this is subject to the hospital's right to refuse to keep any patient who proves unco-operative. This may seriously limit the freedom of action of those patients who have nowhere else to go. Those who do fall within the criteria for compulsion, on the other hand, may be subjected to whichever procedure is appropriate to their case. Such patients are colloquially termed "sectionable," after the three sections of the 1983 Act which provide for compulsory admission. But as a preliminary measure to prevent their leaving hospital before there can be "sectioned," they may be detained for a short period under section 5.

3. Detention of "In-patients" under Section 5

Section 5(1) makes it clear that an application for compulsory "admission" may be made in respect of a patient who has been informally admitted to hospital. This cannot be done with a detained patient, except that an application for long term admission for treatment may be made while a patient is detained short term for assessment (s.5(1) and (6)). But if the authorities are not immediately able to complete an application, perhaps because a relative or social worker is not available, section 5 provides two procedures for keeping an informal patient in the hospital for a short time. Neither can be used to prolong the detention of a patient whose "section" is about to expire (s.5(6)) and neither gives any statutory power to impose treatment without consent (s.56(1)(*b*)).

Both powers apply only to some-one who is already an "in-patient," a term which is not defined. In ordinary language, it is usual to distinguish between an"out-patient," who attends for an appointment with a specialist or for emergency treatment in casualty, and an in-patient, who has been allocated a bed in a ward. It may take no more than the stroke of an administrator's pen to convert one into the other. But it is unlikely that the law would accept that a volitional patient can become an in-patient without agreeing to do so. Thus it would be most unwise to use these powers as a way of preventing a would-be suicide from leaving casualty when he comes round after having been "washed out." It would also be most unwise to use them to convert a day patient into an in-patient.

Under section 5(2), the doctor in charge of an in-patient's treatment may furnish the hospital managers with a report which authorises the patient's detention in the hospital for 72 hours from the time when the report is "furnished." Presumably this means the time when it reaches the administration. The section is not specific about who may do the detaining (compare section 6(2) on page 204). For example, could the doctor authorise the staff to detain the patient even though the hospital managers wished to release him? The doctor "in charge" is thought to mean the consultant (or other) on whose list the patient is; but he may nominate *one* other doctor on the hospital staff to act for him in his absence (s.5(3)).

The criterion for making these reports is simply that "it appears to" the doctor concerned "that an application ought to be made" for compulsory admission under the Act. This is not as wide as at first it appears. The words do not suggest that a purely speculative detention of a patient who *might* be liable to compulsion is allowed, still less of a patient whom the doctor does not genuinely believe to be sectionable. The form prescribed (Mental Health (Hospital, Guardianship and Consent to Treatment) Regulations 1983, Form 12) requires him to explain the reasons for his opinion, including why informal treatment is not or is no longer appropriate. Nevertheless, the power does apply to *any* doctor in charge of *any* patient in *any* hospital. It would certainly allow, for example, an obstetrician to detain a woman whom he believed had become "sectionable" after child-birth.

Section 5(4) permits even swifter action by a registered first level nurse trained in nursing the mentally ill or the mentally handicapped (see the Mental Health (Nurses) Order 1983). The in-patient must already be "receiving treatment for mental disorder." The nurse must believe: "(a) that the patient is suffering from mental disorder to such a degree that it is necessary for his health or safety or for the protection of others for him to be immediately restrained from leaving the hospital; and (b) that it is not practicable to secure the immediate attendance" of the doctor who could act under section 5(2). The power is clearly aimed at patients who are threatening to leave the hospital at any minute. It should not be used to restrain or seclude patients during an episode of disturbed behaviour.

The nurse must record her belief on the prescribed form (Form 13), but this does not require reasons. There is then immediate authority to detain the patient in the hospital for six hours or until the earlier arrival of the doctor (the time of lapse must be recorded on Form 16 by the same nurse or by an authorised nurse of the same class: reg. 4(5)). The initial record must be delivered to the managers, either by the nurse or some-one authorised by her, as soon as possible after it is made. Once again, it is not clear what would happen if they disagreed. When the doctor arrives, he may invoke the power under section 5(2), although in theory the patient might disappear while he is doing so. The 72 hours are calculated from the time when the nurse made the record (s.5(5)). If the doctor does nothing, the patient is free to go.

Both powers envisage a decision by a doctor or nurse who is on the spot (see, for example, the reference to the "attendance" of the doctor in section 5(4)). It is clearly unlawful to leave blank forms ready signed to be used by other staff as and when needed. The Act does not specify (as it does elsewhere) that the doctor must have examined the patient, but it is probably unlawful to rely on hearsay information, for example over the telephone. There have been suggestions of both these tactics (Miller, 1975) and, more seriously, of using the power as a handy substitute for the full compulsory procedures, for example by persuading a patient to enter hospital informally and making a report the same day (Bean,

1980), or as a periodic means of persuading long-stay patients to co-operate with their treatment. It is important to remember that it is nothing more than a holding power, giving no right to impose treatment.

Section 5(2) appears to have been very little used, although recorded instances rose from 79 in 1970 to 299 in 1979 (DHSS and others, 1981), but many may go unrecorded. No doubt doctors, and now nurses, are most reluctant to jeopardise their relationships with informal patients by holding this sort of threat over them but the patient who knows that the power exists may not appreciate this. The problem would have far less substance if the law made it easy to distinguish the sectionable from the unsectionable patient. Doctors may well feel that this is perfectly possible in practice and that the majority of patients are in no danger at all. In law, however, as we shall see in Chapter 2, this is very far from so. The common law's distinction between the dangerous lunatic and the harmless eccentric has not survived in the modern legislation.

4. *An Outline of the Compulsory Powers*

Although the great majority of patients are admitted informally, the numbers of psychiatric admissions are such that compulsion is still a relatively frequent experience. In 1973, for example, there were around 4,000 *more* compulsory admissions to mental hospitals than there were sentences of immediate imprisonment. The total number of admissions to mental hospitals has fluctuated considerably in recent years, but the number of compulsory admissions has shown a continuous downward trend (DHSS and others, 1981). There were more than 33,000 in 1970, but fewer than 19,500 in 1981. Before the details are examined in later chapters, it may be helpful to summarise the various provisions under which such admissions can take place and in particular the statutory criteria for invoking them. For completeness, the much more remote possibility of compulsory care outside hospital will also be mentioned. The powers fall into four broad categories.

(a) *Civil commitment under Part II of the 1983 Act*

The great majority of patients (around 15,800 of those compulsorily admitted in 1981) are committed for their own or other people's good as a result of an "application" made by the nearest relative or a social worker and supported by one or two doctors, but without the intervention of a court or other judicial authority. If accepted by the hospital to which it is addressed, the application is sufficient authority to detain and sometimes to treat the patient against his will. The assumption is that the independent decisions of applicant, doctors and hospital, coupled with the possibility of subsequent review by an independent tribunal, will secure the patient's admission as quickly, privately and painlessly as possible, while safeguarding his civil liberties. There are three procedures for applying, which are colloquially known as "sections." The fourth relates to guardianship in the community.

(i) Under section 2, an application for admission for assessment authorises the patient's detention for up to 28 days. Most forms of treatment for his disorder may be given without his consent during that time. The application must be supported by recommendations from two doctors, one an approved specialist in mental disorder, to the effect that:

> (a) the patient "is suffering from mental disorder of a nature or degree which warants the detention of the patient in a hospital for assessment (or for assessment followed by medical treatment) for at least a limited period; and
> (b) he ought to be so detained in the interests of his own health or safety or with a view to the protection of other persons."

(ii) Under section 4, an application for admission for assessment may be made in an emergency with the support of only one medical recommendation. The doctor need not be an approved specialist, although he should, if possible, have previous acquaintance with the patient. The grounds are the same as for a section 2 admission, but both applicant and doctor must also state that "it is of urgent necessity for the patient to be admitted and detained under section 2" and that "compliance with the provisions . . . relating to applications under that section would involve undesirable delay." The application authorises detention for up to 72 hours, but the admission may be converted into an ordinary section 2 admission by the provision of a second medical recommendation within that time. Unless and until that is given, however, there is no statutory power to impose treatment without consent.

(iii) Under section 3, an application for admission for treatment may again be made either by the nearest relative or by a social worker. However, if the nearest relative objects to the admission, the social worker must seek authority from the county court. The patient may be detained in the first instance for up to six months. Then the detention may be renewed, on the advice of the consultant, for a second six months and thereafter for a year at a time. Most forms of treatment for his disorder may be given to the patient without his consent. The initial application must be supported by recommendations from two doctors, one an approved specialist, to the effect that:

(a) the patient "is suffering from mental illness, severe mental impairment, psychopathic disorder or mental impairment and his mental disorder is of a nature or degree which makes it appropriate for him to receive medical treatment in a hospital; and

(b) in the case of psychopathic disorder or mental impairment, such treatment is likely to alleviate or prevent a deterioration of his condition; and

(c) it is necessary for the health or safety of the patient or for the protection of other persons that he should receive such treatment and it cannot be provided unless he is detained under this section."

(iv) Under section 7, an application for the reception of the patient into the guardianship of a local social services authority or private individual may be made in the same way as an application for admission for hospital treatment but to the authority rather than the hospital. The disorders covered are the same but the "treatability" test does not apply. It must be "necessary in the interests of the welfare of the patient or for the protection of other persons that the patient should be so received." The patient must be at least 16 years old.

(b) *Powers relating to persons accused of crime*

A much smaller number of patients (under 1200 in 1981) are admitted as a result of the orders of a court or the directions of the Home Secretary, after they have been accused of criminal offences or, if juveniles, found to be in need of care or control. These powers are largely contained in Part III of the 1983 Act, although some derive from other statutes.

(i) Under section 37 of the 1983 Act, all courts may make ordinary hospital orders over certain criminal offenders, and under section 1 of the Children and Young Persons Act 1969, juvenile courts may make such orders over persons under 17 found to be in need of care or control. The effect is almost identical to that of an admission for treatment under section 3 of the 1983 Act, so that the patient's fate is controlled by the medical authorities rather than the court. The grounds are that:

> "(a) the court is satisfied, on the written or oral evidence of two registered medical practitioners, that the offender is suffering from mental illness, psychopathic disorder, severe mental impairment or mental impairment and that . . . (i) the mental disorder from which the offender is suffering is of a nature or degree which makes it appropriate for him to be detained in a hospital for medical treatment and, in the case of psychopathic disorder or mental impairment, that such treatment is likely to alleviate or prevent a deterioration of his condition; . . . and
>
> (b) the court is of the opinion, having regard to all the circumstances including the nature of the offence and the character and antecedents of the offender, and to the other available methods of dealing with him, that the most suitable method of disposing of the case is by means of an order under this section."

(ii) Under section 41 of the 1983 Act, the Crown Court may make a restriction order if, in addition to the grounds for making an ordinary hospital order, it "appears to the court, having regard to the nature of the offence, the antecedents of the offender and the risk of his committing further offences if set at large, that it is necessary for the protection of the public from serious harm." A restriction order removes the usual power of the medical authorities to decide whether a patient may move or leave: the former is the exclusive province of the Home Secretary and the latter is decided either by the Home Secretary or by specially constituted mental health review tribunals: either may grant an absolute or conditional discharge, but a conditionally discharged patient remains liable to be recalled to hospital by the Home Secretary.

Under section 43, a magistrates' court which has the evidence required for a hospital order may commit an offender to the Crown Court with a view to a restriction order being made. Under section 44, the committal may be to hospital if a bed is available.

(iii) Under section 48 of the 1983 Act, the Home Secretary may direct the transfer to hospital of remand and civil prisoners or persons detained under the Immigration Act 1971 who are suffering from mental illness or severe mental impairment of the appropriate nature or degree and who are in urgent need of medical treatment. Under section 47, he may direct the transfer of persons serving custodial sentences who are suffering from mental illness, psychopathic disorder, severe mental impairment or mental impairment where the other medical criteria for a hospital order are fulfilled. Under section 46, he may direct the detention in hospital of persons detained during Her Majesty's Pleasure under the enactments relating to discipline in the armed forces. These last, and transferred remand prisoners, must be made subject to restrictions, but with the others the Home Secretary may choose whether or not the patient should be restricted. Any restrictions must cease when the imprisonment would have ceased, but patients transferred under section 47 may remain subject to an ordinary hospital order even though the restrictions have come to an end. Patients transferred with restrictions may be returned to the prison system if the transfer is no longer warranted on medical grounds.

(iv) Once section 36 of the 1983 Act is brought into force, the Crown Court itself will be able to remand to hospital for treatment where it has evidence from two doctors, one an approved specialist, that an accused is suffering from mental illness or severe mental impairment of the appropriate nature or degree. Once section 35 is in force, all courts will be able to remand to hospital simply for reports, where they have evidence from one specialist doctor that there is reason to suspect that the accused is suffering from mental illness, psychopathic disorder, severe mental impairment or mental impairment, and the court believes that it would be impracticable to make such a report if he were remanded on bail. And once section 38 is in force, all courts will be able to make an interim hospital order, for up to six months in all, over a convicted offender (or a juvenile brought before the court in care proceedings), where they have evidence from two doctors, one approved, that he is suffering from mental illness, psychopathic disorder, severe mental impairment or mental impairment and that there is reason to suppose that the condition is such that a hospital order may be appropriate.

(v) The Crown Court may find an accused unfit to plead because of mental disorder, or not guilty by reason of insanity of behaviour which would otherwise be a crime. Under section 5 of the Criminal Procedure (Insanity) Act 1964, these people are detained subject to the Home Secretary's directions with the same status as restricted patients, but those found unfit to plead may have to return to face trial should they become fit to do so.

(vi) For completeness, it should be recalled that all courts have power to make probation or supervision orders with a condition that the patient undergoes some psychiatric treatment. Section 3 of the Powers of Criminal Courts Act 1973 permits this for most criminal offenders and the Children and Young Persons Act 1969 for juvenile offenders or those found in need of care or control under section 1 of that Act. There must be evidence from one specialist doctor that the person is suffering from mental disorder which requires and may be susceptible to medical treatment but which does not warrant a hospital order. If the patient is admitted to hospital, however, he is an informal patient unless other compulsory powers are taken and thus there is no statutory power to impose treatment without his consent, although his failure to co-operate may sometimes be a breach of the order.

(vii) Under section 37 of the 1983 Act, the courts also have power to place offenders under the guardianship of a local social services authority or private individual. The grounds are the same, save that instead of (a)(i) (page 18 above) the condition is "(ii) in the case of an offender who has attained the age of 16 years, the mental disorder is of a nature or degree which warrants his reception into guardianship under this Act." This is also possible for 16 year olds found in need of care or control under the 1969 Act.

(c) *Detention in a "place of safety"*

Apart from the power to hold for a short time those who are already in-patients in a hospital (discussed on pages 12 to 15 above), there are two provisions under which a person may be detained for up to 72 hours in a "place of safety," which includes (among other places) both a hospital and a police station. These give no authority to treat the patient without his consent.

(i) Under section 136 of the 1983 Act, if a police officer finds in a place to which the public have access a person who appears to him to be suffering from mental disorder and to be in immediate need of care or control, he may, if he thinks it necessary in the interests of that person or for the protection of other persons, remove the person to a place of safety. This power is discussed along with those relating to criminal offenders in Chapter 5.

(ii) Under section 135(1) of the 1983 Act, a social worker may apply to a magistrate for a warrant which will permit a police officer to enter premises by force if need be. The social worker must swear that there is reasonable cause to suspect that a person believed to be suffering from mental disorder (a) has been, or is being, ill-treated, neglected or kept otherwise than under proper control, or (b) being unable to care for himself, is living alone. The police officer must be accompanied by a social worker and a doctor, but once entry has been gained, the person may, if thought fit, be removed to a place of safety without being formally "sectioned." This power is discussed further in Chapter 4, along with the general problem of gaining access to premises and patients.

There are other powers in the Act to detain people for the purpose of getting them to and from their places of detention, or pending their arrival there, but these only arise once some other power has been invoked and will therefore be discussed with those powers.

(d) *Powers under other legislation*

Some people who are suffering from mental disorder may find themselves subject to detention in hospital, or elsewhere, under quite different legislation. These powers give no right to impose treatment without the patient's consent. The two major examples relate to the young and the old respectively.

(i) Children who are subject to orders placing them in the care of a local authority under the Children and Young Persons Act 1969, or to local authority resolutions assuming parental rights over them under the Child Care Act 1980, may be placed in hospital by the authority in much the same way as parents may "volunteer" their children. But the authority has rather more extensive control over them than their parents would have had, and the two are compared in Chapter 2.

(ii) Under section 47 of the National Assistance Act 1948, a local authority may apply to a magistrates' court for the removal to hospital or other suitable place of a person who, according to the certificate of the community physician, (a) is suffering from grave chronic disease *or* being aged, infirm or physically incapacitated, is living in insanitary conditions; *and* (b) is unable to devote to himself, and is not receiving from other persons, proper care and attention. The initial order is for up to three months, but it may be renewed for further periods of up to three months at a time. If the evidence of two doctors is available, there is an emergency procedure under the National Assistance (Amendment) Act 1951 for applying to a single magistrate without giving notice to the person concerned. These procedures will be compared with the process of "sectioning" a patient under the Mental Health Act in Chapter 4.

5. *Hospitals*

Another consequence of the 1959 Act was to sweep away the legal categorisation of hospitals which had had such a restricting effect upon the treatment available in the past. In section 145(1) of the 1983 Act, a hospital is defined as:

> "(a) any health service hospital within the meaning of the National Health Service Act 1977; and
> (b) any accommodation provided by a local authority and used as a hospital by or on behalf of the Secretary of State under that Act."

This definition includes the four special hospitals, which are provided by the Secretary of State under section 4 of the 1977 Act as part of his general duty to provide a comprehensive health service (under section 1 of that Act). Finally, by virtue of section 34(2) and Schedule 1 to the 1983 Act, the definition of a hospital includes a private mental nursing home, provided that it is specially registered to receive compulsory patients under the Nursing Homes Act 1975.

Thus, in theory, there is no longer any category of patient who must be sent to a particular type of hospital and the reverse is almost, but not quite, true. Ordinary NHS hospitals are free to accept any type of patient, informal or compulsory. Private mental nursing homes may accept informal patients and any category of compulsory patient, except for prisoners transferred under sections 46, 47 and 48 of the 1983 Act (which expressly exclude the possibility). The maximum security special hospitals may accept any legal category of compulsory patient who fulfills their criteria (see page 29 below) but cannot admit patients informally.

This theory, however, works out very differently in practice. This is because no hospital is under any legal duty to accept any patient unless it has agreed to do so. This was an obvious corollary of the desegregation principle introduced by the 1959 Act. A maternity hospital, for example, could not be made to admit a violently psychotic man. Unfortunately, however, hospitals are equally free to refuse patients for whom their facilities may well be suitable. And there are some prospective patients, particularly those who have appeared before the courts, for whom no suitable facilities are provided at all.

This section will be concerned with the problems of finding a bed, particularly for a compulsory patient, in an ordinary NHS hospital, a special hospital, a regional secure unit, or in a mental nursing home, and with some possible legal solutions. The decision to accept or reject any patient is technically one for the hospital "managers." Many of their other functions will appear in later chapters. By section 145(1), the district or special health authority responsible for its administration are the managers of an ordinary NHS hospital or of a regional secure unit, the Secretary of State for Social Services is the manager of a special hospital (but for Rampton until mid 1984 the functions are carried out by the Review Board), and the "person or persons registered" are the managers of a mental nursing home. The registration and control of mental nursing homes is also dealt with in section (d) below.

(a) *Ordinary NHS hospitals*

The "open door" policies which accompanied the 1959 Act have affected the willingness of ordinary hospitals to accept compulsory patients in two ways. In looking at these, we must distinguish between mental illness and mental handicap hospitals. Although the 1959 Act made a determined attempt to integrate the separate legal systems relating to "lunacy" and "mental deficiency," the two have remained largely separate in practice, because they present such very different problems.

The first effect of the "open door" has been a dramatic drop in the numbers of hospital beds for in-patients, particularly in mental illness. It was originally hoped that the old mental illness hospitals, the former asylums, could be run down and closed, to be replaced with psychiatric units in district general hospitals and by smaller community hospitals. Certainly, the number of mental illness hospital in-patients has fallen from almost 150,000 in 1955 to around 73,000 in England in 1981. But the smaller community hospitals did not materialise, while the district general hospital units deal mainly with the acute and more easily treatable cases. They will often take only short-stay patients and some will not accept compulsory patients at all. Yet the major mental illnesses such as schizophrenia remain an intractable problem and the numbers of elderly and demented patients have been rising steadily. The result is that the old specialised hospitals have not been closed and it is now accepted that they will continue to be needed for the chronic long stay patients (DHSS, 1981a). This in itself separates patients by category and can easily lead to a two-tier, two-quality service. As the Royal Commission on the National Health Service Act (Merrison, 1979) point out, standards in the specialised hospitals have not been helped, either by the expectation that they would eventually be closed, or by the widely-held view (founded on the work of sociologists such as Erving Goffman) that such places are inevitably harmful to their patients. What began as a plan to provide flexible services to meet the needs of all kinds of patients has not necessarily worked out as originally intended.

There has not been anything like the same decline in the number of mental handicap hospital beds. There were just over 58,000 resident patients in England and Wales at the end of 1954, and by 1981 this had fallen to just over 43,000 in England. Although there are many hospital residents who suffer from multiple handicaps requiring skilled nursing and medical care, most mentally handicapped people require no more medical attention than anyone else. It is now seen as an "accident of history" that so many of those in residential care are in institutions which have been inherited by the health service (Merrison, 1979). *Care in the Community* (DHSS, 1981a) estimated that up to 15,000 could be discharged immediately if appropriate services were available in the community. In 1983, it cost £25 a day to keep a patient in hospital, even in the "Cinderella" of the hospital services, but only £12 a day in local authority residential accommodation. Transferring funds and facilities from the health service to local authorities is a slow and complex business, but recently the funds available for joint financing have been increased. The Health and Social Services and Social Security Adjudications Act 1983 will allow NHS funds to be used for housing and education, as well as for social services, where the health authorities may in effect pay for each patient who is transferred into local authority residential accommodation. Allied to these developments is the growing feeling that detention in hospital is hardly, if ever, appropriate for mentally handicapped people. But they have not yet been entirely removed from the compulsory powers in the 1983 Act, as we shall see in the following chapter.

This leads us to the second effect of the "open door." The policy not only hopes to return patients to the community but perhaps even more importantly to maintain open conditions within the hospital itself. The old custodial or "asylum" role has been rejected in favour of a more conventional picture of hospital treatment and cure. Some of the more difficult patients who could quite easily have been contained within asylum conditions can no longer be managed on an ordinary ward within normal staffing levels. This has had two results. One was a considerable rise between the early 1960s and the early 1970s in the numbers of patients transferred from ordinary mental illness hospitals to the maximum security special hospitals (Parker and Tennant, 1979; see further below). The other was an increasing reluctance to accept offender patients, particularly on restriction orders but even on ordinary hospital orders. According to the Home Office criminal statistics, the number of orders dropped from 1440 in 1966 to 759 in 1979. (DHSS figures indicate a fall from 1517 to 975 over the same period, but a rise to 1169 in 1981.) The fall was particularly marked in mental handicap hospitals.

Two sections of the 1983 Act are aimed at meeting the most obvious difficulties but are scarcely effective in doing so. First, as there is nowhere which can be forced to accept a patient in an emergency, section 140 obliges every regional health authority (and every district authority in Wales) to notify all the local social services authorities in its region or district of those hospitals where there are arrangements to receive patients in cases of "special urgency." This covers both informal and compulsory admissions but stops far short of a positive obligation to supply a bed. During the passage of the 1982 amendments, however, strenuous demands were made for such an obligation, at least towards those disordered offenders who might otherwise have to be sent to prison. These were backed by numerous examples reported by and to MIND (see Gostin, 1977), where judges had felt forced to send abnormal offenders to prison simply because no suitable bed could be found. As we shall see in Chapter 5, however, the recent case law suggests that the prisons should not be used to fill the gaps in the hospital and social services. There are still cases where the court will have little option. To meet these demands, section 39 of the 1983 Act allows any court which is minded to make a hospital order or interim hospital order to seek information from the regional health authority where the patient lives or last lived, or from any other which it thinks appropriate, about hospitals in the region or elsewhere which might be prepared to take the patient. The authority has a duty to supply whatever information it has or can reasonably obtain, but not, of course, to supply a bed.

Under section 1 of the National Health Service Act 1977, however, the Secretary of State has a duty to provide a comprehensive health service. Under section $3(1)(a)$ this includes a duty to supply hospital accommodation to the extent which he considers necessary to meet all reasonable requirements. If a patient whose requirement is quite obviously reasonable has been refused a bed, or kept in a special hospital longer than necessary because a bed in a more suitable local hospital has not been provided, or even been sent to prison because no hospital will have him, has this duty been broken? This point arose in *Ashingdane* v. *Department of Health and Social Security and others*, Court of Appeal, February 18, 1980. A Broadmoor patient was refused a bed in his local hospital because of a ban on restriction order patients operated by the nurses' trade union. He launched actions against the union branch secretaries, but also against the DHSS and the area health authority. He claimed that the Secretary of State was in breach of the duty under the 1977 Act and that it was *ultra vires*, or outside the powers, of both the Secretary of State and the health authority to take any account of the union ban in reaching their decisions. The actions against the DHSS and the health authority were stayed, for at that time the 1959 Act gave them virtual immunity from suit. As we shall see in Chapter 10, that immunity has now been removed and more such actions may be brought.

They would undoubtedly encounter great difficulties. In *R.* v. *Secretary of State for Social Services ex parte Hincks*, April 1980, [1981] C.L.Y. unreported cases 274, the Court of Appeal rejected an allegation of breach of this same duty made by four patients who had been waiting for orthopaedic operations for up to three years because of a shortage of beds in their area. The courts have often taken the view that the allocation of funds for any particular area of social need is primarily a matter for political control through Parliament rather than judicial control through the courts. But it is no simple matter to determine how far this principle goes. If the duty in question has been placed on local authorities, but the responsible government Minister may intervene if they default, it has usually been held that aggrieved individuals must pursue this remedy instead (the leading case is *Pasmore* v. *Oswaldtwistle Urban District Council* [1898] A.C. 387, but see also *Wyatt* v. *Hillingdon London Borough Council* (1978) 76 L.G.R. 727). This argument has much less force where the duty lies on the Minister himself, for the remedies of complaint to the Community Health Council or Health Service Commissioner are without teeth. Where the decision is a purely political judgment about how much taxation should be levied and how those taxes should be spent, the Minister's responsibility to Parliament can be the only solution. But where the Minister's decision is outside the powers which Parliament has given him, there is every reason for the courts to intervene. Indeed, in the difficult case of *Meade* v. *Haringey London Borough Council* [1979] 1 W.L.R. 637, the Court of Appeal went so far as to suggest that the "alternative remedy" argument did not apply where a local authority's decision to close schools during an industrial dispute was *ultra vires*. In the *Hincks* case, Lord Denning might well have allowed the case to proceed had there been any suggestion that the decision was so grossly unreasonable that no reasonable Secretary of State could have made it. It is "trite law" that the courts must not interfere with the perfectly proper exercise of a discretion which Parliament has conferred on some other body. But that body must not exercise his discretion so as to frustrate the purpose of Parliament in conferring it (*Padmore* v. *Minister of Agriculture, Fisheries and Food* [1968] A.C. 997). He must apply his mind to the question. He must apply the right law to the question. He must take into account the relevant considerations and exclude the irrelevant. Even if he has done all this, his decision might still be *ultra vires* if it is a decision which no reasonable body in his position could have taken (*Associated Provincial Picture Houses Ltd.* v. *Wednesbury Corporation* [1948] 1 K.B. 223).

Even accepting all this, the patient would still have to convince the court that it was proper to allow him to challenge the decision. Where there is breach of a statutory duty which is owed to a particular individual, he may have a right to damages for the injuries which he has suffered as a result. This depends upon the presumed intention of Parliament, but is usually limited to highly specific duties owed to clearly defined groups of individuals, of which the Housing (Homeless Persons) Act 1977 provides the best modern example. But the question of whether a person may claim damages for breach of duty is quite separate from the question of whether he may apply to the High Court for judicial review of an administrative action. In *Cocks* v. *Thanet District Council* [1982] 3 W.L.R. 1121, the House of Lords decided that a local authority's decision-making process under the Housing (Homeless Persons) Act 1977 could only be challenged through the procedure and on the normal principles applicable to judicial review, although if a breach of duty were established it might then give rise to a private right to damages. The duty to provide hospital accommodation cannot be defined in the same way that the duty to house homeless persons is defined, so there is little scope for a private right to damages. But it is certainly possible that patients with a reasonable requirement of hospital treatment have a legitimate expectation that decisions relating to their individual claims will be taken in accordance with the principles outlined earlier. The courts may therefore be prepared to entertain applications for judicial review. But it is clear from both *Cocks* and the very different case of *O'Reilly* v. *Mackman* [1982] 3 W.L.R. 1096 that where no private rights are involved, claims that public bodies have acted *ultra vires* must be made under the judicial review procedure in Order 53 of the Rules of the Supreme Court (and provided for in section 31 of the Supreme Court Act 1981). The appropriate remedies are within the court's discretion, but would be a declaration that the decision was unlawful, coupled with an order to take it again but this time applying the right principles.

It will appear from all of this that there are numerous factual and legal obstacles in the way of such a claim as Ashingdane's against the DHSS and health authorities. As we shall see in the next section, however, special hospital patients have an additional basis for challenging the DHSS decisions which could prove more fruitful. English law is far better adapted to telling public authorities what they must *not* do than to forcing them to do anything. But if the hospital managers are prepared to offer a bed and a court is therefore able to make a hospital order, it is possible that staff who obstruct the patient's admission are guilty of contempt of court (see the remarks of Lawton L.J. in *R.* v. *Harding* (*Bernard*), *The Times*, June 16, 1983). In those rare cases where an accused is found unfit to plead or not guilty by reason of insanity, the Home Secretary has to find a bed for the patient and all involved could be guilty of contempt if none can be found.

(b) *The special hospitals*

Under section 4 of the National Health Service Act 1977, the Secretary of State has a duty to provide special hospitals "for persons subject to detention under the Mental Health Act 1983 who in his opinion require treatment under conditions of special security on account of their dangerous, violent or criminal propensities." They are managed directly by the DHSS (which also decides whether to accept a particular patient) rather than by the district health authorities which are responsible for ordinary NHS hospitals. But the Report of the Rampton Review Team (Boynton, 1980) found that this had led to a lack of leadership and purpose, which they thought responsible for many of the short-comings in the "system" and in the quality of patients' lives. At their suggestion, the Rampton Review Board has been set up for a limited period (until June 1984) to try to ensure that the reforms which they recommended are carried out. This example has not yet been followed in the other three hospitals, which may be ripe for similar exposure (see, for example, Cohen, 1981).

The first "state asylum" was Broadmoor, which was opened in 1863 in response to pressure from the lunacy commissioners and others to make special provision for dangerous criminal patients. Rampton and Moss Side were opened between the wars to cater for difficult subnormal patients but they have always been able to take non-offenders. An advance unit of the new Park Lane hospital was opened in 1974. It is still being developed to relieve the overcrowding in Broadmoor and in response to the continuing but changing pressures being placed upon the special hospitals.

There is not, and never has been, any category of patient who must be sent to a special hospital. In 1962 to 1964, and again in 1972 to 1974, nearly all the ordinary hospital order patients were first admitted to ordinary NHS hospitals, although the proportions of restriction order patients they admitted were respectively 54·4 per cent. and 41·7 per cent. (Parker and Tennant, 1979). Roughly two-thirds of all restricted patients are in special hospitals (Home Office, 1982). Equally, roughly two-thirds of special hospital patients are restricted. Since 1959 there has been no category of compulsory patient who cannot be sent to a special hospital. Between 1962 to 1964 and 1972 to 1974, the proportion of special hospital patients admitted from mental illness hospitals rose from 9·9 per cent. to 15·6 per cent., although the proportion coming from mental handicap hospitals fell from 25 per cent. to 14·2 per cent. But whereas in 1962 to 1964 less than half of these transfers were non-offenders, by 1972 to 1974 nearly three-quarters had been committed under civil powers. The special hospitals were increasingly being asked to take those patients whom the ordinary hospitals found too difficult to manage in open conditions. The size of the special hospital population has been reduced from 2,500 to around 2,000 since 1950 and the DHSS undoubtedly became stricter in their criteria for acceptance during the 1970s. Nevertheless, at the end of 1982, there were approximately 370 special hospital patients who had not been admitted through the criminal process. As many as a quarter of Rampton's patients are non-offenders (Boynton, 1980). Others in special hospitals have not yet been tried because they are unfit to plead, sometimes to charges which are quite trivial or of which they could be innocent.

Even some of those who have been convicted have committed relatively minor offences.

The best known example is Nigel Smith, for he is referred to by Scarman L.J. in *R.* v. *McFarlane* (1975) 60 Cr. App. Rep. 320 at 324. Smith was admitted to Broadmoor on a restriction order after committing a relatively minor series of frauds. He had no prior history of violence or mental illness, but he did make the mistake of confessing violent feelings towards his mother during an interview in prison with a Broadmoor psychiatrist. Scarman L.J. remarked that "one wonders how the criteria indicated" in what is now section 4 of the 1977 Act "could have been said to have been met." But because there was no other suitable place for him to go, "inevitably he goes to the sort of hospital which should not be cluttered up with cases of his sort."

There is nothing in the 1983 Act to prevent the DHSS from accepting patients such as this. Could it be *ultra vires* the Secretary of State to detain there a patient who did *not* require treatment under conditions of special security on account of dangerous, violent or criminal propensities? Once again, a private action for damages for false imprisonment is unlikely to succeed, for that tort is not committed where the complaint is against the conditions rather than the fact of confinement (see *Williams* v. *Home Office (No.2)* [1982] 2 All E.R. 564). Although there may come a point at which they are so bad as to render the detention unlawful, the same proposition would defeat an application for habeas corpus (see *R.* v. *Commissioner of Police for the Metropolis ex parte Nahar and another, The Times*, May 28, 1983). In the case of *B.* v. *United Kingdom*, applic. no. 6870/75, the European Commission on Human Rights declared admissible a complaint that the patient's detention in a special hospital constituted "inhuman or degrading punishment or treatment," contrary to Article 3 of the European Convention on Human Rights. The complaint was based partly on the conditions in Broadmoor, which had appalled the Butler Committee on Mentally Abnormal Offenders (1974 and 1975) and many others, and partly on the deleterious effects of being confined in a place which was inappropriate both to his offences and his needs. The Commission proceeded to investigate the facts, but decided by eight votes to five that there had been no violation of Article 3. The case may nevertheless have had some effect in speeding up the improvements in Broadmoor. An individual patient might still seek judicial review in an attempt to quash the Secretary of State's decision to admit or keep him there. The 1977 Act is far more precise about the criteria for special hospital admissions than it is about those for providing hospital beds, so that it may be easier to show that no reasonable Minister could reach the decision in question. There must come a point at which the patient does not require any "special security" and the lack of alternative secure facilities becomes irrelevant.

Despite all this, the obstacles to transferring patients out of special hospitals remain enormous (Dell, 1980). Many patients will be unable to cope if they are released directly into the community from the highly structured environment of the special hospital (see Boynton, 1980 and Cohen, 1981 for descriptions). The public outcry should they offend again will be much louder than the concern at their continued imprisonment. But transfer to an NHS hospital may encounter opposition both from the staff and the local community. Some of this will be pure prejudice but some will be based on a genuine lack of resources to cater for any difficulties which might arise (Gunn, 1979). Strenuous efforts have been made since Boynton reported on the "scandal" of the Rampton patients who should not be there. But at the end of November 1982, there were still 200 patients in special hospitals (around 10 per cent. of the whole) awaiting transfer. Fifty six of these had been waiting for more than two years. Around the same time, there were 286 prisoners thought by their prison medical officers to be suffering from mental disorder within the meaning of the 1959 Act, although there were only 12 officially waiting for a hospital transfer. This is almost certainly a gross underestimate of the number of prisoners with some form of psychiatric disorder. Whether they would be better off in a special hospital is a tricky question, to which we shall return in Chapter 5. There is no doubt that many special hospital patients would be better off elsewhere.

(c) *Regional secure units*

As far back as 1961, the Working Party on the Special Hospitals (Emery, 1961) foresaw the problems which the open door policy would bring and recommended secure provision within the NHS. The Butler Committee were so horrified by what they found at Broadmoor that they rushed out an interim report (1974) recommending the setting up of secure units in each NHS region as a matter of urgency. The revised Report of the Working Party on Security in NHS Psychiatric Hospitals (Glancy, 1974) did the same. Between 1976 and 1982, the government provided a total of £9½ million in capital and £44 million in revenue to develop and run these facilities. Several interim units were opened, providing around 600 beds, but by the end of 1982 there was still only one permanent unit, with 30 beds available. Of all the revenue allocated, only £18 million had been spent on security and another £14 million on other psychiatric services. Some regional health authorities undoubtedly did not respond to the government's wish that they should spend this money on security, or at least on psychiatric services, and found other more pressing needs. But they are now spending a much higher proportion for this purpose. Eight more units are at least being built and it is expected that by the end of 1985 there will be 12 permanent units completed, offering over 600 beds.

Whether they will solve the many and varied problems which they are expected to solve is quite another matter. They will be highly selective in the patients they accept and are unlikely to take those who might have to stay a long time. Health authorities may well be tempted to use them to remove problem patients from the ordinary hospitals rather than to provide a half-way house for special hospital patients or transferred prisoners, especially those with personality disorders which may take a long time to improve. Experience of Eastdale, the half-way house for special hospital patients at Balderton hospital, suggests that it is social skills training, rather than security, which is most important. Other special hospital patients (particularly the severely handicapped, whom Boynton thought should never be there) need neither security nor a half-way house, but a permanent home with appropriate care. It seems safe to assume that the courts will continue to find it difficult to secure for offenders places which both the courts and the health authorities consider suitable.

(d) *Mental nursing homes*

Another possibility is to enter a private mental nursing home. These may admit informal patients and, provided that they are registered to do so, all types of compulsory patient except those transferred from prison under sections 46, 47 and 48 of the 1983 Act. There is, of course, no question of such hospitals having any duty to take an individual patient unless they have agreed to do so. If a private hospital is prepared to offer a bed, for example to an offender who might otherwise have to go to prison, the health authority has power (under the National Health Service Act 1977) to pay the bill. There is, however, nothing in either the mental health or the NHS legislation to oblige them to do so.

Mental nursing homes were, at first, those former licensed houses and charitable hospitals which were not taken over by the NHS. The private sector is now playing a growing role in all forms of health care. It has always been heavily involved in the care of the elderly, where the boundaries between nursing and residential homes are by no means easy to draw. All are subject to some form of central or local government control through the requirements of registration, which is an increasingly important function. Mental nursing homes are defined in section 2(1) of the Nursing Homes Act 1975 as:

> "Any premises used, or intended to be used, for the reception of, and the provision of nursing or other medical treatment (including care and training under medical supervision) for, one or more mentally disordered persons (meaning persons suffering, or appearing to be suffering, from mental disorder), whether exclusively or in common with other persons."

NHS hospitals and any other premises managed by a government department or provided by a local authority are expressly excluded (s.2(2)). A mental nursing home must be registered under the 1975 Act, whereas a residential home must be registered under the Health and Social Services and Social Security Adjudications Act 1983 (which is due to replace the Residential Homes Act 1980 early in 1984; this text assumes that the 1983 Act, including amendments made to the 1975 Act, is in force). The distinction between them lies in the fact that the former does but the latter does not provide "nursing or other medical treatment," although that term is widely defined in section 2(1). A mental nursing home is only exempt from registration under the 1983 Act if it is used solely as such. That Act introduces the possibility of dual registration, even for those homes which at the time are being used solely for the one purpose. This is most welcome. The dividing line between a "patient," who is receiving nursing or other medical treatment, and a resident, who is receiving other forms of special care, may be very difficult to draw. And many homes will wish to continue to provide care for those residents, particularly the elderly, who cross the line. Residential homes are covered in Chapter 9.

The line between a nursing home which caters for the mentally disordered and other nursing homes is also important. Both must be registered under the 1975 Act, but a mental nursing home must be registered as such, because inspectors have an additional power to examine patients. Otherwise, the requirements are very similar (since amendments made to the 1975 Act by the Health Services Act 1980 and the 1983 Act) and the DHSS advise that homes accommodating elderly people who are mentally confused need not necessarily register as mental nursing homes. It depends upon the number of such patients and the seriousness of their condition (DHSS Circular HC(81)8, LAC(81)4). The dividing line in law is whether the home caters for people suffering, or appearing to be suffering, from mental disorder. So here we have yet another problem in distinguishing mental order from mental disorder (see further in Chapter 2).

Any person (including a company) carrying on a mental nursing home must be registered with the Secretary of State (1975 Act, s.3), who has delegated this function to district health authorities. Registration may be refused if the applicant, his staff or his premises are unfit for the purpose or his staff are not suitably qualified. There must be either a doctor or a qualified nurse in charge (who need not but in a small home may be the "person registered") and the authority may insist upon qualifications suitable for the home in question, for example in nursing the mentally ill or mentally handicapped. The authority may also specify the number and qualifications of nurses required (s.4). It must specify the maximum number of patients and may impose other conditions about the type and age-range of patients who may be accommodated (s.8). Authorities are therefore advised to develop and publish guide-lines for acceptable standards of accommodation and staffing, which should be comparable to those in the NHS. If a home is to take compulsory patients it must be registered in a separate part of the register (s.3(4)(*b*)) and the authority will be interested in the security arrangements. As always, it is hoped that these can be kept to a minimum.

The Secretary of State makes regulations about the details of applying for registration, record-keeping, visiting and inspection (s.6), and about the general conduct of and level of services to be provided in nursing homes of all types (s.5). Under the Nursing Homes and Mental Nursing Homes Regulations 1981 (which may be replaced when the 1983 Act comes into force), homes must keep a register of all patients, case records on each patient, and a full record of all staff, and these must be retained for at least a year after the last entry or the patient's departure (reg. 6). Regulation 10 prescribes a long list of facilities and services which must be provided and in mental nursing homes particular importance will be attached to recreational and occupational facilities, as well as such obvious things as furniture, food and fire precautions. Health authorities must inspect homes at least twice a year (reg. 9) and have powers of entry, not only to registered homes but also to homes which they reasonably believe are being used as nursing homes (reg. 8). They may decide whether to visit outside normal working hours and whether or not to give advance warning. The inspector may require records, registers and any other information he needs for the inspection, but not clinical records unless he is a doctor. The inspector of a mental nursing home may visit and interview patients in private, and if he is a doctor he may examine them and their medical records, in order to investigate their complaints or where it is suspected that they are not being properly cared for (s.9(2)). This is in addition to the very similar powers of the new Mental Health Act Commission in respect of any patients who are compulsorily detained under Mental Health Act (see further in Chapter 6) and to those of any health authority which is maintaining a compulsory patient in the home and therefore has an independent power to discharge him from compulsion (see further in Chapter 7).

Failure to register or to display a registration certificate (ss.3, 10 and 11), breach of the conditions relating to patients (ss.8 and 15), contravention of the regulations relating to record-keeping, inspection or the provision of services and facilities (ss.5, 6 and 14 and reg. 11), and obstructing the visiting of mental nursing homes and their patients (ss.9 and 16) are all criminal offences, although the penalties are not severe. There is a new offence of holding out a place as a mental nursing home when it is not registered as such (s.3A(2)).

Registration may be cancelled if the "person registered" is convicted of any of these offences, which include the failure to provide all the "adequate" facilities and services listed in the regulations, or if anyone else has been convicted of an offence under the Act in relation to the same home, or if the conditions relating to patients have been broken, or on any ground which would have entitled the authority to refuse registration in the first place (s.7). In urgent cases where there is a serious risk to the life, health or well-being of patients, this may be done by a single magistrate (s.8A). Otherwise, the authority may do so according to statutory procedures which are designed to ensure a fair consideration of the case (ss.8B, 8C and 8D). These latter procedures also apply to the initial decision to refuse registration or to any later variation of the conditions. There is a right of appeal against all these decisions, including that of a magistrate, to the registered homes tribunal (s.8E), to be constituted under the Health and Social Services and Social Security Adjudications Act 1983 (which introduces all these new procedures). If a home has compulsory patients in it when registration is cancelled or the registered person dies, the registration continues in force for two months to enable alternative arrangements for them to be made (s.10).

In practice, of course, health or social services authorities will have to make alternative arrangements for every patient if registration is cancelled. Unfortunately, experience in the child care sector suggests that it is difficult to impose high standards upon the private sector if the controlling authority will be faced with having to provide for any patients or residents who are displaced. These difficulties are compounded when, as is all too well known, standards of care in public hospitals for the mentally disordered may leave something to be desired.

2 Mental Disorder and the Grounds for Compulsion

1. *Psychiatry is a Problem*

Defining mental disorder is not a simple matter, either for doctors or for lawyers. A disorder of the "mind" is not the same thing as a disorder of the "brain," although the former may be caused by the latter. The dictionary definition of mind includes "the seat of consciousness, thoughts, volitions and feelings." But how are we to know when these functions have become so abnormal as to warrant the term "disorder or disability?" It is often said (in the psychiatric textbooks) that with a physical disease or disability, the doctor can presuppose a state of perfect or "normal" bodily health (however unusual that may be in practice) and then point to the ways in which the patient's condition falls short of this. A state of perfect mental health is probably unattainable and certainly cannot be defined. The doctor has instead to presuppose some average standard of mental functioning; and it is not enough that the patient deviates from this, for some deviations are in the better-than-average direction. Even if the patient is below average, the doctor still has to decide how far below is sufficiently abnormal, among the vast range of possible variations, to be labelled a "disorder or disability."

If this be so, it must cast doubt upon the *validity* of many diagnoses of mental disorder, for they could never have the scientific objectivity of a finding of physical disorder. However, the distinction between them in practice is nothing like as clear cut. A very similar relativity is involved in determining whether a failure in bodily functioning is thought bad enough to be called a disorder. The patient's evaluation, and to some extent the doctor's, will be influenced by social and cultural norms. The diagnosis will at first be a hypothesis, which will act as a guide to treatment and may give some indication of the future course of the disorder, but may well have to be modified as more is learnt about its underlying causes, either in the particular case or in general.

Some disorders of the mind are the result of bodily defects (such as syphilis or arterio-sclerosis) and can be approached in much the same way: by alleviating the painful or distressing symptoms while recognising the connection between them and the underlying defect, which may (or more often may not) be capable of remedy. There is a school of psychiatric thought which believes that all mental disorders worthy of the name will eventually be traced to physical or organic causes and can thus be fitted into this simple disease model. On this view, where the cause is not yet known, psychiatry is simply at the same stage as medicine has been (and still is) with many physical disorders: the stage of minute observation and recognition of distinct clusters of symptoms, categorising them into discrete syndromes, alleviating the pain and distress which they cause to the patient and attempting to predict the future course from similar cases, while at the same time searching for some clue to the underlying defect. Obstetricians do not, for example, refuse to treat the effects of toxaemia of pregnancy simply because they do not yet know what causes it.

The advantage of this model of mental disorder from the legal point of view is that it is *potentially* capable of limiting the scope of psychiatric intervention and competence—it lays no claim to solving all the ills that flesh is heir to. The disadvantage is that it enables physical treatments whose effects are scarcely understood to be employed for disorders which have not yet been shown to have a physical cause. This is all very well if the patient understands the position and agrees. It is not so obvious why the hypothesis of a physical cause should justify the imposition of such treatment against the patient's will. Nor does it explain why the doctors are so sure that a physical cause will some day be found for some disorders but not for others. Even in the case of the most serious illnesses, schizophrenia and the affective (mood altering) psychoses, the hypothesis upon which the whole edifice is built has yet to be conclusively demonstrated.

Thus there are other schools of psychiatric thought which, in varying degrees and varying combinations, reject the notions of organic causes, of discrete disease entities, and of the more radical physical treatments. They seek other causes and other solutions. Their various therapies may be aimed at the patient's individual psyche or at its interaction with family or societal pressures. The disadvantage of these psychotherapeutic models from the legal point of view is that they can carry the province of psychiatry far beyond the normal concerns of the medical profession, into the wider ills of the family and society. There is no necessary connection with medicine at all. This could be a serious objection if these models are used to give a spurious scientific objectivity to attempts to explain or to excuse an offender's behaviour. From the patient's point of view, however, the advantage is that their methods of treatment can usually only succeed with his free co-operation.

There is yet a third school of thought, which concentrates, not on the causes of the disorder, but on attacking its behavioural manifestations. This school has developed systems of behaviour modification which rely upon the consistent reinforcement of desired behaviour and the equally consistent discouragement of bad (see Royal College of Psychiatrists and others, 1980; Boynton, 1980). Lawyers may find it particularly curious that offenders are removed from the penal system (which claims very similar objectives) for this purpose, but in theory the treatment is much more intensive and aimed at the particular problems of the patient himself. It can claim to do wonders for just those patients whom many more conventional psychiatrists now admit that they cannot treat, those whose disorders are manifested mainly by their anti-social or inadequate behaviour. Unless it is allied to a clear distinction between the normal and the abnormal, therefore, it is an obvious recipe for enabling offenders to escape their just deserts while confining some relatively harmless non-offenders.

These various models offer ample scope to the anti-psychiatrists within the profession itself, let alone to outsiders. The organically-minded are accused, for example, of failing to enter into the patient's own view of his life and to grasp the underlying rationality of what he says and does (found particularly in the work of Laing); or of perverting the concept of disease or illness to justify the imposition of treatment upon socially inconvenient people, both for their own and society's ends (found particularly in the work of Szasz). Those attacked, on the other hand, tend to accuse the anti-psychiatrists of ignoring the problems of the really ill and concentrating on the much pleasanter (and in America at least more profitable) task of ministering to the neuroses of the middle classes. Clare (1980), for example, points out that the countries in which the practice of psychiatry is most controversial are also those (the U.S.A. and the U.S.S.R.) in which the widest definitions of the most serious illnesses are employed.

He argues that the majority of those in the NHS would claim to do their best to incorporate the good features of every approach into their clinical practice. The so-called "medical model" is not synonymous with the organic theory of mental disease, for it can encompass a sympathetic understanding of the patient's experience, a broad-minded evaluation of the complex of possible causal factors, and a cautious approach to treatment. But its prime claim is to apply the ordinary medical methods to the identification of the disorder, so that, for example, no-one is labelled a schizophrenic without exhibiting the precise symptoms which have been agreed to indicate this particular diagnostic category. Once criteria have been laid down and practitioners properly trained in their use, psychiatric diagnosis can indeed become very *reliable*. In other words, the chances of two or more psychiatrists coming up with the same label for the same patient become as good as, if not better than, those in any other branch of medicine.

Unfortunately, however, this does nothing to answer the question of its *validity*. If we all agree what a table looks like we have a fairly good chance of identifying a particular object as a table and our disagreements will be about not-quite-table-like objects. We will also be better at table-spotting than anyone else because we have had so much training and experience at it. We may even have acquired a certain skill in making tables better. (Psychiatrists will quite properly say all of these things.) None of that proves that our account of a table has any validity. A high degree of reliability in the identification of witches was achieved by the witch-hunters of the seventeenth century in just the same way.

These accounts of the nature and causes of mental affliction provide us with no sort of justification for allowing psychiatrists to confine and treat patients against their will. We do not permit surgeons to remove appendices simply because they are better at identifying when an appendix is diseased and at performing the operation. When neither the disease nor the cure is universally agreed, there is even less justification. This is certainly not to argue that a justification does not exist, merely that it does not lie in the expertise of the psychiatrist alone. But before considering what it might be, we must consider what English law has to say on the subject.

2. *The Legal Categories of Mental Disorder*

The Act makes two vital distinctions. First, for admission for assessment (ss.2 or 4) or removal to a place of safety (ss.135 or 136), the patient need only be suffering from some "mental disorder." For longer term admission for treatment (s.3), or reception into guardianship (s.7), or for a court hospital or guardianship order (s.37), interim hospital order (s.38), or transfer during sentence (s.47), he must have one of the four specific forms of mental disorder: "mental illness," "severe mental impairment," "psychopathic disorder," or "mental impairment." Secondly, admission for treatment, hospital orders (but not interim hospital orders), and transfers during sentence all distinguish between the *major* disorders of mental illness and severe mental impairment, which justify admission even if hospital treatment is unlikely to do the patient any good, and the *minor* disorders of psychopathic disorder or mental impairment, which only justify admission if treatment is likely to make him better, or at least prevent his getting worse. Similarly, remands to hospital for treatment (s.36) and transfers of unsentenced prisoners (s.48) can only happen where the patient is suffering from a major disorder.

As well as the implications for the liberty of the subject, therefore, the precise meaning of these terms has great practical importance. But added to the intrinsic difficulties of defining them is the fact that the Act does *not* distinguish between the forms of disorder which justify long term civil commitment and those which permit the therapeutic rather than penal disposal of criminal offenders. Many people might wish to take a narrower view of the grounds for forcibly detaining a non-offender than of the circumstances justifying a court in sending an offender to hospital rather than to prison. The only scope for this, however, lies in the additional criteria for civil commitment (under all three sections), which replace the discretion of the court or the Home Secretary in criminal cases and are intended to keep civil compulsion to a minimum. In reality, as we shall see, they may have this effect, but for all the wrong reasons.

(a) *"Mental disorder"*

Section 1(2) of the Act defines "mental disorder" as "mental illness, arrested or incomplete development of mind, psychopathic disorder and any other disorder or disability of mind." Quite clearly, therefore, it is more than a handy collective noun to embrace all the four specific forms of disorder mentioned in some sections of the Act: "arrested or incomplete development of mind" is wider than "severe mental impairment" and "mental impairment"; and "any other disorder or disability of mind" takes in conditions which are not included in any of the other terms. Section 1(3) does, however, provide that a person cannot be dealt with under the Act as suffering from mental disorder, or from any specific form to it, "by reason only of promiscuity or other immoral conduct, sexual deviancy or dependence on alcohol or drugs."

There are two possible reasons why mental disorder sufficient for the short term powers is so much wider than the four forms needed for the long term powers. First, what is now "admission for assessment" used to be "admission for observation," with the clear implication that a short period of observation might be needed before a firm diagnosis could be made. Secondly, removal to a place of safety gives no right to impose treatment without consent, and there used to be considerable doubt about whether admission for observation did so: detention and observation may be thought justified where forcible treatment is not. But under the 1983 Act patients admitted for 28 days of assessment may be treated in exactly the same way as those admitted for treatment (s.56(1)). And in practice the initial compulsion is usually what matters. Most patients having been taken to hospital will remain there until discharged by the hospital: it is not surprising that, for example, in England and Wales in 1981 there were more than 14,000 admissions for observation but just over 1,700 admissions for treatment. The remainder cannot all have been cured and discharged within the 28 days. But whether they agreed to stay through ignorance, inertia, the effects of treatment or a genuine willingness to do so cannot be known. There is also the problem, well-documented in the United States but probably less acute in the NHS, that once the label "patient" is attached to any person, not only do medical and nursing staff interpret his behaviour in that light, but he too may adopt "patient like" behaviour in order to conform to their expectations and make life more tolerable.

We must therefore consider first what the law means by the four specific forms of disorder, and then consider the two terms which make mental disorder into a wider concept.

(b) *"Mental illness"*

Although the law regards it as a major disorder, "mental illness" is nowhere defined in the Act. The Percy Commission (1957) were much more concerned with the definitions of subnormality and psychopathic disorder and assumed that mental illness would be construed in the same way as "unsoundness of mind" and "lunacy" had been construed in the past. They also assumed that these were limited to severe defect or loss of reason or intellect, and could not encompass disturbances of personality or behaviour. These were dangerous assumptions, for there is evidence that during the nineteenth century lunacy had been stretched, from its common law origins in dangerous madness, so as to enable families and workhouses to unload their enfeebled elderly or incorrigibly troublesome members onto the asylums (Scull, 1979). Similarly, some modern psychiatrists may assume that mental illness simply refers to whatever disorders are left once the various forms of handicap and psychopathic disorder are subtracted (Rollin, 1969).

One solution would be to ask the psychiatrists themselves to distinguish the concept of "illness" from that of "disorder." Thus the organically inclined might agree that the major disturbances of mental functioning now called psychoses can properly be termed "illnesses," because they are a "mental change involving an obvious departure from normal health" (for which in due course an organic cause is likely to be found); whereas other conditions are not illnesses but "extreme variations in personality from a hypothetical norm." This approach coincides with that of the Butler Committee (1975), who defined mental illness as a "disorder which has not always existed in the patient but has developed as a condition overlying the sufferer's usual personality."

But this approach would not be sufficient to limit the concept to the psychoses (principally schizophrenia, endogenous depression and manic-depressive psychoses, and the various psychotic disorders associated with physical conditions, such as senile dementia or delirium tremens). Neuroses (such as anxieties, hysteria, phobias, obsessions, reactive depression and the like) are dealt with alongside personality disorders in the International Statistical Classification of Diseases and in most psychiatric textbooks. But some doctors would assert that at least some of the neuroses (perhaps particularly depression which often cannot be neatly categorised) also result from a "change involving an obvious departure from normal health"; and that because they can be just as disabling as a mild form of psychosis, and some sufferers can have just as little realisation of the need for treatment, they are equally valid candidates for compulsion. Certainly, the diagnostic categories of those admitted to special hospitals during 1978 do not suggest that mental illness is in practice limited to psychoses. Only six of the 83 admissions to Broadmoor were categorised as psychotic, five had personality or behaviour disorders (probably recorded as psychopathy for legal purposes), and all the others were in the residuary category, which includes depression not specified as neurotic or psychotic, epilepsy, undiagnosed cases and admission for other than psychiatric disorders (DHSS, 1983). Yet, in law, all Broadmoor patients should be suffering from "mental illness" or "psychopathic disorder" if they are not mentally handicapped. Part of the explanation no doubt lies in psychopathy (see section (c) below); but part will lie in the tendency to apply more elastic concepts of mental illness for the purpose of saving a criminal offender from prison than would be thought appropriate in compelling a non-offender to accept treatment.

Particular examples are alcohol or drug abuse and some forms of sexual deviation. These have commonly been thought to be "all in the mind" and thus treatable by psychiatric methods. Yet to include them suggests that a man may be insane simply because of his inconvenient, damaging or self-destructive behaviour. Because of this, the DHSS (1978) suggested that they should be excluded from the definition of mental disorder for the purposes of civil commitment, but that the courts should remain free to impose a hospital order after a criminal offence. In fact, however, section 1(3) excludes those whose *only* problem is promiscuity, immoral conduct, sexual deviancy, alcohol or drug from *all* the categories of mental disorder, and thus from the possibility of therapeutic court disposal unless there is some other mental disorder as well. But it does not exclude other conditions of a similar nature where the temptation to diagnose "mental illness" may be similar. Nor does it tell us how a sign of mental illness may be differentiated from its social and behavioural results.

It is for these reasons that there was some hope that the law might supply a more precise definition. The opportunity for the courts to do so arose in the case of *W.* v. *L.* [1974] Q.B. 711 (see also, on another point, at page 86):

The patient, a young man of 23, had put a cat in a gas oven; had later made a cat inhale ammonia and then cut its throat with a cup; had hanged a puppy in the garage; had strangled a terrier with wire; had threatened his wife with a knife; and last had threatened to push her downstairs as a means of disposing of the baby she was expecting. This was clearly enough to fall within the definition of psychopathy (below, section (c)); but at that time, being over the age of 21, he could not be obliged to remain in hospital for longer than 28 days unless he committed a criminal offence or could be termed "mentally ill." The doctors were divided in their opinions, but there was one who described him as suffering from an "episodic epileptoid psychosis."

The Court of Appeal decided that he was both psychopathic and mentally ill. Lawton L.J. provided the only authoritative statement in English law on the meaning of "mental illness:"

> "The words are ordinary words of the English language. They have no particular medical significance. They have no particular legal significance . . . ordinary words of the English language should be construed in the way that ordinary sensible people would construe them. . . . I ask myself, what would the ordinary sensible person have said about the patient's condition in this case if he had been informed of his behaviour to the dogs, the cat and his wife? In my judgment such a person would have said 'well, the fellow is obviously mentally ill'."

It is impossible not to think of this as the "man-must-be-mad" test. It simply adds fuel to the fire of those who accuse the mental hygiene laws of being a sophisticated machine for the suppression of unusual, eccentric or inconvenient behaviour (and in this country without due process of law). It pays scant regard to the painstaking efforts of psychiatrists to distinguish mental health from mental illness by means of carefully described deficiencies, not in behaviour, but in mental functioning. It tells us nothing about why some people who are cruel to animals should be regarded as responsible for their actions and some should not.

Thus the DHSS Consultative Document on the 1959 Act (1976)

canvassed the possibility of a closed definition of mental illness which would require one or more of the following characteristics: (i) more than temporary impairment of intellectual functions shown by a failure of memory, orientation, comprehension and learning capacity; (ii) more than temporary alteration of mood of such degree as to give rise to the patient having a delusional appraisal of his situation, his past or his future, or that of others or to the lack of any appraisal; (iii) delusional beliefs, persecutory, jealous or grandiose; (iv) abnormal perceptions associated with delusional misinterpretation of events; (v) thinking so disordered as to prevent the patient making a reasonable appraisal of his situation or having reasonable communication with others. (This was identical to that suggested by the Butler Committee for the purposes of a verdict of "not guilty by reason of mental disorder," save that "more than temporary" is substituted for "lasting"). In the event, however, the attempt was abandoned, ostensibly because the lack of definition was not thought to have caused any difficulties in practice (DHSS, 1978).

Of its very nature, lack of precise definition will not cause problems to the people who operate the law; but it may very well do so for their patients. It is to be hoped that practitioners will limit their intervention to cases exhibiting mental symptoms which bring them within the precise and recognised categories of mental disease. They might also bear in mind the definition suggested by the Northern Ireland Review Committee on Mental Health Legislation (MacDermott 1981):

> " . . . a state of mind of a permanent or temporary (but not merely transient) nature in which the individual exhibits such disordered thinking, perceiving or emotion as impairs his judgment of his situation to the extent that he requires care, treatment or training in his own interests or in the interests of other persons."

At least these focus attention upon *why* it is that some people may be treated differently by the law from all the others whose actions are inconvenient or damaging either for themselves or for others.

(c) *"Psychopathic disorder"*

This same problem arises in even more acute form with the "minor" disorder of psychopathy, defined in section 1(2) of the

Act as "a persistent disorder or disability of mind (whether or not including significant impairment of intelligence) which results in abnormally aggressive or seriously irresponsible conduct on the part of the person concerned."

In the nineteenth century, the term "moral insanity" was coined to describe cases which did not exhibit the obvious symptoms, such as delusions or hallucinations, associated with lunacy. It originally meant "madness, consisting in a morbid perversion of the natural feelings, affections, inclinations, temper, habits, moral dispositions, and natural impulses, without any remarkable disorder or defect of the interest or knowing and reasoning faculties. . . . " (Prichard, 1835). This may approximate to the modern concepts of neurosis and personality disorder but has no specific connection with anti-social behaviour. "Moral" in those days meant "emotional" or "psychological" rather than the reverse of "immoral." In Germany the term "psychopathy" or "constitutional psychopathic inferiority" was used for a whole range of conditions where the patient's personality deviated from some supposed biological norm.

The idea of a specific disorder closely associated with anti-social behaviour seems to have stemmed from the observation that there were people whose persistent and apparently incorrigible misbehaviour began at a very early age. In England, these were termed "moral imbeciles," with the obvious risk of confusion with the originally wider concept of moral insanity and the quite different condition of intellectual imbecility. Because neither were thought to be covered by the concept of "lunacy," the Mental Deficiency Acts of 1913 and 1927 were passed to provide for the confinement of both the intellectually and the morally defective. The two were defined separately in the Acts, but their association led inevitably to doubts about whether the morally defective could be confined even though they were not intellectually subnormal.

The Percy Commission (1957) wished to make it clear that disordered personalities of normal intelligence could be dealt with under the new Act. By that time the concept of psychopathy had changed radically. The theory of a constitutional origin had been challenged. Efforts to categorise and define specific personalities which might be called pathological had concentrated on predominantly "aggressive" or predominantly "inadequate" characteristics. From this it was a short step to the Percy Commission's conclusion that there was a mental *disorder* called psychopathy, which could be defined largely in terms of the adequacy of the person's social functioning. Hence they suggested a third category of mental disorder, after mental illness and severe mental subnormality, covering "any type of aggressive or inadequate personality which does not render the patient severely subnormal but which is recognised medically as a pathological condition." If it included "marked limitation of intelligence" the term "feeble-minded psychopath" was proposed. But because of the obvious libertarian objections, the Commission proposed age limits on the prolonged detention of those who had not offended against the criminal law (see further section 3(b) below).

The Commission were still attacked for suggesting too wide a criterion for compulsory hospitalisation, and for failure to distinguish sufficiently clearly between personality disorder and mental handicap. The resulting statutory definition of psychopathy therefore emphasised the connection with serious anti-social behaviour, and provided for a separate definition of non-severe mental handicap. It is questionable, therefore, how far the concept has come from the old idea of "moral imbecility" (Anderson, 1962). Yet the original meaning had been quite different, and psychiatrists are by no means agreed on the existence of a specific clinical entity corresponding to the statutory definition.

But whereas the concept might be thought too wide to justify civil commitment, it has been particularly criticised in its application to criminal offenders. Why should this particular group of offenders be singled out for special treatment? Are they a particular group at all? How is it possible to distinguish the mentally disordered psychopath from the mentally normal recidivist? Is it not circular to conclude that a person is disordered because he commits crimes and then conclude that his disorder should at least partially excuse those crimes (see particularly Wootton, 1959)? Even if the psychiatrist can point to signs of mental pathology which are independent of the tendency to commit crimes, such as the lack of normal feelings or motivations associated with his behaviour, the case for special treatment is still not made out. A psychopath who has been made the subject of a hospital order is apparently no more likely to go on behaving badly in the future than is a similar but "normal" offender who has been sent to prison (Walker and McCabe, 1973). Yet few of them respond to any of the more conventional forms of psychiatric treatment and they are often the most troublesome and inconvenient patients.

The result of all this is that, far from amounting to an excuse, the label "psychopath" is likely to do an offender more harm than good. Few hospitals will be prepared to admit him from the courts, but if they do, he may have more difficulty than a mentally ill patient in proving that it is now safe to let him out. If a hospital place cannot be found, the court may be tempted to impose a prison sentence at the top end of the range because, by definition, he is more than usually dangerous. Indeed, few hospitals are prepared to admit psychopaths at all. They made up only 1,600 of some 207,800 admission of all types in England in 1981. Significantly, some 17 per cent., an unusually high proportion, were under compulsory powers.

The Butler Committee wished to make it clear that responsibility for psychopathy lay with the prison rather than the hospital services. They suggested that a hospital order should not be made unless there was at least a suspected additional mental or physical illness or disability *and* a prospect of benefit from hospital admission. The DHSS (1976 and 1978) recognised that "psychopath" had become a damaging label involving much stigma. But they did not want to remove the possibility of treatment from those few who are admitted to hospital, so they sought in vain for a less damaging label. Unfortunately, it is impossible to provide a less insulting term without also providing a less insulting definition. That, of course, would have broadened the scope of both civil and criminal commitment to an unacceptable degree. The statutory definition therefore remains in essence what it has been since the 1959 Act.

(d) *Mental impairment and severe mental impairment*

The common law distinguished "idiots" (who have no understanding from birth and are presumed incurable) from "lunatics" (who may have lucid intervals or even be cured). The early lunacy legislation included idiots along with lunatics, but the Idiots Act 1886 was the first to provide separately for the confinement of both idiots and "imbeciles." This left out of account people who were neither mad nor severely handicapped, but suffered from disturbed or inadequate personalities, manifested mainly in the quality of their social functioning. Hence the Report of the Royal Commission on the Care and Control of the Feeble-Minded of 1904 to 1908, the Radnor Commission, recommended that local authority institutions be provided for them as well as for the idiots and imbeciles.

The Mental Deficiency Acts of 1913 and 1927 defined four categories of mental defect, itself defined in 1927 as "a condition of arrested or incomplete development of mind existing before the age of 18 whether arising from inherent causes or induced by disease or injury." The first category were "idiots," who were unable to guard themselves against common physical dangers, such as fire, water or traffic. Their mental age when adult would still be that of a pre-school child. "Imbeciles" could guard against physical dangers but were incapable of managing themselves or their affairs. Their mental age would be about that of a kindergarden or infant school child. The "feeble-minded" were the largest group. Though neither idiot nor imbecile, they were thought to require care, supervision or control for their own protection or that of others. The last group were the "moral defectives," whose mental defect was coupled with strongly vicious or criminal propensities (and who became the psychopaths of today).

The Percy Commission wanted to sweep away this outdated terminology and also the strict legal separation between the care for lunatics and that for defectives. Hence they recommended a uniform set of procedures to cover both mental illness and mental handicap. The main result of this was to remove psychopathy from its association with mental handicap and it is now usually regarded, if anything, as a psychiatric disorder. The 1959 Act also replaced the three grades of handicap with the major disorder of "severe subnormality" and the minor disorder of "subnormality." Both required limitation of intelligence. For severe subnormality, this had to be such that the patient was incapable of leading an independent life or guarding against serious exploitation.

In the debate before the 1982 amendments, mental handicap organisations campaigned hard for it to be taken out of the Act altogether. They disliked the association with mental illness. This may suggest that handicapped people are invariably disturbed in their thinking, feeling or behaviour, when this is very far from true. They argued that the need for civil commitment, if it arose at all, stemmed not from the handicap as such, but from some additional psychiatric or behaviour disorder (which might even be the result of how supposedly normal people had reacted to their handicap). Mental handicap cannot be "cured" in the way that psychiatric disorders can be cured, although the patient's level of functioning can be improved by long and careful training. If they are committed to hospital, therefore, they will find it much harder to obtain their release. This is a particular problem with hospital orders. Courts may wish to make a therapeutic disposal, partly because they are distressed by the thought of exposing a handicapped person to the rigours of prison, and partly because they hope that it will improve his chances of learning to survive in society. But the handicapped person knows only too well that, although hospital may be a pleasanter place than prison, he may have to stay there for a great deal longer. And a special hospital is by no means well adapted to improving his chances of surviving in society (see Boynton, 1980). Indeed, the Rampton Review Team recommended that severely handicapped patients should not be in Rampton at all. In fact, as we know only too well (see further in Chapters 1 and 5), courts have often been cheated of their humane intentions by the reluctance of NHS hospitals to accept handicapped patients from the courts. The proportion of compulsory admissions of all types to mental handicap hospitals and units has been steadily falling, from 9.3 per cent. in 1970 to 1.7 per cent. in 1981. In terms of numbers, the fall was from 1,082 to 412. In effect, there was little need to compel the non-offenders and the offenders were not wanted.

However, the Butler Committee (1975) had not wanted to deny them the chance of a therapeutic disposal, although they did recommend that the court should have evidence from a specialist in mental handicap. The DHSS (1978) concluded that non-offenders might still have to be compelled in order to protect them from exploitation. MIND (Gostin, 1978) responded that "it is a curious society which, in order to prevent abuse of its vulnerable citizens, suggests confinement for the abused, while allowing freedom for those who exploit." Of course, the same could be said of those who abuse children. The removal of the child, even against his will, is not always worse than leaving him in the detrimental environment. Nor does compulsion inevitably mean confinement in an institution. Guardianship (see further in Chapter 9), at least in its 1959 Act form, provides a measure of protection while leaving the patient in the community. The community is where it is now generally agreed that the great majority of mentally handicapped people belong.

The end result has been a most unsatisfactory compromise. The 1983 Act defines "severe mental impairment" as "a state of arrested or incomplete development of mind which includes severe impairment of intelligence and social functioning and is associated with abnormally aggressive or seriously irresponsible conduct on the part of the person concerned" (s.1(2)). "Mental impairment" is "a state of arrested or incomplete development of mind (not amounting to severe impairment) which includes significant impairment of intelligence and social functioning and is associated with abnormally aggressive or seriously irresponsible conduct on the part of the person concerned" (s.1(2)). This means that for all the longer term powers, admission for treatment under section 3, hospital orders and transfers from prison, but also guardianship, the patient's mental handicap *must* be associated with psychopathic behaviour. It may not make much difference in criminal cases (see further in Chapter 5), but it will inhibit still further the use of hospitalisation and, more importantly, guardianship, to protect and support a handicapped non-offender. And as we have already seen, the psychopathic conduct may provide an additional reason to want to lock some-one up, but it certainly does not hold out much more hope of a cure.

The changed definitions also emphasise that there must be impairment of social functioning as well as of intelligence. But they certainly do not make it any easier to distinguish the major disorder of "severe" impairment (which does not have to be "treatable" for long term admission) from the minor disorder of merely "significant" impairment (which does; see section 3(b) below). Still less do they make it easy to distinguish the significantly impaired person from the "dull but normal." This was never an easy matter, even in the days when it was thought to be governed by the scientific measurement of intelligence. The Percy Commission thought that all the former idiots and imbeciles and some of the feeble-minded would be in the severely subnormal category. They suggested a mental age of below about seven and a half to nine, or an I.Q. of 50 to 60, would be a "strong pointer" to severe handicap. They made no suggestion at the upper end. The International Statistical Classification puts "borderline mental retardation" at an I.Q. of 68 to 85. The latter must be too high, for it would include around 17 per cent. of the population. Psychiatrists and psychologists would now doubt that the concept of intelligence is capable of governing the matter. A person with an I.Q. score in the 80s may be handicapped by the inadequacy of his social functioning, while a person with a lower score may be much more capable. It may be as well that the new definitions bring this out into the open. But they do serve to emphasise how subjective and value-laden the assessment of a "significant" impairment can be. The same can be said of the distinction between "significant" and "severe" but this is now less important than it used to be.

(e) *Arrested or incomplete development of mind*

The mental handicap lobby did not succeed in excluding mental handicap from the short term powers of compulsion. "Arrested or incomplete development of mind" remains an ingredient of "mental disorder" which is sufficient for admission for assessment or removal to a place of safety. There is no reason to suppose that it is limited to "severe mental impairment" and "mental impairment" within the meaning of the Act. If it were, the Act would have said so. The phrase dates back to the old mental deficiency legislation (see page 51 above) when it certainly included everything which we would now understand by the term "mental handicap." It would seem to cover any appreciable failure to meet the normal milestones of mental development, whether this is caused by genetic or constitutional factors, or by environmental shortcomings in childhood, or by damage to or disease of the brain. But it would *not* cover the subsequent degeneration of a mind which had been fully developed. The mental infirmities of old age would not be included here, although they may be included as a mental illness, at least if they amount to a psychosis, and they might amount to "any other disorder or disability of mind."

Arrested or incomplete development of mind might, however, cover things other than intellectual handicap. When it was used in the definition of mental defect, it included "moral defect." Could it apply to people whose only disorder is an ingrained tendency to anti-social conduct, such that an incomplete development of the capacity to make moral judgments must be suspected? This would be a dangerous widening of the concept of psychopathic disorder (which is already controversial enough). Fortunately, section 1(3) excludes people whose only problem is promiscuity, immoral conduct, sexual deviancy or alcohol or drug abuse.

(f) *Any other disorder or disability of mind*

Once again, this residuary category is sufficient for the short term powers and there is no reason to suppose that it is simply a handy collective noun for the four specific disorders. The example given in Parliament during the passage of the 1959 Act was brain damage caused by an injury or physical disease such as encephalitis (although the results of this might often amount to one of the other disorders). As ordinary words of the English language, "any other disorder or disability of mind" seem to mean any mental condition which deviates sufficiently from the supposed norm to be called abnormal and which is sufficiently deleterious (as abnormally high intelligence, for example, usually is not) to be called a disorder.

If so, this is both too wide and too vague to justify even the shortest invasion of liberty, let alone detention for up to 28 days with the risk of forcible psychiatric treatment. The DHSS (1976) argued that to be more specific, but to include all the suitable candidates for compulsion, might in practice *extend* the categories of those at risk. As it is, many psychiatrists probably do not address their minds to the law's distinction between mental illness and mental disorder and only recommend any form of compulsion for people whom they consider to be mentally *ill*. On the other hand, they probably do not restrict that concept to the psychotic illnesses (as was the Percy Commission's original intention). For the short term powers, it may not matter so much that they are prepared to include other disorders under the umbrella of "illness," for the law allows them to do so (whether it should is another question). If so, a mental disorder in practice probably means a condition of mind which has been recognised and described by psychiatrists sufficiently often to appear in the standard psychiatric textbooks. But is that any improvement on the lawyer's definition attempted above?

In fact, the best known exceptions to the practice of equating mental disorder with mental illness were alcoholics and drug addicts, who might be admitted to detoxification units for short periods (perhaps by the police acting under section 136; see Chapter 5). It is curious, therefore, that they have been expressly excluded by section 1(3), along with the promiscuous, immoral or sexually deviant. The DHSS (1978) maintains that these are "social and behavioural problems" rather than mental disorders. These apart, however, the law has still not acknowledged that such a distinction exists.

3. *The Additional Criteria for Civil Commitment*

In 1957, the Percy Commission set out the principles which they believed would still justify the use of compulsion in a world where all care and treatment was, if possible, to be provided without it. First and foremost, there had to be a pathological mental disorder for which the patient required hospital or community care. Secondly, this care could not be provided without compulsion because the patient or his family would not accept it. So far, so good: but the Commission went on to suggest two additional requirements which were crucial. Thirdly, if the patient would not accept treatment, there should be "at least a strong likelihood that his unwillingness is due to a lack of appreciation of his own condition deriving from the mental disorder itself." Finally, there should be one of two advantages to be gained: *either* a "good prospect of benefit to the patient from the treatment proposed—an expectation that it will either cure or alleviate his mental disorder or strengthen his ability to regulate his social behaviour in spite of the underlying disorder, or bring him substantial benefit in the form of protection from neglect or exploitation by others;" *or* a "strong need to protect others from anti-social behaviour by the patient."

However, the Commission did not suggest that these principles should be expressed. Instead, they recommended a scheme which distinguished between the various types of disorder in a way which they believed would translate their views into action. Their third principle would be achieved by restricting long term treatment to the mentally ill or severely subnormal. Their fourth principle would be achieved by the additional criteria in the grounds for commitment. As modified in the 1983 Act, there are now *three* matters of which the recommending doctors must be satisfied, in addition to the diagnosis of mental disorder already discussed. These are summarised below, before the full meaning of each is discussed:

(i) For admission for *assessment,* the patient's disorder must be "of a nature or degree which warrants the detention of the patient in a hospital for assessment (or for assessment followed by medical treatment) for at least a limited period" (s.2(2)(*a*)). The 1959 Act contained a similar formula for admission for *treatment.* But under the 1983 Act, the particular form of the patient's disorder must be "of a nature or degree which makes it appropriate for him to receive treatment in a hospital" (s.3(2)(*a*)). (The same formula is applied to court hospital orders, transfers from prison and remands for treatment, but not to the exploratory remands for reports or interim hospital orders; these are all discussed in Chapter 5).

(ii) For an admission for *treatment,* if the patient is suffering from *psychopathic disorder* or non-severe *mental impairment,* medical treatment in a hospital must be "likely to alleviate or prevent a deterioration of his condition" (s.3(2)(*b*)). (The same "treatability" formula is applied to court hospital orders and transfers of sentenced offenders from prison).

(iii) For an admission for *assessment,* it is required that the patient "ought to be so detained in the interests of his own health or safety or with a view to the protection of other persons" (s.2(2)(*b*)). The equivalent in an admission for *treatment* is that "it is necessary for the health or safety of the patient or for the protection of other persons that he should receive such treatment and it cannot be provided unless he is detained under this section" (s.3(2)(*c*)). (There is no equivalent in court orders or transfers from prison, for the offence or alleged offence already places the patient at the disposal of the authorities).

Because the definitions of the various forms of mental disorder are so wide, it is these three additional requirements that distinguish the "sectionable" from the "unsectionable" patient. But how effective are they in doing so?

(a) *"Of a nature or degree . . ."*

This is meant to ensure, at the very least, that the *type* or *severity* of the patient's disorder is such that he ought to be in hospital, for a short or a long time as the case may be. Compulsory admission should not be used if the patient could equally well be cared for in the community. This criterion does go some way towards insisting that patients are cared for in the "least restrictive environment" possible. In practice, doctors in NHS hospitals will insist that they are not going to admit any patient who does not need to be in hospital, because pressure on their beds is so great.

Unfortunately, however, there are some cases where it may be necessary for the patient to be in hospital, even though he *could* be cared for outside. First, of course, the community may not have the facilities which he requires. We have already seen in Chapter 1 that there are large numbers of hospital patients, particularly in mental handicap hospitals, who could be transferred to the community tomorrow if only the right facilities were there. If any of these are compulsory patients (whether civil or criminal, for this requirement applies to both), it is at least arguable that they are unlawfully detained, because their disorder is not bad enough to warrant their being in hospital.

Secondly, and this applies particularly to the mentally ill, it may be necessary for the patient to be in hospital because only in hospital can he be forced to accept medical treatment whether he likes or not. There are undoubtedly hospital patients who could survive quite well in the community if only there were some way of insisting that they had their regular injections of the long-acting drugs which keep their symptoms under control. Under the 1959 Act, it was theoretically possible to do this by transferring them into guardianship, although in practice it was hardly ever done. Now even that possibility has been removed. Under the 1983 Act, a guardian has no right to force the patient to accept treatment, although he may insist that the patient goes to a clinic where treatment is available, or is visited by a community nurse. As will be seen in Chapter 9, there are two views about whether patients *should* be obliged to accept treatment in the community. Given that they cannot be, however, is continued detention in hospital lawful, even though in theory their condition is not bad enough for them to be there? These patients are different from those in the first group, because their condition would be bad enough were it not for the treatment. The answer, then, is probably "yes."

But might this requirement go further than requiring that the patient's condition is bad enough for him to be in hospital? If it must be bad enough to *"warrant his detention"* does this not ask for a *moral* judgment about whether it is bad enough to *force* him to go? Beebe, Ellis and Evans (1973) provide an illustration in the case of Mrs. X., who was a socially isolated 65-year-old Viennese refugee Jewess. Her G.P. reported to the mental welfare team that she was again becoming paranoid. The team agreed (with some reservation because of cultural factors). Paranoia is undoubtedly a mental disorder, although it may either be a personality disorder or a psychotic paranoid state. Mrs. X. would probably have been better off in hospital for her own sake. Nevertheless, the team thought themselves unable to compel her to go, because "she was sufficiently in contact with reality."

Taken seriously, this requirement could come close to the Percy Commission's third principle: that the patient's unwillingness to enter hospital should result from a failure to appreciate his need for treatment, which failure is caused by the mental disorder itself (and not, for example, by ordinary independence of mind, dislike of hospitals, or distrust of doctors). For an admission for assessment (whether or not in an emergency), the law still requires that the patient's condition is bad enough to "warrant his detention," in other words to force him to go. This is indeed welcome, because the only diagnosis required is one of "mental disorder," which is a concept of unlimited potential.

But this is no longer required for an admission for treatment. The changed wording simply insists that the patient's condition is bad enough to "make it appropriate for him to receive medical treatment in a hospital." There is no mention of its being appropriate to *compel* him to go. The law-makers must have assumed that whenever a patient was suffering from one of the four specific forms of disorder which was bad enough to require hospital treatment, it was bound to be bad enough to force him to go. But is that right? A doctor might well describe Mrs. X.'s paranoia as a mental illness, but does that amount to a moral justification for putting her in hospital against her will?

(b) *Treatability*

This requirement has now been introduced into the law for a very different reason from that originally proposed by the Percy

Commission. They put it forward as a condition for the commitment of *all* patients, apart from those whose detention was necessary to protect other people from anti-social behaviour. But the present requirement applies only to the long term detention of psychopathic or non-severely impaired patients. In civil commitment, it replaces the age limits which were contained in the 1959 Act. Yet those age limits were put there to meet a serious libertarian point. These patients are not suffering from those gross distortions of perception, thinking or mood which are (or at least ought to be) involved in a finding of mental illness. Nor are their capacities so impaired that they are no more capable of looking after themselves than a child of seven or eight. Their disorders consist of an apparently pathological inability to avoid "abnormally aggressive or seriously irresponsible behaviour." The Percy Commission believed that to allow such people to be detained *before* those tendencies had manifested themselves in a criminal offence had exposed a wide range of social misfits to confinement without trial. This had certainly happened to some unmarried mothers, confined for their "moral defect." The Commission did believe that it was permissible to detain such people in hospital after they had committed crimes or for a short period of observation. They also believed that a long term effort to improve the patients' behaviour was permissible while they were still growing up. But once they were adults, they were entitled to the same presumption of innocence as the rest of us. Hence they could not be compelled to enter hospital for treatment after the age of 21, although if they had been admitted before that age they could be kept until 25, and even beyond if they were actually dangerous.

In the years that followed, this point was forgotten. The age limit was seen as an arbitrary restriction upon the hospitals' power to provide treatment where they thought it might do good. Some people (for example, the judges in the Court of Appeal in *W*. v. *L*. [1974] Q.B. 711, page 46 above) clearly thought that there ought to be some form of preventive detention available for people who were not mentally ill but whose doctors thought them dangerous. The doctors, on the other hand, did not want to be expected to provide preventive detention, even if the person had committed a crime (*particularly* if the person had committed a crime). They wished it to be emphasised that they could not be expected to receive such patients unless there was some prospect of benefit from treatment. But if there was such a prospect, they saw no reason for limiting civil compulsion to the young.

Hence the age limits have been swept away. But for both an admission for treatment and a hospital order the psychopathy or impairment must be such that hospital treatment is "likely to alleviate or prevent a deterioration of his condition." This concept of making the patient better, or at least preventing him getting worse, is difficult to apply where the condition is of constitutional origin and cannot be "cured" by conventional psychiatric treatment. Many hospitals have been reluctant to accept these patients for years. Some, however, may be able to offer treatment which is designed for the modification of behaviour (although it is not always easy to distinguish this from providing an environment which simply reduces the possibilities for it to occur, which is certainly what happens in special hospitals). Whether a person should be obliged to accept this when he has not offended the criminal law (or even when he would rather be punished) is certainly questionable. In effect, then, the new "treatability" test is designed to protect the hospitals from any responsibility towards patients whom they do not want, but it provides no protection at all for the patient who does not want the hospital (Gunn, 1979).

The 1983 Act has however gone some way towards meeting the original purpose of the treatability test by applying it to the *renewal* of both an admission for treatment and an ordinary hospital order (though not a restriction order) for patients of all types (s.20(4); see further page 122 below). But in the case of mental illness or severe mental impairment, an alternative is that the patient would be unlikely to be able to care for himself, to obtain the care which he needs or to guard himself against serious exploitation.

There are two very curious features about all this. The first is that the Percy Commission proposed treatability as an *alternative* to the need to protect other people. But in the 1983 Act it is a condition in its own right. That means, for example, that even the detention of a mentally ill hospital order patient cannot be renewed unless treatability (albeit with the alternative of inability to care for himself) can be shown. On the other hand, treatability has *not* been written into the circumstances in which a mental health review tribunal *must* grant a discharge (s.72(1)(*b*) see further on page 271), although the tribunal must take it into account in exercising its discretion to discharge (s.72(2)(*a*)). Thus a tribunal may refuse to discharge a patient who could not have been admitted in the first place and who will have to be released at his next renewal date.

(c) *"In the interests of his own health or safety or for the protection of other persons"*

This requirement was the one designed to implement the Percy Commission's fourth and final principle of "treatability" or protection. In practice, however, psychiatrists commonly believe that it means that the patient must be dangerous to himself or others (see even Clare, 1980). Bean (1980), for example, found that, while a high rating for psychiatric disorder was needed before the patient would be admitted to hospital at all, whether he was admitted informally or compulsorily depended mainly on his "dangerousness" rating. These psychiatrists are to be commended for their caution, although they may be using the term dangerousness in a very loose sense. But in fact this is *not* what the law requires.

The Act uses the criterion that the patient is likely to "act in a manner dangerous to other persons or to himself" for the quite different purpose of preventing his nearest relative from discharging him (s.25(1); see further on page 235). Where an Act of Parliament uses two different phrases it is presumed to mean two different things. In this case, it is clear that the criteria for the initial admission to hospital were meant to be broader than those for keeping him in against the wishes of his family.

The difference between the two phrases is quite obvious. A patient is only dangerous *to himself* if he is likely to kill or injure himself, either deliberately or through extreme self-neglect. But a patient may need hospital treatment "in the interests of his own health or safety" whenever this is the best way of providing the appropriate care or treatment or of safeguarding him against the risks, temptations or other stresses to which he might be subjected outside. Once the doctor has reached the conclusion that the patient's disorder is bad enough to make it appropriate for him to receive treatment in a hospital, it follows that this is necessary in the interests of his own health or safety, and if he will not go voluntarily, it follows that detention is necessary for the same purpose. The new wording of section 3(2) (above page 57) makes this process quite plain.

Of course, there may be some patients whose condition is not bad enough to warrant hospital admission for their own sake but is bad enough to warrant it for the sake of other people. If the law required such patients to be *dangerous,* there would obviously have to be a risk that they would attack and harm some-one. But the Act simply requires that it be necessary to "protect other persons." This leaves it to practitioners to decide who those other persons might be and what they are entitled to be protected from. A good illustration (from personal experience) is Mrs. Y. She displayed none of the first rank symptoms of schizophrenia (thought control, auditory hallucinations or delusions) but was described by the psychiatrist as "bats." She was a very bad house-keeper, was loud, argumentative and often irrelevant in conversation, and made a thorough nuisance of herself by pestering and arguing with her neighbours. Significantly, her own psychiatrist remarked that it had been a mistake to give her a "good" council house with house-and garden-proud neighbours. Most of the usual drugs had been tried and he did not suggest that keeping her in hospital was likely to do her any good at all.

So how far was he entitled to go in trying to protect other people from her? Does the Act simply intend that they should be protected from physical harm? Or can it at least be extended to protecting families from the enormous physical and mental strain which caring for a disordered relative, particularly a senile parent, can impose? Or from the emotional and sometimes financial suffering caused by living with some-one who is clearly going out of his mind? Or from the developmental damage suffered by the children of parents who cannot cater adequately for their intellectual and emotional needs? Or from the irritation and nuisance suffered by neighbours of people like Mrs. Y.? The general consensus would propably stop at around the third point on this scale but the law does not insist that the psychiatrist does.

Thus it is clear that this requirement provides no extra protection for those patients who will undoubtedly be helped by going into hospital. And it provides only very limited protection for those whose families and neighbours will be helped even if they will not. The only confident statement is that the protection of property alone is not enough.

(d) *Consenting or incapable patients*

The patient may be suffering from mental disorder; it may be bad enough to warrant hospital admission or make hospital treatment appropriate; if he is psychopathic or impaired, he may be "treatable"; and the admission or treatment may be necessary in his own interests or those of others. But should he be compelled, even if all these conditions are fulfilled, if *compulsion* is not necessary, either because he is willing to go or because he is in no state to object?

Of course, there may be cases in which the compulsion of an apparently willing, or a non-objecting incapable, patient is in fact necessary. There may be well-founded fears that he will soon change his mind. Beebe, Ellis and Evans (1973) give the examples of the schizophrenic woman who asked for the security of the hospital but warned that her voices might tell her to leave, or the alcoholic who had frequently left before and was plagued by intrusive thoughts that he should kill his wife and child. The patient may be willing to stay in hospital but unwilling to accept the medical treatment which his doctor thinks necessary. The patient may be incapable of expressing a view either way, but the doctor may consider that he needs treatment which goes beyond the narrow bounds of the common law doctrine of necessity (see further in Chapter 6). In these cases, the compulsion is as necessary as the admission or the treatment and the law will allow it.

But what is the position where an informal admission is only inappropriate for administrative reasons? Tales abound of hospitals which will not admit patients out of normal hours, or without a prior interview with the hospital psychiatrist, or during industrial action, without the clear mark of urgency which a compulsory admission provides. And what is the position when the psychiatrist concentrates on discovering symptoms of mental disorder and whether the patient is "dangerous" without exploring his willingness to seek treatment? (For examples, see Chief Medical Officer, 1966; Oram, 1972; Roy, 1968; Bean, 1980).

Section 2 (admission for assessment) requires that the patient's condition warrants his *detention* and that he ought to be so *detained* in the required interests. If the only reason that detention is thought warranted is that the hospital has administrative objections to an informal admission or no-one has bothered to consult the patient, these conditions have not been fulfilled and he should not be sectioned. Section 3 (admission for treatment) does not use those words, but does require that the appropriate hospital treatment "cannot be provided unless he is detained under this section" (s.3(2)(c)). Those words are meant to limit the use of compulsion to those cases in which the compulsion as well as the treatment is necessary. Unfortunately, they might be stretched to include the administrative cases, although not the cases where no-one has bothered to consult the patient.

Of course, if the patient is willing to enter hospital, he may also be willing to be "sectioned" if this is necessary to secure him the appropriate bed. As section 131(1) says (page 5 above), "Nothing in this Act shall be construed as preventing a patient who requires treatment for mental disorder from being admitted . . . without any application . . . rendering him liable to be detained. . . . " This was meant to make it clear that there was nothing to prevent hospitals admitting patients informally if they wished. It was not meant to mean that patients could be railroaded against their will into hospital without bothering to use the compulsory procedures. But does it also mean that the Act's procedures cannot be used if they are not necessary to overcome his objections? The point may be academic, because no wrong would be done to the patient if he were prepared to consent to *all* the implications of a "section." But those who sectioned him might be guilty of the offence of making a false statement in the admission forms, contrary to section 126(4) (see page 340 below).

4. *Commentary*

Despite all this debate, the grounds for admission (especially admission for treatment) amount to little more than this. The doctor must find evidence of a condition which he is prepared to call a mental disorder (or for treatment, a mental illness). He must conclude that the best place for the patient, either in the patient's own interests or those of other people, is in hospital. And compulsion must be the only way of getting him there, or persuading him to stay, or giving him the necessary treatment. In practice, psychiatrists in the NHS will probably take a far more restricted view than the letter of the law requires. The law in effect allows them to use compulsion whenever *they* need to do so in order to give the patient the treatment which they think he needs. There must be more to it than that. We must start from the assumption that mental patients are people like anyone else and entitled to the same rights as other people and then ask what will entitle us to take away those rights. We must also remember that this discussion is not concerned with people who have committed criminal offences. People who do not conform to the fundamental obligation to obey the criminal law may raise different questions.

The Act suggests two justifications for civil commitment, which must be treated separately. The first is the person's own health or safety. The problem here is whether it is ever justifiable to take away a person's freedom solely for his own sake. Mill (1859) argued that self-protection was the only object for which mankind was justified in interfering with another. A man must be allowed to go to the devil if he wishes, provided that he does not infringe the equal rights of other people in the process. The argument is familiar in the seat-belt and smoking controversies of today. The usual answer is that these particular examples of self-neglect result in a disproportionate claim on the resources of the NHS, to the detriment of other patients or taxpayers. But in the case under discussion, the result will probably be a smaller rather than a greater claim on public expenditure. Indeed, Sedgwick (1982) has pointed out that some of the implications of anti-psychiatry, although it has been enthusiastically espoused by many on the left, are extremely attractive to those on the right who wish to limit the provision of public facilities for the disordered. Nevertheless, the libertarian argument must still be answered.

The easy answer is that it was never intended to apply to people who are incapable of participating in the system of rights and duties implied by the concept of equal freedom. The obvious example is a child. He must be brought up and educated to a point where he is capable of participating. Both he and his parents must accept this. We must want for him the very minimum that he would want for himself, whatever else he might want (Freeman, 1980). Can we apply the same idea to mentally disordered people? The difficulty is that childhood can be defined by reference to some objective and easily proved criterion. It is also clear that the purpose of the intervention is to enable the child to take his place as a fully responsible member of society. Both are problematic in relation to mental disorder, whether illness or handicap.

To take the second problem first, it is here that some of the arguments of the anti-psychiatrists are particularly relevant. If mental illness is defined by reference to the psychiatrist's own standards of normality, by definition he takes no account of the standpoint of the very person he is supposed to be helping. The patient's conduct appears irrational or inappropriate because the doctor cannot put himself in the patient's place. For these reasons, he can do little to help. In fact, he can only make matters worse. The label "mentally ill" places the patient too low, and indeed may imprison him in an institution which can only do damage (Goffman, 1961), while the label "psychiatrist" places the doctor so high, that effective communication between them is ruled out (Laing, 1959; Laing and Esterson, 1971). This must be doubly so where the normal relationship of trust between doctor and patient is destroyed by the imposition of compulsory powers.

It is indeed curious that two centuries of laws have been designed on the assumption that psychiatrists can cure their involuntary patients. Yet in the nineteenth century the percentage of cures was extremely low, particularly among pauper patients (Scull, 1979). Even today, numerically the most important problems are the incurable diseases of old age and the major functional psychoses, where the symptoms may be treated but not the cause. But there are still many patients whom the doctors can help and in some cases, particularly depression, they can be tolerably confident that they will be able to produce such an improvement that the patient will reach the point where he is glad that his wishes were overborne. The same can apply to mentally handicapped people. They, like children, can respond to long and skilful training for participation in society, although this is not a task for the medical profession.

But is the fact that the doctor can bring about such a cure that the patient will thank him in the end enough? Of course it is not. I may be glad when the dentist has taken my teeth out, but he cannot do so by force. There has still got to be something which disqualifies the patient from the right to make that choice. The law pays far too little attention to the precise mental qualities which add up to a disqualification. It assumes that a diagnosis of mental illness or mental disorder is enough. It also assumes that once such a diagnosis has been made, we can take it for granted that the refusal to accept help is the result of that diagnosis, rather than of ordinary stubbornness, political or religious conviction, or a different approach to the calculation of the odds. We have already seen how totally inadequate the legal definitions are, although practitioners will probably be much more cautious. They realise that the fact that the patient is not quite like other people is not enough. Labelling his condition an "illness" may have made other people more inclined to concede their right to intervene, although no such right is conceded for physical illness. But by itself, it takes the argument no further.

Frankly, no-one has yet taken the argument much further. There are several possibilities. We could look at the usual criterion for enjoying ordinary legal rights, such as the capacity to make a will (page 321 below). This depends upon understanding in broad terms what is involved in making the decision and the effects of making it. Eccentricity, caprice, forgetfulness, the inability to make choices which others regard as sensible or wise or good, these do not disqualify. The minimum requirement is to know what one is about. This is a very useful criterion when it comes to dealing with the status of mentally handicapped people, because their disorder consists mainly in a deficiency in just this quality. Once they have reached a certain point, there is no reason to believe that the handicap alone will distort their capacity to participate in the system of rights and duties of which we speak.

The same could be applied to mental illness. But the patient's consciousness may be unimpaired and his understanding distorted in a rather different way. He knows where he is and what he is about, but the way in which he perceives his situation, and the way in which he thinks about things, may be quite different from those of other people. It is not, or should not be, that he has different moral, political or religious views. It is that the kinds of perception and the kinds of thinking which lead him to those views are not the same as other people's. The Butler Committee's attempted definition of serious mental illness (page 47 above) came some way towards this idea. It may strike a chord with those who are actually dealing with patients, rather than simply thinking about them. There is still a great deal of work to be done on the question.

But suppose that we have disqualified the patient on some sort of test or other. This must be a minimum requirement for compulsion, even if we know that we can do him good. Equally, however, even if we know that we cannot do him any good, he is still disqualified. Is there any reason why we should not treat him as a perpetual child? The justification for helping the child to reach maturity is not there, but neither is the qualification for participation in legal rights and duties. We would obviously still owe him the duties of humanity, treating him with the same kindness as we would treat a child, providing him with the necessities which might promote the development of his physical, mental and emotional health as best we can. There is no reason at all to do this in a particularly restrictive environment, out of touch with everyday life. We ought never to give up hope that one day he might progress towards a limited maturity, and this can best be promoted by as much contact with ordinary life as is possible. But it need not involve recognising the right to equal freedom until he becomes qualified to exercise it. We must still beware setting that threshold too high.

These arguments apply to the compulsion of mental patients wherever it is to take place. They do not lead to their being locked up in secure institutions, unless these are more likely to make them better or are in fact more humanitarian than the alternatives. They do allow patients to be kept in surroundings which are as conducive as possible to their successful rehabilitation. But what about the other possible justification for compulsion? The Act refers to the protection of other persons. For people who reject what has gone before, this is the only possible reason for intervention. But what are other people entitled to be protected against? They are certainly entitled to some protection against conduct which the law defines as criminal. There is a need for society to admit that in some cases it can protect itself against these, even though it cannot demonstrate the offender's blameworthiness in the usual way (Kittrie, 1971). But outside the confines of the criminal law, how far are we entitled to go? As we have already seen (page 63 above), the law does not tell us and it certainly should. It goes far beyond "dangerousness" and indeed there are other things against which people may legitimately claim protection. But we ought to know what they are. The other question is whether the machinery of civil commitment either can or should be used for this purpose. It has, as we shall see, enormous advantages over the criminal process, not only for the authorities but also for the person concerned. But the risks involved are also manifest. If in effect we are creating a special sort of crime called "anti-social mental disorder," should we not admit it?

3 The Role of Social Workers, Relatives and Doctors

Each of the three procedures for compelling a non-offender to go into hospital consists of an application made to the hospital managers, either by the patient's nearest relative or by an approved social worker, supported by the recommendations of one or two doctors. There are two curious features about this. The first is that the doctor never has the final word. He cannot force either the relative or the social worker to act. The second is that the final decision can either be made by a detached professional or by a lay person who is closely involved with the patient. The reasons for this lie in the different procedures laid down for private and pauper patients in the old lunacy legislation.

1. *Patients and Paupers*

The common law allowed anyone to restrain a dangerous lunatic. Any relative, friend or neighbour who was prepared to foot the bill could arrange for him to be confined in a private madhouse or public hospital, without going to the trouble and expense of invoking the Crown's ancient jurisdiction over the person and property of those found lunatic by inquisition. Libertarian lawyers such as Lord Mansfield (see *Coate's Case* (1772) Lofft 73) were clearly troubled by this and the first Act for regulating Madhouses (1774) made it unlawful for them to take patients without the written and sealed order of a physician, surgeon or apothecary. In 1828, the Act to regulate the Care and Treatment of Insane Persons in England extended this idea to the public subscription hospitals (but not yet to Bethlem) and laid down a procedure which was remarkably like that of today. An order was made by the person who would see that the bill was paid, and supported by two medical certificates (except for a short term emergency confinement, where one was enough). This pattern continued, with refinements, until 1890. Then for the first time, it was laid down that the initial petition should, if possible, be made by the husband or wife or a relative of the patient and, except in an emergency, the order of a judicial authority was required. At first, the doctors had been seen as a protection against unscrupulous families and madhouse keepers. By the end of the nineteenth century, the patient was thought to need protection against unscrupulous doctors as well.

For pauper or vagrant lunatics, however, the position was quite different. The earliest Acts expressly dealing with the confinement of lunatics were the Vagrancy Acts of 1713 and 1744, which were designed to prevent a variety of social misfits wandering about and becoming a charge on parishes other than their places of origin. Two justices were allowed to confine "persons who by lunacy or otherwise are furiously mad or so disordered in their senses that they may be dangerous to be permitted to go abroad" even if they were not chargeable to the parish as paupers. Those who were might in any event be disposed of as the parish officials thought fit. Increasingly, this meant confinement, usually in the poorhouse or workhouse, although some were sent to charitable hospitals and more and more to the private madhouses. There, the condition of pauper lunatics was so terrible that the first aim of the reform movement was to set up county asylums where they might be better cared for. The next step was to devise procedures which would oblige the poor law officials to identify suitable candidates and send them there. These generally involved the parish overseers, and later the relieving officers, in bringing pauper or vagrant lunatics before the justices, who could then direct them into an asylum. The early nineteenth century reports and statutes chronicle the battle between the reformers' ambition to secure proper care and treatment (as they saw it) in an asylum or hospital and the more economically-minded poor law authorities. As early as 1811, however, the justices had to call for medical assistance before issuing a warrant to take the patient to an asylum. The patient's family had nothing to do with it, unless they were prepared to assume financial responsibility, in which case they were allowed to discharge him if he was not actually dangerous. The Lunacy Act 1890 brought together all the procedures for both paying and non-paying patients, but the differences between them remained until the National Health Service Act 1946.

The procedures under the Mental Deficiency Act 1913 allowed

parents to commit their young or severely handicapped children without any judicial order, provided that there were two medical certificates. More commonly, defectives were committed by judicial order on the petition of a relative, friend or relieving officer, again with two medical certificates. It was this Act which introduced the idea that one of the doctors should be specially approved for the purpose. But it also allowed a policeman or relieving officer to take an abandoned, neglected or illtreated defective to a place of safety without any medical certificate at all.

With the dismantling of the old poor law administration following the Local Government Act 1929, the relieving officer became the local authority public assistance officer, but he continued to be "duly authorised" under both the lunacy and mental deficiency legislation to operate the admission procedures for non-paying patients. Under the Mental Treatment Act 1930, "pauper lunatics" became "rate-aided persons of unsound mind" but it also became possible to admit them direct to certain hospitals for a short period without any medical certificate at all.

That Act began to make cautious moves in the direction of community care, authorising local authorities to establish psychiatric outpatient clinics and to arrange after-care. Already, with the setting up of the first training course for psychiatric social workers, at the London School of Economics in 1929, there was an idea that social workers might have a professional role to play in the care of the mentally disordered. With the establishment of the NHS in 1948, the responsibilities of local health authorities to provide services for the care and after-care of many types of patient were expanded. The particular function of arranging the compulsory admission of mental patients was given to them, shorn of its connection with the financial relief of need, which was transferred to central government. Many of the former public assistance officers stayed as mental welfare officers, duly authorised as before. But the authorities' other duties meant that they were now recruiting an entirely different type of worker to undertake social case work as part of their care and after-care functions. Their training, skills and outlook were radically different from those of the former public assistance officers and although in many places the two were integrated in the new service, in some they operated quite separately until the 1959 Act.

That Act swept away the need for any judicial involvement in compulsory admission (unless it was necessary to gain entry to private property by force). The Percy Commission (1957) thought the magistrate more of a rubber stamp than a genuine safeguard. The best protection was "that the working of the new procedures should be in the hands of people who have the sort of knowledge and experience needed to form a sound judgment of the questions at issue." The Commission had no doubt that these people were doctors. Stronger safeguards would be provided by requiring more than one medical opinion, by insisting that one of the doctors was specially qualified to give it, and by doing away with the power to detain patients without medical advice.

The report gives little attention to why, in that case, it was necessary for the relative or mental welfare officer to continue to be involved at all, although there is discussion of the means of overcoming the relative's objections. It was assumed that the age old practice of an application by the relative or local official should continue. Much emphasis was given to improving services for patients in the community. But it does not seem to have occurred to the Commission that trained and experienced social workers might not be content to see themselves as errand boys for the family or the doctors. Nevertheless, although "no responsible relative or mental welfare officer would lightly disregard or dissent from the doctors' advice," the report conceded that in the last resort they must be free to do so. In the years that followed, social workers have increasingly asserted both their professional independence and the importance of the judgments which they are qualified to make. This has called in question the role of the relative, whose only qualification is proximity to the patient. Not only may this "distort detached perception," but he "may himself be an integral part of the patient's mental disorder" (Gostin, 1975).

2. Social Workers and Relatives

(a) The approved social worker

The emphasis given in 1959 to the development of community care coincided with the restructuring of the profession and training of social workers in the local authority health and welfare services, following the Younghusband Report (1959). In 1971, however, their functions were transferred to the new all-purpose social services departments, set up under the Local Authority Social Services Act 1970 following the Seebohm Report (1968). These would, it was thought, provide a more efficient service aimed both at prevention and at meeting the needs of the family as a whole. Specialised training courses gave way to all-purpose generic training and existing field-workers might no longer be able to concentrate on areas where they had special knowledge and experience. When the health service was reorganised in 1973, hospital social work was transferred to local social services departments. Hospital social workers with particular skills in the field of mental disorder became eligible for appointment as mental welfare officers.

Under the 1959 Act, local authorities were free to appoint any or all of their social workers as mental welfare officers as they thought fit. Practice varied. Some appointed all their field-workers. Some appointed only those with a special interest in the work, who might include former untrained "duly authorised officers" as well as trained psychiatric or hospital social workers. Some appointed only those who, in addition to their generic training, had taken a further course of in-service preparation for the task. Some considered that hospital social workers might be too closely identified with the clinical team to play a fully independent role in compulsory admission, others saw the advantage of having a specialist on the spot to deal with patients already in or at the hospital. The medical profession complained that the old experienced officers had given way to the young and inexperienced. In part at least, this was because the new social workers' training had led them increasingly to question the authority of the medical profession, without always giving them the knowledge and skills to do so properly.

A further problem was the ambiguity of the social worker's role under the 1959 Act. Was he simply a substitute for the absent or reluctant relative? Or a junior member of the clinical team devoted to providing for the patient's needs as the doctors saw them? Or a truly independent professional with skills which were just as relevant to the decision as those of the doctors? The 1983 Act tries in two ways to shift the emphasis towards a fully independent professional role.

As from October 28, 1984, the functions which were previously entrusted to mental welfare officers are to be carried out by approved social workers. The 1983 Act also gives the approved social worker some new duties. (Until October 28, 1984, mental welfare officers will carry out both the old and new duties.) An approved social worker is an officer of a local social services authority appointed by his authority for this purpose (1983 Act, s.145(1)). Authorities must appoint sufficient social workers for the task (s.114(1)), but these must be people whom the authority can approve "as having appropriate competence in dealing with persons who are suffering from mental disorder" (s.114(2)). In doing so they must have regard to the matters directed by the Secretary of State (s.114(3)), the scheme of training and assessment in fact devised by the Central Council for Education and Training in Social Work (see CCETSW, 1983). This expects both ordinary teaching and in-service observation and practice, leading to formal examinations and assessment. It is intended to ensure an understanding of mental disorder within "family, social and cultural contexts," of the facilities and services available to provide care, treatment or support for patients and relatives, of the legislation and possible alternatives, and the respective roles of the various professions involved.

The legislation gives the approved social worker a variety of jobs, but these fall into three broad categories. In the first are those which enable him to gain access to mentally disordered people living in the community who may need his help. He has power to enter and inspect any place in his area (apart from a hospital) where a mentally disordered person is living, if there is reason to think that the patient is not being properly cared for (s.115). If there is reason to think that a person who may be mentally disordered is being neglected or ill-treated or "kept otherwise than under proper control," or is living alone and unable to care for himself, the social worker may apply to a magistrate for a warrant to gain entry to private premises and, if necessary, remove the patient to a place of safety (s.135(1)). A full account of these powers is given in Chapter 4.

A second category consists of his powers to apprehend absconders. An approved social worker is amongst those who are entitled to recapture compulsory patients who escape from a variety of situations: on the way to a hospital or place of safety or between the two, from that hospital or place of safety, or when in breach of the conditions attached to leave of absence from hospital or the directions of a guardian (ss.18 and 138). A full account appears in Chapter 7. This sort of police activity is not very popular either with hospitals or with social workers. It is only infrequently undertaken, save where the absconder is a criminal offender (and not always then) or has escaped from a maximum security special hospital (when there is likely to be a considerable hue and cry in which the police will be involved).

The third and most important category consists of the social worker's role in the process of arranging compulsory admission to hospital. He has a similar but much less frequently invoked role in arranging reception into guardianship in the community, and in that case he is also likely to be involved in carrying out the responsibilities of a guardian on behalf of his authority or in supervising the work of a private guardian. This is discussed in Chapter 9. But where a social worker has been involved in compelling a patient to go into hospital, he will have very little part to play in what happens thereafter. He may be asked to supply a social inquiry report for the hospital (see below) or for a mental health review tribunal (see Chapter 8) or to arrange the after-care for which his authority is responsible when the time comes for the patient to be discharged (see Chapter 9), but these tasks may also be given to non-approved social workers. The approved social worker has no legal voice in the treatment of the patient while in hospital or in whether the patient is ready to be discharged. This is one reason why social workers find their role in compulsory admission so much more troubling than their role in taking children into local authority care. It is some explanation for the uneasy relationship between social workers and doctors, which is explored in section 5 of this chapter.

Another problem for social workers arranging compulsory admission is that the patient's nearest relative not only retains a parallel power to do so but also has a limited right to discharge the patient from hospital. This fact obviously devalues the apparent importance attached to the social worker's professional contribution, although both in law and in practice the position is rather more complex. Before examining the inter-relationship of the social worker and the nearest relative in the process of compulsory admission, therefore, we must find out who the nearest relative is and what he can do.

(b) *The patient's nearest relative*

The patient's nearest relative is normally determined by taking whoever comes first on the list of relatives (s.26(1) and (3)). However, a person who does not "ordinarily reside" in the United Kingdom, Channel Islands or Isle of Man must be ignored if the patient does reside here (s.26(5)(*a*)). A person under the age of 18 must be ignored unless he is the patient's spouse (or recognised cohabitant, see under spouse below) or parent (but who would "section" a two-year-old child?) (s.26(5)(*c*)). A new provision in the 1983 Act promotes to the top of the list any relative (or relatives) who is looking after the patient or with whom the patient ordinarily resides (or, if now an in-patient, last lived with or was looked after by) (s.26(4)). This is particularly likely to affect people caring for their elderly and demented relatives, who might otherwise yield to an older brother or sister or an estranged spouse. It does not, however, promote relatives who look after a patient while he is in hospital unless they did so before he went in. Curiously, a relative who is himself a mental patient (informal or compulsory) is not automatically ignored, although he may be replaced by the county court (see section 2(d) below). The list of relatives is as follows:

Spouse. A husband or wife comes first even if aged under 18, but must be ignored if they are permanently separated, either by agreement or under the order of a court, or if one of them has deserted the other (s.26(5)(*b*)). These are not exactly easy questions for a social worker or hospital to determine, especially at short notice. Desertion involves an intentional withdrawal from cohabitation, without the other's consent or a good excuse. To be separated by agreement or court order normally means that the agreement or order must formally relieve the parties of their duty to live together. But most agreements to separate these days are quite informal and the only court orders (apart from divorce) which release from the duty to cohabit are decrees of judicial separation or anti-molestation injunctions granted in the county court, and (possibly) exclusion orders granted in a magistrates' court. Ordinary maintenance and custody orders do not. However, it is probably safe to disregard a spouse if they are in fact separated and the separation is likely to be permanent. If the patient is unmarried, or if the spouse can be disregarded under these rules, then a *cohabitant* who has been living with the patient as husband or wife for at least six months and is still doing so (or was until the patient went into hospital) must be treated as a spouse (s.26(6)).

Son or daughter. This includes adopted children, but not step-children or a man's illegitimate children (s.26(2)). If there are several, the eldest is preferred regardless of sex (s.26(3)), subject now to the preference given to the "caring" relative.

Father or mother. The 1983 Act now places father and mother on an equal footing, so the elder or carer will take priority (s.26(3)), but fathers of illegitimate children (s.26(2)) do not count, and those divested of authority over the patient by an order under section 38 of the Sexual Offences Act 1956 (s.26(5)(*d*)) must be ignored. For reasons which are explained in section 2(e) below, children under 18 are hardly ever compulsorily admitted, but in some circumstances their oldest parent will not be nearest relative. If there is a court order granting custody or guardianship to someone else (for example, to the mother in divorce proceedings), that person will be "nearest relative" even if not a relative at all. The same is true of people made guardians by deed or will of either parent or given custody in a separation agreement between the parents (s.28). If a local authority has parental rights over a child or young person, either by a care order under the Children and Young Persons Act 1969 or a resolution under section 3 of the Child Care Act 1980, the local authority is nearest relative unless there is another parent whose rights have not been assumed by the resolution or the patient has a spouse (s.27). If the child has been made a ward of court, no application for compulsory admission to hospital can be made without the court's leave and the functions of nearest relative can only be exercised by or with leave of the court. Reception or transfer into Mental Health Act guardianship is not possible at all, presumably because the child is already in the guardianship of the court (s.33).

Brother or sister. Grandparent. Grandchild. Uncle or aunt. Nephew or niece. Within these categories, the principles applicable to sons or daughters also apply. The eldest in any category usually comes first, regardless of sex, relatives of the whole blood are preferred to those of the half-blood, and illegitimate children are treated as if they were the legitimate children of their mothers, but are unrelated to their fathers (s.26(2) and (3)), and the caring relative is promoted (s.26(4)).

Non-related caretakers. The list now ends with any person who is *not* a relative within any of the above categories, but with whom the patient ordinarily resides (or did so before he was last admitted to hospital) and has done so continuously for at least five years (s.26(7)). This rule is quite different from the preference given to the *relative* who has been looking after the patient. These non-relatives will only count as nearest relative if there is no-one else on the list and can never be treated as the nearest relative of a married patient unless the spouse can be ignored because of permanent separation or desertion.

Authorising another to act. The legal nearest relative can always authorise someone else to perform his functions (under regulation 14 of the Mental Health (Hospital, Guardianship and Consent to Treatment) Regulations 1983), provided that that person is not excluded under section 26(5). The authority must be in writing and given to the person authorised, with notice to the hospital managers if the patient is already detained in hospital, to the local social services authority if the patient is in the authority's guardianship, and to both local social services authority and the guardian if the patient is in private guardianship. Authorisation can be revoked at any time in the same way. This is obviously a sensible provision for the nearest relative who has little contact with the patient. But there is no requirement to register the authorisation with the local authority before any question of compulsion arises. A social worker may perhaps only discover that it has been given when he contacts the nearest relative, which rather defeats the object of the exercise.

Appointment by the county court. If there is no nearest relative or the nearest relative is in some way unsuitable, the county court has power to appoint some-one to perform the task. This is more frequently used as a method of overriding the wishes of the patient's family and will be discussed in section 2(d) below.

The nearest relative has a role parallel to that of an approved social worker in arranging the patient's compulsory admission to hospital or reception into guardianship. The former is discussed in section 2(c) below and the latter in Chapter 9. Unlike the approved social worker, however, he also has power to discharge a civil patient from compulsion, although this may be prevented if the patient would be likely to act dangerously were he to be released. This is discussed in Chapter 7. Moreover, the general principle is that whenever the nearest relative cannot himself discharge the patient from hospital, he may apply for the case to be reviewed by a mental health review tribunal. The only exception is where he has been barred from discharging a patient admitted for up to 28 days' assessment. A full account of the powers and procedures of tribunals appears in Chapter 8.

In the debates leading up to the 1982 amendments, many had suggested that the powers of the nearest relative should be removed. An independent social assessment was certainly needed in addition to the medical opinions, but the relative could not supply it. He had no professional knowledge, either of mental disorder or of the facilities available for treatment. He was too closely involved with the patient to judge the situation dispassionately and might easily assume that the only response to a crisis was immediate admission to hospital. Yet it was for exactly the same reasons that the DHSS (1978) argued that the relative should retain his powers. "Some relatives may prefer to feel that they are in control of the situation, and they will be in the best position to judge when they are unable to cope any longer with the patient." Despite this, the DHSS also hoped that the strengthened role and expertise of the social worker would in fact lead to their making even more of the applications than they already do. The inconsistency of this attitude is obvious and does nothing to help either the social worker or the relative to understand what is really expected of him.

(c) *Arranging compulsory admission: the relative and the social worker*

Under section 11(1) of the 1983 Act, applications for compulsory admission to hospital either for assessment or for treatment may be made either by an approved social worker or by the patient's nearest relative. Even if the professional opinion of the social worker is that the application should not be made, he cannot prevent the relative from making it (perhaps, in the case of an emergency application, on the recommendation of the family G.P. or of a locum with no previous knowledge of the family at all). In practice, of course, the social worker is the person who carries the necessary forms and knows about the admission policies of the local hospitals. He may therefore be tempted to deny the relative access to these. This would be most improper, for the Act gives the relative the right to apply whatever the social worker may think.

However, wherever a patient is compulsorily admitted on the application of his nearest relative (except on an emergency application), section 14 now insists that the managers notify the local social services authority, for the place where the patient lives, as soon as practicable. The authority must then arrange as soon as practicable for a social worker to interview the patient and provide the hospital with a report on his social circumstances. This need not be done by an approved social worker, but it will be all the more helpful if it is. The hospital doctors require as much information as possible about the context in which the incident or behaviour which triggered the admission took place, and also about other methods of handling the problem, and this is what an approved social worker should be trained to assess. It was obviously intended that this duty should apply to all compulsory admissions except those which only last for 72 hours. Unfortunately, the section does not make it entirely clear whether it applies when an emergency admission is automatically converted into an ordinary admission for assessment by the provision of a second medical recommendation during the first 72 hours. Ideally, the hospital should have an objective social assessment as soon as possible after any admission in which it was not available beforehand (or if available was ignored).

On the other hand, the nearest relative cannot prevent the social worker from making an application for admission for assessment. But either before or within a reasonable time after making such an application, section 11(3) now requires the social worker to do what he can to inform the person (if any) who appears to be the patient's nearest relative, not only of the admission but also of the relative's right to discharge the patient. As an admission for assessment only lasts for 28 days, or 72 hours if in an emergency, "within a reasonable time" must mean as soon as possible. But when telling the relative of his power to discharge, it would be wise also to tell him that the patient's doctor may prevent this if the patient "would be likely to act in a manner dangerous to other persons or to himself" (s.25(1)).

However, if a social worker is proposing to make an application for the patient's long term admission for treatment (or, for that matter, reception into guardianship), he *must* consult the person (if any) who appears to be the nearest relative. The only exceptions are where this is not reasonably practicable or would involve unreasonable delay (s.11(4)). In theory, this should hardly ever be so, because an admission for assessment gives ample time to trace and consult the relative. In practice, admission for assessment is often used as a short term admission for treatment, after which it is hoped that no further compulsion will be necessary. There is still little excuse for not consulting the family about the possibility of longer detention.

Whether or not he has been consulted in this way, the nearest relative has the right to prevent an admission for treatment (or a reception into guardianship) if he objects to it. He must notify his objection, either to the social worker who proposes to make the application, or to the local social services authority (s.11(4)). The Act does not insist that the social worker obtains the relative's positive consent, but he must record in the application whether he has consulted the relative and, if so, that the relative does not object (see Mental Health (Hospital, Guardianship and Consent to Treatment) Regulations 1983, Form 9). If the relative does object, the social worker cannot make the application (s.11(4)). He may, however, apply to the county court for the relative to be replaced, on the ground that the objection is unreasonable (see section 2(d) below). If this is done while the patient is still detained for assessment, the patient may be detained and treated until the dispute is settled, even though the normal 28 days have gone by.

More commonly, however, the patient's relatives are anxious for him to be admitted, but would like the social worker to take the responsibility. This is natural enough. The social worker is familiar with the procedures and relatives are often anxious that the patient should not feel betrayed or let down, or even know that his family no longer feel able to cope with him. Some social workers believe that it is good practice to encourage the nearest relative to face facts and to take responsibility for an admission which the family wants. The more common view (shared by the DHSS, 1978) is that the social worker should shoulder the burden. His professional training should enable him to withstand and overcome any antagonism from the patient. Even if he cannot do this, it is far more important for the patient's own future health and well-being that he should retain a good relationship (if he has one) with his family than with his social worker.

Social workers can come under a great deal of pressure to act, not only from families but also from some doctors. What is their legal position? The 1983 Act now insists that they do at least consider the case. If the nearest relative of a patient living in the area of a local social services authority "requires" this, the authority *must* direct an approved social worker as soon as practicable to consider the patient's case with a view to making an application (s.13(4)). There is no discretion to refuse, however unreasonable the demand. But the duty does only apply to a "patient," who is defined (in section 145(1)) as a "person suffering or appearing to be suffering from mental disorder." The social worker is under no duty to make the application, but if he decides not to do so, he must give the relative a written explanation.

Section 13(1) does impose a positive duty upon an approved social worker to make an application, but only if three conditions are fulfilled. First, the patient must be physically present in the area covered by the social worker's local authority (this means their whole county or metropolitan district, not simply the area covered by the social worker's "area team"). Section 13(3) makes it clear that an approved social worker also has power to act outside his own local authority. This is most desirable if the patient is his own client, but there is no legal duty to do so. Secondly, the social worker must be "satisfied" that the application ought to be made. He has no duty to act in any case which he does not himself judge to merit it, whatever the family or the doctors may say. Thirdly, if he is satisfied that the application should be made, he has the duty to make it himself if he "is of the opinion, having regard to any wishes expressed by relatives of the patient or any other relevant circumstances, that it is necessary or proper for the application to be made *by him*" (s.13(1); emphasis supplied). This is a clear hint that he should be ready to do the job himself if this is what the family wants, rather than expect them to do it.

However, before an approved social worker makes any application for admission to hospital, he *must* "interview the patient in a suitable manner and satisfy himself that detention in a hospital is in all the circumstances of the case the most appropriate way of providing the care and medical treatment of which the patient stands in need" (s.13(2)). This is a most welcome recognition of the professional contribution which a properly trained social worker has to make, although it has a slightly hollow ring when that contribution can easily be avoided by getting the relative to apply instead. The interview itself may certainly present difficulties, both legal and practical.

What is meant by an "interview"? We tend to think of a two-way oral exchange, such as happens on television or radio or when we apply for a job. It is certainly intended that the social worker should find "suitable" means of communicating with, for example, a deaf and dumb person or a foreign language speaker, if necessary through an interpreter. But what if the patient cannot communicate at all or (perhaps understandably) refuses to do so? The Oxford English Dictionary contains old definitions which involve only a personal meeting, or getting a "view, glance or glimpse." Could that be enough to be "suitable" in such cases? The problem with this suggestion is that the Act already requires that any applicant, whether relative or social worker, has "personally seen" the patient, either within the 14 days which end on the date of the application (s.11(5)) or, in an emergency application, within the past 24 hours (s.4(5)). An interview suggests something more, although possibly only an attempt by the social worker to communicate in the best way possible with the particular patient before him.

In addition to the interview, although not necessarily as a result of it, the social worker must be satisfied that detention in hospital is the most appropriate way of providing the care and medical treatment which the patient needs. There is more than a faint suggestion here that it is the doctor's task to decide what care and treatment the patient needs and the social worker's task to decide the best way of providing it. However, as we shall see in section 5 of this chapter, although the relationship between the social worker and the doctors is by no means an easy one, there are elements in the determination of the patient's needs on which the social worker is certainly entitled to have a view. In law, the social worker may disagree with both the family and the doctors. In practice, he should be sure of his ground before doing so.

(d) *Replacement of the nearest relative by the county court*

The county court may appoint an acting nearest relative, under section 29 of the 1983 Act, either as a way of supplying a relative for a patient who has none, or more commonly of overriding the wishes of the relative which he has. Proceedings are very rare. There were 9 cases in 1979, 15 in 1980, and none at all in 1981, according to the Judicial Statistics. Application to the court may be made by any relative, any other person with whom the patient is living or was living just before going into hospital, or an approved social worker (s.29(2)). There are four possible grounds (s.29(3)):

(a) that the patient has no nearest relative or that it is not reasonably practicable (perhaps because of the patient's mental condition) to discover whether he has one or who it is; or

(b) that the nearest relative is incapable of acting because of mental disorder or other illness; or

(c) that the nearest relative unreasonably objects to the making of an application for admission for treatment or for reception into guardianship; or

(d) that the nearest relative has exercised, or is likely to exercise, the power to discharge the patient without due regard to the patient's welfare or the interests of the public.

The situation in ground (c) is the only one in which the health or social services are likely to be seriously troubled. But when is a relative being unreasonable? There are two reported cases in which the Court of Appeal has considered the question.

The most important is *W.* v. *L.* [1974] Q.B. 711 (see also on page 46, in connection with the definition of mental illness). The patient, who was adjudged both psychopathic and mentally ill, had indulged in a variety of sadistic acts towards animals and had threatened his wife and the baby she was expecting. His admission for observation was about to run out and the baby had been born. His wife objected to an admission for treatment. She was confident that she could keep him under control with the drugs prescribed. No doubt she did not wish to break up the family and jeopardise her husband's employment just at the birth of their first child.

The Court of Appeal decided that the test was not what the relative subjectively considered reasonable, but what an objectively reasonable relative would do in the particular circumstances of the case. In this case, a reasonable person would regard it as too great a risk, particularly to the baby, to have the husband home until he had been cured. The wife was therefore replaced as nearest relative so that the application could be made.

But will it ever be reasonable for the relative to disagree with the professional opinions? The second Court of Appeal case was concerned more with a technicality than with the substance. In *B. (A.)* v. *B. (L.)* (*mental health patient*) [1980] 1 W.L.R. 116, the law report does not explain why both the doctors and the social worker considered an application necessary. Two doctors had recommended it, but as their examinations had been more than seven days apart, their recommendations were not technically sufficient to found an application. The mother objected and the county court judge thought her objection unreasonable. On appeal, the mother complained that she had not seen the medical opinions and that she could not be unreasonable if these were not sufficient. The Court of Appeal held that it was enough that her solicitor had seen the reports and that the applicant did not have to "get his tackle in order" before going to the county court. That may be done after the court has ruled on whether the objection is unreasonable.

The second point is fair enough, for the evidence on which the social worker takes the case to court will probably be out of date before he comes to make the application. Unfortunately, the judgment in this case is couched in such a way as to suggest that the mother *must* have been unreasonable, simply because the two doctors had recommended admission. This cannot be right. First, the Act's scheme relies upon the independent concurrence of the applicant and doctors as an effective protection for the patient. It was never intended that the decision should be left solely to the doctors. As the Act gives the relative a veto unless the court decides otherwise, it clearly contemplates that the court should evaluate the reasonableness of the relative's attitude in the light of all the available evidence, and not simply rubber-stamp the original doctors' views. Secondly, in *W.* v. *L.* the Court had likened the process to that of dispensing with a parent's agreement to an adoption order on the ground that the agreement is unreasonably withheld. In adoption cases, the court is not allowed simply to substitute its own judgment for that of the parent. It must decide whether the parent's decision falls within the range of possible decisions which a reasonable parent might make. Sometimes, there are two reasonable views open to such a person, and the court must not then interfere simply because it would have chosen the other one *Re* W. (*an infant*) [1971] A.C. 682).

There is one reported example of a county court judge declining to find the nearest relative unreasonable. In *S*. v. *G*. [1981] J.S.W.L. 174, the judge took as his starting point the merits of the doctors' case for detention, stating that "it is vitally important that matters about which doctors have to be satisfied should be clearly proved." The doctors did disagree about the precise diagnosis, but they had no doubt that the patient was mentally ill. Equally, however, his detention was no longer necessary in the interests of his own health or safety. The question was whether it was necessary for the protection of other persons. The judge concluded from the evidence that it was not. Hence the father's objection could not be unreasonable. The judge did not have to consider whether there might be two reasonable views.

This case is only an illustration of the approach which the county court judge may take, for it cannot bind others. But it would seem logical for him to consider whether there is a case for the admission for treatment before deciding whether the relative's attitude to it is reasonable. In this case, the father had obtained an adjournment in order to seek evidence from two other psychiatrists and they had reached a different conclusion from the recommending doctors. If the judge had heard the case when it was first listed, he would have granted the application. But the situation may change very rapidly and a short delay before the hearing may well strengthen the relative's case.

In the meantime, section 29(4) provides that if the patient is detained for assessment and an application for the replacement of the nearest relative on ground (c) or (d) is made before the 28 days run out, the patient may still be detained for assessment (which includes treatment) until the application has been finally disposed of. This includes the time limited for appealing from the county court to the Court of Appeal and the time taken for any such appeal to be heard or withdrawn. If the nearest relative is replaced, the patient may be detained for a further seven days to enable the formalities of an admission for treatment to be completed.

The court may appoint either the applicant or any other able and willing person to act as nearest relative, but if the applicant is an approved social worker the court must appoint his local authority rather than him (s.29(1)). If a local authority is given the powers of a nearest relative, it must arrange for the patient to be visited in hospital and do whatever else would be expected of the patient's parents (s.116). This obviously involves far more than the legal functions of a nearest relative. The displaced nearest relative can apply for the patient's case to be reviewed by a mental health review tribunal once in every 12 month period after the order (s.66(1)(h) and (2)(g)). However, if he was displaced on ground (c) or (d), he cannot apply to the county court for the order to be discharged (see s.30(1)(b)). The order will automatically lapse when the patient ceases to be liable to be detained (or subject to guardianship) or if no application is made for his detention or guardianship within three months of the order (s.30(4)).

If the order was made on ground (a) or (b), the court itself may specify a maximum duration (s.29(5)) and the displaced relative can apply for it to be discharged (s.30(1)(b)). If the person displaced has ceased to be the nearest relative under section 26, for example because the patient has married, the new nearest relative may apply for the order to be discharged (s.30(1)(b)). The person appointed as acting nearest relative may always apply for discharge (s.30(1)(a)) or for its variation to appoint someone else instead (s.30(2)). So may any relative if the person appointed dies (s.30(3)). An approved social worker may apply for the variation of the order, but not for its discharge (s.30(2)). Thus a person displaced for unreasonableness cannot regain his position unless the patient is discharged.

Nevertheless, the commitment procedures assume that the patient is an irrational being whose liberty may properly be removed by extra-judicial process. His nearest relative, on the other hand, is assumed to be a rational individual, whose voice in the patient's future may only be removed after due process of law. In some families, it must be difficult to decide who should be labelled "patient" and who "relative," but the consequences of that initial allocation are crucial for all concerned.

3. *Parents, Children and Local Authorities*

Mental Health Act compulsion is hardly ever used for patients under the age of 16, for two reasons. The first is that there are other means of overcoming any opposition from the child or his family to whatever care or treatment is thought most appropriate to his needs. If the child is under 17, he may be brought before a juvenile court in care proceedings under section 1 of the Children and Young Persons Act 1969. The applicant will usually be the local social services authority, although proceedings may be brought by a police officer or the N.S.P.C.C. The ground alleged would be that the child's "proper development is being avoidably prevented or neglected or his health is being avoidably impaired or neglected or he is being ill-treated." This can include neglect of his mental and emotional health or development was well as purely physical neglect or ill-treatment (*F.* v. *Suffolk County Council* (1981) 79 L.G.R. 554). It must also be shown that the child is "in need of care or control which he is unlikely to receive unless the court makes an order under this section in respect of him" (s.1(2)).

The orders available include both a hospital and a guardianship order under the 1983 Act (s.1(3)(*d*) and (*e*)). However, the conditions required for these orders in criminal cases must be fulfilled (s.1(5)(*b*)). These insist on medical evidence of the child's mental condition and they also limit the use of guardianship to people who have reached the age of 16 (see further in Chapter 5). Alternatively, the court may make a care order (s.1(3)(*c*)). This vests parental powers and duties in the local authority, usually until the child is 18, but in some cases until 19, unless the court discharges the order earlier (Child Care Act 1980, s.10; 1969 Act, ss.20 and 21). The local authority then has a wide discretion to decide where the child shall be placed (1980 Act, s.21). A hospital order, on the other hand, may be renewed indefinitely by the hospital authorities for as long as the patient's condition warrants it. But it provides for no other form of care should the patient be discharged from hospital. The juvenile court is therefore allowed to make both a care order and a hospital order (1969 Act, s.1(4)). The local authority is then the patient's nearest relative for as long as the care order is in force (1983 Act, s.27) and can make other provision for the child when the doctors decide that he is ready to leave hospital. In practice, however, most of the same objectives can be secured simply by making a care order, for which no complicated medical evidence is required.

Another method of overriding parental wishes for any child under the age of 18 is to apply for him to become a ward of the High Court. Any interested person may do this. If the Court decides to intervene, it becomes the child's guardian and all important decisions must then be referred to the Court. The welfare of the child is the "first and paramount consideration" in any question concerning his custody or upbringing (Guardianship of Minors Act 1971, s.1). The procedure has been used to challenge particular decisions of parents whose general care of the child cannot be criticised. Thus the Court can prohibit a treatment proposal supported both by the parents and the doctors. This happened, for example, when Heilbron J. decided that the sterilisation of an 11-year-old girl with Sotos' syndrome was not in the child's best interests (*Re D. (A Minor) (Wardship Sterilisation)* [1976] Fam. 185). On the other hand, the Court may decide to allow treatment which the parents oppose. This happened, for example, when the Court of Appeal sanctioned an operation to save the life of a Down's syndrome baby after the parents had decided that it would be kinder to allow her to die (*Re B. (A Minor) (Wardship: Medical Treatment)* [1981] 1 W.L.R. 1421). Where a child is a ward of court, Mental Health Act guardianship is impossible, compulsory admission to hospital requires the Court's leave, and the functions of nearest relative can only be exercised by or with leave of the Court (s.33). In practice, however, none of the compulsory procedures is necessary for the Court can sanction whatever it thinks best. The Court's power to coerce its wards is, it appears, more extensive than a parent's power to coerce his child (see *Hewer* v. *Bryant* [1971] 1 Q.B. 357, *per* Sachs L.J.).

However, parents do possess some coercive powers over their children and these are the second reason why Mental Health Act compulsion is usually quite unnecessary. The simplest account of these regards the age of 16 as a straightforward dividing line, below which children are subject to their parents' control and above which they are not (see, for example, Gostin, 1975). Certainly, if a 16 or 17 year old is capable of expressing his own wishes and wishes to go into hospital, his parents cannot prevent him (1983 Act, s.131(2)). Further, his consent to any surgical, medical or dental treatment which would otherwise be a trespass to his person is as effective as it would be if he were of full age (Family Law Reform Act 1969, s.8(1)). The common law requires only a broad understanding of what is proposed in order for any consent to be effective (see further in Chapter 6). Most 16 and 17 year olds will therefore be in the same position as any other informal patient.

It has been argued (*cf.* Foulkes, 1970) that a parent may give a consent which will prevail over the objections of a capable but protesting 16 or 17 year old. This is because the provision validating such a child's consent does not invalidate any consent which would otherwise have been effective (1969 Act, s.8(3)). However, the common law does not grant parents the right of physical coercion over children who have reached the age of discretion (see again *Hewer* v. *Bryant* [1971] 1 Q.B. 357 *per* Sachs L.J. and the authorities quoted there). For a capable child, the age of discretion is certainly no older than 16 and for boys it may be 14. It is therefore safe to assume that a capable 16 or 17 year old is master of his own fate unless a court order or the Mental Health Act procedures are used. The more difficult question is whether a capable child *below* the age of 16 is able either to consent or to object to proposed medical treatment. Writers on the law of tort or crime (for example, Williams, 1983; Skegg 1973; *cf.* Samuels, 1983) tend to take the view that he may give a valid consent to anything which he is capable of understanding. Consent is, after all, only required because the treatment would otherwise be a crime or a tort against the child. It is not a crime or tort against the parent. This view was recently supported by Woolf J. when he refused a declaration that the NHS advice on giving contraceptive treatment in confidence to girls under 16 was unlawful (*Gillick* v. *West Norfolk and Wisbech Area Health Authority* [1983] 3 W.L.R. 859). If the child is old enough to consent, then logically he is also old enough to object, but if he does not do so, the *Gillick* case suggests that the parent's consent may suffice as an alternative to his. Where a child is not capable of giving a valid consent to treatment, his parents can undoubtedly either consent or object on his behalf. These powers almost certainly persist up to the age of 18 if the child remains incapable, either of consenting to treatment or of "expressing his own wishes" as the case may be.

The practical answer, therefore, is that where a child is capable but strongly protesting it will usually be unwise to proceed without invoking compulsory powers; where he is capable and consenting it will usually be safe to proceed; and where he is incapable the parents' wishes will prevail unless the compulsory powers are used. However, the parents' powers are always subject to the power of the Court to intervene if they are not acting in the child's best interests. Does this mean that the child could sue if no one invokes the court's powers and the treatment is carried out? The parent's consent will not protect a doctor who has advised or carried out treatment in breach of his duty to take reasonable care of his patient. But there are cases, of which sterilisation is a prime example, where the doctor is not in breach of his duty of care but the treatment may not be in the child's best interests. Where there are good therapeutic reasons for a treatment, it is probably safe to proceed where the parent and doctor *reasonably believe* that it is in the child's best interests. The same is probably true of harmless non-therapeutic procedures, such as male circumcision. But an irreversible treatment for which there are no good therapeutic reasons should not be given unless all concerned are satisfied that it is *in fact* in the best interests of the child. Such cases will exist, but *Re D.* (above) was not one of them. When in doubt, the safest course is to seek the views of the High Court.

These principles still leave a great deal of discretion in the hands of parents and doctors. There is every reason to believe that parents of handicapped or mentally disturbed children will find it hard to put their children's interests first all the time. Equally, the children's welfare may be damaged even further if they are forced into confrontation. Hence Gostin (1975) argued that parents should not be able to "volunteer" their children for admission to mental hospitals without some additional check, such as an automatic review by a mental health review tribunal. In *Parham* v. *J.L. and J.R.* 444 U.S. 584 (1979), the United States Supreme Court accepted that these children did have liberty interests which required protection. But the majority considered that the independent judgment of the hospital's medical superintendant was sufficient, not only where the child was in the care of his parents but also were he was a ward of the state. The minority accepted that a prior hearing might do more harm than good to relationships within the natural family but argued for a subsequent review. Where the child was a ward of the state, however, there were no such relationships to be damaged. Nor could it be assumed that the authorities would share the natural inclination of parents to put their children's interests first. Thus the minority considered that children in care should not be admitted to mental hospitals without a prior judicial hearing.

These arguments are particularly relevant now that the Criminal Justice Act 1982 has placed restrictions upon the circumstances in which children in care may be kept in "accommodation provided for the purpose of restricting liberty." It has been assumed that this means secure accommodation provided in community homes and youth treatment centres for children in care. But there is nothing in the Act to exclude locked wards in mental hospitals, regional secure units, and other secure facilities. Thus children should not be admitted to such places unless they are either absconders or likely to injure themselves or others if kept anywhere else (1982 Act, s.25). They cannot be kept there for longer than 72 hours without the authority of a juvenile court. If the court considers that the grounds exist, it must authorise further detention for a specified period of not more than 3 months but this may be extended for a further six months (Secure Accommodation Regulations 1983).

These regulations operate as a check upon the normal power of a local authority to decide where any child in its care is to be accommodated (Child Care Act 1980, s.21). They do not operate where there is some other authority for placing the child in a secure hospital, such as a hospital order or a compulsory civil commitment. Nor, of course, do they prevent a local authority from arranging for any child in its care to be admitted to an ordinary mental hospital or to some other place which is designed to offer treatment for his mental condition. However, there is no reason to suppose that a local authority has any greater power than a parent to impose medical treatment upon the children in its care. If a capable 16 or 17 year old objects to treatment, it should not be given without recourse to the compulsory procedures in the Mental Health Act (and this, of course, requires that he be admitted to a hospital within the meaning of that Act). Even below that age, it will depend on the child's capacity. Where the child is in voluntary care (under section 2 of the Child Care Act 1980) the authority can only authorise day-to-day treatment and such other measures as the parents allow. All of this will have important implications for the treatment of disturbed adolescents in community homes or youth treatment centres. The one consolation to local authorities is that if they *are* acting within their powers (that is, where they have parental rights over a child who has not reached the age of discretion) the High Court will be most reluctant to allow the parents or anyone else to use the wardship procedure to challenge them (*A*. v. *Liverpool City Council* [1982] A.C. 363). Where a local authority has parental rights over a child patient, it must arrange for him to be visited in hospital and do whatever else would be expected of his parents (1983 Act, s.116).

The import of much of this is that it may be necessary to invoke the Mental Health Act procedures a little more frequently than has previously been thought. From the child's point of view, this is by no means a bad thing, for he will then have access to the Mental Health Act Commission, to the mental health review tribunal, and to the greater safeguards applicable to the medical treatment of detained patients (see Chapters 6 and 8). There would, indeed, be something to be said for regarding all child patients as detained patients for these purposes. Their numbers are not large, for strenuous efforts have recently been made to get them out of hospitals and back into the community. But these in no way mitigate the situation of those who remain, often effectively abandoned by their parents and the child care authorities alike.

4. *The Doctors*

(a) *Their qualifications*

Applications for admission to hospital under section 2 (for assessment) or section 3 (for treatment), or for reception into guardianship under section 7, must be supported by the recommendations of two doctors (ss.2(3), 3(3) and 7(3)). An application for admission for assessment in an emergency under section 4 requires the support of only one (s.4(3)). A warrant under section 135(1) to gain entry to private premises and remove the patient to a place of safety can only be executed if a doctor is present (s.135(4)), although the patient can be taken to hospital without any formal recommendation. Medical evidence is also required for an order to remove a person to a hospital or other place under section 47 of the National Assistance Act 1948 (discussed in

Chapter 4), although in this case it is the normal procedure which requires one doctor and the emergency version which requires two. The only compulsory civil procedure in which the support, or at least the presence, of a doctor is not required is the police power to remove a person from a public place to a place of safety under section 136 (discussed in Chapter 5).

Whenever the Mental Health Act requires the recommendations of two doctors, one of them must be on the list of those approved under section 12(2) "as having special experience in the diagnosis or treatment of mental disorder." Approval is a function of the Secretary of State, carried out by district health authorities, who must obtain the agreement of at least two members of an advisory panel, set up for each district by the regional health authority, for any particular appointment (DHSS Circular HSC (IS)18, 1974). The Percy Commission (1957) did not suggest that approval should be limited to consultant psychiatrists, but that it could include other hospital psychiatrists and specialists with suitable experience, psychiatrists in private practice, local authority and school medical officers (who are now community physicians), and some general practitioners and prison medical officers. The DHSS guidance takes the same view and stresses that there should be enough approved doctors, distributed conveniently over the country, with at least two on the staff of every hospital which takes detained patients. Approval is usually for a period of five years at a time.

It may come as a surprise that all approved doctors are not at least qualified psychiatrists. The problem is that there are only some 2,000 psychiatrists, both qualified and in training, with only some 200 in mental handicap hospitals. The Royal College of Psychiatrists came into being in 1971 and has made strenuous efforts to bring post-graduate training in line with that in other medical specialisms. They have suggested that approval be limited to doctors who are, or are eligible for, membership of the College (or the former equivalent qualification of the Diploma in Psychological Medicine), or other equivalent psychiatric experience or training. Others have gone further and suggested that current practice in psychiatry should be required. It would obviously be sensible for mental handicap admissions to be considered by doctors with special experience in this very different field. Despite all this, the DHSS has not changed its guide-lines, nor does the Act allow health authorities to impose conditions upon approval. Even approval does not guarantee that the doctor will be familiar with the legal requirements: indeed, an approved social worker may well be more knowledgeable than the doctor about this aspect of the matter. But there are still too few approved doctors to go round, which is undoubtedly one of the reasons why emergency admission is used so much more frequently than the other procedures.

In all applications, one of the doctors must, if practicable, have "previous acquaintance" with the patient (s.12(2)). If it has not been possible to use such a doctor, the applicant must explain why (Mental Health (Hospital, Guardianship and Consent to Treatment) Regulations 1983, Forms, 1, 2, 5, 6, 8, 9, 17 and 18). This is thought particularly important in an emergency application, where the solitary doctor need not be an approved specialist, although previous acquaintance is still only required if practicable (s.4(3)). Sometimes an approved doctor will know the patient beforehand, for example because of previous treatment in hospital or a domiciliary visit. But it was originally expected that the patient's general practitioner would supply the second recommendation, having the background knowledge to set the psychiatric symptoms in context. Whether this is any sort of safeguard for the patient must be doubted. A G.P. (significantly now called a family practitioner) usually has little knowledge of psychiatry or experience of mental disorder. He is under much more pressure than the hospital psychiatrist to consider the welfare of his other patients in the family or neighbourhood. Psychiatrists often claim that they spend more time resisting the pressure to admit patients than forcing them in (see, for example, Bean, 1980). But once the specialist has decided to admit the patient, the G.P. is unlikely to disagree. Whatever his experience, qualifications or private views, the structure of relationships between specialists and G.P.s is not such as to encourage him to do so.

Even so, there will still be emergency admissions where the patient has neither the protection of a specialist nor of a doctor who knows him. Many psychiatric emergencies arise in inner cities with floating populations, at times when one doctor is deputising for another, or where there is no psychiatric emergency team to make domiciliary visits at all hours. But these admissions may not always be lawful. It could well be "practicable" for the proposed applicant to chase up a doctor who does know the patient, even though that doctor is not on duty or does not usually make domiciliary visits. Administrative arrangements are not the sole criterion for what is practicable in the eyes of the law.

In practice, of course, it is often extremely difficult to obtain a hospital bed unless a doctor from that hospital has already seen the patient. The law, however, does not insist that one of the doctors must be on the hospital staff. Indeed, it starts from the presumption that both of them should be independent of it. This is because of the spectre of collusion which dominated the procedures for paying patients in the past. Thus no recommending doctor may be, or be related to, a person who receives or has an interest in the receipt of any payments made on account of the maintenance of the patient (s.12(5)(*d*)). This would include having a financial interest in an admitting private mental nursing home. More importantly, the doctor may not be on the staff of the admitting hospital or nursing home, or be related to a doctor who is (s.12(5)(*e*)), although relationship to any other member of the hospital staff does not matter.

Despite this, it was always intended that the great majority of compulsory patients would be admitted on the recommendation of their hospital doctor. Thus, provided that the patient is to be admitted to an NHS hospital as a non-paying patient, *one* of the recommending doctors (or the sole doctor in an emergency) may be a member of its staff (s.12(3)). The 1983 Act goes further. For these patients, *both* doctors may be on the hospital staff, provided that three conditions are fulfilled: (a) getting an outside doctor would cause a delay involving *serious* risk to the patient's health or safety; (b) one of them works at that hospital for less than half the time that he is contracted to work for the NHS; and (c) if one of them is a consultant, the other does not work (either there or elsewhere) in a grade in which he is under that consultant's direction (s.12(4)).

For the purpose of all these rules, however, a G.P. who works part time in a hospital is not regarded as a member of the hospital staff (s.12(6)). But it is difficult to know what the rules can hope to achieve. They prevent a doctor recommending the admission of some-one who is to be his private patient and they prevent a consultant getting together with his registrar or houseman or even another full time consultant at that hospital. But if the aim was to provide two genuinely informed opinions, these might have been more satisfactory than the consultant and G.P. If, on the other hand, the aim was to reassure the patient, he is unlikely to appreciate the niceties. In any event, the rules do not prevent action which he may find equally suspicious. There is, for example, nothing to stop a consultant at the admitting mental hospital from joining with his houseman at the general hospital from which the patient is to be transferred.

There are other rules aimed at securing the doctors' independence. They cannot be partners (s.12(5)(b)), nor can one be employed as an assistant by the other (s.12(5)(c)), and they must not be related to one another, or to a partner or assistant of the other (s.12(5)). A recommending doctor cannot be the applicant (s.12(5)(a)), the applicant's partner (s.12(5)(b)), or employed as an assistant by the applicant (s.12(5)(c)), nor can he be related to any of these people (s.12(5)). Finally, no recommending doctor can be related to the patient himself (s.12(5)). "Related" means being the husband, wife, father, father-in-law, mother, mother-in-law, son, son-in-law, daughter, daughter-in-law, brother brother-in-law, sister or sister-in-law of the person concerned.

No doubt these rules do an excellent job in ensuring that a psychiatrist does not conspire with his assistant to place his wife in a mental nursing home which he runs, but they also invalidate the recommendation of a doctor who happens to be the brother-in-law of some totally disinterested doctor on the hospital staff.

(b) *The medical recommendations*

Each doctor must have "personally examined" the patient (s.12(1)). The Act does not define an examination, which presents much the same difficulty as the social worker's interview. An interview might include holding a conversation through a locked door, but an examination implies that the doctor must at least see the patient. On the other hand, it is difficult to hold an interview with someone who cannot or will not speak, but it may be possible to examine him. If there are two doctors, their examination may be joint. But if they examine separately, not more than five days may elapse between the days on which their examinations took place (s.12(1)).

The Act does not specify that the recommendation must be

signed at the same time as the medical examination. But it is important to state both dates accurately on the forms, for two reasons. First, the recommendations must be *signed* on or before the date of the application itself (s.12(1)). Clearly, one should not make an application and then go looking for evidence to support it. Secondly, the application only remains valid for 14 days, beginning with the date of the last medical *examination*, or in an emergency admission, for 24 hours beginning with the time when the examination actually took place or the application if earlier (s.6(1)). If the patient does not arrive at hospital within these time-limits, it is unlawful either to take him or to detain him there. The only exception to this timetable is where a second medical recommendation is provided after an emergency admission to convert it into an ordinary admission for assessment (s.4(4)). This can obviously happen after the application has been signed, but in all other respects it must comply with the Act's requirements.

Medical recommendations may be single or joint but must be in the forms prescribed by the Mental Health (Hospital, Guardianship and Consent to Treatment) Regulations 1983. Recommendations on forms required for one section cannot be used for another, which may be important to the social worker choosing between ordinary and emergency admissions for assessment. For admission for assessment, the Act only requires them to confirm that the statutory grounds are made out (s.2(3)). The forms do not expressly require them to give any diagnosis or reasons for their opinions about this, but they must explain why informal admission is not suitable (see forms 3 and 4). In an emergency application, the Act similarly does not require reasons (s.4(3)), but the prescribed form requires the doctor to state how long a delay would be caused by waiting for another doctor, why this might result in harm, and whether that harm would be caused to the patient, to those now caring for him, or to other people. He must also state when he first learned that the patient's condition was causing such anxiety that it might warrant an immediate admission to hospital—that day, the day before, within the last week, or more than a week ago (form 7). In an admission for treatment, or reception into guardianship, the Act itself requires the doctors to give grounds for their opinions on the patient's state of health and (where applicable) treatability (ss.3(3) and 7(3)). The forms therefore insist on a clinical description (forms 10, 11, 19 and 20).

They must also explain why hospital detention is necessary, indicating whether other methods of care or treatment (such as out-patient treatment or local authority social services) are available and if so why they are not appropriate, and why informal admission is not appropriate. Guardianship recommendations must explain why the patient cannot appropriately be cared for without powers of guardianship.

(c) *The responsible medical officer*

Once the patient is in hospital, many important legal functions are carried out by the responsible medical officer (RMO), who may well have been one of the recommending doctors. These are discussed in Chapters 6 and 7. The RMO is defined in the Act as the doctor in charge of the patient's treatment (s.34(1)). This must mean the doctor who is formally and professionally responsible for the patient in the hospital.

5. *Doctors and Social Workers*

The social worker and the doctors can themselves override any objections of the nearest relative to an admission for assessment. They will probably be able to persuade a county court judge to override his objections to an admission for assessment or a reception into guardianship. But what can a doctor do if neither the relative nor the social worker is willing to apply? Many doctors have an invincible belief that they have a "common law" duty to treat their patients and they also have a very natural professional desire to do so. The common law does indeed impose upon them a duty to take reasonable care of their patients. But this means taking the care that a reasonable doctor would take in advising and carrying out treatment and care which the patient wants. Apart from a very limited doctrine of necessity (discussed in Chapter 6), it does not entitle a doctor to impose treatments which his patient does not want, still less to interfere in the life of a person who has not even agreed to become his patient. The whole point of the Mental Health Act procedures is to allow medical intervention in circumstances far wider than those which the common law would allow. Those procedures accept that any individual social worker may refuse to act on the medical recommendations. The doctor then has two possible courses of action. He may try to find another social worker who will act or he may complain to the local authority or, of course, combine the two.

This is not an empty threat. It is one thing to say that the social worker has the right to act independently and quite another thing to put it into practice. The doctors are likely to see the social worker, at best, as a junior member of a professional team which is devoted to securing the best possible care and treatment for the patient. At worst, they will see him as little more than a messenger to supply the forms, arrange transport to hospital, and smooth over any difficulties with the patient and his family (see Bean, 1980). The social worker is bound to share something of the medical approach. He is professionally concerned with the assessment of need and the provision of care. Any professional person is likely to believe that his expert knowledge and experience make him better equipped to solve a problem than are the lay people whose problem it is. The law in fact gives social workers much more power to impose solutions upon their clients than it gives to doctors.

However, although the old poor law or duly authorised officer probably had few qualms about taking a patient to hospital against his will, the modern social worker is likely to find this much more difficult. It is not only that "to be able to impose a course of action by physical force if necessary upon another human being is such a violation of the rights of personality that in normal conditions the social worker's integrity no less than the patient's would suffer emotional damage" (Le Mesurier, 1949). Any sensitive person might feel the same, but traditional social work training was based on the principles of casework, which had much in common with those of psychoanalysis. The implied condemnation of the patient's character and behaviour is the opposite of a non-authoritarian or "non-judgmental" attitude towards him and compulsion scarcely allows him any "self-determination." It can also seem a confession of the failure of the social worker's or a colleague's casework techniques and one which could jeopardise the building of a successful relationship with the client in future. The social worker is also committing his client to a situation which is quite outside his control, yet with modern open door policies the patient may be out of hospital and needing his support in a relatively short time. Casework principles no longer figure so prominently in social work training, but any modern course is bound to include sociology, in which the views of the "anti-psychiatrists" (diverse though these are) will certainly be aired. They may learn of research which suggests that the roots of compulsory admission lie far below the comparatively late appearance of the psychiatrist upon the scene, in the "complex struggles and negotiations in families and other social groups about behavioural norms." It also suggests that "the issue of compulsion arises mainly when the 'patient' refuses to accept the definitions of 'illness' and 'health' insisted upon by his significant others" (Jordan, 1981; see Bott, 1971; Lawson, 1966). They will be aware of class biases in both the recognition and treatment of mental disorder and most of them will have come into the profession with a commitment of redressing the more glaring inequalities in society.

Nevertheless, the job inevitably places the approved social worker in a position of authority over his client. If he believes that all mental illness is a myth invented by psychiatrists as part of the structure of social control over the disenfranchised classes, the job is not for him. Part of his task is to reconcile his assessment of the patient's needs with his respect for the patient's rights and integrity. In this he is no different from the doctors, who are by no means insensitive to these issues. The other part of the social worker's task is to reconcile the different pressures from the patient, his family, the doctors and his own assessment of the situation. This in the end comes down to identifying a proper sphere of professional competence within which the social worker may disagree with the doctors, for of his right to disagree with both patient and family there can be no doubt.

The law is not very helpful. It reserves the social worker's right to refuse the medical advice. But the forms expect the doctors to certify that the grounds for admission exist and to explain why informal admission or other solutions are not appropriate. The applicant has only to confirm the procedural details and explain why (if this be so) he could not find a doctor who knew the patient beforehand. He is not expected, by the forms at least, to address his mind to whether a case for compulsion exists. Section 13(2) does now expect the social worker to interview the patient and satisfy himself that detention in hospital is the most appropriate way of providing the care and medical treatment which the patient needs. But it stops short of requiring the social worker to satisfy himself about what that care and treatment is or why it is needed. Yet it is essential for practitioners to confront the issue of what is properly a medical problem and what is properly a social problem or a mixture of the two. The CCETSW scheme for approval goes some way towards this, in the skills which it requires the social worker to show.

These contain such obvious things as being able to carry out the compulsory procedures, to provide the required social reports, to ensure that due regard is paid to the legal rights of clients, to interpret these rights to clients and relatives, and to understand the roles, responsibilities and language of other professionals and to communicate and work effectively with them. But they also include several other skills which are directly relevant to the assessment of whether the grounds for a compulsory admission exist. In fact, each of the three main components in those grounds can contain both a medical and a social element.

The first is a diagnosis of mental disorder or a specific form of it. The doctors involved may be most reluctant to concede the social worker any voice in this question and the latter must obviously tread delicately. But there are cases in which it is necessary to set the patient's behaviour into its social, familial and cultural context in order to make a proper assessment of its meaning. CCETSW expects approved social workers to be able to recognise behavioural symptoms of mental disorder and mental impairment, and to appreciate the impact of the cultural and ethnic background of clients.

The next component is that the disorder is bad enough to warrant (or make appropriate) the patient's detention in hospital. Unfortunately, this assessment must be affected by the fact that enforced medical treatment can only be provided in hospital. Much will therefore depend upon whether medical treatment is needed and the social worker will rarely be in a position to challenge the doctor's opinion about certain types of treatment. He may, however, be able to suggest and arrange for others to be given and in different settings. CCETSW expects him to be able to formulate and execute, in consultation with other professionals, a social care plan including alternatives to compulsory admission to hospital when these are desirable.

The final component is that detention is necessary in the

interests of the patient's own health or safety or for the protection of others. The social worker may not be able to disagree with the opinion that certain treatments are necessary for the patient's own health, but even here he may be able to ascertain whether it is necessary to use compulsory admission in order to secure them. Sometimes it may be possible to do so in less restrictive conditions. Sometimes it may be possible to explore whether the patient is prepared to accept treatment voluntarily. Bean's research (1980) suggests that this issue is not always adequately covered by the doctors, who concentrate upon finding symptoms of mental illness and assessing "dangerousness." In practice, he found, it is the dangerousness rating which determines whether an admission is informal or compulsory. The social worker obviously has a part to play in assessing this. There may be specific features of a particular illness about which the psychiatrist will be more knowledgeable, but in general "psychiatrists have not shown themselves to be particularly skilled at predicting dangerousness. Nor have they been too astute in distinguishing the potential suicide from the pretender" (Clare, 1980). According to Clare, the reason for the popular belief that they have some special skill lies in the equally erroneous belief that most psychiatric patients are actually or potentially violent. Few psychiatrists have gone as far as he in attempting to dispel this faith in their omnicompetence, but there is a great deal of American research casting doubt upon it (see, for example, Steadman, 1979). It is equally doubtful whether social scientists have any sufficiently precise knowledge of the causes of dangerous behaviour to enable them to make valid predictions (compare Prins, 1975, with Webb, 1976). But if these are possible at all, they must be based upon the interaction between the patient and his social circumstances (see, for example, Hepworth, 1982). It is right that CCETSW should expect an approved social worker to be able to assess the situation of clients and to record the evidence for that assessment.

Above all, perhaps, CCETSW expects a professional ability to manage and contain a crisis situation. It is to be hoped that all the professionals involved will bring this quality to their very anxious task. But if all these complex and difficult skills are expected of both the doctors and the social workers, what can be the justification for the continued involvement of the patient's nearest relative? If there is a case for lay involvement, it is as a counterweight to the overmighty power of those who know what's best for us. The relatives are the very last people who can supply the detached but confident judgment which would be necessary to do this. That is what mental health review tribunals are designed to do.

4 The Machinery of Civil Commitment

There are several routes along which a patient may become liable to detention in hospital because of mental disorder, without ever being accused of a criminal offence. The grounds upon which applications for compulsory admission under the Mental Health Act may be made, the role of social workers, doctors and relatives in making them, and the short term power to detain an existing hospital patient for the purpose, have already been covered in earlier chapters, but there are many procedural details still to be mentioned. These include the process of getting the patient to hospital, the duration and possible renewal of his detention there, and the monitoring of the admission documents. The alternative procedure for admitting some people, particularly the elderly, under the National Assistance Act 1948 is also covered. But before all this, we must first consider how the doctors and the social workers can gain access to the patient in a crisis.

1. *Gaining Access*

The three "sections" in Part II of the 1983 Act will not always give the authorities adequate power to deal with a psychiatric crisis. There is no power to apprehend or detain a person until an application has been "duly completed" (see s.6(1)). This cannot be done unless the applicant has had an opportunity of personally seeing the patient (s.11(5)) and a social worker applicant must also interview the patient (s.13(2)). Any application must be "founded on" the requisite medical recommendations (ss.2(3), 3(3), and 4(3)). To give this the doctors must have personally examined the patient (s.12(1)). The difficulty is illustrated by the case of *Townley* v. *Rushworth* (1963) 62 L.G.R. 95:

The defendant's wife had signed an application form for his emergency admission but the doctor had not yet made the medical recommendation. When he went to the house with another relative and two policemen, the defendant told them to leave. The doctor replied that the defendant must go to hospital whether he wanted to or not and began to prepare an injection. One of the policemen restrained the defendant from leaving the room. Seeing a scuffle, the other policeman came up and the defendant punched him on the nose. The doctor then injected the defendant and summoned an ambulance. Only after that did the doctor sign the medical recommendation. Subsequently, the defendant was charged with assault occasioning actual bodily harm to the policeman and convicted by the magistrates. When he appealed to the Divisional Court, however, it was held that as the application form had not been duly completed by the addition of the medical recommendation, the four people in the house had no power to restrain the defendant, and indeed were trespassers. As they were trespassers, the defendant was entitled to use reasonable force to resist them. So, "unless it is to be said that a householder is to sit down and submit, not only to his liberty being infringed in his own house, but also to assault by injection, and to his liberty being removed in hospital, I cannot say that to hit out with the fist is an unreasonable use of force" (Lord Parker of Waddington C.J., at p. 98).

Lanham (1974) has argued that the decision is wrong and that the Act itself authorised the doctor to do what he did. He suggests that because the recommendation can be signed after the application form (provided that both are on the same day) a signed application is enough to authorise the doctor to enter the premises and make his examination. This cannot be right. An application does not authorise anything until it is duly completed and the provisions quoted above (as well as the prescribed application form itself) indicate that this cannot happen until the recommendation has been made. Indeed, the court itself went too far, because Lord Parker assumed that all would have been well if the doctor had signed the recommendation beforehand. This, of course, he was not entitled to do unless he had examined the defendant very recently. But in any event, under section 6(1) a duly completed application merely authorises the taking and conveying to hospital of the patient. There is no reference to entering premises, which is provided for elsewhere by the procedure for getting a magistrate's warrant if entry is refused (see below). Practitioners should not assume that completing the forms, even if it can lawfully be done without seeing the patient immediately, is sufficient to justify entry to private premises, with or without force.

(a) *Common law powers of detention*

On the other hand, the court in *Townley* v. *Rushworth* (1963) 62 L.G.R. 95 did not consider whether the common law might have provided lawful justification for what was done. Although Carson (1982) has argued otherwise, the common law undoubtedly permitted that a "private person may without an express warrant confine a person disordered in his mind who seems disposed to do mischief to himself or any other person" (Bacon's Abridgement, cited in Clerk and Lindsell, 1982, both works of authority). It was this, rather than any statutory authority, which justified the admission of non-pauper patients to madhouses and hospitals in the early days. It could easily be taken too far—hence Lord Mansfield's strictures in *R.* v. *Coate* (1772) Lofft 73 that keepers of madhouses should be taught "that the circumstances of the case alone could support their action," that "everything must appear strictly, with all diligence and due advice, to be done for the best" and that "all unnecessary severity, all confinement other than for the best purpose of the unhappy person's recovery" would be subject to censure; but he had no doubt that such a power existed. And when the Act for regulating Madhouses was passed in 1774, it was designed to provide additional procedural protection, but left the common law grounds for confinement untouched (see s.31). Lord Campbell C.J. was still displaying a similar approach to the Lunacy Act of 1845, which did provide statutory protection to people acting under the certificates and orders which it prescribed, but not to the people actually making the orders. Thus in *Fletcher* v. *Fletcher*(1859) 1 El. & El. 420, he found for a plaintiff against an uncle, who had committed the nephew in the reasonable belief that the nephew was insane but who did not allege that there was actual insanity at the time: "By the common law of England no person can be imprisoned as a lunatic unless he is actually insane at the time." There are several cases dealing with the effect of failure to comply with the Act's procedures and taking contradictory views. But both Lord Denman C.J. in *Shuttleworth's Case* (1846) 9

Q.B. 651 and Coleridge J. in *R. v. Pinder, Re Greenwood* (1855) 24 L.J.Q.B. 148 stated that the common law would permit them to refuse to release an insane person who was dangerous either to the public or to himself. And in *Scott* v. *Wakem* (1862) 3 F. & F. 147, Bramwell B. directed the jury that if the defendant (who was a surgeon) "had made out that the plaintiff was, at the time of the original restraint, a dangerous lunatic, in such a state that it was likely that he might do mischief to any one, the defendant would be justified in putting a restraint upon him, not merely at the moment of the original danger, but until there was reasonable ground to believe that the danger was over" (indeed, he went further than this, and suggested that if the plaintiff's wife had called the defendant in to cure her husband of delirium tremens, or if the plaintiff himself had afterwards approved of what was done, the defendant would have been justified, providing that he did no more than was necessary and proper in the circumstances). Finally, in *Symm* v. *Fraser* (1863) 3 F. & F. 859, Coleridge C.J. directed the jury that the defendant doctors might have succeeded in a plea of justification (they had in fact pleaded that they were not responsible for what was done by attendants whom they had sent after being called in by the plaintiff herself), because what they had done had resulted in the preservation of her life and health, and the prevention of serious mischief to herself or others, while she was suffering from delirium tremens.

Subsequent legislation has at least made it clear that those who operate the statutory procedures correctly have lawful justification for what they do. It even provides some protection for those who operate them incorrectly (as we shall see in Chapter 10). But it does not remove the power to act independently of the statutory procedures and under the common law. It is safe to assume from the cases above that, at the very least, the common law permits any person to restrain a person who is actually insane and who seems disposed to do mischief to himself or others. A reasonable belief in insanity is not enough. And as the common law tended to contrast the dangerous lunatic with the harmless eccentric it may be that a reasonable belief in dangerousness is also not enough. In *Sinclair* v. *Broughton* (1882) 47 L.T. 170, the Judicial Committee of the Privy Council stated that there was no law permitting a magistrate or policeman (in India) to confine a person "in consequence of a bona fide belief that a person is dangerous by reason of actual lunacy; . . . a fortiori, this cannot be done in the case of a bona fide belief of danger from impending lunacy." But these remarks could be understood in several ways. In any event, it is clear that the powers are limited to doing what is necessary and proper for as long as the danger lasts.

It is not at all clear whether it gives a right of entry to private premises. Lanham (1974) has argued that "where a person has a power to arrest the insane and dangerous he can also enter the latter's premises to make the arrest." He bases this on the analogy of the common law power to break into premises to prevent a felony and arrest the offender or to follow a felon into his house in order to arrest him. But a power of arrest does not invariably carry with it the right to enter premises by force and there is no case acknowledging this right in relation to the insane. Indeed, in *Anderdon* v. *Burrows* (1830) 4 C. & P. 210, Lord Tenterden C.J. acknowledged the difficulty, but later said that "the proper course is, if access cannot be obtained, to apply to the higher authority, which has cognisance over such matters, to get the party taken up in order that he may be examined" (this is probably a reference to the judges' powers as delegates of the Crown's prerogative jurisdiction over the person and property of lunatics and idiots, which can no longer be exercised). It would be most unwise to assume that the common law gave any person, relative, doctor or policeman any right to enter premises even where the common law power to arrest exists.

Of course, there may be some other occupier of the premises who is entitled to grant entry. If the defendant in *Townley* v. *Rushworth* (1963) 62 L.G.R. 95 had owned his house jointly with his wife, she could at least have prevented their being trespassers, although there might still have been an assault before the forms were signed. Indeed, it ought to be the case that a wife's rights to occupy the matrimonial home also give her the right to license visitors whether her husband likes it or not (and this was held to be so, at least in the case of domestic violence against her, in *R.* v. *Thornley* (1980) 72 Cr. App. R. 302). Similarly, a patient living in a flat or bed-sitter may not always have exclusive rights of occupation, so that the landlord may be entitled to authorise entry. Otherwise, a police officer does have power to gain entry for the purpose of arresting a person for certain serious offences (and this is to be extended by the Police and Criminal Evidence

Bill 1983–84). But as Carson (1982a) points out, a person damaging his own property or about to commit suicide is not committing a crime at all. The police may have a common law power of entry where a serious breach of the peace is being committed (although if so, they have shown remarkable reluctance to exercise it for the protection of battered wives). But the essence of a breach of the peace is putting other people in fear for themselves and the disturbed behaviour of a patient alone in a locked room can scarcely do this. A warrant is the only answer.

(b) *Entry under section 115*

Section 115 empowers an approved social worker to enter and inspect any premises which are not a hospital and in which a mentally disordered patient is living, if he has reasonable cause to believe that the patient is not under proper care. The premises must be in the area of the local social services authority which appoints him, and he must, if asked to do so, produce some duly authenticated document (for which no statutory form is laid down) showing that he is such a social worker. Section 145(1) defines a "patient" as a person who is suffering or appears to be suffering from mental disorder: but the addition of the words "mentally disordered" in section 115 could limit this power to those who are in fact disordered.

The power is undoubtedly useful, but it is aimed at discovering and protecting patients who for some reason may not be receiving proper care, and not at producing a situation in which the patient may lawfully be "sectioned." Thus, it relates only to an approved social worker, although once there he may be able to persuade the occupier to allow entry to a doctor as well. Secondly, it is only exercisable "at all reasonable times" and it is debateable whether this includes the middle of the night, even if a serious psychiatric emergency threatens, although in that case it probably does. Finally, while it might grant a defence to a social worker who entered without permission or stayed when asked to leave, it certainly does not permit him to gain entry by force. If he is acting within his powers, however, it is an offence for anyone to obstruct him without reasonable cause (s.129).

(c) *Warrants under section 135(1)*

Under section 135(1), an approved social worker may lay an information on oath before a magistrate, at any time or at any place. It must appear "that there is reasonable cause to suspect that a person believed to be suffering from mental disorder—(a) has been, or is being, ill-treated, neglected or kept otherwise than under proper control, in any place within the jurisdiction of the justice, or (b) being unable to care for himself, is living alone in any such place." The magistrate may then issue a warrant, which need not name the patient (s.135(5)) but must specify the premises to which it relates. It is addressed to a named constable, not to the approved social worker, but in executing it the policeman must take with him an approved social worker (not necessarily the informant) and a doctor (s.134(4)). The warrant authorises the policeman to enter, by force if need be, the specified premises, and, if thought fit (it is not clear by whom), to remove the person to a place of safety, with a view to the making of an application under Part II of the Act, or of other arrangements for his treatment or care (s.135(1)).

A "place of safety" is defined for the purpose of this section (and of section 136, see Chapter 5) as "residential accommodation provided by a local social services authority under Part III of the National Assistance Act 1948 or under paragraph 2 of schedule 8 to the National Health Service Act 1977 (see Chapter 9), a hospital as defined by this Act (see Chapter 1, section 5) a police station, a mental nursing home (see Chapter 1, section 5), or residential home for mentally disordered persons (see Chapter 9), or "any other suitable place the occupier of which is willing temporarily to receive the patient" (s.135(6)).

A patient who is removed to a place of safety under this section may be detained there for up to 72 hours (s.135(3)). There is therefore no need to "section" the patient once entry has been gained to the premises, even if he is reluctant to come to hospital. Neither this section nor an emergency admission under section 4 gives any statutory power to treat the patient without his consent, and there is much to be said for delaying the stigmatising process of "sectioning" until the situation has cooled down somewhat.

This provision is the obvious answer to the problem of gaining entry. Social workers should certainly not attempt forcible entry by themselves, and as we have seen, the police power to do so without a warrant is extremely limited. But getting a warrant is bound to cause some delay, which could be dangerous if the patient is suicidal or destructive. Even then, Carson (1982a) has pointed out that the grounds are not apt to cover every case in which a compulsory admission might be appropriate. A seriously ill, depressed or suicidal person may be quite able to care for himself and may not be ill-treated or neglected by anyone else. What then is meant by "being kept otherwise than under proper control?" Does it mean that somebody is controlling him improperly or can it include cases where some control would be proper but is not being employed by anyone?

The Act would therefore appear insufficient to give doctors and social workers the power to deal promptly with a crisis on private premises to which they are denied access (compare the powers of the police to remove people found in places to which the public does have access, in Chapter 5). Very few people are admitted to hospital under section 135(1), although an unknown number of other warrants may result in "sections," informal admission, removal to another place, or no action being taken at all. But this does not necessarily mean that there is no problem: it could just as easily mean that the law is being flouted by social workers, doctors or the police.

(d) *Warrants under section 135(2)*

Section 135(2) deals with the problem of entry once a patient has become liable to compulsion under the Act (or under the Mental Health (Scotland) Act 1960, as amended): any constable or other person who is authorised under the Act to take a patient to any place, or to take into custody or retake a patient who is liable to be so taken or retaken, may lay information on oath to a magistrate: (a) that there is reasonable cause to believe that the patient is to be found on premises within the magistrate's jurisdiction, and (b) that admission to the premises has been refused or a refusal is apprehended. Once again, the warrant authorises the policeman (who must be named) to enter the premises, by force if need be, and remove the patient. The policeman may be accompanied by a doctor and by any person authorised to take or retake the patient, but it is not essential (s.135(4)).

2. *Ordinary and Emergency Admission for Assessment*

(a) *Ordinary admission under section 2*

An ordinary application for admission for assessment must be made on Form 1 (prescribed by the Mental Health (Hospital, Guardianship and Consent to Treatment) Regulations 1983, reg. 4(1) and Sched. 1), by the patient's nearest relative or someone authorised by him or by a county court to act, in which case the authorisation must be attached, or on Form 2 by an approved social worker (s.11(1)). The applicant must have personally seen the patient within the 14 days ending on the date of the application (s.11(5)). Form 2 requires the social worker to state whether or not he has yet told the nearest relative about the application and power of discharge, but he has no obligation to consult the relative beforehand. The application must be "founded on" two medical recommendations each in Form 4, or a joint medical recommendation in Form 3, complying with the requirements of section 12. The application is made to the managers of the particular hospital and must be personally delivered to their authorised officer (reg. 3(2)).

A duly completed application is sufficient authority for the applicant, or any person authorised by the applicant, to take the patient and convey him to hospital (s.6(1)). The forms no longer state that they are accompanied by the medical recommendations, but it is hard to see how an application can be founded on something that has not yet been done. The documents give no authority to take the patient anywhere other than the named hospital. This has caused problems where physical treatment (for example for an attempted suicide) is urgently needed, but it is known that the general hospital will not admit compulsory patients. Should the application be made to that hospital, so that the patient can be taken there for life-saving treatment in casualty, and then a fresh application made so that he can be taken to the psychiatric hospital which will admit him? Or should the application be made to the psychiatric hospital, with the intention of taking a detour to the general hospital en route? The former is more in keeping with the letter of the law, but the problem is one which the administrators should not allow to arise.

Although getting the patient to hospital is the applicant's task, he may authorise others, such as the ambulance service or the police, to help him. It is advisable to do so in writing. No more force may be used than is reasonably necessary to effect the purpose (for an example, see *Allen* v. *Metropolitan Police Commissioner* [1980] Crim. L.R. 441) but the applicant should not be held responsible for the excesses of delegates whom it was reasonable to call in and who should have known better. If the patient escapes, either before he can be apprehended or on the way to hospital, he may be recaptured by the person who had his custody immediately before the escape, or by any police officer, or by any approved social worker (s.138(1)(*a*) and s.137(1)). But this only applies during the period of 14 days beginning with the date of the second medical examination. If the patient does not arrive at the hospital by then, there is no longer any power to take him there, or to admit him if he gets there (s.6(1) and (2)). If the proposed patient learns of the application before he is taken, and consults a solicitor, it is obvious what the solicitor's advice should be.

It is lawful to take a patient to the named hospital, even though that hospital has not already agreed to admit him. But unless the hospital did agree, the patient would have to be released immediately on arrival. It is therefore most advisable to have arranged the bed in advance. Although the Act contemplates that the applicant will decide whether and how to complete the form, in practice it is more usual for the doctors to arrange a bed. If the patient is admitted, the managers must make a record of this in Form 14 (reg. 4(3)) and of the receipt of the medical recommendations in Form 15 (reg. 4(4)).

Once admitted to hospital, the patient may be detained there for up to 28 days, beginning with the day on which he was admitted (s.2(4)). But he may be discharged before then, either by the responsible medical officer, or by the hospital managers, or (in certain cases) by his nearest relative (see Chapter 7) or by a mental health review tribunal (see Chapter 8). If he wishes to apply to a mental health review tribunal, he must do so within 14 days. Once the 28 days have elapsed, the patient may remain in hospital informally (s.131(1)) but he cannot be further detained unless other compulsory powers are taken *before* the admission for assessment runs out (s.2(4)). There is no power to renew an admission for assessment and it is clear from section 5(1) and (6) that an expiring admission for assessment cannot be replaced with a second admission for assessment or with a "holding power" under section 5(2) or (4). Thus, unless the patient becomes subject to a court order or Home Secretary's direction, any further detention must be by an application for admission for treatment, the grounds for which are more restricted. The only situation in which the admission for assessment can itself extend beyond 28 days is where before that date an application has been made to the county court for the replacement of the nearest relative.

Unfortunately, however, the Act does not specify what period must elapse between separate admissions for assessment. A series of these, interspersed with periods in the community or as an informal patient, might effectively evade the more stringent criteria of admission for long-term detention and treatment. This may no longer be a serious omission, now that patients admitted for assessment may apply to a mental health review tribunal. But the practice is to be deplored.

The hospital managers have a duty to do what they can to ensure that the patient understands his position and his legal rights (see Chapter 6) as soon as possible after he is admitted. There is no specific duty to remind him that he is free to go once the 28 days are up. They must, however, tell him about the treatment which he may lawfully be given in hospital; and this, as we shall see in Chapter 6, is now the same as that which may be given to patients admitted long-term for treatment. For this reason, it has been argued that admission for assessment should have been abolished. It allows a serious intervention with the patient, but the grounds for admission are more appropriate to a short period of observation and nothing like as strict. Perhaps the true distinction should have been between those grounds and procedures justifying a very short "cooling-off" period, and those justifying a long term attempt to treat the patient's underlying problems. That distinction does to some extent exist in the difference between an emergency admission and the others, but its value is effectively destroyed by the continuing existence of this 28 day "short treatment" admission.

(b) *Emergency admission under section 4*

This is simply a short cut version of an ordinary admission for assessment. By itself, it lasts for no more than 72 hours, and gives no power to impose treatment. But it may easily be converted into an ordinary 28 day admission, with power to treat, once the patient is in hospital.

The application must be made on Form 5 or 6 and the applicant must have seen the patient within the previous 24 hours (ss. 11(5) and 4(4)). Only one medical recommendation is required, and the doctor need not be an approved specialist, but he must "if practicable" know the patient beforehand (s.4(3)). If he does not, the applicant must explain why it was not practicable to use one who did. It may be "practicable" to use the patient's own doctor if he can easily be traced but does not wish to come out because he is not "on call." Both applicant and doctor must state that in their opinion it is of urgent necessity for the patient to be admitted and detained under section 2 *and* that compliance with the Act's requirements for that section would involve "undesirable" delay. This can only refer to the need to obtain two recommendations, one from an approved specialist. Thus it is clear that section 4 should only be used where the need for admission is so urgent that a second or approved doctor cannot be found in time. The doctor must explain this further (see Chapter 3, section 4).

The procedure for removing the patient and admitting him to hospital is the same as for an ordinary section 2 admission. But the patient must arrive at the hospital within the period of 24 hours beginning at the time of the medical examination or at the time of the application, whichever is the earlier (s.6(1)(b) and (2)). It will be recalled that the application may be signed before the recommendation, provided that they are signed on the same day (s.12(1)).

An emergency application ceases to have effect once 72 hours have elapsed from the time of the patient's admission to hospital, *unless* a second medical recommendation is given and received by the managers within that time, and the two medical recommendations together comply with all the usual requirements of section 12 (apart, of course, from the requirement that both must be signed on or before the date of the application) (s.4(4)). Once that recommendation is given and received, therefore, the admission is *automatically* converted into an ordinary section 2 admission. The authority to detain is extended to 28 days, but beginning on the day on which the patient was originally admitted under section 4; and the patient may be treated in the same way as an ordinary section 2 patient. There is no need to bring in the nearest relative or an approved social worker to make a fresh application. Indeed, as the patient has already been admitted for assessment, the effect of section 5(1) and (6) is that this cannot be done without allowing the emergency admission to lapse for some time.

Once again the patient must be informed of his position by the hospital and this includes his right to apply to a mental health review tribunal. He must apply within 14 days of an admission for assessment and there is nothing to prevent his doing so the moment he is admitted. If the second medical recommendation is not forthcoming, of course, the application will be otiose. But if the recommendation is given, valuable time may be saved.

(c) *The choice between sections 2 and 4*

Emergency admission is the most controversial of the three "sections," yet it has always been the most frequently used: nearly 61 per cent. of all admissions for observation (as it then was) in England and Wales in 1970, up to 64 per cent. in 1975, and down to 58·4 per cent. in 1978. But during the same period, the proportion of compulsory admissions in mental illness fell from 17·5 per cent. to 10·3 per cent. and in mental handicap from 9·3 per cent. to 3·0 per cent. (DHSS and others, 1981). If compulsion is reserved for those cases where it is genuinely essential, it is not surprising that it often happens in an emergency. However, there are considerable regional variations, not only in the use of any form of compulsion, but also in the relative use of the various sections. It is extremely unlikely that the incidence of "sectionable" mental disorder varies to anything like the same extent, and even less likely that the incidence of genuine emergencies does so. Whatever may be the explanation for the differing use of compulsion, this clearly has no connection with the differing use of emergency admission. The Mersey region had, in 1978, the highest rate of *admissions* to mental illness hospitals in England (416·62 per 100,000 population); but 91·5 per cent. were admitted informally, while the national average was 89·7 per cent.; and only 38·4 per cent. of those admitted for observation were brought in under the emergency procedure, while the national average was 58·4 per cent. The Trent region, on the other hand, had the lowest rate of admission (329·70 per 100,000); but was slightly below the national average with 88·9 per cent. of them informal; and very much above the average with 69·9 per cent. of its admissions for observation under the emergency procedure (DHSS, 1983).

The obvious explanation lies in the different policies of hospitals in the various regions and their procedures for handling emergencies. In Camden in 1966 (Roy, 1966) virtually all "night calls" which required compulsion were handled under the emergency procedure; but by 1969 to 1971 (Beebe, Ellis and Evans, 1973) a policy of using approved psychiatrists whenever possible on emergency calls had been introduced. A much higher proportion of ordinary admissions for observation was the result, although it seems also to have led to a significant increase in the use of compulsion.

The main criticism of emergency admission is that the patient may be deprived of the protection of a psychiatric opinion before his admission to hospital. The obvious risk is that partisan or inexperienced relatives, social workers and G.P.s will react to a crisis with an over-hasty admission, after which the damage is done. The patient is stigmatised, may even fall victim to the tendency of some doctors (perhaps not only those on the other side of the Atlantic) to over-diagnose those already labelled "patient," or may no longer feel able to leave the hospital once the 72 hours are up. The "best" solution might be an emergency admission on the recommendation of an approved psychiatrist, for this could give the minimum intervention with the maximum protection. But this suggestion ignores the ease with which an emergency admission can be converted into one giving the full power to treat. Further, while the evidence suggests that psychiatrists *may* be an effective safeguard against inappropriate *admission*, it does not suggest that they are such an effective safeguard against inappropriate *compulsion*.

Clearly, therefore, no-one should choose an emergency admission unless there is a genuine and urgent need to admit the patient before the right two doctors can be found, and without realising that the consequences for the patient may be just the same as in an ordinary admission for assessment. Nor, on the other hand, should it be used as a short term expedient to compel treatment—for until it has been converted, it gives no power to impose treatment without consent. It might be a useful method of getting a would-be suicide to the hospital against his will, but once there, the hospital would have to rely on common law powers to save his life. If all these matters are given their proper weight, the proportion of emergency admissions ought to be much smaller than it is.

3. Admissions for Treatment under Section 3

There have always been far fewer admissions for treatment than for observation (now assessment). There were 1,214 and 28,403 respectively in England and Wales in 1970, and 1,712 and 14,094 respectively in 1981. But whereas admissions for observation almost halved during the decade, admissions for treatment fell somewhat, only to rise again beyond 1970 level by 1980. In 1970, they were only 4 per cent. of the total under all three sections, but in 1981 they were 7·4 per cent. Obviously, patients admitted under the long term powers constitute by far the greatest proportion of resident compulsory patients (particularly as these are counted on New Year's Eve each year). At the end of 1981, there were 3,211 residents detained under the fore-runner of section 3 and only 947 under the fore-runners of sections 2 and 4 (the remainder were mainly offenders).

(a) *Application and admission*

The application may be made either by the patient's nearest relative, or some-one authorised by that relative or a county court to act as such, on Form 8, or by an approved social worker on Form 9. The relative must usually be consulted and may either object or signify his lack of objection. This and the means of overriding the relative's objections are discussed in Chapter 3.
The applicant must have seen the patient within the 14 days ending on the date of the application (s.11(5)) and a social worker applicant must have interviewed the patient (s.13(2)). Two medical recommendations complying with section 12 are necessary and Forms 10 or 11 require them to be far more explicit than for an admission for assessment. The procedure for taking the patient to hospital, recapturing him if he absconds before getting there, and admitting him to the hospital is the same as in an ordinary admission for assessment. He must therefore arrive at the hospital within the period of 14 days, beginning on the date of the second medical examination (s.6(1)(*a*)).

(b) *Duration and renewal*

The rules governing what may happen to the patient in hospital are the same as those for an ordinary admission for assessment (see Chapter 6). The differences between them lie in the grounds for admission and in the potential duration of the patient's detention. Once admitted to hospital for treatment, the patient may initially be detained for six months beginning with the day on which he was admitted (s.20(1)) but he may be discharged before then, either by the responsible medical officer, or by the hospital managers, or (in certain cases) by his nearest relative (see Chapter 7), or by a mental health review tribunal (see Chapter 8). He may apply to a tribunal at any one time during those first six months. He may remain in hospital informally after the authority for his detention has lapsed or he has been "discharged" from detention (s.131(1)).

Once the patient has been detained for six months, the authority for his detention can be renewed for a further period of six months and thereafter for periods of one year at a time (s.20(2)). The responsible medical officer must examine the patient within the period of two months ending on the day on which the authority to detain would expire. If the RMO considers that the requisite conditions are fulfilled, he must make a report to the managers on Form 30 (s.20(3) and reg. 10(1)). But before making the report, he must consult one or more other people who have been professionally concerned with the patient's medical treatment. These may be other doctors, nurses, psychologists or other therapists (s.20(5)).

Their views may be particularly important now that the criteria for renewing the patient's detention have been specified and tightened up. In all cases, the RMO must believe that it is necessary for the patient's own health or safety or for the protection of other persons that he should receive medical treatment in a hospital and that it cannot be provided unless he continues to be detained (s.20(4)(c)). Where the RMO is of the opinion that the patient is suffering from mental illness or severe mental impairment of a nature or degree which makes it appropriate for him to receive such treatment in a hospital, the responsible medical officer must also believe *either* that such treatment is likely to alleviate or prevent a deterioration of his condition *or* that the patient, if discharged, is unlikely to be able to care for himself, to obtain the care that he needs or to guard himself against serious exploitation (s.20(4)(*a*) and (*b*)). Where the RMO is of the opinion that the patient is suffering from psychopathic disorder or mental impairment of the appropriate nature or degree, the RMO must also believe that medical treatment in a hospital is likely to alleviate or prevent a deterioration of his condition (s.20(4)(*a*) and (*b*). Thus the same conditions which were necessary at the initial admission must also be fulfilled at its renewal, but the "treatability" test is now also applied to the "major" disorders, unless the patient would be unable to fend for himself if discharged. Whether this will make much difference in practice, given the lack of facilities for giving patients the care they may need outside hospital remains to be seen.

If the report is made to the managers, the authority for the patient's detention is renewed automatically for the appropriate period from the expiration of the current period (s.20(2) and (8)), *unless* the managers decide to discharge the patient despite the RMO's advice (s.20(3)). If the detention is renewed, the patient must be informed and a new right to apply to a mental health review tribunal will arise.

(c) *Reclassification*

At renewal, the RMO may decide that the patient is suffering from a different one of the four forms of disorder from that which was originally specified. If the additional criteria appropriate to the new form of disorder are also satisfied and the detention is renewed, the application will be amended accordingly (s.20(9)). There is also a procedure for reclassifying the form of the patient's disorder at other times (s.16). Again, the RMO makes a report to the hospital managers, this time on Form 22 (prescribed under reg. 6), after consultation with one or more other professionals involved with the patient's medical treatment (s.16(3)). The effect of a reclassification "downwards," from mental illness or severe mental impairment to psychopathic disorder or mental impair-ment, is that the RMO must also report whether further medical treatment in hospital is likely to alleviate or prevent a deteriora-tion of the patient's condition. If the patient is not "treatable," his detention is automatically ended (s.16(2)). A reclassification "upwards" has little practical effect. The major disorders are subject to a less stringent "treatability" test at renewal, but the RMO will have to reconsider the whole case then anyway and could always change his mind about the form of the patient's disorder once more. Nevertheless, the patient and his nearest relative must be informed of *any* reclassification under this section (s.16(4)) and each has a right to apply to a mental health review tribunal. It will therefore be much simpler to leave the question of reclassification until renewal. Otherwise, a great deal of extra work may be caused by something which will have no practical effect except for a very few psychopathic or mildly impaired patients, whom the RMO might just as well have discharged instead.

4. *Transfer from Guardianship*

Under section 19(1)(*b*), a patient under guardianship may be transferred to hospital. The transfer is effected by the responsible local social services authority on Form 27, but only after a procedure which is virtually identical to an ordinary admission for treatment (reg. 8(3)). An approved social worker must make the application on the usual form, and the usual rules about consulting the nearest relative and the duties of the social worker apply. The application must be founded on medical recommendations in Forms 28 or 29, which are virtually identical to those for an admission for treatment. The application must be accepted by the hospital and the local authority must be satisfied that a bed will be available within 14 days beginning with the day on which the transfer is signed. The authority must also have taken such steps as are practicable to inform the nearest relative of the proposed transfer. Once the transfer has been authorised, the patient may be taken to hospital by an officer of the local authority or by anyone authorised by them, but must arrive there within the 14 days beginning with the date of the second medical examination (reg. 9(1)(*b*)). The hospital must then record the admission on the usual form.

This suggests that the patient will then be regarded as an ordinary admission for treatment on that date. He certainly has the usual right to apply to a tribunal within six months. But section

19(2)(*d*) provides that Part II of the Act is to apply to him as if the original guardianship application were an application for admission for treatment and he had been admitted to hospital at the time when he was originally received into guardianship. Strictly speaking, the renewal dates should be calculated from the reception rather than from the admission. In practice, no one in the hospital will know when that was.

5. *Patients detained before the 1983 Act*

Among the 7,000 or so resident compulsory patients in mental hospitals are over 200 who have been detained there since before the 1959 Act came into force: there were 210 of these in the special hospitals alone in 1978. Some had been transferred from the penal system and are now treated as though they were subject to a transfer direction, with restrictions, under section 46, or 47 or 48 with 49, as appropriate (1983 Act, Sched. 5, para. 37; see also paras. 38 and 39). Some of these "mental defectives" might remain subject to civil compulsion after their court orders ceased, and they are like ordinary hospital order patients today, in that their nearest relatives have no power to discharge them (para. 34(4)). In other respects, however, both they and the patients originally admitted under the civil powers in the Lunacy and Mental Deficiency Acts are to be treated as if they had been admitted for treatment under Part II of the 1983 Act (para. 34(1)). The only difference between them and patients admitted since the 1959 Act is that the authority for their detention may still be renewed for periods of two years at a time (paras. 34(2) and 33(1), (2) and (4)). However, the procedure for renewal is the same, and this includes the new criteria laid down in section 20(4) (para. 34(3)). Thus some patients may have to be released from compulsion when their next renewal comes round, for example, because their mental handicap does not amount to "mental impairment" under the new definition, or because they are not treatable in a hospital. There were many of the former "feeble-minded" or "moral defectives" who under the 1959 Act were automatically released at 25, unless they were either dangerous, or were incapable of caring for themselves and could not be found a place where they would be likely to remain voluntarily (this still applies in the unlikely event that there is anyone now below the age of 25 who was compulsorily admitted before the 1959 Act came into force: see paras. 34(3) and 35)). Some of the latter may well become eligible for release at their next renewal.

Those originally admitted for treatment for "minor" disorders under the 1959 Act, however, will lose the benefit of the now-repealed age limit of 25, and may be detained until their detention next comes up for renewal. For all the patients admitted under the 1959 Act, the current period of detention will remain at its original length (which is twice that laid down in section 20(1) or (2) of the 1983 Act), with one exception. If the period is two years and less than 16 months had expired by September 30, 1983, the period is reduced to 18 months (para. 9). Until renewal comes round, the criteria for detention will remain as they were under the 1959 Act (paras. 6 and 7). But the next renewal will be governed by the 1983 Act procedure, with the new criteria in section 20(4).

6. *Scrutiny and Rectification of Documents*

The 1959 Act removed the central check on the validity of admission documents which had been exercised by the Board of Control, and the job is now done by the hospital management (reg. 4(2)). The new Mental Health Act Commission might undertake some scrutiny as part of its general powers of review, but is unlikely to have the resources to deal with every case. There are a few circumstances in which minor mistakes in applications or medical recommendations can be rectified, under section 15(1), or a fresh medical recommendation substituted for one which is insufficient, under section 15(2) or (3). These do not apply to orders made by a court, which may on occasions be just as defective.

Section 15(1) permits any application or recommendation "which is found to be in any respect incorrect or defective" to be amended by the person who signed it, provided that the hospital managers consent. This may be done within 14 days of the patient's admission (although of course an emergency admission can never last longer than 72 hours unless it is converted into an ordinary admission for assessment).

"Incorrect" probably means "inaccurate" in the sense of misstating names, dates, places or other details which had they been correctly stated would have justified the admission. It does not mean that a document which accurately reflects the facts can be rectified if those facts do not fall within the legal requirements. For example, a frequent fault is that the medical recommendations are undated or dated later than the application (see s. 12(1)). If in fact they were signed on or before the date of the application, the mistake can be rectified. But if they were signed later, then the application is invalid and the detention illegal.

"Defective" probably means "incomplete" in the sense that all the information required in the forms has not been given. It cannot mean that forms which are complete and accurate statements of the facts can be falsified in order to provide legal justification for detention where none exists. Thus a form may be amended if a vital date or qualification is omitted: but not if the date which is accurately stated contravenes the Act's time limits or if the person signing the document is not qualified to do so. But there is one mistake in the form filling which must surely invalidate the application, and that is forgetting to sign it: it cannot then be regarded as an application or recommendation at all.

In one respect, however, section 15 does permit the remedying of a genuine deficiency which might otherwise invalidate the admission. If one of the two medical recommendations required for an ordinary admission for assessment or for admission for treatment is "insufficient to warrant the detention of the patient," the matter can be cured by obtaining a fresh recommendation which is sufficient. The hospital managers should notify the applicant (not the person who signed the document as under section 15(1)) and if a fresh medical recommendation is received within 14 days of the patient's admission, the application is treated as if it had been valid from the outset (s.15(2)).

This procedure may be used where one (but only one) of the recommendations does not disclose adequate grounds for the admission. This is unlikely in an admission for assessment, where all the doctor has to do is put his signature to a printed form containing all the necessary statements, although he does now have to explain why informal admission is not appropriate. It is more likely in an admission for treatment, where he has to give a clinical description of the patient's mental condition and elaborate on other possible methods of care as well as the suitability of informal admission. If he fails to convince the scrutinising officer (who should in the DHSS view be a doctor), then the recommendation may be "insufficient" but could be remedied by a fresh one, provided of course that the facts warranted it. The new recommendation could be provided by the same or a different doctor.

The same procedure can be used where the two recommendations are good in themselves but taken together do not fulfill the Act's procedural requirements (s.15(3)). The obvious example is where neither doctor is an approved specialist, but the section may also apply where the dates of their examinations were too far apart (see s. 12(2) and (1)). A fresh recommendation may cure this, and it need not comply with the requirements about the interval between the examinations or about signing the recommendation on or before the date of the application (s.15(2)(*a*)). But together the new recommendation and the old must comply with every other requirement in the Act (s.15(2)(*b*)).

One discrepancy which can never be cured in this way is where the doctors do not agree on at least one of the four forms of mental disorder in an admission for treatment (s.15(4)). Nor can the procedure apply where it is the recommendation in itself, rather than in its relationship with the other one, which is bad: for example, where one of the doctors is not qualified at all, or where he is disqualified from making the recommendation because of his relationship with one of the other people involved. It could certainly not be used to render lawful the detention of a patient who had arrived at hospital more than fourteen days after the date of the second medical examination, for it is not then the recommendation which is insufficient. Thus the mistakes which can be put right under section 15 are very limited.

7. *The National Assistance Act Procedures*

There were 121 admissions to mental hospitals in 1981 under "other" compulsory powers, a figure which has shown a steady decline over the decade. But some of these, perhaps the majority, were under section 47 of the National Assistance Act 1948 and its emergency version in the National Assistance (Amendment) Act 1951. These allow a person to be removed to other suitable places besides a hospital, often to a local authority elderly person's home. It is not known how many orders are made each year. But it does seem clear that they almost always relate to elderly or aged people who are living alone and are no longer looking after either themselves or their homes as well as the people around them would wish. Grey (1979) traces the origin back to the Webbs' Minority Report of the Poor Law Commission of 1909, which referred to the need "for some power of compulsory removal of infirm old men or women who refuse to accept an order for admission to the workhouse, and who linger on, alone and uncared for, in the most shocking conditions of filth and insanitation." But they saw this, not as an aspect of poor relief, but of public health. And it was in that guise that forerunners of the present provision appeared in local Acts for Bradford and London (and perhaps other places) during the 1920s. There is obviously a delicate borderline between the physical and the mental infirmities of old age, and there will certainly be cases in which the National Assistance Act and Mental Health Act procedures will be alternatives. The relative merits and demerits are, however, by no means easy to assess.

(a) *The grounds*

The grounds for proceeding under the 1948 Act have three components: (i) that the person is suffering from grave chronic disease *or*, being aged, infirm or physically incapacitated, is living in insanitary conditions; *and* (ii) that the person is unable to devote to himself, and is not receiving from other persons, proper care and attention; *and* (iii) that his removal from home is necessary, either in his own interests or for preventing injury to the health of, or serious nuisance to, other persons (s.47(1) and (2)).

It is important to remember that the person *must* either be suffering from "grave chronic disease" or living in "insanitary" conditions. Harvey (1979) gives as a typical example of the use of the power an old lady called Agnes. She was apparently quite fit, but gave concern to neighbours and her doctor by "her occasional reluctance to turn off the gas." Yet she had a home help and was apparently very critical of the quality of the help's work. Where was the evidence, either of grave chronic disease or of her living in insanitary conditions? At its widest, insanitary may mean "injurious to health," but it is normally associated with the spread of infection or lack of proper sanitation.

It is also necessary that the person be unable to look after himself *and* not receiving proper care from other people. This raises even more explicitly than the Mental Health Act the question of whether the person could cope at home if only the right sort of community services were available: "the definition of need is a function not only of the person's disability but of the level of services available in the community" (Grey, 1979). Although the Act refers only to what is, or is not, being provided, it would be as well to consider also what *could* be provided before taking such a drastic step.

It also now known (see Norman, 1980) that removing elderly people from their own homes, particularly when they are reluctant to accept this, is likely to lead to a swifter deterioration than leaving them at home would have done. It may therefore be difficult to say that removal is necessary in their own interests, and conditions would have to be very bad indeed before they constituted a risk to the health of other people, or even a serious nuisance to them. A "nuisance" is something which causes either physical damage to the neighbours' property or a substantial interference with its use and enjoyment. None of this, therefore, suggests that section 47 is simply a way of overcoming the reluctance of an old lady who might be safer or more comfortable in an old people's home.

(b) *The full procedure*

The full procedure under the 1948 Act is initiated by the district community physician, who is now an employee of the health service and not the local authority. He certifies in writing to the district local authority that the grounds exist. But in the non-metropolitan counties the district local authority is not the local social services authority which is responsible for the old people's and other residential homes, as well as for the provision of social services to people in their own homes. Thus, although the local authority makes the application to the local magistrates' court, the social workers who may have been helping the old person will not necessarily be involved.

Seven clear days' notice of the hearing must be given to the person concerned "or to some person in charge of him" (s.47(7)(*a*)). This last is a curious idea, as by definition the proposed patient is not being properly looked after by those around him, so that it seems most unjust to deprive him of his right to notice by giving it to them instead (as we shall see, however, there is another and more popular way of depriving him of notice). Seven clear days' notice must also be given to the "person managing" the place to which it is proposed to remove the patient, unless that person is heard in court (s.47(3)). The "manager" of a hospital is a person with whom we are familiar under the Mental Health Act (see Chapter 1) but who is the person managing a local authority old people's home? The officer in charge may be extremely reluctant to receive a resident in defiance of the normal principle that these are voluntary residences with none of the authoritarian connotations of the workhouses of the past. But his local authority employers, in whose name the home is managed, may on occasions think differently. It would seem that the authority, rather than the individual, is the "person managing" for this purpose. But even though they must be given a hearing, the section does not expressly state that they must agree to accept the resident.

The court must hear oral evidence of the allegations in the certificate. If they are then satisfied of these, and that it is "expedient" to do so, they may order the removal of the patient to a "suitable hospital or other place" (s.47(3)). The actual "removal" is the task of an officer of the applicant local authority, who must be specified in the order, but who may call upon the ambulance service to provide transport (s.47(2) and (10)). The court fixes the duration of the order, up to a maximum of three months (s.47(4)). But the court may extend this for further periods of up to three months, provided once again that the patient or some person in charge of him (who could presumably be the officer in charge of the home) is given seven clear days' notice (s.47(4) and (7)). On the other hand, once six weeks have gone by since the original order or any extension, the patient (or someone acting on his behalf) may apply to the court for the order to be revoked (s.47(6)). This time, seven clear days' notice must be given to the community physician (s.47(7)). In practice, however, the chances of rehabilitating an old person who has been removed from home in this way are extremely slim. He will probably remain where he is whether or not the order continues in force. There is no other right of appeal, save on a point of law to the High Court.

The magistrates' court may vary the place at which the person is to be kept, provided once again that the manager is either heard or given notice (s.47(5)). If the person is kept in hospital, the accommodation is free. If he is in a local authority home, the usual procedure for levying charges from him applies. If he is somewhere else, the local authority must pay, but can seek to recover from the person by those same procedures (s.47(8) and (9); see Chapter 9). This has obvious echoes of the procedure for recovering the cost of removing lunatics to asylums under the old lunacy legislation, but nowadays it looks more like adding injury to insult.

(c) *The emergency procedure*

However controversial and deficient the full section 47 procedure may be, it does at least provide one form of judicial hearing, usually with notice to the person whose life is to be disrupted. There is, however, an emergency version in the National Assistance (Amendment) Act 1951, which is probably more frequently used. The district community physician and a second doctor (usually, but not necessarily the G.P.) must both certify that in their opinion the person fulfills conditions (i) and (ii) for the full procedure and that it is necessary to remove him in his own interests and without delay (s.1(1)). This then permits several modifications to the basic procedure.

First, the application may be made by the district community physician himself, provided that the local authority has given him general authorisation to do so (s.1(3)). Secondly, it may be to a single justice, rather than to a full magistrates' court (s.1(3)). The requirement of seven clear days' notice to the person concerned is waived (s.1(1)), and the order can in fact be made *ex parte* (s.1(3)), that is without any notice at all. The requirement of notice to the manager of the hospital or home is also waived, provided that it is shown that he has agreed to have the person (s.1(2)). The magistrate must still have oral evidence of the grounds. Any order made under the emergency procedure can only last for up to three weeks (s.1(4)) and the right to apply for revocation after six weeks is therefore inapplicable. An application to the full court, with the appropriate notice, is necessary to obtain an extension. But an extension may very well not be necessary once the initial break with home has been achieved.

(d) *What does an order allow?*

The Acts are by no means clear about what may be done with the person once he has been removed. Section 47(1) of the 1948 Act declares that the purpose of the provisions is to secure "the necessary care and attention" for the people concerned; and section 47(3) provides that the court may order their removal to the hospital or home, and their "detention and maintenance therein." It seems that the 1951 Act was expressly passed because a doctor had been unable to persuade a person with a broken leg to go to hospital for treatment. Yet the Acts say nothing about imposing medical treatment, as opposed to care, attention and maintenance, without the patient's consent. In this they are very like the Mental Health Act 1959, which seems to have assumed that getting the patient to hospital was the only problem: what happened once he was there could safely be left to the clinical judgment of the doctors. Nowadays, however, we are very much less inclined to read such powers into statutes which do not expressly contain them (see Jacob, 1976), and it would be most unwise to go beyond the limits of what is permitted by these Acts and by the common law.

8. *Commentary*

Which would you rather be? Admitted to hospital or old people's home under the National Assistance Act or committed to mental hospital under the Mental Health Act? The National Assistance Act conforms much more closely to the model of due process, because it involves an arbitration by an independent outsider. In practice, however, the person most nearly affected is not usually given notice of the proceedings, and no arbitration takes place. The Percy Commission thought that the intervention of a judicial authority in such circumstances was little more than a rubber stamp and they were probably right. It would be different if the person concerned were given notice, the right to representation, and a full-dress hearing before his liberty is infringed. But that has never been on offer to mental patients since the procedure for finding lunatics by inquisition was abandoned, even during the so-called triumph of legalism under the Lunacy Act 1890. The biggest objection to the present commitment procedures is that the patient's rights are so crucially affected by the initial decision that he is a "patient." This defines whether he or his nearest relative is to be regarded as a rational human being. This defines whether he can be taken to hospital, detained, and given treatment without anything at all in the nature of due process ever having taken place. And the label "patient," as we all know, is extremely sticky.

That apart, the procedure does have enormous attractions. It is quick. It is private. It was naive of the Percy Commission to believe that it would do away with the stigma of certification, for there is certainly a stigma in being "sectioned." But it could be less than that involved in any of the previous procedures, if only because the consequences are now so much less drastic. It is meant to protect both his liberty and his needs better than a trial would do, by involving just those people who might be expected to assess them both properly. Above all, their judgment is now to be subjected to the independent review of a tribunal specially designed for the purpose, at which the patient can appear and be represented and meet all of the arguments.

Until that last development, the sectioning procedure was much more open to attack. It assumed that all the participants would be able to act independently of one another. But in fact the only entirely free agent is likely to be the hospital consultant, who controls access to his own beds. Other doctors will find it hard to disagree with him. Relatives and social workers may find it easier to do so, but their dual responsibility places both in a difficult position. The social worker's duty to interview is an important step in involving the patient in his fate. But where everyone is concerned to balance the competing values of the patient's liberty and his needs, one or the other can be knocked off balance. But Bean (1980) suggests that if other doctors and social workers are permitted to disagree with the consultant, "unstable interaction" is caused, to the detriment of the patient. If that were always so, there would be no point at all in any legal formalities. As it is, it is far too tempting to regard them as pieces of paper that have to be filled in properly, as a timetable that must be kept, but not as a mechanism for substantial consideration of whether the case for intervention exists.

Even if in fact everyone involved bends over backwards to avoid railroading the patient into hospital, these make good reasons for the European Convention on Human Rights to insist on a speedy judicial review of the merits of the patient's detention (Art. 5(4)) and for mental health review tribunals to be given the job. The patient admitted for assessment will still have to ask for it, and it may take place almost at the end of his detention. But it should have a retrospective effect on how everyone sees his case and a prospective effect on how others are seen in the future. There is much to be said for the English way of doing things. But all the procedures in the world will be of no use if we have not got the substance right, and that is another story.

5 Mentally Disordered Offenders

The fact that a person who is alleged to have committed a criminal offence may be mentally disordered can affect the normal processes of the law at several points. He may never be reported to the police, if the people aggrieved do not consider him morally responsible for what he has done. The police may decide not to prosecute, for they have almost complete discretion and a variety of alternatives. If a prosecution is launched, a few may be transferred to hospital before being dealt with, or be found unfit to stand trial. At the trial, mental disorder may occasionally provide a defence to the charge, although the consequence will then usually be worse than being found guilty. Much more frequently, it will allow the court to impose a therapeutic rather than a penal sentence. Even if a prison sentence is chosen, the Home Secretary may later transfer the prisoner to hospital. When none of these is available, the court will have to consider the alternatives in the light of circumstances which include the offender's mental condition. Some of the reforms of the hospital order system which were proposed by the Butler Committee on Mentally Abnormal Offenders (1975) are contained in the 1983 Act. But we are still waiting for a thorough-going reform of the whole system.

1. *Police Powers*

(a) *Detention under section 136*

A police officer may remove to a place of safety any person whom he finds in a "place to which the public have access" and who appears to be suffering from mental disorder and in immediate need of care or control, provided that the officer thinks the removal is necessary in the interests of the person concerned or for

136

the protection of other persons (s.136(1)). There is no need for the officer to suspect that a criminal offence has been committed, let alone an arrestable offence. No magistrate's warrant, written application or medical evidence is required, as it would be if the person were on private premises. A "place to which the public have access" covers more than public highways and open spaces where all are free to come and go as they please. It includes places like railway platforms and football grounds and car parks, to which members of the public are admitted on payment, or shops and public houses, which are only open at certain times of day. These are not included at other times, but while they are open the concept may cover parts of the premises to which general access is denied. Even if some members of the public are not allowed in, a place may qualify if others are admitted *qua* public. But if people are only admitted as lawful visitors to private premises, for example when passing through a garden to get to the front door, then the public do not have access. Lifts, landings and staircases serving a block of flats could be private premises, while open walkways linking dwellings on a modern housing estate could be public (*Knox* v. *Anderton* (1983) 76 Cr.App.R. 156).

A place of safety includes both a hospital and a police station, as well as local authority residential accommodation of all types, private or voluntary residential or nursing homes for the mentally disordered, and any other suitable place the occupier of which is willing temporarily to receive the patient (s.135(6)). Once at the place of safety, the person may be detained for up to 72 hours "for the purpose of enabling him to be examined by a registered medical practitioner and to be interviewed by an approved social worker and of making any necessary arrangements for his treatment or care" (s.136(2)). The section gives no power to impose medical treatment without consent (s.56(1)(*b*)). The DHSS view (1978) is that once the person has been examined by a doctor and interviewed by a social worker the authority for his detention lapses automatically, even if the 72 hours are not over. This can only be right where they decide that no further arrangements for his treatment and care are necessary.

The statistics suggest that this section is hardly ever used outside London. The four Thames regions accounted for 85·6 per cent. (1368 out of 1598) of the admissions in 1979, 83·1 per cent. (1563 of 1880) in 1980, and 84·4 per cent. (1609 of 1906) in 1981. These figures do point to an increase, but otherwise they are totally misleading. They refer only to hospital admissions. Cases where the person is taken to a police station or elsewhere are not centrally recorded. Even if he is later admitted to hospital, this may well be under a different section or as an informal patient. The practice in any area will depend upon the willingness of local hospitals to accept patients direct from the police, the availability of doctors and social workers to go to police stations if asked, the policies of the particular police force and the attitudes of individual police officers. The Butler Committee (1975) concluded that, despite the figures, the section was in fact widely used.

Whether its use is regarded as an abuse depends upon the purposes for which the police in fact employ it. Despite its broad terms and complete lack of procedural safeguards, both Rollin (1969) and Walker and McCabe (1973) thought that it was not abused. They found that the police treated it mainly as an alternative to arrest and prosecution for an obvious offender who seemed equally obviously disordered. Even if prosecution is never contemplated, Walker and McCabe point out that the police could almost always have arrested instead. "Almost any behaviour of a markedly abnormal kind in a public place can be made the basis of some sort of charge." Also, most of the patients admitted in this way had been in hospital before. The police seemed reluctant to put a person in hospital without medical advice, unless he was known to have a history of hospital treatment or his behaviour was so obviously bizarre that the "man must be mad" test would apply. But if the section's main purpose is indeed to allow the police to keep their options open when they discover a possible mentally disordered offender, it is hard to understand why the government refused to implement the Percy Commission's original recommendation that there should always be grounds for arresting the person instead.

The DHSS (1978), however, thought that the power most often arose "where a person's abnormal behaviour is causing nuisance or offence." This is certainly borne out by the one reported case. In *Carter* v. *Metropolitan Police Commissioner* [1975] 1 W.L.R. 507, a woman with no history of mental disorder was taken to hospital by the police following a dispute with her neighbours. Her version was that at the time she was standing calmly in the doorway of her own flat. The police version was that she had telephoned them to say that there was trouble but that she had "not started screaming yet" and was found on the communal landing, shouting abuse and with excrement on her hands. The court found the police version more credible and refused her application for leave to sue (under what is now section 139; see Chapter 10). Given that the dispute clearly had racial overtones, it is doubtful whether the court could properly assess which version was the more credible on the written affidavits alone. Nor was it considered whether the landing was a "place to which the public have access." But even if both points were decided in favour of the police, why should the law permit them to solve this sort of problem by making an instant diagnosis and arranging detention in hospital without any sort of medical or social work advice?

The DHSS (1978), however, did not see any problem with the underlying principle, but with the implementation. This could be solved partly by emphasising the very limited and short term purpose of the detention and partly by issuing guidance upon where the person should be taken. The first may be welcomed. The second is more controversial. Both in 1976 and 1978, the DHSS obviously thought that a hospital or other accommodation was more suitable than a police station for a "sick person." Yet this assumes that the police diagnosis is right and that the label "patient" should be thus summarily applied to someone who may not be sick at all. Sick or not, the person concerned may not prefer to spend up to 72 hours in a mental hospital to having the matter sorted out in a police station. There is much to be said for taking him to the police station first, so that a properly considered choice may be made, between treating him as a medical problem, or as a penal problem, or as no problem at all. In any event, as MIND (Gostin, 1975) suggested, the maximum period of detention could easily have been reduced to 24 hours.

(b) *Diversion, interrogation and prosecution*

There are several alternatives open to the police when they encounter a possible offender who may be mentally disordered. If he is known to be an absconding compulsory patient, they may simply detain and return him to hospital under sections 18 or 138 (see Chapter 7). Even if he is not technically absent without leave, they may contact the hospital to recall him, so that section 18 will apply. If he is not already a compulsory patient, they may be able to persuade him to co-operate while they set in motion the processes for an ordinary informal or compulsory admission. If he is "found in a place to which the public have access," they may make use of their powers under section 136, either to deliver him direct to the hospital, or to take him to the police station for further inquiries as to his mental state. If he "seems disposed to do mischief to other persons or to himself," they may even rely upon the common law power to arrest the insane (see Chapter 4), although this will afford them no protection if it turns out that he was not actually insane at the time. Alternatively, they may make use of whatever powers of arrest exist for the particular offence suspected, or of their powers in the prevention of crime or a breach of the peace. Finally, of course, they may simply request that he accompanies them to the police station to "assist in their inquiries."

Theoretically, if the person is detained, the police must tell him at the time under which of these powers they purport to act. Nor does the initial use of a criminal arrest preclude a later decision to divert out of the criminal process, any more than the initial use of a diversionary procedure precludes a later decision to prosecute. In practice, one suspects that a police officer may refrain from putting a label on the detention until the decision between arrest and diversion has been made, after which it is unlikely to be changed.

Part of the process of deciding will be the interrogation of the suspected offender. It seems only recently to have occurred to the police (and even higher authority) that the confessions of mentally disordered people, particularly if they are mentally handicapped, are not the most reliable. It is all too easy for a police officer to extract admissions from a vulnerable or pliant person and then thankfully regard the case as closed without checking the story further. The best known example is the case of Colin Lattimore. He was convicted almost entirely on his own admission of taking part in the killing of Maxwell Confait, although this happened at a time when Colin Lattimore could not possibly have been there. Following Sir Henry Fisher's report on the case (1977), guidelines on the interrogation of mentally handicapped people were included in the Home Office administrative directions to the police, which are annexed to the Judges' Rules (1978).

The guidelines apply whenever it appears to a police officer that a person whom he intends to interview (whether as a suspect or a witness) has a mental handicap which raises doubts about whether he can understand the questions put to him or is likely to be especially open to suggestion. The officer must then take particular care in putting the questions and accepting the answers. As far as practicable, a mentally handicapped adult should only be interviewed in the presence of his parent, or some other person in whose care, custody or control he is, or another responsible person (such as a social worker) who is not a police officer. The same applies to interviews with children, whether mentally handicapped or not. But any document which results from an interview with a mentally handicapped child or adult should be signed by the parent or other responsible person present, as well as by the person making the statement. Even then, it will still be necessary to take care to verify the facts admitted and to find corroboration if possible. All this is, of course, in addition to the normal rules and directions about questioning.

A breach of the rules or directions does not necessarily render a statement inadmissible. But a confession must be excluded unless the prosecution can prove that it was "voluntary in the sense that it was not obtained by fear of prejudice or hope of advantage excited or held out by a person in authority or by . . . oppression" (*D.P.P.* v. *Ping Lin* [1976] A.C. 574). Breaches of the rules can certainly combine with other circumstances to amount to oppression, which "excites hopes (such as the hope of release) or fears, or so affects the mind of the subject that his will crumbles and he speaks when otherwise he would have remained silent" (*per* Lord MacDermott, adopted in *R.* v. *Prager* (1971) 56 Cr. App. R. 151). A good example is *R.* v. *Westlake* [1979] Crim. L.R. 652, in which the accused was arrested for the attempted murder of Michelle Booth. He had a mental age of 11 or 12 and was kept in custody for 24 hours before his interrogation. He was then questioned repeatedly over the next five days. No attempt was made to have his father present, although this was practicable. There were frequent breaches of the rules and directions and the judge found the form of questioning itself oppressive. If the judge "thinks it possible that the confession was obtained by inducement or oppression, he has no discretion, he *must* exclude it" (*per* Hodgson J.). Even if there is no inducement or oppression, the judge still has a discretion to exclude evidence which is more prejudicial than probative (*R.* v. *Sang* [1980] A.C. 402). An example of this is *R.* v. *Stewart* (1972) 56 Cr. App. R. 272, where the accused was so severely handicapped that his understanding and language were those of a child between three and five. However sympathetic the questioner, this must cast doubts upon the reliability of the answers. Unfortunately, however, there does seem to be some judicial confusion between mandatory and discretionary exclusion (see *R.* v. *Platt* [1981] Crim.L.R. 622). It is also possible that their particular applicability to mentally handicapped people will be forgotten in the court's quite natural anxiety to ensure that perfectly voluntary and reliable confessions are not excluded simply because the police cannot prove that the rules were adhered to in every particular.

The Police and Criminal Evidence Bill 1983–84 intends to replace the common law rules on the admissibility of confessions (cl. 69). The Judges' Rules and administrative directions are to be replaced by some statutory provisions and a code of practice (cl. 59). Breach of the code is to be a disciplinary offence and to be taken into account if thought relevant in any question arising in court proceedings (cl. 60). The draft code (Home Office, 1983) deals with both mental illness and mental handicap. If there is any suspicion that a person in custody is either mentally ill or handicapped, a parent or responsible person should be informed, or failing them the local social services department. If mental illness is suspected, the police surgeon should be called. Whether or not they are in custody, such people should not be questioned without a responsible person present, to whom the statutory right to legal advice should be explained. If the responsible person thinks that legal advice is desirable, the interview should not begin. But it may proceed without either a responsible person or a lawyer if an officer of the rank of Superintendant or above reasonably believes that delay would involve a risk of harm to persons or serious loss of or damage to property.

Except where the consent of the Director of Public Prosecutions is required for a particular prosecution, the police have an almost unfettered discretion to choose between criminal proceedings and diversion in any individual case. Such evidence as there is (principally Rollin, 1969, and Walker and McCabe, 1973) suggests that the two most important factors are the nature of the offence and the police knowledge of the offender's history. Rollin found that a much higher proportion of the prosecuted offenders in his group had committed crimes against property than had the unprosecuted. These are probably seen by the police as more blameworthy, involving a higher degree of thought and planning, than are the public order offences common amongst the unprosecuted group, which often involved outstandingly abnormal behaviour. The unprosecuted offenders were more likely to be seriously ill (or soon discovered to be so) but also less likely to have a serious criminal record.

Nevertheless, there is also evidence that chance plays a large part in these decisions. Whitehead and Ahmad (1970) were concerned that so many of their hospital order patients appeared to have committed minor public order offences directly related to their disorder (such as shouting at their "voices"). Walker and McCabe (1973), on the other hand, discovered several unprosecuted offenders whose crimes were very serious. Beebe, Ellis and Evans (1972) illustrate the way in which some offenders can manipulate the system: a man picked up as drunk and disorderly announced suicidal intentions and was pronounced "mental" by the police surgeon. The psychiatric team called to the police station took a different view, as he seemed to have definite plans for the next day and merely wanted them to save him from the magistrate. Because of this disagreement, he probably escaped official action altogether.

That case also illustrates the dilemma in which the police may place the social worker and doctor called to the police station. In more serious cases, the police could so easily say "section him or we prosecute." The team may be tempted to comply in order to save the patient from a worse fate. But prosecution is by no means invariably a worse fate than being "sectioned" and patients should only be compelled to enter hospital if the circumstances genuinely warrant it. If "Her Majesty's courts are not dustbins into which the social services can sweep difficult members of the public" (in the famous words of Lawton L.J. in *R.* v. *Clarke* (1975) 61 Cr. App. R. 320), neither are the hospitals. They are places for the medical treatment of people suffering from mental disorder within the meaning of the Act.

The D.P.P. has a set of guidelines on whether to prosecute in the serious cases with which he is concerned, and these have recently been commended to the police by the Attorney-General (Home Office Circular 26/83). Apart from such generally applicable factors as the sufficiency of the evidence, the gravity of the offence, and the likely penalty, concern is shown for the likely effect of prosecution upon the young, old, infirm or mentally ill. For the last, however, the D.P.P. usually requires independent evidence of both the illness and the likely adverse effects of prosecution. He may be sceptical about these if the illness (such as depression) could be the result of being found out. And if there is no adverse prognosis from prosecution, he does not usually think it right to take the illness into account, because the mental instability could increase the likelihood of reoffending.

These guidelines fall far short of the Butler Committee's recommendation that mentally disordered people should not be prosecuted if this would serve no "useful public purpose." If there was no need for a restriction order, and the court was likely to choose a therapeutic order in any event, the same result might be achieved without prosecution. Sometimes, however, prosecution may be preferable. Even the most disturbed patient may feel a sense of grave injustice at prolonged detention in hospital without trial. Many professionals now believe that handicapped people should be prosecuted and held responsible where responsibility exists. This is an essential element in recognition as a human being. But at the same time we must beware the temptation to believe that mentally disordered people are more likely than others to commit crimes. Mostly, they are not. And those that do, seem to do so for reasons which are more like those of other "normal" offenders than to do with their disorder. A person with paranoid delusions is neither more nor less likely to attack his tormentors than is a person who is in fact being persecuted. While diversion out of the criminal justice system may be of benefit to some, we should not forget the advantages of a proper investigation of the evidence and of the alternative disposals.

2. *Procedure before Trial*

(a) *Obtaining the medical evidence*

Medical evidence will obviously be required where there is a possibility that the accused is unfit to plead or the defence of insanity or diminished responsibility may arise. A court cannot make any order which will result in compulsory admission to hospital, or in psychiatric care in the community, without the prescribed medical reports. The written or oral evidence of two doctors is required for any type of hospital order (an ordinary hospital order under section 37, a restriction order under section 41, or an interim order under section 38), for a remand to hospital for treatment (under section 36) or a committal to hospital with a view to a restriction order (section 44), or for a guardianship order (section 37). Only one doctor is required for a probation or supervision order with a condition of psychiatric treatment, or for a remand to hospital for reports (section 35).

Where two doctors are required, one of them must be on the list of those approved for their special experience in the diagnosis or treatment of mental disorder. Where only one is required, he must also be on that list (s.54(1)). The procedure and criteria for approval have already been outlined in Chapter 3. They do not ensure that the doctor is a consultant psychiatrist, or even a specialist in the particular form of mental disorder which is suspected. The Butler Committee (1975) suggested that one solution to the special problems posed by mental handicap, of which more anon, was to have evidence from a specialist in that field. In practice, the court is unlikely to find a bed for a mentally handicapped offender without it.

None of the other rules governing who may make medical recommendations for civil commitment apply, no doubt because collusion is not thought to be a problem. There is nothing to stop their being related to one another, or to the patient, or, more importantly, being employed at the same institution. The DHSS (1978) thought that they should not both come from the same prison or hospital (whether or not it was the admitting hospital). This has not been embodied in the Act, but there is nothing to stop the profession and the courts observing it in practice.

Equally, the Act does not insist that the doctor who gives evidence of the defendant's mental condition should be on the staff of the admitting hospital. In *R.* v. *Blackwood* (1974) 59 Cr. App. R. 246, the Court of Appeal stressed that this was particularly desirable where the court was contemplating a restriction order. There should be no doubt about whether the patient was suitable for this and whether the hospital was willing to have a patient whom the doctors could not discharge when they thought fit. The Butler Committee (1975) proposed that the consent of the receiving doctor should be required, not only to the admission, but also to any restrictions. In *R*. v. *Royse* [1981] Crim. L.R. 426, however, it was pointed out that the need for restrictions is a matter for the court rather than a medical judgment. The committee's proposal has therefore not been adopted.

However, no court can send a defendant to hospital unless it has evidence that a bed in that hospital will be available within a stated time. That evidence must now be given either by the doctor who would be in charge of the patient there or by some other representative of the hospital managers (ss.35(4), 36(3), 37(4), 38(4) and 44(1)). As that doctor is extremely likely to be on the approved list, it will often be more convenient for him to supply the necessary evidence of the defendant's mental condition as well. He could then make observations about the need for restrictions and the suitability of the hospital if restrictions were made.

Oral evidence of the accused's mental condition will obviously be required where a jury has to decide on his fitness to plead, insanity or diminished responsibility. One of the two doctors must give oral evidence if the court makes a restriction order (s.41(2)). Otherwise, the evidence required for Mental Health Act orders may be given in writing, although the court may always insist on the doctor's attendance if it wishes. Written evidence from a doctor or representative of the hospital managers may be admitted without formal proof of the signature or qualifications (s.54(2)). If the report is not presented on behalf of the defendant, it must be disclosed to his legal representative. If he has none, the substance must be disclosed to him personally, or to his parent if he is a juvenile. The defence is entitled to insist that the doctor gives oral evidence, so that he may be cross-examined, and to call evidence to rebut what he says (s.52(3)). This does not apply, however, where the doctor's evidence relates solely to the availability of a bed.

It is important to realise that the medical evidence is not sacrosanct. Reports may be obtained either by the prosecution, or by the defence, or at the request of the court. The defence need not accept the prison doctor's verdict that the accused is fit for disposal as the court thinks fit and can shop around for more favourable reports (although they may have difficulty in persuading the legal aid authorities to pay for these unless they can show a good reason). This is one explanation for the frustration which can arise when the court is faced with clear evidence that the defendant's mental condition warrants an order but no evidence that a suitable hospital is willing to have him. However, lawyers should also be prepared to subject "favourable" reports to critical scrutiny. They should guard against the assumption that a hospital order is always a soft option or in fact what the client wants. They should also recall that once the possibility is raised, a Crown Court judge may well consider adding a restriction order (see Gostin, 1977).

There is a long-standing view (discussed, for example, by Kenny, 1983) that expert evidence is not suitable for adversarial combat and should be called to assist the court rather than the parties. This assumes that the court's expert is right and anyone else is wrong, which in a field like psychiatry is manifestly absurd. Judges themselves seem to veer from an exaggerated contempt to an equally exaggerated respect (see, for example, King, 1980). The Butler Committee rejected proposals for a panel of psychiatrists to advise the courts. Rightly, they did not wish to deny the accused the opportunity of calling his own evidence if he wished. But they comforted themselves that the unedifying "battle of the experts" had diminished, since the abolition of the death penalty and the shift of most decisions to the disposal stage. Yet it is not at all clear why the medical evidence should be thought less reliable when the question is, for example, whether the "Yorkshire Ripper" should be convicted of murder or manslaughter, than it is when the question is whether an otherwise petty offender should be sent to Broadmoor indefinitely. It deserves careful and unprejudiced scrutiny in each case.

The Butler Committee, however, were more concerned that many defendants who might benefit from psychiatric treatment could slip through the net. A busy magistrates' court, dealing with an unrepresented defendant on a minor charge, is unlikely to think of getting medical reports unless he shows obvious signs of disorder (Donovan and O'Brien, 1981). The police, prison authorities and even a legal representative may not know of any psychiatric history, unless there is a previous psychiatric disposal which shows up on the criminal record. The Committee recommended that the police should make a brief note on the record of any treatment which came to light in the course of proceedings. There is plenty of evidence (see, for example, Boehringer and McCabe, 1973) that such people appear in the courts time and again without the opportunity for treatment being taken. Magistrates, however, seem to be more impressed by the defendant's demeanour in court, than by his previous history or the nature of the offence, when making their decisions to call for reports.

The Butler Committee advocated a much greater use of social inquiry reports, particularly on charges which often involve mental disorder, in order to isolate those cases where a medical opinion is warranted. The Court of Appeal has advised that there should be a psychiatrist's report in cases of arson (*R.* v. *Calladine, The Times,* December 3, 1975). Prisons tend to obtain at least the medical officer's view on people remanded on charges of murder or serious sex offences. Where a person charged with murder is granted bail, the court must now make it a condition that he is examined by two doctors, one of them approved, unless satisfactory reports have already been obtained (Bail Act 1976, s.3(6A)).

This leads us to the Butler Committee's second concern, which was with the conditions under which a report is prepared. If an accused is remanded in custody, it may be easy to obtain a report, but prison is scarcely the most favourable environment in which to make a psychiatric assessment. If the accused is remanded on bail, the court may make whatever condition appears necessary to ensure that he makes himself available, so that a report may be made to assist the court in dealing with him for the offence (Bail Act 1976, s.3(6)(*d*)). This can include a condition of residence in hospital, but unless the accused is separately "sectioned" he is an informal patient whom the hospital cannot detain. All courts have a specific power to remand offenders for reports after conviction. Magistrates may do so (for three weeks at a time in custody and four on bail) without convicting, if they are satisfied that the defendant did the act or made the omission charged (Magistrates' Courts Act 1980, s.30). The usual presumption in favour of bail applies to all these remands (Bail Act 1976, s.4(4)).

The Butler Committee thought that the courts should be able to remand to hospital for reports if a remand on bail is impracticable. This is now provided for in section 35 of the 1983 Act, but will not be implemented until there is enough regional secure accommodation. The Crown Court will be able to remand anyone awaiting trial or sentence for a prisonable offence, unless the penalty is fixed by law. This excludes murder, which is extraordinary. Alleged murderers do not have to be remanded to prison and there is no reason to restrict hospital remands to people who can be given Mental Health Act orders (which again are not available where the penalty is fixed by law). Magistrates will only be able to remand after convicting the accused of a prisonable offence, or finding that he did the act or made the omission charged, or with his consent (s.35(2)). These remands can only be made where bail would be impracticable, so prison would almost always be the alternative. Nevertheless, it was thought that a normal offender might resent being sent to hospital, so the court must have written or oral evidence from one approved doctor that there is reason to suspect that the accused is suffering from mental illness, psychopathic disorder, severe mental impairment or mental impairment (s.35(3)). There must also be evidence from the doctor who would be making the report, or some other representative of the hospital managers, that a bed will be available within seven days, beginning with the date of the remand (s.35(4)). Between them, these requirements may ensure that few such remands are made.

The accused may be kept in a "place of safety" before he is taken to hospital. But for this and other orders under Part III of the Act, a place of safety is a police station, prison or remand centre, or another hospital which is willing to have him for the time being (s.55(1)). Once in hospital, he must be detained (s.35(9)) and if he escapes he may be arrested without warrant and must then be brought back to court (s.35(10)). But there is no statutory power to force him to accept treatment (s.56(1)(*b*)). The Act expressly allows him to obtain his own medical report at his own expense, so that he can ask for the remand to be ended (s.35(8)). A remand under this section cannot last for more than 28 days at a time (s.35(7)), but the accused may be remanded again and again if the doctor states that this is necessary (s.35(5)). He need not be brought back to court for the purpose, provided that he has a legal representative who is given an opportunity of being heard (s.35(6)). But the total period cannot be longer than 12 weeks in all and the court can always end it earlier (s.35(7)).

(b) *Hospital care while awaiting trial*

At present there is no power, in a case where bail is not appropriate, for the court to remand the accused to hospital instead of prison. All that can happen is that the Home Secretary may direct his transfer to hospital under section 48. This applies to civil prisoners, people detained under the Immigration Act 1971, people remanded in custody by a magistrates' court, and any other person who is detained in a prison or remand centre but not serving a custodial sentence (s.48(2)). In practice, the last means people awaiting trial or sentence in the Crown Court. The Home Secretary must have reports from at least two doctors, one approved, that the prisoner is suffering from mental illness or severe mental impairment, of a nature or degree which makes it appropriate for him to be detained in hospital for medical treatment, and that he is in urgent need of this treatment (s.48(1)). The doctors must agree on one form of disorder, even if one of them thinks he is both mentally ill and severely impaired (s.47(4)).

All transfers have the same effect as a hospital order (s.47(3)). The patient may be treated, but he may also apply to a mental health review tribunal, even during his first six months in hospital (see Chapter 8). The transfer of a civil or Immigration Act prisoner can never last longer than his detention would have done (s.53(1)) and the Home Secretary may choose whether to transfer him as an ordinary hospital order or as a restriction order patient (s.49(1)). If restricted, he may be transferred back to prison, if the Home Secretary is notified by the RMO, any other doctor, or a mental health review tribunal, that he no longer needs treatment for mental disorder or that no effective treatment can be given in that hospital (s.53(2)). The transfer of remand prisoners *must* take effect as a restriction order (s.49(1)) and (2)), but the precise consequences depend upon which court he is waiting to appear in.

If the patient is waiting to appear in a magistrates' court, the transfer lasts as long as the remand, unless the court remands him again (which it may do in his absence if he has appeared before the court within the last six months) or commits him for trial in the Crown Court (which again it may do in his absence if the RMO reports that he in unfit to take part). But the magistrates themselves may end the transfer, even if the remand has not expired or the patient has been committed to the Crown Court, if the RMO reports to them that the patient no longer needs treatment for mental disorder, or that no effective treatment can be given in that hospital (s.52). If and when the magistrates finally deal with a transferred patient, they may be able to make a hospital order, sometimes without in fact convicting him, but they cannot do so in his absence (see below).

If the patient is waiting to appear in the Crown Court (or elsewhere), the transfer lasts until the court disposes of the case. But the Home Secretary has power to transfer him back to prison, if notified by the RMO, any other doctor or a mental health review tribunal that he no longer needs treatment or that no effective treatment can be given (s.51(3)). The Court itself may end the transfer if notified to the same effect by the RMO, but it may choose to release him on bail rather than transfer him back to custody (s.51(3)). However, if the patient is still in hospital when he comes up for trial or sentence, the Court may make a hospital order in his absence and without convicting him, provided that three conditions are fulfilled. First, it must be impracticable or inappropriate to bring him before the court. Secondly, there must be written or oral evidence from at least two doctors, one appoved, that he is suffering from mental illness or severe mental impairment of a nature or degree which makes it appropriate for him to be detained in hospital for medical treatment. Lastly, the Court must think that this is proper, after considering the depositions and any other documents sent to court (s.51(5) and (6)). The order may be with or without restrictions.

The effect of all this is that both a magistrates' court and the Crown Court may make a hospital order over a transferred remand prisoner without ever trying him. The Crown Court does not even have to be satisfied that he did the act or made the omission charged. This may be a more satisfactory alternative than finding the accused unfit to plead (see below), because there need not be restrictions. But it is subject to exactly the same disadvantage of indefinite detention without trial. Indeed, the transfer alone may have this result, for the court may be persuaded to go on remanding the patient, or to refrain from listing his case, until he recovers enough to be tried (see Gostin, 1977). The Home

Secretary is unlikely to agree to a discharge, however long the patient has spent in hospital. Legal advisers should do their best to get the case to court, so that decisions on his guilt and the most appropriate disposal can be made.

The Butler Committee (1975), on the other hand, were more concerned that disordered people might be languishing in prison without proper treatment while waiting for their cases to be heard. The only circumstance at present in which a court may remand or commit an accused person direct to hospital is where a magistrates' court decides to commit an offender to the Crown Court with a view to a restriction order being made (s.43). The magistrates must already have convicted the offender and received the evidence necessary for a hospital order. If they wish to commit to hospital, they must also have evidence from the doctor who would be in charge, or some other representative of the hospital managers, that a bed is available, but in this case there is no 28 day time limit (s.44). Once again, the committal has the same effect as a restriction order, which is scarcely an inducement to bring the case quickly before the Crown Court.

Section 36 of the 1983 Act introduces a very limited power to remand direct to hospital, which again will not be implemented until the facilities exist. It applies only to people waiting for trial or sentence in the Crown Court. The offence must be punishable with imprisonment, but fixed penalty offences like murder are again excluded. The evidence of mental condition is the same as that required for a transfer from prison, except that there is no need for the treatment to be urgent. There must be the usual evidence from the hospital that a bed will be available within seven days. As the object is to secure treatment for the patient's disorder, the usual provisions about medical treatment of detained patients apply (see Chapter 6). Apart from that, however, the effects of the order, its duration and renewal, are the same as in a remand to hospital for reports.

As three months is by no means a long time to be waiting to appear in the Crown Court these days, these patients may well have to be returned to prison, unless the Home Secretary can be persuaded to make a transfer direction. It is ironic that a transfer ordered by the Crown Court should be so much less drastic in its effects than one which is directed by the Home Secretary. It scarcely indicates a consistent view about whether it is worse to languish in prison without treatment or to languish in hospital without trial.

(c) *Fitness to plead*

This issue relates solely to the ability of an accused to participate in his trial. It has nothing to do with his state of mind at the time of the alleged offence. The question is whether he can plead to the indictment and understand the proceedings sufficiently to be able to challenge jurors, take in the evidence, and make a proper defence (*R*. v. *Pritchard* (1836) 7 C. & P. 303). Someone suffering from amnesia about the relevant events, but who can understand the trial, is fit to be tried (*R*. v. *Podola* [1960] 1 Q.B. 325). An illiterate deaf-mute, or someone who is incapable of communicating with the court or his legal advisers, may not be tried (*R*. v. *Sharp* (1957) 41 Cr. App. R. 196). A severely subnormal or psychotic patient might not be fit. But the fact that he is highly abnormal and cannot act in his own best interests does not necessarily mean that he cannot understand the trial (*R*. v. *Robertson* (1968) 62 Cr. App. R. 690).

The issue is usually brought up either by the prosecution or by the defence before the accused is arraigned, but it may be raised by either side or by the court at the trial (*R*. v. *MacCarthy* [1967] 1 Q.B. 68). It must normally be tried by a jury as soon as it arises (Criminal Procedure (Insanity) Act 1964, s.4(3)). If this is on arraignment but the accused is found fit, he will be tried for the offence by a different jury (s.4(4)). But the judge may postpone the decision on the fitness issue until any time up to the opening of the case for the defence (s.4(2)). If the issue has to be decided at any time after arraignment, the judge may choose whether it should be tried by the trial jury or by a separate one (s.4(4)).

If the accused is found unfit to plead, or more properly under disability, there can be only one consequence. He is ordered to be detained in a hospital specified by the Home Secretary, with the same status as a patient on a restriction order of unlimited duration (s.5(1) and (3) and Sched. 1). He must be found a bed within a maximum of two months from the order, but the situation arises so rarely that the authorities' ingenuity is unlikely to be too severely taxed. The patient may remain in hospital until the Home

Secretary either agrees to his discharge or transfers him back to the penal system for trial (s. 5(4)). Apparently, the latter is "sparingly used" (Home Office evidence to the Butler Committee, 1975), generally where his mental condition improves rapidly. Otherwise it may be difficult to try the case so long after the event. However, the patient now has the right to seek an absolute or conditional discharge from a mental health review tribunal (see Chapter 8). This does not inevitably result in his being transferred back to the penal system for trial, although he could presumably be arrested again for the original offence.

There is dispute about the criteria for a finding of disability, and in particular whether amnesia should be excluded. If genuine, it can obviously make it impossible for the accused to defend himself and is quite different from mere forgetfulness (Walker, 1981). But the main difficulty with the present law is its all or nothing attitude. The accused may be able to understand a trial on a simple charge, but not on a more complicated matter. He may also have a perfectly good defence to it. The judge's power to postpone the issue of fitness where this is "expedient and in the interests of the accused" (s.4(2)) may provide some solution to both of these problems, but it is obviously not a complete answer. The accused may also be detained for a great deal longer than is appropriate either to his alleged offence or to his mental condition, although it is not unknown for the Home Office to agree to a discharge in a very short time and he can now apply to a tribunal as well. But in some cases, detention in a mental hospital may be wholly inappropriate.

Curiously in view of their attitude to other forms of diversion, the Butler Committee thought it wrong that the accused should feel that he had been indefinitely imprisoned without trial. They suggested that the issue of fitness should normally be decided by a judge, unless the medical evidence is not unanimous and the defence calls for a jury. If there is some prospect of recovery, the court should be able to postpone the trial for up to six months and send the accused to hospital in the meantime. If there is no such prospect or he remains unfit, there should always be as good a trial of the facts as is possible in the circumstances. The accused should be represented, even if he cannot or will not instruct a lawyer himself. He may then be entitled to an acquittal or a finding that he should be dealt with as a person under disability. The latter should allow the court to impose any appropriate non-penal order, such as a hospital order (with or without a restriction order), an order for out-patient treatment, guardianship, or a discharge. A similar procedure should be available in magistrates' courts.

In fact, it now turns out that the magistrates can produce a similar result. They have power to make a hospital order (without restrictions) over a mentally ill or severely impaired defendant without convicting him, provided that they are satisfied that he did the act or made the omission charged (Mental Health Act 1983, s.37(3); the Crown Court can only do this if the patient has been transferred from prison to hospital before trial, s.51(5) and (6)). In *R. v. Lincoln (Kesteven) Magistrates' Court, ex parte O'Connor,* [1983] 1 W.L.R. 335, the accused was so severely handicapped that he was unable to understand what it meant to consent to summary trial on a charge of assault occasioning actual bodily harm to a nurse at the hospital where he was an informal patient. The magistrates therefore were unable to try the case and so refused to make a hospital order. In the Divisional Court, however, Lord Lane L.C.J. and Ackner L.J. held that they could have made an order without holding a trial, although it was stressed that the circumstances in which this would be appropriate were very rare and would usually require the consent of those acting for the defendant.

This may be a practical result. The Court obviously felt that a restriction order would have been wholly disproportionate, both to the offence charged and to the defendant's mental condition. It is still difficult to understand how the magistrates can be satisfied that he did the deed without holding some sort of trial. In practice, one suspects that a great many more defendants are unfit to stand trial than the one or two dozen who may be found so each year. Where they have a legal representative, he will obviously do his utmost to avoid producing the inevitable result, save on a murder charge where the alternative might just be worse. Where they have no legal representative, the penalty may not be great and the problem may even pass unnoticed. To insist that magistrates invariably provide a lawyer for a defendant whom they have reason to believe is suffering from severe mental illness or mental handicap might be the most practical solution. Furthermore, the mere fact that it is difficult to try someone does not necessarily mean that the various psychiatric disposals are appropriate.

3. *Mental Disorder as a Defence*

(a) *Insanity*

Most people seem to have a vague sense that a person who by reason of mental disorder is not responsible for his actions should not be visited with the full consequences of the criminal law. Yet neither would they wish an individual who is liable to commit criminal acts to be left at large. The result has been the special verdict of "not guilty by reason of insanity" (Trial of Lunatics Act 1883, s.2(1)). After this, the defendant must be ordered to be detained in a hospital specified by the Home Secretary, with the same status as a restriction order patient (Criminal Procedure (Insanity) Act 1964, s.5(1) and Sched. 1). Now that the courts have power to opt for therapeutic rather than penal measures when sentencing a wide range of disordered defendants for most offences, the defence of insanity is only worth raising when the prospect of indefinite detention in Broadmoor is preferable to the sentence which the court would otherwise be obliged by law to impose. Nowadays in practice this means murder, where the sentence is fixed at life imprisonment. But here the alternative verdict of guilty to manslaughter by reason of diminished responsibility provides a wider and more flexible alternative. We therefore have the intriguing spectacle of the prosecution alleging that the accused is "not guilty by reason of insanity," while the defence offers a plea of guilty to manslaughter. The draconian effect of an insanity verdict also means that in lesser charges the important distinction is not between guilt and insanity but between innocence and insanity. Again we have the intriguing spectacle of defendants rapidly changing their plea to guilty if the judge rules that their defence amounts to one of insanity.

Thus defendants are only too pleased that the present defence has always been thought very limited. It is a typical lawyer's attempt to relate the defendant's mental state at the time of the guilty deed to the lawyer's concept of a blameworthy or guilty mind. The accepted formulation is that given by the judges in response to questions from the House of Lords in *M'Naghten's Case* (1843) 10 Cl. & Fin. 200. The accused must prove on the balance of probabilities (or if he claims diminished responsibility or automatism the prosecution may prove, but beyond reasonable doubt that at the time of his act he was "labouring under such defect of reason from disease of the mind as not to know the nature and quality of the act he was doing, or, if he did know it, that he did not know it was wrong." This provides two rather different defences. An example of the first is assaulting someone with an axe believing him to be a block of wood. The disorder has negatived the existence of the guilty mind which would normally be required for a conviction. An example of the second is killing someone in the belief that one is God and thus entitled to do it. To that extent, the person with a diseased mind is relieved from the presumption that we all know and understand the law and its relationship to our actions. But strictly speaking, neither limb of the defence will excuse a man who knows what he is doing and knows it to be against the law, even though he is acting on the orders of his "voices," or under the delusion that his victim is persecuting him, or in the belief that he has a divine mission to exterminate prostitutes. Still less does it excuse a man whose perception, knowing and reasoning faculties are unaffected, but whose capacity to resist his impulses or conform his behaviour to the law is substantially impaired. Attempts to refine the defence in the United States (see for example, Morris, 1978) tend to concentrate on whether these sorts of case should be included. In this country, we have been preoccupied since the abolition of the death penalty with the fact that insanity is in practice not an excuse at all.

Most of the English case law, therefore, is concerned with the distinction between the man who does not know what he is doing because of "disease of the mind" and the man who has lost control of his bodily functions for some other reason (such as a fit of sneezing) and is entitled to an ordinary acquittal because of "non-insane automatism." But what does the law mean by a "disease of the mind"? Is it limited to mental illnesses in the psychiatric sense, which was certainly what the judges were dealing with in M'Naghten's Case? Or can it include physical and neurological conditions which impair mental functioning, either temporarily or permanently? The judges approach this question in the light of what they now acknowledge to be the purpose of the special verdict, which is not to excuse but to protect society against the recurrence of dangerous conduct.

In *R.* v. *Kemp* [1957] 1 Q.B. 399, Devlin J. defined "mind" in its ordinary sense of the mental faculties of reason, memory and understanding. Insanity could therefore include a malfunctioning of these faculties brought on by arterio-sclerosis. This definition was adopted by Lord Diplock in the unanimous House of Lords decision in *R*. v. *Sullivan* [1983] 3 W.L.R. 123, which concerned the unconscious violence of an epileptic in the post-ictal stage of grand mal. The defence argued that the M'Naghten Rules did not apply at all to unconscious movements, as opposed to those carried out in a deluded state of consciousness. But the House held that "not to know the nature and quality of the act" did include not knowing what he was doing at all. The defence also argued that the loss of consciousness was not caused by mental illness, for this could not include a loss of faculties which lasted for such a short time. Doctors would certainly draw such a distinction. But their lordships decided that "if the effect of a disease was to impair those faculties so severely as to have either of the consequences referred to in the latter part of the rules, it mattered not whether the impairment was organic, as in epilepsy, or functional, or whether the impairment was permanent or was transient and intermittent, provided that it subsisted at the time of the commission of the act."

However, they did not want to rule out the possibility of non-insane automatism if a temporary impairment resulted from some external factor, such as a blow on the head or the therapeutic administration of drugs. Such a transitory malfunctioning was held not to be disease of the mind in *R*. v. *Quick* [1973] Q.B. 910, which concerned hypoglycaemia brought on by a combination of insulin, alcohol and lack of food. But a diabetic who knows that this might make him aggressive or uncontrolled could be sufficiently reckless to justify a conviction for a crime which does not require any specific intent (*R*. v. *Bailey* [1983] 1 W.L.R. 760). But why is an epileptic insane, while a diabetic is either innocent or guilty, when in each case the basic problem is the inter-relationship between a physical condition and the drugs or other things that they take? A "disease of the mind" is loss of mental functioning, yet the probable explanation is that one is a condition of the brain while the other is a condition of the pancreas.

Transitory malfunctionings which are totally unrelated to any condition of the brain or to any psychiatric illness should lead to an acquittal, for example where the accused was sleep-walking. So should failure to use one's mental faculties, for example when walking out of a shop without paying in a fit of absence of mind, even if this is exacerbated by depression (*R.* v. *Clarke* [1972] 1 All E.R. 209). The so-called hysterical dissociated states can cause difficulty, not least to those judges who find it hard to believe that the accused was indeed unconscious of what he was doing. If a man, for example, is driving purposefully, "hysterical fugue" is no defence to a charge of doing so recklessly (see *R.* v. *Isitt* (1977) Cr. App. R. 44). There is nothing to stop the judges holding that hysteria, at least if it is prone to recur, is a disease of the mind, for they have not yet turned their attention to the types of functional disorder which might be included.

The Butler Committee (1975) proposed a special verdict of "not guilty on evidence of mental disorder" in two situations. The first is where evidence of any type of disorder is put forward to negative the existence of the state of mind required for the particular offence. This would be roughly equivalent to the first limb of the rules but somewhat broader. In particular, it would bring in, they thought, *all* cases of non-insane automatism. In practice, the House of Lords has virtually done this for them, but even on their proposals there are surely some automatons who are *not* suffering from mental disorder? We have not quite reached the position where all loss of control over one's bodily functions is regarded as a mental *disorder*. The Committee, like the courts, also favoured a specific exception for transitory states produced by the use or non-use (for example by diabetics) of drugs or alcohol, or by physical injury.

The second proposal was much more radical. The defence should be available whenever the accused was suffering from severe mental illness (their definition is quoted on page 47) or severe mental handicap (which they would not have limited to mental impairment under the 1983 Act). There would be no need to prove any causal connection between the disorder and the offence, for lack of any real blameworthiness could be assumed. This reflects the humane concern of doctors and others who do not like to see the poor in mind even put on trial, let alone punished (indeed when some give evidence about such things as hysterical dissociation, it seems that they do not like to see anyone punished). Nor do they like to be asked to speculate about precisely what the accused was thinking as he wielded the axe.

This solves everyone's problems, but does not provide an answer in principle to the question of criminal responsibility.

The Committee also suggested that the court should have a discretion to impose any non-penal order after a special verdict. This would certainly make the defence a great deal more attractive. It would also have the merit, when combined with a wider definition, of forcing the authorities to make more facilities available (Walker, 1981). The courts would not be able to send a person to prison when he ought to be elsewhere. The disadvantage is that it assumes that hospital is the right place for those offenders who cannot be set free, and that is not an assumption which the hospitals share.

(b) *Infanticide*

This offence was created in 1938 to mitigate the then mandatory death sentence for murder (although these women were always reprieved). It applies where a woman kills her child of under 12 months when her mind is "disturbed by reason of not having fully recovered from the effect of giving birth to the child or by reason of the effect of lactation consequent on the birth" (Infanticide Act 1938). The court can then impose any penalty it thinks fit and imprisonment is now quite rare. The offence may be ripe for abolition, now that much the same ground is covered by the defence of diminished responsibility, which can also refer to the killing of a child over 12 months or of a different child. The Criminal Law Revision Committee (1980a) wished to retain it, apparently because the psychiatrists had suggested several examples which would be infanticide but not diminished responsibility. These all related to the stresses caused by having to cope with a new baby in poverty-stricken or other socially deprived environments, or by not being able to cope with these pressures or to relate properly to the new baby. Clearly, the offence is now being used in circumstances far wider than those originally intended. But would not these stresses, or at least some of them, amount to mental disorder for the purpose of diminished responsibility? And if they do not, should they amount to an excuse at all? If they should, why should they not apply to fathers? Or to other people who are driven to killing by the intolerable pressures of their surroundings although unprovoked by their victims?

(c) *Diminished responsibility*

This defence was also introduced to mitigate the mandatory sentences of death or life imprisonment for murder. It results in a conviction for manslaughter, for which the sentence is quite at large. From the defence point of view, it is usually preferable to an insanity verdict. Although there was originally some reluctance to do so, it is now accepted that the judge may agree to the plea without a trial where the medical evidence is not challenged (*R*. v. *Cox* (1968) 52 Cr. App. R. 130; see also *R*. v. *Vinagre* (1979) 69 Cr. App. R. 104). In 1976 and 1977, for example, the defence was only challenged by the prosecution or the judge in 29 out of the 194 cases in which it was raised, and failed in 18 of these, giving an overall failure rate of less than 10 per cent. (Dell, 1982). Technically, the accused must be "suffering from such abnormality of mind (whether arising from a condition of arrested or retarded development of mind or any inherent cause or induced by disease or injury) as substantially impaired his responsibility . . . " (Homicide Act 1957, s.2).

"Abnormality of mind" has been widely construed as a "state of mind so different from that of ordinary human beings that a reasonable man would term it abnormal" (*R*. v. *Byrne* [1960] 2 Q.B. 396). This is similar to, but even wider than, the "man must be mad" test for mental illness, because it can clearly cover disturbed personalities including psychopathy, and transient abnormalities of the sort which may result in mercy killings or battered babies. But the required causes for the abnormality have to be stretched if they are to cover such cases, and there is ample evidence that doctors do this. They, and the Criminal Law Revision Committee (1980a), would prefer to replace the medical criterion with mental disorder as defined in the Mental Health Act. The second element, substantial impairment of responsibility, is a moral question on which doctors have no particular expertise, although they are often asked to express an opinion. Logically, it should have some connection with the legal definition of responsibility for the offence. The problem is then very similar to that in insanity. If someone knows what he is doing, knows it to be wrong, and could have prevented himself if he chose, how can we say that he was not responsible? And how is it possible to have degrees of such responsibility? What the defence is really getting at is degrees of moral turpitude, which is quite a different matter.

The Butler Committee, and others (Walker, 1981; Dell, 1982, for example), would prefer to solve the problem by abolishing the mandatory sentence for murder and leaving it to the discretion of the judge. This would certainly remove the need for a statutory formulation which would be acceptable to Parliament and cover all the killings in which there is substantial mitigation. But it would not absolve the judge from the need to apply fair and consistent principles in sentencing. At the moment, that need has been somewhat obscured by the finding of diminished responsibility. It is sometimes assumed that the accused was not responsible at all, and requires treatment or sympathy rather than punishment. But the incorrigibly dangerous may merit life imprisonment and sometimes there is a degree of blame which merits a determinate sentence (*R.* v. *Chambers* [1983] Crim.L.R. 688). Abolition of the mandatory sentence would force the judiciary to think clearly about what those degrees of blame might be. The Criminal Law Revision Committee (1980a) were divided on the question of abolishing the mandatory sentence, but wanted to retain the diminished responsibility defence in any event. They thought that juries might shrink from convicting of murder in such cases and also that the judge would benefit from the jury's view that responsibility was diminished. The first could be solved by substituting on all-purpose "homicide" verdict. The second argument applies to all offences, although in practice there is hardly ever a trial even in diminished responsibility cases. Walker (1981) has suggested that the defence should apply to other charges, not so as to produce a conviction for a lesser offence, but so as to halve the maximum penalty available. Coupled with the proposed extension of the insanity defence, this would have a dramatic effect on the criminal liability of mentally disordered people. The practical problem would still be to find an appropriate disposal.

4. *Sentencing*

While the law has so far stuck to a very strict view on criminal responsibility, it has now been provided with a wide range of non-penal methods of disposal after conviction. There are five specifically psychiatric orders, and also the possibility that an offender who is sent to prison may later be transferred to hospital.

We must also consider what the court might do if a therapeutic disposal was neither available nor appropriate. It cannot defer sentence on condition that the offender attends a mental hospital (*R.* v. *Skelton* [1983] Crim.L.R. 686).

(a) *Psychiatric probation or supervision orders*

Probation orders require an offender to be under the supervision of a probation officer for a specified period of between six months and three years. They may be made in any court for any offence other than one with a fixed penalty (which in practice means murder), but there is no power to order probation without convicting (Powers of Criminal Courts Act 1973, s.2). Supervision orders are the equivalent for offenders under the age of 17, and also for juveniles found in need of care or control in care proceedings (Children and Young Persons Act 1969, ss.7(7)(*b*) and 1(3)(*b*)). There is no minimum duration for a supervision order (s.17) and the supervisor may (and if the child is under 13 and no probation officer is working with the family must) be a local authority social worker rather than a probation officer (s.13).

The variety of conditions which may be inserted in these orders has been steadily growing, but requirements for psychiatric treatment have a longer history than most. Probation was first introduced in 1907 and with the growth of psychiatric outpatient clinics and voluntary hospital treatment in the 1930s, some enterprising magistrates began to use it as an unofficial means of persuading disordered offenders to seek treatment. The position was regularised in 1948, when express power to insert such conditions was granted. The present law is contained in section 3 of the 1973 Act and section 12(4) and (5) of the 1969 Act.

The court must have evidence from one "approved" doctor: neither Act states that this may be written or oral, but juvenile courts have a general power to admit written medical evidence in care proceedings (Children and Young Persons Act 1963, s.26) and written reports are commonly agreed for the purposes of sentencing. The 1973 Act obviously contemplates that written reports will be admitted, for it provides that section 54(2) and (3) of the Mental Health Act shall apply (see page 146 above) (s.3(7)). The doctor must state that the person's mental condition "is such as requires and may be susceptible to treatment but is not such as to warrant his detention in pursuance of a hospital order" (1973

Act, s.3(1); 1969 Act, s.12(4)). Strictly, then, the court cannot choose between the two as the medical requirements are mutually exclusive. If satisfied that arrangements for the treatment have been made, the court can then insert one of three conditions: in-patient treatment in a hospital (but not a special hospital) or mental nursing home, out-patient treatment at a specified institution or place, or treatment by or under the direction of a named doctor. Further than this, the court is not allowed to be precise: the doctor himself may direct analysis or other forms of therapy by another professional under medical supervision. The condition may be imposed for the whole or only part of the period of the order, but a psychiatric condition in a supervision order cannot continue after the patient reaches 18 (1969 Act, s.12(5)). An existing order can be varied to include one of the conditions, but only within three months, which may be too early for the supervisor to discover the need (1973 Act, Sched. 1, Para. 3(2)(c); 1969 Act, s.15(1)).

The court must explain all the requirements of a probation order and obtain the offender's consent (1973 Act, s.2(6)). This does not apply to supervision as such, but the consent of a person of 14 or over must be obtained for a psychiatric condition (1969 Act, ss.12(5) and 16(7)). The doctor in charge of a probationer may himself make arrangements for the patient to be treated in a different place from the one specified in the order, provided that the patient agrees. This can include arranging in-patient treatment at a place which could not have been specified in the original order. It is unlikely that this means that doctor and patient can agree on in-patient treatment even though the court required only out-patient attendance. It is also unlikely that they can agree on treatment in a special hospital (these are reserved for detained patients), but they might choose a place which was not a hospital or mental nursing home. These changes do not have to be reported to the court, but the doctor must tell the supervisor, and the treatment is then automatically deemed part of the order (1973 Act, s.3(5) and (6); there is no equivalent for supervision orders).

The doctor can also report to the supervisor if for any reason he is no longer willing to be responsible for the patient; or if he thinks that the treatment should continue beyond the period specified, or that the patient needs a different one of the three kinds of treatment, or that he is not susceptible to or no longer requires treatment. The supervisor must then apply to the court for the condition to be varied or cancelled accordingly. The Act does not insist that the court does so, but usually it will have little choice (1973 Act, Sched. 1, para. 4; 1969 Act, s.15(5)).

So what is to happen if, having given his consent in court (which many might do to avoid a worse fate), the patient later changes his mind and refuses to co-operate with his doctor? Variation or cancellation negates the court's object; and even if the requirement is for in-patient treatment, the admission will normally be informal, so that the hospital can neither detain him or treat him against his will. The doctor can only report to the supervisor, who may take proceedings for breach: in a probation order, or a supervision order made in criminal proceedings, the present sanctions are a fine of up to £50, an attendance centre order if the offender is under 21 (though not in the Crown Court), or to sentence him afresh for the original offence if the offender is 17 or over (1973 Act, s.6(3) and (6); 1969 Act, s.15(2) (2A) and (4)). There are no sanctions at all for a child under 18 who is in breach of a supervision order made in care proceedings, although the court could make use of its general power to substitute a care order if the child is unlikely to receive the care or control which he needs without it (1969 Act, ss.15(1) and 16(6)). But it is expressly laid down that a probationer cannot be dealt with for breach of the order if all he has done is to refuse to undergo any surgical, electrical or other treatment, if the court decides that the refusal is reasonable in all the circumstances (1973 Act, s.6(7)).

Not surprisingly, therefore, opinions differ as to the efficacy of the order. Therapeutically, it may be preferable to a hospital order because there is less and less need for even the most seriously disordered to be detained in hospital and the order allows a flexible combination of medical care and supervision. On the other hand, evasion is relatively easy, and there have been failures of communication between the medical and supervising authorities. The supervisor is expressly precluded from actively supervising an in-patient (1973 Act, s.3(4)), and the hospital is not always quick to inform him of discharge or non-cooperation. It would help if a much clearer indication of exactly what was expected of patient, doctor and supervisor were given at the outset (Lewis, 1980). Despite their possible shortcomings from a penal point of view, these remain the most popular form of psychiatric disposal.

(b) *Hospital orders*

The 1959 Act gave the courts power to send a wide range of mentally disordered offenders to hospital. Similar powers had existed before then only in relation to "mental defectives," although these (as we have seen in Chapter 2) included what are now called psychopaths. In theory the choice was now a simple one: either the offender was "bad" and should receive the penalty appropriate to the gravity of his offence and his previous record, or he was "mad" and should be committed to the medical authorities for as long as was necessary to cure him. Unless extra restrictions were needed to protect the public, the policy was to make those for whom the courts had chosen a therapeutic rather than a penal disposal as similar as possible to those admitted for treatment under civil powers.

A hospital order can be made for any offence, apart from one with a fixed penalty (in practice, murder), provided that the trial court could have sentenced the offender to imprisonment, or some other form of custody, instead (1983 Act, s.37(1)). The Crown Court must actually convict the offender, unless he has already been transferred from prison to hospital before trial or committed to hospital by the magistrates with a view to a restriction order being made (see section 2(b) above). Magistrates, however, may impose a hospital order on a mentally ill or severely impaired defendant without recording a conviction, provided that they are satisfied that he did the act or made the omission charged (s.37(3)). It now appears that they can do this without holding a trial in the strict sense (*R.* v. *Lincoln* (*Kesteven*) *Magistrates' Court, ex parte O'Connor* [1983] 1 W.L.R. 335; page 155 above). It therefore gives them a rather unsatisfactory alternative to finding him unfit to plead or not guilty by reason of insanity, neither of which is open to them at present. Juvenile courts may make orders over young offenders under section 37, but also over juveniles found in need of care or control in care proceedings under the Children and Young Persons Act 1969 (see further in Chapter 3).

The medical criteria. Two doctors, one of them approved, must state that the offender is suffering from mental illness, psychopathic disorder, severe mental impairment or mental impairment.

The disorder must be "of a nature or degree which makes it appropriate for him to be detained in a hospital for medical treatment." In the case of psychopathic disorder and mild mental impairment, this treatment must be likely to alleviate or prevent a deterioration of his condition (s.37(2)(*a*)(i)). The doctors must agree on one of the four forms of disorder, although they may differ about whether he also suffers from any other. The court must specify its conclusion on this (s.37(7)).

The definitions of the various forms of disorder have already been discussed in Chapter 2, but several points are particularly important here. The residuary category of "any other disorder or disability of mind" is not enough for a hospital order, and neither is the broader concept of mental handicap. The patient must either be mentally ill or he must exhibit abnormally aggressive or seriously irresponsible conduct. The latter may either be the result of a persistent disorder or disability of mind (psychopathy) or allied to severe or significant impairment of intelligence and social functioning (s.1(2)).

Because the broader categories are excluded, doctors may well have been tempted to apply a very wide concept of mental illness. There is certainly evidence of this in Walker and McCabe's study (1973), particularly in relation to sex offenders and drug addicts. The 1983 Act now excludes people whose only problem is promiscuity or other immoral conduct, sexual deviation or dependence on alcohol or drugs (s.1(3)). If a doctor wishes to recommend a hospital order for such people, he will have to give evidence of some specific psychiatric illness or psychopathic disorder.

It is difficult to tell what the effect of the much narrower definition of mental handicap will be. Perhaps most crimes are "seriously irresponsible" even if they are not "abnormally agressive." But it is just these inadequate and inconvenient offenders who reveal the greatest gap between the expectations of the courts and the policies of the health service. The courts do not like sending handicapped people to prison, and are proving increasingly reluctant to do so (see section 4(f) below). NHS hospitals do not like having them. This is only partly because they may be difficult to manage. More and more, the place for able-bodied mentally handicapped people is in the community, rather than in a hospital, where they can rarely be cured by conventional psychiatric treatment and may have to stay for a very long time before anyone can be satisfied that they are unlikely to offend again.

The new "treatability" test reflects the hospital view. It will reduce still further the scope for sending the less severely handicapped offenders to hospital. But it was mainly introduced because the Butler Committee were persuaded that the responsibility for dealing with dangerous psychopaths should be squarely placed on the prison rather than the hospital service. Having once been quite anxious to claim that they could alter aberrant personalities, the medical profession are now ready to admit that there is usually little they can do. They wished it to be clear that they could no longer be expected to take a patient unless they could either make him better or at least prevent his getting worse.

In practice, however, there is a second medical element in the grounds which enables the profession to pick and choose. A hospital order cannot be made unless the court has evidence, either from the doctor who would be in charge of the patient or from another representative of that hospital, that a bed will be available for him there within 28 days (s.37(4)). The difficulties in finding a bed, and the court's power to seek information from the regional health authority, have already been discussed in Chapter 1. The decision to offer a bed is clearly that of the hospital managers, acting on the advice of the clinical team under the leadership of the RMO. Consultant psychiatrists these days recognise that other professions, particularly the nursing staff who will have day-to-day contact with the patient, must have a voice in deciding who can be accepted on to their wards. But if the hospital decides to offer a bed and the nursing or other staff continue to object, they may effectively frustrate the intentions of the court. In *R. v. Harding (Bernard) The Times,* June 15, 1983, Lawton L.J. warned that the time had come for people who resisted admissions to secure units to appreciate that, once a hospital order had been made, anyone who obstructed its execution or counselled or procured others to obstruction, might be guilty of contempt of court. Whether the Crown Court would carry out such a threat is open to doubt. It is equally doubtful whether this or any other measure will arrest the long term decline in hospital orders, which have fallen by at least a third during the 1970s.

The judicial criteria. Once it has the required medical evidence, the court must decide whether the order is the most suitable way of disposing of the case, having regard to all the circumstances including the nature of the offence, the character and antecedents of the offender, and to the other available methods of dealing with him (s.37(2)(*b*)). The court cannot impose a fine, custodial sentence, probation, supervision or parental recognisances order on top of a hospital order, although it can make other additional orders, for example for compensation or local authority care (s.37(8)).

In principle, the court should decide whether punishment or treatment is appropriate and make its choice accordingly. In *R.* v. *Gunnell* (1966) 50 Cr. App. R. 242, it was held that an offender who deserved punishment could be sent to prison, even though he qualified for a hospital order and a suitable bed was available. Once it has been decided that treatment is appropriate, the court can go on to consider whether a restriction order should be added to the basic hospital order. In practice, however, these neat distinctions are not so easy to apply, partly because an offender could be both "mad" and "bad" (Rollin, 1969), and partly because of the scarcity of hospital beds which the courts regard as suitable.

The court is entitled to take into account the need to protect the public (*R.* v. *Higginbotham* [1961] 1 W.L.R. 1277). And in *R.* v. *Gardiner* [1967] 1 W.L.R. 464, the Court of Appeal drew attention to all the deficiencies of an ordinary hospital order in this respect. The hospital may discharge the patient at any time and is quite likely to do so within a year. It may make little attempt to recapture him if he absconds, and he can obtain his discharge simply by remaining at large for 28 days. Under the 1983 Act, his detention cannot be renewed beyond the initial six months unless the medical criteria still exist. These include a treatability test which even applies to mentally ill and severely impaired patients, although in a more limited way. Once the patient ceases to be liable to detention, there is no power to recall him to hospital, and usually no compulsory after-care. Even a restriction order (see below) no longer solves all of these problems. In any event, it deals only with the patient's legal status. Unless a bed is found in a special hospital or secure unit (for which a restriction order is not essential) the practical problem of security will remain. Hence the deciding factor for the court is often, not whether a bed is available, but whether a bed which the court thinks sufficiently secure is available (see *R.* v. *Morris* [1961] 2 Q.B. 237; *R.* v. *Cox* (1967) 52 Cr. App. R. 130; *R.* v. *McFarlane* (1975) 60 Cr. App. R. 320; *R.* v. *Harding* (*Bernard*), *The Times,* June 15, 1983).

On the other hand, if such a bed can be found, the courts seem only too happy to accede to the medical recommendations. They have been as vociferous as any in pressing for more medium secure accommodation. In *R.* v. *Harding* (*Bernard*), *The Times,* June 15, 1983, Lawton L.J. remarked that it was a form of cruelty to keep a mentally sick person in prison. The idea that a hospital order may be equally severe in some cases does not seem to have occurred to them. Some offenders are likely to remain in hospital for a great deal longer than they would have stayed in prison, and in these days of increasing alternatives to custody they might well have avoided prison altogether. The utilitarian answer (Walker and McCabe, 1973) is that, however it may seem to the patient, it is not unjust to make the commission of an offence the "occasion" for sending to hospital a patient who ought to be there and who could just as easily have been "sectioned" under civil powers. This is a little too neat. The patient might never have been considered a suitable case for compulsory hospitalisation had it not been for the offence. And the offence will undoubtedly colour the views of both the hospital and any mental health review tribunal about whether he should be discharged. For as long as his disorder continues, the burden will be upon him to show that he can be trusted outside.

The law itself is a little inconsistent about the "justice" of imposing a hospital order. The offence must now be punishable with imprisonment. But the courts do not seem to take the triviality of the offence into account and the Court of Appeal has refused to regard a hospital order, even with an unlimited restriction order, as "more severe" than a prison sentence (*R.* v. *Bennett* [1968] 1 W.L.R. 988; *R.* v. *Sodhi* [1978] Crim.L.R. 565). This means that it can be substituted for a custodial sentence on appeal.

The Butler Committee were similarly ambivalent. In general, they approved heartily of the hospital order system, which accords well with their mixture of therapeutic positivism and concern for the protection of the public. But they did recommend that handicapped people should not be sent to hospital without the evidence of a specialist in mental handicap, because they were concerned about the possible injustice. They also proposed that a hospital order should not be substituted on appeal without the offender's consent. Gostin (1977), however, has suggested that a hospital order should never be made without consent. This is not as radical as it seems. Hospitals much prefer their patients to be receptive to the idea of treatment and consent is already needed to the rather more common probation order with a condition of psychiatric treatment. The notion that an offender should not be allowed to choose his punishment, while it may have merit, cannot be applied to orders which are not supposed to be punishments at all. The question is, rather, whether a person whom we are prepared to call an offender should be entitled to the benefit of the normal principle of proportionality in sentencing, unless both he and the court are prepared to waive it.

The legal effect. Ordinary hospital orders are almost indistinguishable from admissions for treatment under civil powers. All the rules relating to the duration and renewal of detention, reclassification, leave of absence, absconding, and discharge by the authorities are the same (1983 Act, s.40(4) and Sched. 1, Pt. I; see Chapter 4). There are now only two important differences. First, the patient's nearest relative cannot discharge him, but can instead apply for the case to be reviewed by a tribunal within the same periods that the patient himself can apply (s.69(1)(*a*); see Chapter 8). Secondly, the offender has the same right as any other to appeal to a higher court against the order, although for an appeal from the Crown Court to the Court of Appeal, leave will be required unless a point of law is involved. But he no longer has the same right as a civil patient admitted for treatment to apply to a tribunal within the first six months of his admission. This was removed from ordinary hospital order patients when restriction order patients were given rights of application (as a result of the decision of the European Court of Human Rights in *X.* v. *United Kingdom,* applic. no. 6998/75, (1981) 4 E.H.R.R. 181). Understandably, the government did not see why restriction order patients should be allowed to go to a tribunal within six months of a court's decision that they were a serious risk to the public. But the right to a review is one of those "set forth in the Convention" and under Article 14 these must be enjoyed by all "without discrimination on any ground such as sex, race, colour, language, religion, political or other opinion, national or social origin, association with a national minority, property, birth or other status." It was feared that restricted patients might complain of discrimination if ordinary hospital order patients could apply when they could not. Hence a right which had existed since the 1959 Act, had never been known to cause difficulties, but might benefit a few patients (of whom Michael Fagan, the Queen's intruder, was one) was taken away.

The hospital order is authority for a police officer, approved social worker or any other person directed to do so by the court, to take the patient to the named hospital within 28 days, and for the hospital to detain him (s.40(1)). Once he is admitted, any previous compulsory admission or hospital order ceases to have effect, unless the new order is quashed on appeal (s.40(5)). The patient can be kept in a place of safety in the meantime (s.37(4); for the definition, see page 149 above). If the Home Secretary finds that, because of an emergency or some other special circumstances, it is not possible to admit him to the named hospital, he may arrange admission to another one (s.37(5)).

(c) *Interim hospital orders*

The stark choice between treating an offender as mad or bad was thought, by the Butler Committee and others, to present another difficulty. Unlike a probation order, a hospital order gives no means of returning to court for a more suitable disposal if it turns out that a mistake has been made. It may not matter if an offender is discharged from hospital in a very short time because his illness has been cured or brought under control. But it does matter if there has been a mistaken diagnosis (perhaps brought about by his own deception), or if there is no suitable treatment, or if he has refused to co-operate with any sort of treatment. The power to remand to hospital for reports or for treatment may help to avoid these mistakes, but the 1983 Act also allows the courts to have a "second bite at the cherry" through the medium of interim hospital orders under section 38. This again will not be implemented until there are suitable facilities, although the need for security is not so great on a trial order as it is on a remand. The order will be available when the court has actually convicted the defendant of an offence which would qualify for a full hospital order. There must be evidence from two doctors, one of them approved, and at least one of them must be employed at the hospital which is named in the order (s.38(3)). They must state that the offender is suffering from mental illness, psychopathic disorder, severe mental impairment or mental impairment. There is no room here for a tentative diagnosis, as there is in a remand for reports. There must also be "reason to suppose that the mental disorder from which the offender is suffering is such that it may be appropriate for a hospital order to be made in his case" (s.38(1)). There must be the usual evidence from the proposed RMO or the hospital managers that a bed will be available within 28 days (s.38(4)). The court's power to require information about possible beds from the regional health authority applies to interim as well as full hospital orders (s.39). The court then has a complete discretion to try an interim order before finally deciding how to deal with the offender.

If an interim order is made, the patient can be kept in a place of safety before he is taken to hospital by a police officer, approved social worker or other person directed to do so by the court. The hospital must then detain him in accordance with the order (s.40(3)). The usual provisions about the medical treatment of detained patients apply (s.56(1)). Otherwise, however, the order is not like an ordinary hospital order. Neither the patient nor his nearest relative may apply to a mental health review tribunal. No one has any right to discharge the patient or even to grant him leave of absence. If he absconds, a police officer may arrest him without warrant and must then bring him as soon as practicable back to the court which made the order (s.38(7)). The order lasts in the first instance for whatever period the court specifies, up to a maximum of 12 weeks. The court may renew it for further periods of 28 days at a time, up to a maximum of six months in all, if the RMO reports that this is warranted (s.38(5)). The patient does not have to be there at renewal, provided that he has a legal representative who is given an opportunity of being heard (s.38(6)). The court may even replace the interim order with a full hospital order without the patient being there, but with the same proviso (s.38(2)). But he must be brought back to court for the decision about what to do instead, if the RMO reports against renewing the interim order or making a full order, or if the court wishes to do something different.

Once an interim order is at an end, the court has a completely free choice among the disposals available for the offence in question. If the evidence is there, it may make a full hospital order. This means that the patient will have to spend another six months in hospital before his case can be reviewed by a tribunal. On the other hand, the court could choose to impose a penalty. This may be all very well if the offender turns out not to have been mentally disordered after all or to be unsuitable for medical treatment. Even then, it seems undesirable to impose a further custodial sentence if only a short period in custody would have been appropriate. It would be quite wrong to impose an alternative penalty if the hospital order turns out to have been such a wise choice that the offender has already been cured. The court may be tempted to make a probation order with a condition of some form of psychiatric after-care in such a case. But it should not be forgotten that the court could not have done this had it made a full hospital order in the first place.

(d) *Restriction orders*

Restriction orders are the most controversial form of psychiatric disposal. They were originally an attempt to combine the advantages of a hospital order with the advantages of indefinite preventive detention coupled with a power of recall after release. But the decision of the European Court of Human Rights in *X.* v. *United Kingdom,* applic. no. 6998/75, (1981) 4 E.H.R.R. 181, has forced a reconsideration of this.

The court's powers. A restriction order can only be made in the Crown Court (s.41(1)). But if magistrates have convicted an offender aged 14 or more, and have the evidence required for a hospital order, they may commit him to the Crown Court with a view to a restriction order being made (s.43(1)). If a bed is available, this can be direct to hospital (s.44). If the Crown Court disagrees with the magistrates, it may only impose an order or penalty which they could have imposed, unless the magistrates have also committed with a view to a greater penalty than they can give. The Crown Court can remand to hospital for reports or treatment, or make an interim order, as if it had itself convicted the offender (s.43(2), (4) and (3)).

The court must always have the evidence required for an

ordinary hospital order and one of the doctors must attend to give evidence in person (s.41(2)). This does not have to be the doctor who would be in charge of the patient, although the court must have the usual evidence that a bed will be available. It is obviously important to have the hospital's views about whether restrictions are appropriate, but in the end the matter is one for the judge (*R.* v. *Blackwood* (1974) 59 Cr. App. R. 246; *R.* v. *Royse* [1981] Crim. L.R. 426).

The court must consider the restriction order necessary to protect the public from serious harm, having regard to the nature of the offence, the antecedents of the offender, and the risk of his committing further offences if set at large (s.41(1)). In *R.* v. *Gardiner* [1967] 1 W.L.R. 464, the Court of Appeal stated that judges should have compelling reasons if they did not impose restrictions in cases of crimes of violence or the more serious sexual offences, particularly if the offender has a similar record or a history of mental disorder involving violent behaviour. But under the 1959 Act, these were not the only cases justifying restrictions. In *R.* v. *Toland* (1974) 58 Cr. App. R. 453, it was said that any seriously anti-social conduct from which the public required protection, such as repeated burglaries, was sufficient.

However, the earlier cases must now be read subject to the 1983 Act's insistence that the restrictions be necessary to protect the public from *serious harm*. We shall have to await guidance from the Court of Appeal on whether this is limited to offences against the person, or may extend to serious damage to property (such as arson), or to offences of dishonesty (such as burglary and fraud). The Butler Committee believed that orders were being made in cases where their severity was not appropriate. Gostin (1977) could certainly supply examples. Amongst the most obvious was Nigel Smith, referred to by Scarman L.J. in *R.* v. *McFarlane* (1975) 60 Cr. App. R. 320. He was a "petty fraudster" with no history of violence or even mental illness, who found himself not only in Broadmoor, but also under a restriction order of unlimited duration. Once a court has imposed restrictions, the burden on the offender to justify his release becomes very considerable. Nevertheless, even before the 1983 Act, restriction orders were becoming less frequent. Hospital orders of all kinds fell by more than a third during the 1970s, but the proportion of restriction orders also fell. They were 21·1 per cent. (278 out of 1317) of those made in 1970, but only 15·3 per cent. (156 of 1017) in 1975, and 13·4 per cent. (102 of 759) in 1979. The trend seems clear, even though the fall was not in an entirely straight line. Partly, of course, the hospitals are even more reluctant to accept potential restriction order patients than they are to accept other offenders. But it may be that the legal profession has become more aware of the draconian effects of a restriction order (compare some of the case histories given by Gostin, 1977) and the courts may also have become more discriminating in their use. The proportion of restricted patients entering hospital after committing burglary, theft or handling certainly fell between 1971 and 1981 (Home Office, 1982). But this includes all types of restricted patient, less than half of whom are now admitted on restriction orders.

Effects. Restrictions may be imposed for a definite period or without limit of time (s.41(1)). Unlike prison sentences, the purpose is not to reflect the gravity of the offence in their length but to ensure that the patient is not discharged until he is ready. As there is usually no means of knowing when this will be, the Court of Appeal stated in *R.* v. *Gardiner* [1967] 1 W.L.R. 464 that unlimited orders should be made unless the doctors could confidently predict a recovery within a limited period. The Butler Committee considered that the power to prescribe a time limit was illogical and should be abolished. This has not been done, but the courts seem likely to persist in the *Gardiner* approach (*R.* v. *Haynes* [1982] Crim.L.R. 245).

The Home Secretary can lift the restrictions at any time, if he is satisfied that they are no longer necessary to protect the public from serious harm (s.42(1)). If the patient is still in hospital when the restrictions end, either because the court specified a limited duration or the Home Secretary has lifted them, he is treated as if he had been admitted under an ordinary hospital order on the day the restriction order ended (ss.41(5) and 42(1)), but he will be able to apply to a tribunal during the first six months. If, however, the patient has been conditionally discharged from hospital before the restrictions end, he will achieve an automatic absolute discharge on that date (s.42(5)).

While the restrictions last, they are still severe. The patient cannot be discharged, transferred to another hospital, or even given leave of absence, without the Home Secretary's consent (s.41(3)(*c*)). Either the Home Secretary or the RMO may recall him from leave, and the former is not bound by the usual six month time limit (s.41(3)(*d*)). Absconders can be recaptured at any time and so cannot obtain their "discharge by operation of law" by staying at large for 28 days (s.41(3)(*d*)). The Home Secretary has an independent power to discharge the patient, which is more commonly used because the discharge may be absolute or conditional (s.42(2)). A conditionally discharged patient is subject to compulsory after-care (although not medical treatment) and may be recalled to hospital at any time (s.42(3)). All of these matters are discussed further in Chapter 7.

The other crucial difference between an ordinary hospital order and a restriction order is that the latter continues indefinitely. For as long as the restrictions last and the patient has not been absolutely discharged, there is no need for his detention to be periodically renewed under section 20 (s.41(3)(*a*)). This means that no one is under any statutory obligation to consider whether the criteria for detaining him still apply. It also used to mean that the Home Secretary did not feel under obligation to agree to a discharge simply because there were no longer any medical grounds for keeping the patient in hospital. He might require to be satisfied, not only that the patient was sane, but also that he was safe. Gostin (1977) collected many examples where the Home Secretary refused or delayed a discharge, even though the RMO or a tribunal had reported that the patient no longer suffered from a mental disorder which warranted his detention in hospital for treatment. A reported case is *Kynaston* v. *Secretary of State for Home Affairs* (1981) 73 Cr. App. R. 281, in which it took two years from the RMO's report that the patient was no longer disordered for the Home Secretary and his advisers to agree that it was safe to discharge him. However, in the subsequent litigation (which was blocked because of the immunity in what is now section 139), the Court of Appeal did suggest that Kynaston could not have been detained if he had indeed been cured. This is, however, extremely difficult to prove if, as was thought by the Home Office advisers, the patient's problem is a psychopathic personality.

Because it appeared that a restricted patient might be detained for much longer than was justified by his mental condition, Gostin (1977) argued that the restriction order was not a therapeutic disposal, but a penalty equivalent to a sentence of life imprisonment. It should therefore be governed, if not by the usual principle of proportionality, then at least by the maximum term of imprisonment applicable to the offence. The point was reinforced by those offenders transferred from prison to hospital. No matter what their condition, their restrictions must cease when their imprisonment would have ceased (see below). Gostin's suggestion, however, was directly contrary to the approach of the Butler Committee. They were more troubled that dangerous offenders had to be released from prison at the end of their sentences and recommended the extension of the principle of indeterminate detention to them.

In the event, the decision of the European Court of Human Rights in *X.* v. *United Kingdom,* applic. no. 6998/75, (1981) 4 E.H.R.R. 181, has put a different complexion on the matter. Having been convicted of a serious attack upon a workmate, X spent two-and-a-half years in Broadmoor before his conditional discharge in 1971. After three apparently blameless years in the community, he was recalled in April 1974. It later turned out that this was because of the alarming things which his wife said to his supervisor when announcing her intention of leaving him. Habeas corpus proceedings were unsuccessful and under the 1959 Act, his right to seek reference to a tribunal did not arise until six months after his recall. Even then the tribunal could only advise the Home Secretary, who took no action until it tallied with the advice of the RMO.

The main plank of his complaint of breaches of the European Convention on Human Rights, and the one on which he succeeded, was the lack of any judicial review of the merits of his recall and detention. This has now been remedied by giving restricted patients rights of application to and review by mental health review tribunals, although the tribunals' powers are more limited than with ordinary hospital order and civil patients (see Chapter 8). But the patient also complained that his second period of detention in Broadmoor was in breach of Article 5(1) of the Convention, which states that: "No person shall be deprived of his liberty save in the following cases . . . (a) the lawful detention of a person after conviction by a competent court; . . . (e) the lawful detention . . . of persons of unsound mind . . . " (none of the other cases applied). In the earlier *Winterwerp Case,* applic. no. 6301/73, (1979) 2 E.H.R.R. 387, the European Court had laid down three minimum conditions to be satisfied for the lawful detention of persons of unsound mind. Except in an emergency, the person must be reliably shown to be of unsound mind, that is, a true mental disorder must be established on the basis of objective medical expertise; the mental disorder must be of a kind or degree warranting compulsory confinement; and the validity of the continued confinement will depend upon the persistence of such a disorder. The government argued that because X's detention had been ordered after conviction by a competent court, it was justified under Article 5(1)(*a*) and these requirements did not apply. The European Commission on Human Rights argued that, because the court had chosen a therapeutic disposal, the detention could only be justified under Article 5(1)(*e*) and therefore these requirements must apply. Somewhat puzzlingly, the European Court considered that the detention before his conditional discharge fell within both (*a*) and (*e*); they were less sure whether the detention after his recall did so; but they found this unnecessary to decide, because in any event the requirements of (*e*) would have to be satisfied. On the facts, however, they found no reason to disagree with the Broadmoor doctor's judgment that these did exist when X was recalled to hospital.

The message of this is plain. If the patient is no longer suffering from mental disorder of a nature or degree which makes his detention in hospital appropriate, he can no longer be detained there, no matter how dangerous he may be. The Act now provides that the RMO must examine the patient and report to the Home Secretary at such intervals as the latter may require, but not exceeding a year (s.41(6)). There is still no formal renewal procedure and no express requirement for the Home Secretary to agree to the discharge of a patient who no longer meets the criteria. No doubt the Home Secretary will continue to seek the views of others before reaching a decision. But it is now clear, from both the *X* and *Kynaston* cases, that he must apply those criteria to that decision.

It will be interesting to see whether these changes have any effect upon the practice of the courts. The old style restriction order was a remarkably effective method of protecting the public. It will now be more difficult to work out whether that protection will be better achieved by a prison sentence with the possibility of a transfer to hospital than by the new style restriction order.

(e) *Transfer from prison*

Any prison officer will tell you that many of his prisoners are "only 16 shillings in the pound." Prison medical officers are more cautious. They now make six-monthly returns to the Home Office of prisoners whom they consider to be mentally disordered within the meaning of the 1983 Act. On September 30, 1982, for example, they reported only 286, of whom 210 were mentally ill. Even if these prisoners are placed in the hospital wing of a prison where the medical officer has psychiatric experience, they cannot expect to receive the treatment which they would get in hospital. For one thing, there is no statutory power to impose treatment without their consent (Brazier, 1980). However, the Home Secretary can direct that offenders serving prison sentences be transferred to hospital under section 47 of the 1983 Act. This includes offenders serving other types of custodial sentence, those who do not comply with an order to enter into recognisances to keep the peace or be of good behaviour, and those imprisoned for non-payment of fines (s.47(5)). (Other prisoners may be transferred under the more limited power in section 48, which has already been discussed with the pre-trial procedures).

The Home Secretary must have reports from two doctors, one of them approved. The prisoner must be suffering from mental illness, psychopathic disorder, severe mental impairment or mental impairment, and the other conditions are also the same as for an ordinary hospital order. Once again, therefore, if the "16 shillings in the pound" offender is not mentally ill and does not behave in an abnormally aggressive or seriously irresponsible manner, he cannot be transferred. If he is only psychopathic or mildly impaired, he cannot be transferred unless hospital treatment is likely either to make him better or at least prevent his getting worse. In addition to the medical criteria, the Home Secretary must consider the transfer "expedient," having regard to the public interest and all the circumstances (s.47(1)). The patient must arrive at the hospital within 14 days of the direction (s.47(2)), so the Home Office must have secured a bed for him beforehand. He may be transferred either with or without restrictions (s.49(1)).

A transfer without restrictions has the same effect as an ordinary hospital order (s.47(2)). It is normally chosen if the prisoner is coming to the end of his sentence, but it can mean that he will remain legally liable to be detained in hospital beyond the time when he would have been released from prison. He may, however, be discharged at any time and will be able to apply to a tribunal even during his first six months (see Chapter 8). As with an ordinary hospital order, his longer detention is not thought unjust, because he could in any event have been compulsorily admitted under civil powers. He will not necessarily see it that way, especially if he is detained in a secure unit or special hospital.

Restrictions are normally imposed if the sentence has some time to run, but they cease automatically at the end of the sentence (s.50(2)). This date must now be calculated with all the remission which the patient would have had if he had stayed in prison (s.50(3)), but adding on to the sentence any period during which he was absent without leave from the hospital (s.50(4)). The transfer has the same effect as a restriction order (s.49(2)). The patient can apply to a tribunal within the first six months and then as usual, but this does not mean that the tribunal has the power to release him if he is no longer a suitable case for treatment. If advised that he is fit for discharge, the Home Secretary must choose between allowing this or returning him to prison (see further in Chapter 8). Similarly, the RMO must make regular examinations and reports to the Home Office (s.49(3)). If the Home Secretary is advised by the RMO, or by any doctor, or by a tribunal, that the offender no longer requires treatment for mental disorder, or that no effective treatment can be given him in that hospital (which is not quite the same thing as saying that he is fit for discharge), the Home Secretary can do one of three things. He can leave the patient in hospital for the time being, unless the patient is fit for absolute discharge. Or he can send the offender back to a penal establishment, there to complete his sentence as if nothing had happened. Or he can release the offender on licence, or discharge him under supervision, if there would have been power to do this from the penal establishment (s.50(1)). If the patient is still in hospital when the restrictions cease, he remains liable to be detained under an ordinary hospital order (s.41(5)).

These transfers fell from 89 in 1971, to 37 in 1976, but rose to 70 in 1981 (Home Office, 1982). The Home Office has certainly declared its commitment to getting these prisoners into hospital, although only 12 were officially waiting for a bed at the time when there were 286 mentally disordered people (at the very least) in prison. Parliament may be concerned that these prisoners will have to be released at the end of their sentences, unless they can be transferred beforehand. This is yet another reason for pressing for sufficient secure units to accommodate them.

(f) *Guardianship orders*

Guardianship could be a very useful order, but in practice it is hardly ever used (it never reached double figures in any year during the 1970s). It may be made for the same offences and with the same medical evidence as a hospital order, save that the treatability test does not apply, and the condition must be "of a nature or degree which warrants his reception into guardianship" (s.37(2)(*a*)(ii)), rather than such as to make hospital treatment appropriate. Mental handicap is again limited to impairments which are associated with abnormally aggressive or seriously irresponsible conduct. This could be unfortunate, as handicapped offenders are rarely suitable for hospital treatment, but could benefit from prolonged guidance in the community. The 1983 Act also insists that the patient has reached the age of 16. This again removes the option of long term help for juveniles who ought not to be removed from home, whether as a result of criminal offences or after being found in need of care or control in care proceedings.

The duration, procedure for renewal and rights of application to a tribunal are basically the same in a guardianship order as in an ordinary hospital order. The effect, however, is quite different. The patient is placed in the guardianship either of the local social services authority or of some other individual approved by them (s.40(2)). The order cannot be made unless the proposed guardian agrees (s.37(2)). The details appear in Chapter 9, but the guardian now has three powers over the patient. He may decide where the patient should live, and when and where the patient should go for treatment, occupation, education or training, and he may insist that any named doctor, social worker or other person sees the patient at home (s.8(1)). He cannot insist that the patient accepts any medical or other treatment on offer, although if that becomes necessary and the medical recommendations are available, he may transfer the patient to hospital. The patient may be recaptured and returned if he absconds from the place where he is required to live. Otherwise, however, there are no sanctions against a patient who refuses to co-operate (although other people might be guilty of harbouring him or obstructing the authorities). The order is therefore quite different from a probation order with a condition of psychiatric treatment, and of course it involves local authority social services rather than probation officers and doctors.

This is no doubt why it has been so little used. Community services have been slow to develop. But the order requires liaison between the doctors, who will have to give evidence, the social services authority, which will have to take at least some of the responsibility, and the courts, who will not usually have a representative of that authority on hand to consult. The Butler Committee recommended closer co-operation with a view to using guardianship more frequently, and the DHSS (1978) were similarly encouraging. The new form of order corresponds more closely to their suggested essential powers order than the British Association of Social Workers' (1977) hoped-for community care order, but is certainly less ambiguous than the old. The obvious key to further development is the legal profession, which might be encouraged to investigate the idea on behalf of its clients.

(g) *Alternatives*

Given the slump in hospital orders, the continuing difficulty in finding suitable beds, and the further restriction of the eligible cases by the 1983 Act, it is crucial to consider how the fact that an offender is mentally disordered may affect the court's assessment of the alternatives. In a trivial case, of course, it may incline the court in favour of a lenient course, such as a discharge or probation. But at one time, a disturbed offender who was not sent to hospital was undoubtedly at risk of a heavier sentence than might otherwise have been appropriate. After all, if he was mentally ill, his behaviour might not be subject to the same rational processes by which it is assumed that the rest of us are controlled. If his behaviour stemmed from a disordered or inadequate personality, it was likely to continue until he grew out of it. The courts felt bound to take these possibilities into account when exercising their function of individual deterrence.

This may still be the case where the offences committed are very serious. In *R*. v. *Herpels* (1979) 1 Cr. App. R. (S.) 209, the offences amounted to a kidnap at gunpoint. The Court of Appeal stated that a life sentence might be appropriate for an offender who had committed a serious crime and appeared to be suffering from a psychological condition which could lead to further dangerous offences. However, in *R.* v. *Pither* (1979) 1 Cr. App. R (S.) 209, this was confined to exceptional cases where the offender is subject to a "marked degree of mental instability." Persistent delinquent behaviour is not enough. And in *R.* v. *Spencer* (1979) 1 Cr. App. R. (S.) 75, the Court emphasised that a life sentence should not be imposed unless the offender was also a serious and constant danger to the public. The defendant was a former mental patient who set fire to a car while labouring under a misguided sense of grievance, but he had taken pains to avoid endangering life, and the Court substituted a sentence of five years for one of life imprisonment.

Lower down the scale, there have been cases such as *R.* v. *Arrowsmith* [1976] Crim. L.R. 636, in which a woman with a long history of disturbed and aggressive behaviour was given three years' imprisonment on breach of probation for a minor offence, because the medical and social services could not cope with her any longer. But in *R.* v. *Clarke* (1975) 61 Cr. App. R. 320, Lawton L.J. observed that "Her Majesty's courts are not dustbins into which the social services can sweep difficult members of the public. . . . If the Courts became disposers of those who are socially inconvenient the road ahead would lead to the destruction of liberty. It should be clearly understood that Her Majesty's judges stand on that road barring the way. The Courts exist to punish according to law those convicted of offences. Sentences should fit crimes." A £2.00 fine was substituted for a sentence of 18 months' imprisonment for a former Rampton patient who was admittedly very difficult to handle but had only been convicted of breaking a flower pot.

In *R.* v. *Tolley* (1978) 68 Cr. App. R. 323, the Court of Appeal preferred the approach in *Clarke* to that in *Arrowsmith*. They ordered the immediate release of a man who had been diagnosed schizophrenic and sentenced to two years' imprisonment for possessing a small amount of cannabis, even though he was obviously doing very well in the prison hospital. A fixed term of imprisonment should not exceed a length commensurate with the gravity of the offence. The fact that his mental condition made it likely that if set at large he would be a danger to himself or others did not justify using the penal system to supplement the shortcomings of the social services and mental health system.

These cases may certainly be seen as part of a judicial campaign to keep mentally disordered people out of prison. To the extent that they emphasise that punishments should fit crimes, they are welcome. But they were also part of a campaign to persuade the medical authorities to accept responsibility, primarily by building more secure units to which these patients might be sent on hospital orders of potentially unlimited duration. But no matter how many secure units are built, they will not solve the problem of people like Dawn Clarke, who was repeatedly discharged from Rampton by a tribunal. There are many people who are not dangerous in any sensible meaning of the term, but who are difficult and a nuisance to all and sundry, and for whom there is precious little that hospitals as such can do. Hospitals are not dustbins any more than prisons are. The alternative of good facilities in the community simply does not exist in many places. Even if it did, they would find it hard to cope with such people alongside their more docile residents. The courts, and the rest of us, may have to accept that there are some troublesome people whom we must try to tolerate as best we can.

5. *Commentary*

The law relating to mentally disordered offenders is trying to have the best of all worlds. Within the context of a system which is supposed to do justice, it is trying to cure those who might be cured and to protect society against those who cannot. But once again we can start from the proposition that, just as the defendant has the same rights as everyone else, he also has the same responsibilities. The UN Declaration on the Rights of Mentally Retarded Persons (United Nations, 1971) states that "if prosecuted for any offence, he shall have a right to due process of law with full recognition being given to his degree of mental responsibility." This can go either way. If he did not do it, he should not be convicted simply because he is mentally handicapped. If he did do it, he is entitled to the same treatment as others. People who break their responsibilities towards society are normally punished, but their punishment must be in proportion to the offence. Punishments should fit crimes, whether trivial or serious. If then we are going to hold a man responsible, we should accord him the right to minimal proportionality, as the judges seem prepared to do. He may be prepared to accept the loss of that right, in the hope that a therapeutic disposal will do him some good, or at least be more pleasant than the alternative. But if he is responsible enough to participate in ordinary rights and duties, he should be allowed to make the choice.

But what about the people who are really dangerous? Society may have a right to protect itself against them, whether or not they are responsible, and even if there is nothing the medical profession can do for them. But this should be a very limited category. We should make it quite clear what we mean by dangerousness. We should be sure that the event of danger presented is sufficient to justify the level of intervention (Floud and Young, 1981). And we should be able to separate those who are dangerous from those who are not with a higher degree of reliability than we can at present (Walker, 1978). Mental disorder as such is not the criterion. There are plenty of sane people who are dangerous and plenty of insane people who are not. If we are going to deprive people of either proportionality or the normal principles of guilt and innocence in order to protect society against serious risk, we should be concentrating on the accurate identification and discovery of that risk and on nothing else (for a review of the evidence, see Floud and Young, 1981).

Then we have the people who are not responsible and who are not dangerous. Some of these should be left alone. A person whose mind is not on the job when he does what would otherwise be a criminal act should prima facie be acquitted altogether. The forgetful shopper is not dishonest. The epileptic is not deliberately violent. He is no more a fit candidate for punishment or other intervention than the diabetic. He is in most circumstances an ordinary member of society fully entitled to participate as such. There is, of course, much to be said for holding people liable for at least some of their acts, if they know that carelessness or irresponsibility in taking their prophylactic treatment will produce those acts. If they do not exhibit that carelessness, we have no cause to intervene. They are otherwise fully participant members of society.

Lastly, there are a few who do not qualify as participants in the ordinary system of rights and duties, but who behave in criminal ways. These are very few indeed. Towards them we should probably behave in the same way as we do when considering their ordinary civil rights (see page 69). This does not involve locking them up, unless this is absolutely necessary, but in catering for their needs as humanely as possible and trying to the best of our ability to fit them into ordinary life.

Strange though it may seem, English law already contains within it the capacity to produce most of these results. But it does so in a rather haphazard and chaotic way, which depends more on the discretion of the courts than on any carefully considered principles. The main problem is that it assumes that the solution should be governed by the presence or absence of something the psychiatrists call mental disorder, when we have seen how little that can tell us about the patient or about what they can do for him. The second problem is that it assumes a straight dichotomy between punishment and treatment. There are circumstances when neither is appropriate and nothing should be done. There are circumstances when neither is appropriate but something should be done. And there are circumstances when the subject, rather than the authorities, should be given the choice.

6.   Patients in Hospital

Far and away the most important change of principle introduced under the 1983 Act is the decision to regulate what may happen to compulsory patients while they are in hospital. Under the 1959 Act, it was assumed that they were incompetent to decide upon their medical treatment. It was also assumed that neither they nor informal patients required any special protection against exploitation or abuse. Many matters are still left to the principles of the common law or to the discretion of staff and hospital authorities. But on some points the Act is now quite precise. In any event, the law is now vastly more complicated than it was and everyone is much more conscious of the issues involved. The law is discussed on the assumption that there will be no difficulty in bringing cases before the courts. In Chapter 10, however, we shall see that there are certain restrictions on the liability of individuals for acts concerning compulsory patients and these afford considerable protection to hospital staff who are doing their best. They do not protect those who fail to live up to the standards which can reasonably be expected of them.

1. *Explanations*

Whenever any patient is detained under the Act, one of the first things which should happen is that the hospital managers do their best to ensure that he understands his legal position (s.132(1)). These steps have to be taken "as soon as practicable" after the detention has begun, and again if the section under which the patient is detained changes, for example from a section 2 admission for assessment to a section 3 admission for treatment. The steps required are such "as are practicable to ensure that the patient understands" and they *must* include giving the required information both orally and in writing (s.132(3)). If it is quite impossible to explain matters to the patient when he is admitted, the managers should continue their efforts until it does become possible.

The information required is considerable. The patient must understand under which section he is detained and the effect of that section, and the rights of applying to a mental health review tribunal which are available to him under it (s.132(1)). But the hospital must also explain who has the power to discharge him, including the possible bar on a discharge by his nearest relative and the relative's right to challenge this before a mental health review tribunal; the hospital's powers to censor his correspondence (see section 2 below); the Act's provisions relating to the treatment of detained patients and the extra safeguards where certain treatments are proposed (see section 3(e) below); and the protective powers of the Mental Health Act Commission (see section 5) and the effect of the code of practice (see pages 210 and 223) (s.132(2)). With all this to take in, the patient should not be short of occupation after he is detained.

Unless the patient asks otherwise, the hospital must also "take such steps as are practicable" to supply his nearest relative (if any) with a copy of this information, either at the same time as it is given to the patient or within a reasonable time afterwards (s.132(4)). The Act makes no reference to supplying information to any legal adviser whom the patient may have. Yet a major source of complaint before the European Court of Human Rights in the case of *X.* v. *United Kingdom*, applic. no. 6998/75, (1981) 4 E.H.R.R. 181, was that no explanation had been given of the reasons for the patient's recall to Broadmoor after three years on conditional discharge. This was an alleged breach of Article 5(2) of the European Convention on Human Rights, which requires that "everyone who is arrested shall be informed promptly, in a language which he understands, of the reasons for his arrest and of any charge against him." The Government argued that this only applied to arrest on a criminal charge, and in any event that the patient had been told the reasons for his recall by the RMO in Broadmoor, although he may have been too disturbed to understand this at the time. The European Commission argued that Article 5(2) must apply to all types of detention, and that whatever may have been said to the patient himself, there could be no justification for withholding an official and detailed explanation from his solicitors. Following the Commission's strictures, new

guidelines were introduced for the recall of conditionally discharged patients. Under these, the person (police officer, social
worker or whoever) taking the patient into custody should tell him
in simple terms that he is being recalled on the authority of the
Home Secretary under the Act and that a further explanation will
be given later. A detailed account of the reasons should then be
given by the medical staff of the hospital as soon as possible after
his admission, and certainly within 72 hours. The patient's
supervisor and a "responsible member of his family (or his legal
adviser)" should also be informed of the reasons. In the event, the
majority of the European Court found it unnecessary to rule on
the disputed questions of law and fact under Article 5(2). They
found this a lesser problem which was necessarily encompassed by
the greater problem of failing to provide a speedy judicial review
of the lawfulness of the patient's detention (see page 178 above).
At such a review, an explanation would inevitably have been
forthcoming.

The dissenting member of the court, however, considered that
the right to an explanation "constitutes a safeguard of personal
liberty whose importance in any democratic system founded on the
rule of law cannot be underestimated. Quite apart from enabling
the person detained to make proper preparations for bringing legal
proceedings (under Article 5(4)), it is the embodiment of a kind of
legitimate confidence or expectation . . . in the relations between
the individual and the public powers." This has always been an
important principle in the English law of arrest, and no doubt the
Government shared this view when section 132 was enacted.
However, quite apart from leaving out the patient's legal adviser
(if any), section 132 simply requires an explanation of the patient's
legal position. It does not require any explanation of the factual
reasons for his detention. He is not likely to receive that unless the
hospital medical staff volunteer them in accordance with guidelines for recalled patients or he makes an application to a mental
health review tribunal.

There is also a statutory duty to inform the patient when his
detention for treatment or under an ordinary hospital order is
renewed (s.20(3)), when the form of his disorder is reclassified
(s.16(4)), and when his nearest relative is prevented from
discharging him (s.25(2)). The nearest relative must be informed
in each of the last two cases; and, unless the patient or the relative

has asked that this should not be done, the hospital "must take such steps as are practicable" to warn the nearest relative of the patient's impending discharge from detention, if possible at least seven days beforehand (s.133). There is still no statutory duty to tell the patient *at the time* when the authority for his detention simply runs out, even though this may be long after he was originally informed of the position.

There is also no legal obligation to make the position clear to informal patients. The Scottish Mental Welfare Commission often deal with queries about this, and many other things, from informal patients. But the DHSS has always been anxious to preserve the principle that informal patients receiving treatment for mental disorder should not be treated any differently from patients receiving treatment for physical disorders. Any procedure which singles them out has usually been rejected, although, as we shall see, they are now included in the extra safeguards governing the use of some exceptionally intrusive treatments.

2. Patients' Mail

Under the 1983 Act, the scope for censoring patients' mail has been much reduced. Nevertheless, the managers of *any* hospital or mental nursing home, acting through a member of staff as authorised censor (s.134(7)), may open and inspect *any* postal packet in order to discover whether it qualifies for censorship (s.134(4)). In practice, however, this is unlikely to happen outside special hospitals. In any other type of hospital, the only interference allowed is to withhold from the post office any postal packet which a detained patient has addressed and delivered for dispatch to a person who has asked that communications to him from the patient should be withheld (s.134(1)(*a*)). Such a request must be made in writing, either to the hospital managers, or to the RMO or to the Secretary of State.

This also applies to patients in special hospitals. But their mail may also be withheld from the post office if the censor considers that it is likely to cause danger to any person (including someone on the hospital staff), or to cause distress to any person (other than someone on the hospital staff) (s.134(1)(*b*)). Incoming mail for special hospital patients may be withheld if it is thought necessary to do so in the interests of the safety of the patient or for the protection of other people (s.134(2)). However, neither of these wider powers applies to mail to or from any of the following: a Minister of the Crown or Member of either House of Parliament, a Master or officer of the Court of Protection or Lord Chancellor's Visitor, any of the "ombudsmen" (the Parliamentary Commissioner, Health Service Commissioner and Local Government Commissioners), a mental health review tribunal, a health authority, local social services authority, Community Health Council or probation and after-care committee, the managers of the hospital where the patient is detained, any *legally qualified* person instructed by the patient to act as his legal adviser, and the European Commission or Court of Human Rights (s.134(3)). However, there is nothing to stop any individual named on this list putting in a request under section 134(1)(*a*) that mail from a particular patient be withheld.

If the hospital censor does inspect and open a postal packet, but does not withhold anything, he must put a written note of that fact, along with his name and that of the hospital, inside before resealing it (Mental Health (Hospital, Guardianship and Consent of Treatment) Regulations 1983, reg. 17(1)). If he decides to withhold it, or anything in it, he must enclose a note to the same effect and describing any item withheld. He must also record in a special register the fact that it has been withheld, the date when this was done, the grounds for doing so, a description of the items, and his name (s.134(5) and reg. 17 (2)).

If the packet is withheld on either of the wider grounds applicable only to special hospital patients (s.134(1)(*b*) or (2)) the managers must give notice of this to the patient within seven days, and also to the person (if known) by whom an incoming packet was sent. This must be in writing (s.134(6)) and must also give the grounds for withholding the packet and the name of the censor and hospital (reg. 17(3)) and an explanation of the Mental Health Act Commission's powers of review. These should be included in the note enclosed with the packet, in which case they are sufficient notice to the person to whom it is addressed (reg. 17 (2) and (3)). The sender will require a separate notice. The Commission must review the hospital's decision, if asked to do so (in any way they think sufficient, not necessarily in writing; reg. 18(1)) either by the patient or by the person by whom incoming mail was sent. The application must be made within six months of getting the notice that the mail was withheld, and should include that notice (s.121(7); reg. 18(2)). The Commission can direct the production of any documents, information or evidence that they reasonably require (reg. 17 (3)), including, of course, the offending letter itself. They have a complete discretion to overrule the hospital's decision, for whatever reason they think fit (s.121(8)).

The European Convention on Human Rights, in Article 8, guarantees everyone "respect for his . . . correspondence." Interference by a public body is only allowed where this is "necessary in a democratic society in the interests of national security, public safety or the economic well-being of the country, for the prevention of disorder or crime, for the protection of health or morals or for the protection of the rights and freedom of others." On the face of it, even after the 1983 Act, the censorship of special hospital patients' mail goes rather further than this (and the European Court in the *Golder Case*, (1975) 1 E.H.R.R. 524, considered the list of exceptions closed). In *Y.* v. *United Kingdom*, applic. no. 6870/75, a Broadmoor patient did complain that he had been prevented from sending a telegram to his parents about his appeal. But as he was not apparently prevented from sending a letter and in any event delivered his message to his mother when she visited him two days later, the European Commission decided that there had been no material interference. Each letter has to be considered on its merits and the restrictions imposed must be necessary and proportionate to the legitimate aim pursued (see the *Silver Case*, applic. nos. 5947/72, etc., judgment of the court, March 25, 1983). The *Silver Case* emphasised the need for an effective remedy under Article 13, and the power of the Mental Health Act Commission to quash hospital decisions may supply this.

3. *Treatment and Restraint*

The common law normally respects the right of any person to decide what shall be done with his own body. Thus any action which involves the use or the threat of force, however slight, upon his person will amount to a tort (and often also to a crime) unless there is consent or some specific legal justification for acting without it. There are, of course, many activities in mental hospitals which involve no such force, such as teaching, occupational therapy, or psychotherapy, but these in any event involve the co-operation of the patient. But there are a great many other measures commonly employed which would undoubtedly be tortious. These include medical treatments, such as injections with drugs, operations, and electro-convulsive therapy. They also include the various forms of restraint or confinement used, ranging from the bodily restraint of one person by another, through periods of "seclusion" or "time out" in a locked room, to confinement in a locked ward, or eventually in the maximum security conditions of a special hospital.

Under the old lunacy legislation, there was some regulation of what went on in licensed houses, hospitals and asylums, under the overall supervision of the Board of Control and the law was specific about what should be done when "individual mechanical restraint" was imposed. But this was all swept away by the 1959 Act, which made no provision at all for the care and treatment of hospital patients, whether informal or detained. The official view was that this could safely be left to the clinical judgment of the medical authorities and that detained patients could be given any recognised form of treatment for their disorder, whether or not they consented (although a more cautious view was later adopted towards patients detained "for observation").

Others (notably Jacob, 1976, and Gostin, 1979; but see also the Butler Report, 1975) pointed out that the Act gave no express power to impose such treatment and that the common law might still apply. These doubts obviously increased the attractions of legislating upon proposals for the introduction of express safeguards over the use of the more hazardous or irreversible forms of treatment (see NCCL, 1973; Gostin, 1975). The case for these was accepted by the Butler Committee (1975), the DHSS (1978), and even to some extent by the Royal College of Psychiatrists (1981).

The 1983 Act has therefore revolutionised the law's approach to the care and treatment of patients detained in hospital. It is made quite clear that most types of detained patient can be given most forms of medical treatment for their disorder without their consent. Some treatments, however, including electro-convulsive therapy, can usually only be given either with their consent or with an independent medical opinion. Others, including psycho-surgery, can usually only be given with their consent and a second opinion. This last provision also applies to informal patients. The

Act gives no further statutory power to impose treatment upon anyone. But obviously some measures of confinement and control over all types of detained patient will be justified because the Act gives a statutory power to "detain." Nor does the Act remove those justifications which already exist at common law and apply to all types of patient, whether informal or detained. These are the patient's own consent, express or implied; the power to prevent patients doing harm to other people or to themselves or to property; and a very limited doctrine of necessity. These common law powers are, however, subject to the Act's restrictions on the use of certain specified treatments for certain types of patient and this should be borne in mind in sections (a), (b) and (c) below. All these powers will be discussed, but hospital staff may find that the concluding summary contains most of what they need to know for most practical purposes.

(a) *Common law consent*

The patient may have given his express consent to the invasion of his normal legal rights. This is only a defence where what has been done is what the patient agreed could be done, and it is advisable to avoid future arguments by making this clear at the outset. This could be particularly important where the patient agrees to embark upon a programme of "behaviour modification" (see Royal College of Psychiatrists and others, 1980), which may well involve deprivation of ordinary legal rights through a "token economy" or periods of "time out." This should be made clear at the time when consent is sought.

The law requires that consent be "real." It may therefore be invalid if induced by force or fraud. Clerk and Lindsell (1982) observe that: "it might perhaps be tentatively suggested that the plaintiff cannot give a real consent unless he has in fact the freedom to choose whether or not he should do so." The informal patient who gives his consent under the threat that he will be "sectioned" may well complain that he has been deprived of his freedom to choose. So might a hospital order patient complain, like the prisoner in *Freeman* v. *Home Office* [1983] 3 All E.R. 589, that the coercive nature of the institution, and the power of the RMO to decide whether he should be released, will prevent his consent being freely given. The judge in that case decided that whether or not consent had been given was a question of fact in each case. Presumably there might be cases in which the patient's will has been overborne by such circumstances, but the existence of those circumstances does not of itself prove the patient's case. But it is that fear which has led to the provision in the 1983 Act that certain treatments cannot be given without further safeguards, even if the patient does consent (see section (e) below).

Where the patient's consent is given under the ordinary common law, he must have the capacity to give it. However, although common law requires that the patient's consent be "real," it does not require that it be fully "informed" as to all the arguments for or against a particular treatment. In *Chatterton* v. *Gerson* [1981] Q.B. 432, a patient (who was not a mental patient) was twice treated by intrathecal phenol solution injection for chronic and intractable pain following a hernia operation. She found that the second injection failed to relieve her pain, but left her leg completely numb. She therefore claimed, among other things, that her consent to the injection was invalid, because the doctor had not explained all the possible attendant risks. The judge rejected that claim: "In my judgment, once the patient is informed in broad terms of the nature of the procedure which is intended and gives her consent, that consent is real . . . "

Paradoxically, this much-criticised decision (Robertson, 1981) may help to preserve the autonomy of some mental patients, particularly those who are mildly mentally handicapped. Goldstein (1975) has pointed out that the transatlantic concept of "informed consent" places more emphasis on what the patient can understand than on what he wants. It may therefore encourage the authorities to deprive people who cannot fully understand of their right to choose what they want. But if only a "broad terms" explanation is required in order for consent to be "real," the corollary should be that the patient is capable of giving such consent if he is capable of understanding such a "broad terms" explanation. As Glanville Williams (1983, at p. 572) suggests: "The consent of a subnormal patient is easily obtained, but that fact does not rob the consent of its validity. Mentally disordered persons should have the right both to give consent to therapeutic procedures and to withhold such consent, unless there are extremely good reasons against this."

A patient who has given a "real" consent but who wishes to complain that he was not adequately informed must therefore found his claim in negligence, that is, in the failure of the doctor to take such steps as a reasonable doctor would take in all the circumstances to avoid harming the patient. This means that the patient must prove that the doctor's failure to explain caused the ensuing harm, in other words that he would never have given his consent had he known of the risk. The doctor will also escape liability if a responsible body of medical opinion would support his failure to disclose all the risks in the particular case. Thus in *Bolam* v. *Friern Hospital Management Committee* [1957] 1 W.L.R. 582, a patient had agreed to E.C.T. and was badly injured when it was given without a muscle relaxant. His claim failed, partly because medical opinion was at the time divided about the advisability of using one, and partly because the evidence suggested that he would have agreed in any event.

However, even if a valid consent has been given, it may be withdrawn. A patient may agree to a course of drug treatment or E.C.T. but withdraw his consent before it has been completed. Similarly, he may agree to the hospital's practice of locking the ward door at night, or to a programme of behaviour modification involving a period of seclusion, but change his mind and ask to be released. In principle, a consent can be revoked at any time: the only possible exceptions (deriving from the false imprisonment cases of *Robinson* v. *Balmain New Ferry Co.* [1910] A.C. 295 and *Herd* v. *Weardale Steel, Coal and Coke Co. Ltd.* [1915] A.C. 67) are where the patient has only been let in on terms which restrict his right to get out. But nowadays it is doubtful whether a judge would uphold the hospital's right to use self-help to enforce the patient's promise to remain, particularly where no special effort was required to let him out. The most that could be suggested is that a patient who has freely agreed not to seek discharge during the night *may* not be entitled to call upon the staff to let him out at three o'clock in the morning.

But how does the need for consent fit in with the common law duty of care owed by hospital staff towards their patients? Hospitals undoubtedly have a duty to take reasonable care of their patients, and this involves offering them the care and treatment which they need, and taking reasonable steps to prevent them coming to harm. But this duty of care must always be subject to the patient's right of self-determination (unless, of course, that right has been taken away from him by other means). A confused patient may of course be prevented from wandering about the hospital, for the hospital has no duty to allow him to go wherever he wishes. But neither have they any right to keep him in the hospital if he wishes to leave. Often, what sounds like a desire to leave hospital may simply be a complaint or a passing whim. There is nothing wrong in trying to persuade a patient to remain. "But if the patient cannot be persuaded to remain of his own free will he must either be allowed to leave the hospital or, if the appropriate criteria are met, be detained under the compulsory powers provided by the Act" (DHSS, 1978).

(b) *The prevention of harm*

It is undoubtedly possible to restrain a patient from doing harm to himself or to others, whether or not he is liable to be detained under the Act. Once again, this is subject to the Act's restrictions on the use of some treatments in some cases (see section (e) below). There are four circumstances in which this may be done, but there is a considerable degree of overlap between them, and all are subject to very similar limitations. Each has, however, been devised for a slightly different reason.

The first is the prevention of crime, now covered by section 3(1) of the Criminal Law Act 1967, which provides: "A person may use such force as is reasonable in the circumstances in the prevention of crime, or in effecting or assisting the lawful arrest of offenders or suspected offenders or persons unlawfully at large." This applies only to the *prevention* of a crime which is actually in progress or about to be committed. It cannot apply where there is no crime because the patient is insane within the M'Naghten Rules (see Chapter 5). The second principle was recently outlined by Lord Diplock in *Albert* v. *Lavin* [1982] A.C. 546: "every citizen in whose presence a breach of the peace is being, or reasonably appears to be about to be, committed has the right to take reasonable steps to make the person who is breaking or threatening to break the peace refrain from doing so; and those reasonable steps in appropriate cases will include detaining him against his will." This common law power appears to have survived the 1967 Act, for a breach of the peace is not necessarily a crime, and it may perhaps be caused by one who is insane. A breach of the peace normally takes place in public, but can occur in private property, where "harm is actually done or is likely to be done to a person or in his presence to his property or a person is in fear of being so harmed through an assault, an affray, an unlawful assembly or other disturbance" (*R.* v. *Howell* [1982] Q.B. 416). Once again, the essence of the power is prevention and keeping the peace.

Also distinct from section 3(1) of the 1967 Act is the concept of self or private defence. This will almost invariably involve the prevention of crime. But the object is not to assist in preserving law and order, but to enable individuals to escape being harmed by aggressors, and this includes aggressors who are insane. It is necessary to show at least "willingness to disengage" before meeting force with force. It may also be more appropriate to rely on the defence of crime prevention when going to the rescue of strangers (that is, non-relatives) who are under attack (see *R.* v. *Duffy* [1967] 1 Q.B. 63 and the Northern Irish case of *Devlin* v. *Armstrong* [1971] N.I. 13). The point would only be important where one patient was under attack from another who happened to be insane within the M'Naghten Rules, for hospital staff can clearly act in self defence or in defence of their employers' property. It is inconceivable that the common law would *not* allow a defence in such cases, either under the concept of private defence, or breach of the peace, or under the fourth principle, which is the common law power to detain the insane.

As we have already seen in Chapter 4, the common law allows a private person to confine a person disordered in his mind who seems disposed to do mischief to himself or any other person. This is limited to those who are actually insane, although this is probably wider than the concept of insanity within the M'Naghten Rules. For our purposes it is wider than the preceding three powers, because it enables staff to prevent a patient from doing harm to himself as well as to others. All four powers can probably be summed up by the proposition that there is a right to restrain a patient who is doing, or is about to do, physical harm to himself, to another person, or to property. But it is likely that all four are subject to the same requirements of "reasonableness" as are imposed upon the prevention of crime under the 1967 Act (see Harlow, 1974; *R.* v. *Shannon* (1980) 71 Cr.App.R. 192).

"Reasonableness" involves two separate propositions. The first is that the force used is no more than is in fact necessary to accomplish the object for which it is allowed. Nice calculation is not expected of people responding to an emergency, but neither is gross over-reaction to the danger, or the continuation of force once the need for it is over. None of these powers permit anything in the nature of retaliation, revenge or punishment for what has happened. To seclude a patient, including an informal patient, for a short while to "cool off" is permissible. If this is not practicable for some reason, it may be permissible to administer a short term sedative. But they do not allow a prolonged period of solitary confinement (such as was imposed upon a patient suspected of causing a fire, in the case of *A* v. *United Kingdom*, applic. no. 6840/74).

A prolonged period of confinement or sedation would not be permitted under these principles, even if it was in fact necessary to prevent the patient doing harm. This is because of the second element in "reasonableness," which is that the reaction must be in proportion to the harm threatened. The police cannot shoot to kill in order to prevent someone from riding in a motor vehicle without wearing a seat belt. It would be most unwise to use these common law principles as a warrant for prolonged preventive detention, still less for treatment which might have lasting effects. The justification for such measures is better sought by using the Act's powers to impose detention and treatment.

But what if a nurse makes a mistake, and no harm is in fact threatened at all? Where the *only* defence relied upon is the detention of the insane, it is clear that the patient must indeed be insane and that even a reasonable mistake is no defence (*Fletcher* v. *Fletcher* (1859) 1 El. & El. 420). It is not clear whether the patient must actually be dangerous, or whether a reasonable belief in the danger is enough (see Lanham, 1974). The point is academic, for if a nurse succeeded in convincing the court that he genuinely believed the patient to be dangerous, it would be very hard to show that he was wrong. For the other three defences, a reasonable mistake will certainly suffice, and there is much debate about whether even an unreasonable mistake will do (but doubted in *Albert* v. *Lavin* [1982] A.C. 546). Individual nurses acting in pursuance of the Mental Health Act are in any event protected unless it is shown that they acted in bad faith or without reasonable care (1983 Act, s.139) but this will probably not help them in their dealings with informal patients (*R.* v. *Moonsami Runighian* [1977] Crim. L.R. 361).

These principles would support a practice of working out *in advance*, and by consultation between all the people involved, the appropriate response to each type of incident which may be anticipated on the ward. In this way it should be possible to restrict the intervention to the minimum necessary to prevent the threatened harm, to lay down the maximum response to certain types of incident, and to avoid the risk that any incident, however trivial, is met with a standard and often unnecessary over-reaction.

(c) *Necessity*

But are there any circumstances in which the common law permits intervention without the patient's consent and beyond what is immediately required to *prevent* his doing harm (once again, we must bear in mind the Act's restrictions on the use of some treatments in some cases)? There are two circumstances in which this question is of vital importance to mental hospital staff. The first is the informal patient who lacks even the low degree of capacity needed for a "real" consent and is not "disposed to do mischief to himself or others." Can nothing be done without "sectioning" him? As the DHSS (1978) point out, in such cases an absence of dissent cannot be taken as the presence of consent. But a major object of the 1959 Act was to do away with the need to "section" patients such as the severely mentally handicapped, or the elderly severely mentally infirm. Indeed (as we have seen in Chapter 2) under the 1983 Act some of these cannot be "sectioned" long term at all. The other example is the attempted suicide. As suicide is no longer a crime, can he be prevented from carrying out his intention even if he is not "insane" within the meaning of the common law power to restrain? And if he has succeeded in poisoning or otherwise attacking himself, can steps be taken to save his life against his will and without sectioning him? Indeed, as we shall see later, sectioning will not help where the treatment required is for physical rather than mental disorder.

There are undoubtedly some cases where the common law justifies measures for which no consent has been given, but the underlying principle is not easy to determine. The best example is the unconscious road accident victim. We have no "good

Samaritan" laws making it unlawful to refuse to help him, but it is obviously lawful to intervene without his consent. A less obvious example is the patient who has consented to one operation, during which it is discovered that further treatment is urgently required. The doctor has a duty to prevent his patient coming to harm and the patient might well complain if he suffered as a result of the doctor's failure to act. Once again, we may be sure that the doctor will not be liable if he carries on with something which it would be unreasonable, as opposed to merely inconvenient, to postpone (compare the Canadian cases of *Marshall* v. *Curry* (1933) 3 D.L.R. 260 and *Murray* v. *McMurchy* (1949) 2 D.L.R. 442).

But is the reason for these decisions the patient's implied consent? The patient may indignantly repudiate that suggestion when he comes round, but still the doctor will not be liable (see *Beatty* v. *Cullingworth*, British Medical Journal, November 21, 1896, p. 1525). Or is the reason that the treatment was immediately necessary to save the patient's life or perhaps a serious deterioration in his health? Taken to its logical conclusion, such a doctrine would allow us to overrule the protests of any patient, sane or insane, who wished to decline such treatment (for example, the Jehovah's witness who had conscientious objections to a life-saving blood transfusion; or the elderly person who no longer wished for massive surgical attempts to prolong life).

The most we can be absolutely sure of is this. The doctor may proceed where the treatment is "necessary," in the sense that the patient may die or suffer serious harm if it is postponed until he can be consulted, but only where it is reasonable to assume that the patient would have consented, in other words where he is not known to object. We may also be tolerably certain that the law would not condemn intervention which is absolutely necessary to save the patient's life in some cases where he is known to object. This must be true of the attempted suicide, where in any event it is possible to argue that he did not genuinely wish to succeed, but it is far less obviously true of the known Jehovah's witness who requires a blood transfusion. In all these cases, however, even if there is a technical battery, no jury is likely to convict, and there could be no substantial damages for "wrongful life."

But we cannot be sure how much further these principles will carry us, particularly in relation to patients who are permanently incapable of giving or withholding their consent. The hospital may, and indeed must, do what is necessary to sustain life and prevent their coming to serious harm. But does the law permit more substantial intervention? Skegg (1974) has suggested that "if the patient is likely to be permanently incapable of consenting . . . a doctor should be justified in doing whatever good medical practice dictates should be done in the patient's interests." This is extremely doubtful. It would extend the range of treatments involved, reasoning that it would be unreasonable to postpone them until the patient can be consulted because he can never be consulted. It also assumes that if the patient is incapable of giving a valid consent, his active protests (of which he may very well still be capable) can be overruled. The obvious problem example is a proposed abortion for a severely handicapped woman.

The solution would be much simpler if there were still a procedure available for placing such patients under a guardian who could then act as a parent may act in relation to his child. But this is no longer possible, partly because the 1983 Act has clarified but reduced the powers of a guardian over patients in guardianship under the Act (see further in Chapter 9), and partly because (as we have already seen in Chapter 2) many patients for whom it would be eminently suitable have now been excluded. Even when guardianship was available for this purpose, it was rarely used. There has undoubtedly been a tendency to assume that the power of parents to control their children's lives persists into adulthood if the child is legally incapable of making his own decisions (*e.g.* Stephen, 1950; Kloss, 1965). But there is no authority for that proposition at all. There is nothing in the modern law to suggest that other people may acquire the right to consent to treatment on behalf of any patient who is incapable of giving that consent (see Royal College of Psychiatrists and others, 1980; DHSS, 1978).

We may therefore have reached the ridiculous position that incapable patients cannot be treated without consent, save for the purpose of sustaining life, or perhaps preventing a serious deterioration, or preventing them from harming other people or themselves. Yet no one has the power to consent on their behalf and the Act's compulsory procedures cannot always be invoked to fill the gap. There may be little danger to staff who are acting in the patient's best interests, for no damage will be suffered, and legal action is in any event most unlikely. But that is small comfort to the patient himself, whose rights may be so easily invaded. We clearly need someone to resurrect the ancient prerogative power of the Crown to protect these patients, along similar lines to the modern development of the prerogative jurisdiction to protect wards of court.

(d) *"Detention" under the Act*

It was accepted on all sides before the House of Lords in the case of *Pountney* v. *Griffiths* [1976] A.C. 314 that mental hospitals have powers of control and discipline over all their patients. We have seen in the foregoing section what the common law allows in the case of both informal and detained patients. But how much further than that does the statutory power to detain the patient go? All the compulsory powers discussed earlier in this book, whether or not they permit the compulsory treatment of the patient, allow him to be detained in the hospital for the relevant period. But does this give the hospital *carte blanche* to detain him in whatever conditions it wishes? Could he be kept in indefinite solitary confinement, like the Broadmoor patient in *A.* v. *United Kingdom*, applic. no. 6840/74? Or in the iron cage devised for the Bethlem patient Norris in the late eighteenth century (for an illustration, see Scull, 1979)? It is, of course, a criminal offence for any member of the hospital staff to ill-treat or wilfully neglect any patient (1983 Act, s.127). But that apart, is it open to the hospital to make whatever decision it likes about how a patient should be detained, subject only to the usual principle that the decisions of administrative authorities may be reviewed if they are so unreasonable that no reasonable authority could possibly have taken them?

It is submitted that Parliament cannot have intended to give quite such a broad discretion to the hospital authorities (see further Hoggett, 1984). The only clear power which is given in the Act is to detain the patient *in the hospital*. Section 5(4) (the nurse's holding power discussed on pages 12 to 15 above) refers expressly to the need to prevent the patient from leaving the hospital. Section 6(2) gives the managers power to detain a patient admitted under one of the three "sections" *in the hospital*, while a hospital order (and a transfer direction) gives the managers authority to detain (s.40(1) and (2)). Thus there is obviously power to keep the patient within the named hospital. In a hospital or unit which is itself secure, this is an easier concept to apply in practice than it is when most of the patients are free to come and go as they please. Seclusion may sometimes be the only practicable means of keeping an individual detained patient within that hospital without prejudicing the other patients there, and may to that extent be justified.

Some control may also be incidental to the purpose of treating the patient to the extent that this is permitted by the Act. In *Pountney* v. *Griffiths* itself, visiting time was regarded as an aspect of the patient's treatment, and thus the act of inducing him to return to the ward when visiting time was over was incidental to it. In a hospital such as Broadmoor, where the secure and highly disciplined environment is itself regarded as a therapy for the patients, the dividing line between what is permitted in the name of treatment and what can only be justified in the name of detention is particularly difficult to draw. But neither concept could be used to justify any and every regime, however harsh, arbitrary or oppressive.

Finally, some control and discipline may be necessary to enable the institution to function as a hospital at all. Glanville Williams (1983, at p. 484) suggests that the authorities of a psychiatric hospital possess common law powers of discipline similar to those enjoyed by the master of a ship, which involve "no more than restraining passengers or crew who are endangering the vessel or those aboard, or who are seriously disrupting life aboard." In the case of informal patients who have withdrawn their consent to abide by the hospital's rules, the proper course is not to impose discipline as such, but either to ask them to leave or (where the criteria exist) to impose compulsory powers. Compulsory patients cannot so readily be asked to leave and so cannot be permitted to cause serious disruption to hospital life.

It is suggested that these are the purposes for which the power to detain may be used, and further that it should be governed by the Criminal Law Act concept of reasonableness (see page 199 above)—in other words, that the force used is necessary for the purpose permitted, and proportionate to the harm presented. The nurse in *Pountney* v. *Griffiths* may well have been entitled to take hold of the patient for the purpose of escorting him back to the ward. He would obviously not have been entitled to beat the patient unconscious. Hospital staff should observe the limits of reasonableness just as the police and prison officers must do.

Significantly, following the complaint that the patient's five weeks of solitary confinement in *A.* v. *United Kingdom*, applic. no. 6840/74, amounted to "torture or to inhuman or degrading treatment or punishment," contrary to Article 3 of the European Convention on Human Rights, a friendly settlement was reached (see the Report of the Commission, adopted July 16, 1980) which included new guidelines on the use of seclusion at Broadmoor. The other special hospitals were asked to review their own guidelines in the light of these. These apply when a patient is compulsorily confined to a secure room between 7.00 a.m. and normal bedtime. The room must have at least 4·7 square metres floor space and natural lighting.

The nurse in charge of the ward may make the initial decision to seclude—only where the patient is, or seems likely to become, so disturbed that it is desirable to isolate him for his own safety or for the safety of others. The unit nursing officer and RMO (or his deputy) must be told at once. Where the patient is to be secluded for more than three hours, a programme of care must be drawn up by the nurse in charge in consultation with the RMO and reviewed daily. Patients must at least have pyjamas or other special clothing, mattresses, bedding, disposable bedpans and urinals and lavatory paper. But unless the patient's condition precludes it, he must be allowed out of his room for toilet purposes and at least half an hour's exercise twice a day and to have visitors. He must be observed at least every 15 minutes and special records must be kept. If the patient is secluded for more than 24 hours, the hospital management team must be informed, and if for seven days, the team must report to the hospital managers, then and thereafter weekly.

The interesting thing about these guidelines is not so much the procedural safeguards which they embody, but that the criterion is the patient's own safety or that of others. The suspicion in the case of *A.* v. *United Kingdom* was that the patient had been secluded as a punishment for his suspected involvement in a fire. As has already been suggested, the restraint of patients in order to prevent their doing harm to themselves or to others is a readily acceptable principle, provided that it is not carried too far. The restraint of individual patients in other circumstances must be limited to the purposes discussed here, unless it can be justified as medical treatment. Indeed, the Royal College of Psychiatrists' guidance on the "Isolation of Patients in Protected Rooms during Psychiatric Treatment" (1980) states that isolation should *always* be seen as a necessary therapeutic tool and not as a mere management and control exercise. Any implication of its use as a punitive measure should be strictly prevented. Hence they recommend that every incident of its use should be recorded, followed by a case conference or other discussion by the appropriate multi-disciplinary team of the most suitable way of managing the patient.

(e) *Medical treatment under the Act*

Section 63 of the 1983 Act provides that the "consent of a patient shall not be required for any medical treatment given to him for the mental disorder from which he is suffering, not being treatment falling within [the special safeguards provided by] section 57 or 58 above, if the treatment is given by or under the direction of the responsible medical officer." By section 56(1) this applies to all detained patients, apart from: those held in a "place of safety" under sections 135, 136 or pending admission to hospital under a hospital order; those detained as hospital in-patients under either of the short term holding powers in section 5; those admitted for assessment in an emergency under section 4 where the second medical recommendation converting it into a full admission for assessment has not yet been given and received; those remanded to hospital for reports; and restricted patients who have been conditionally discharged from hospital. The treatment of these excepted groups of patients is governed by the common law principles discussed above. The treatment of informal patients is also governed by those principles, save that they are entitled to the *extra* protection applicable to certain treatments under section 57.

This statutory power to impose treatment without consent upon the majority of compulsory patients is subject to several important limitations. The first is that it must be "medical treatment": this is widely defined in section 145(1) to *include* nursing and "care, habilitation and rehabilitation under medical supervision." As has already been said, it is not always easy to distinguish milieu therapy in a maximum security hospital from a system of detention and discipline for its own sake. But for such a system to qualify as treatment, it must be given by or under the direction of the RMO, and it must be designed as treatment for the specific mental disorder from which the individual patient is suffering. Expecting patients to conform to very high or artificial norms of behaviour, to fit into the system for the system's sake rather than their own, or to be punished for their misdeeds prior to their admission to hospital (all of which were reported by the Rampton review team; see Boynton, 1980) can scarcely qualify as medical treatment even under the widest definition. But a carefully designed programme of behaviour modification which will meet the needs of the particular group of patients to whom it is applied obviously can qualify.

The second important limitation is that the medical treatment must be given for the *mental* disorder from which the patient is suffering. The Act gives no power to impose treatment for physical disorders which are unrelated to any mental disorder within the meaning of the Act. This is not an easy question. Some physical disorders can either be the cause or a symptom of a mental disorder: in that case, treating the cause or the symptom is surely treating the mental disorder. Thus (*pace* Carson, 1983), if a depressed patient becomes alcoholic, the alcoholism may be a symptom of his mental disorder which can be treated along with the depression, even though dependence on alcohol cannot *by itself* amount to a mental disorder under the Act (s.1(3)). But if a severely handicapped woman becomes pregnant, her pregnancy may have been caused by her disorder, but is it a symptom of that disorder? And can terminating it be justified as treatment for her disorder? There probably are circumstances in which an abortion will indeed have a beneficial effect upon her intellectual and social functioning and thus might be justified in these terms. Even more difficult is the case where the patient's mental disorder leads him to decline treatment for a quite unrelated physical disorder. If a schizophrenic refuses to have his appendix out because his thought control forbids this, it is permissible to treat the schizophrenia but not the appendix.

In such cases, if the treatment cannot be brought within the Act's concept of treatment for his mental disorder, it can only be given either with consent or under the common law doctrine of necessity. This, as we have seen, is extremely limited in scope.

Section 58 lays down extra safeguards which must be observed where detained patients (within the definition given in section 56(1) above) are to be given either of two types of treatment. The first is electro-convulsive therapy (E.C.T.) (prescribed by the Mental Health (Hospital, Guardianship and Consent to Treatment) Regulations 1983, reg. 16 (2)). The second is the administration of medicine by any means at any time during a period of detention, once three months have elapsed since the first time *in that period* when the patient was given medicine *for his mental disorder*. These treatments may only be given in either of two circumstances: (a) where the patient consents, and either the RMO or an independent doctor appointed by the Mental Health Act Commission certifies (on Form 38) not only that he has consented but also that he is capable of understanding the nature, purpose and likely effects of the treatment; *or* (b) where the *independent* doctor certifies (on Form 39) either that the patient is not so capable or that he has not consented but that the treatment should be given having regard to the likelihood of its alleviating or preventing a deterioration of his condition. Before giving the second type of certificate, the independent doctor must consult two other people who have been professionally concerned with the patient's medical treatment, one of whom must be a nurse and the other of whom must be neither a nurse nor a doctor. These procedures are subject to various related provisions which are also relevant to the safeguards laid down under section 57.

Section 57 lays down even more stringent precautions which must be observed for any surgical operation for destroying brain tissue or destroying the functioning of brain tissue, or for the surgical implantation of hormones for the purpose of reducing male sexual drive (the latter prescribed by the Mental Health (Hospital, Guardianship and Consent to Treatment) Regulations 1983, reg. 16 (1)). These treatments may only be given if *both* of two conditions are fulfilled: (a) an independent doctor and two other people who are *not* doctors must certify (on Form 37) that the patient is capable of understanding the nature, purpose and likely effects of the treatment and has consented to it; *and* (b) that independent doctor (after the same consultation as is required under section 58) must certify (also on Form 37) that the treatment should be given, having regard to the likelihood of its alleviating or preventing a deterioration of the patient's condition. This section applies not only to detained patients (as defined in section 56(1) above) but also to informal patients (s.56(2)). Thus informal patients are given the benefit of a second opinion in addition to their normal right to give or withhold consent. Detained patients are given both the right to give or withhold consent and the benefit of a second opinion. Incapable patients (perhaps with a rather higher threshhold than that required by the common law, discussed earlier) cannot be given these treatments at all. The effect may very well be that psychosurgery will no longer be possible, a result which would certainly not be universally regretted (see Gostin, 1982).

The reasoning behind section 57 is partly that these treatments are so intrusive that they should never be given without the patient's informed consent, but also that there are circumstances in which even informed consent is not enough. Patients who run the risk of a long period of confinement in a maximum security special hospital if they cannot be cured may be ready to agree to anything which holds out the prospect of cure. For this reason, there would be much to be said for extending similar safeguards to other treatments, but perhaps only where the patient is detained in certain places. An alternative is to list such treatments in the code of practice (see page 223) among those which give rise to special concern and thus "should not be given" without these safeguards, even though it is not unlawful to do so (s.118(2)).

Various other provisions are related to the safeguards laid down in sections 57 and 58. Under section 61, the RMO must report to the Mental Health Act Commission any treatment given to a *detained* patient under section 57 or without consent under section 58. This must always be done when required by the Commission. Otherwise it can wait until the RMO makes his next report to the managers for the purpose of renewing the patient's detention, or, if the patient is restricted, until the end of the first six months after the restriction order or direction, and thereafter until the next time when the RMO makes his annual report to the Home Secretary. Under section 61(3), the Mental Health Act Commission may cancel any certificate given for those treatments. Then the whole procedure will have to be gone through again, unless the RMO considers that the discontinuance of the treatment would cause serious suffering to the patient (s.62(2)).

Section 59 provides that any consent or certificate given under either section 57 or section 58 may relate to a "plan of treatment" under which the patient is to be given one or more of the forms of treatment to which the section applies, and the plan need not have a defined time limit. Section 60 allows a patient who has given consent to a treatment, or to a plan of treatment, under either section 57 or section 58, to withdraw his consent to further treatment. Then the whole procedure will have to be gone through again, unless the RMO considers that discontinuance of the treatment would cause serious suffering to the patient (s.62(2)).

Section 62(1) provides that:

> "Sections 57 and 58 above shall not apply to any treatment—
> (a) which is immediately necessary to save the patient's life; or (b) which (not being irreversible) is immediately necessary to prevent a serious deterioration of his condition; or (c) which (not being irreversible or hazardous) is immediately necessary to alleviate serious suffering by the patient; or (d) which (not being irreversible or hazardous) is immediately necessary and represents the minimum interference necessary to prevent the patient from behaving violently or being a danger to himself or others."

Treatment is "irreversible" if it has unfavourable irreversible physical or psychological consequences and "hazardous" if it entails significant physical hazard (s.62(3)).

This provision can easily be misunderstood. It does *not* amount to a blanket permission to impose treatment upon any patient in those four circumstances. Still less does it limit the emergency treatment which can be justified on other grounds (for example, at common law a nurse may kill a patient if this is the *only* way in which the patient can be prevented from killing him, but there could be nothing more irreversible than that). The effect of section 62(1) is simply to *exempt* those listed emergency situations from the need to comply with the extra safeguards which are laid down either in section 57 or in section 58. The legal justification for using the treatment in question must still be found. For detained patients (within the meaning of section 56(1) above) this is easy, for they may be given any treatment for their mental disorder without consent (s.63). But in the extraordinarily unlikely event that a hospital might wish to use psychosurgery or the surgical implantation of hormones for the treatment of an informal patient in any of those emergencies, the hospital would still have to obtain the patient's consent or find some common law justification for proceeding without it.

In practice, section 62(1) is likely to be most important in relation to the use of drugs in circumstances which might otherwise be caught by the three month rule. All sorts of interesting conundra may be posed. It is clearly lawful to proceed where the *present* injection is necessary for any of the reasons listed. But what is the position if the *first* injection three months ago was given in circumstances covered by section 62(1) and the present one is not? Do the Act's procedures have to be complied with? It could be argued that the first administration of medicine was not "for his mental disorder" but for the purposes of coping with the emergency. On the other hand, the safest course is clearly to go through the Act's procedures whatever the circumstances in which the first administration took place.

(f) *Summary*

The conclusions reached in the preceding discussion can be summarised like this:

(i) Unless this is immediately necessary to save the patient's life, *no* patient may undergo psychosurgery or the surgical implantation of hormones to reduce male sex drive, unless an independent multi-disciplinary team has certified that he is capable of consenting and has consented, *and* an independent doctor has certified after consultation that the treatment should be given.

(ii) Otherwise, *any* patient can be given any treatment to which he has consented, provided that he was capable of doing so, that his consent was real, and that it has not been withdrawn. However, the RMO or an independent doctor will have to certify this, if a detained patient (see page 207) is given E.C.T., or drug treatment once three months have gone by since the first time in his detention that he was given drugs for his disorder.

(iii) A *detained* patient can be given E.C.T. or three months drug treatment without his consent, but unless there is an emergency, an independent doctor must certify that the treatment should be given.

(iv) Treatment given to detained patients under (i) or (iii) must sooner or later be reported to the Mental Health Act Commission, who can cancel the certificates and stop the treatment, unless to discontinue it would cause serious suffering to the patient.

(v) A *detained* patient can be given any other treatment for his mental disorder without his consent.

(vi) *Any* patient can be given any treatment (including (i)) which is immediately necessary to save his life, probably even if he is known to object.

(vii) *Any* patient can probably be given any treatment (apart from (i)) which is immediately necessary to prevent a serious deterioration in his health, provided that he is not known to object.

(viii) A *detained* patient can be kept within the hospital itself. Further restraint or seclusion may be lawful for the purpose of treatment or to prevent serious disruption to hospital life.

(ix) *Any* patient can be restrained from doing immediate harm to himself, to other people or to property, provided that no more force is used than is necessary to achieve the object and is proportionate to the harm threatened, and that the Act's restrictions on the use of certain treatments are observed.

4. *Quality Control*

(a) *General standards*

The old Board of Control combined the roles of overseeing the management and general standards of mental hospitals and protecting the interests of individual patients. In 1959, it was assumed that both could safely be left to the internal machinery of the health service. However, a succession of allegations of neglect and misconduct in mental hospitals (see particularly Robb, 1967, and Morris, 1969) led to inquiries such as those into the Ely, Farleigh and Whittingham hospitals, and to many more in later years (see, for example, Beardmore, 1981). These suggested that some special oversight of standards in hospitals catering for the most vulnerable patients was still needed. An independent advisory service, staffed by teams of health service staff on secondment, was set up in 1969 to advise the Secretary of State on standards of care and management practices in individual hospitals for the elderly or mentally ill. This became the Health Advisory Service in 1976. It is not a formal inspectorate, still less a forum for the redress of individual grievances. It aims to improve general standards through visiting and inspecting hospitals and making confidential recommendations to their managing authorities or to the Secretary of State. Also in 1976, the Development Team for the Mentally Handicapped was set up. This has responsibility for both hospital and community services. The aim is to visit both hospitals and residential accommodation, to provide advice and information, particularly on the joint planning of services, and to encourage good practice. Once again, it is not a forum for the redress of individual grievances.

(b) *Internal complaints machinery*

There is no statutory procedure for handling complaints inside hospitals. Comprehensive recommendations, including a draft code of practice, were made by the Davies Committee on Hospital Complaints Procedures in 1973. They had no doubt that the investigation and satisfaction of complaints was primarily a function of management, but there had certainly been failures in the past and it would be unrealistic to expect that there would not be failures in the future. This is particularly so in the enclosed and isolated world of the mental hospital, where practices can develop which are taken for granted until some outsider comes along to challenge them. Most of the major hospital inquiries have been generated by the reaction of someone from outside the hospital, rather than from individual patients or members of staff inside it. Nevertheless, the guidance given to health authorities by the DHSS (Circulars, HM(66)15, HC(81)5) clearly expects that management both can and should resolve individual complaints, without the need for outside intervention.

Complaints should first be made to the person concerned. If this does not provide a solution, the matter can be taken to a senior member of staff. If this is still not successful, a written complaint should be made to the hospital or district administrator. If the patient cannot write the letter, a member of staff should record it and the patient sign it. The health authority will then investigate the complaint in whatever way it thinks best. Most are investigated informally, but in a very serious case it may set up an independent inquiry. Most of the recent inquiries have been set up by health authorities rather than by the DHSS. Sometimes the results are published and sometimes they are not.

Since late in 1981, there has also been a procedure for handling complaints against the clinical judgment of hospital staff (Circular HC(81)5; DHSS and others, 1983). These should first be made to the consultant in charge of the patient's treatment, or to the health authority, or to one of its officers, either orally or in writing. The consultant will investigate, involving any of the other medical staff concerned, and will try to resolve matters by discussion with the patient. If the patient is still dissatisfied, he may renew the complaint, this time in writing. The regional medical officer (or in Wales, the medical officer for complaints) is informed. The consultant may still be able to resolve the issue by further talks with the patient, but if he cannot do so, the regional medical officer may set up an independent professional review. The case will then be considered by two independent consultants in the same specialty, at least one of them from another health region. They should discuss the problem with the patient, who can have a relative, friend or general practitioner with him at the meeting. If the consultants think that the staff concerned have used their clinical judgment responsibly, they should try to reassure the patient. If they think that there have been inadequacies, they should discuss these with the staff concerned and the patient should be told that steps will be taken to prevent the problem happening again. In either case, a report will be made to the district administrator, who will write formally to the patient and send a copy to the consultant involved.

This procedure is intended for the more serious complaints, but not for those which might be the subject of a formal inquiry by the health authority or litigation in the courts. Pursuing the internal complaints procedure obviously does not prevent the patient from seeking compensation from the courts at a later date. It is normally expected that complaints will reach the health authority within a year of the matter complained about, while legal claims for personal injuries must usually be made within three years. Legal action, and the specific problems facing mental patients, are discussed in Chapter 10.

The final possibility inside the national health service is a full scale inquiry ordered by the Secretary of State under section 84 of the National Health Service Act 1977 or under section 125 of the Mental Health Act 1983. The former applies to any matters arising from the 1977 Act, which limits it to NHS patients. The latter applies to any matter arising under the 1983 Act, which is not confined to NHS patients, but will only apply to informal patients to the extent that they are covered by the Act. However, the new Mental Health Act Commission has been specifically created to safeguard the interests of patients detained under the Act and is likely to take over all complaints which are not satisfactorily resolved by the hospital or health authority.

(c) *The ombudsmen*

Even the best designed internal complaints procedure will sometimes fail to produce results. An external arbiter, in the shape of the Health Service Commissioner (or ombudsman) is provided for in sections 106 to 120 of the National Health Service Act 1977. He is a completely independent figure, with his own staff, and at present combines this role with that of the Parliamentary Commissioner for Administration (the general ombudsman). Earlier holders have been career civil servants, but the present incumbent is a senior Queen's Counsel. His terms of reference cover complaints by or on behalf of a person who has suffered injustice or hardship caused by the health authorities, either through maladministration (which means inefficiency), or failure in the services actually provided, or failure to provide a service which it is their duty to provide.

He can therefore deal with many matters arising in NHS hospitals for which the health authorities are responsible, but a great many things are outside his jurisdiction. These include serious incidents or major breakdown in services which are the subject of inquiries set up by the Secretary of State. Nor can he question the merits of a decision taken in the exercise of an authority's discretion, but only whether the way in which it was taken amounts to maladministration. He cannot deal with matters which could be taken to a mental health review tribunal or to a court, unless he is satisfied that it is unreasonable to expect the complainant to do this. He has, for example, been known to investigate complaints that informal patients have been kept in locked wards and in ignorance of their rights. Another vital restriction is that he cannot investigate "action taken in connection with the diagnosis of illness or the care or treatment of a patient which in his opinion was taken solely in the exercise of clinical judgment" (Sched. 13, pt. II). This clearly excludes individual treatment decisions, which can only be challenged internally, or through the Mental Health Act Commission, or occasionally in the courts. But the dividing line between administrative and clinical matters is not always easy to draw. In a mental hospital, such things as physical surroundings and ward routine, although primarily administrative, may be dictated by the clinical policies of the particular consultant. They may be said to amount to milieu therapy or a token economy or the like. However, the Commissioners have generally not regarded these decisions as "solely" taken in the exercise of clinical judgment and have been prepared to investigate.

The complaint must come from the person aggrieved, unless he is dead or unable to act for himself. The health authorities can themselves refer cases. The Commissioner cannot normally act unless an approach has first been made to the authority complained about, but there is an exception where a health service employee is complaining on behalf of a patient who cannot act for himself and fears victimisation. This could easily apply to a nurse who takes up the cudgels on behalf of a mental patient. Complaints must be made within a year of the facts being known to the person aggrieved. If the Commissioner decides that the matter is within his jurisdiction, he conducts a lengthy and careful investigation and reports his findings to the complainant, any person complained about, the relevant health authority, and that authority's superior (the regional health authority over a district health authority and the DHSS over a regional or special health authority). The authority will probably try to put matters right, but if they have not and will not, the only sanction is to make a special report to the Secretary of State, which must then be laid before Parliament.

Given the limitations on his jurisdiction, and the difficulty in predicting what he will and will not regard as a matter of clinical judgment, detained patients will probably prefer to approach the Mental Health Act Commission in the first instance. But as the Commission is a special health authority under the 1977 Act, their activities are also subject to investigation by the health service ombudsman.

Wearing his Parliamentary Commissioner's hat, the same man also has jurisdiction over complaints of injustice caused by maladministration in government departments, under the Parliamentary Commissioner Act 1967. This will cover the administration of special hospitals by the DHSS and the decisions taken by the Home Office in relation to restricted patients. There is no specific exclusion of matters of clinical judgment. But the Commissioner is still only concerned with administrative shortcomings, and not with the merits of decisions taken without maladministration. Nor can he investigate matters which could be taken to a tribunal or a court of law, unless satisfied that it would be unreasonable to expect the complainant to do so. The Commissioner was prepared to accept a complaint from Sam Kynaston about a delay of nearly two years between his RMO's recommendation that he be conditionally discharged from a special hospital and the Home Office decision to do so, even though this complainant later sought (but was refused) leave to pursue this in the courts. However, the conclusion was that there had been no maladministration because of the extensive consultations required. Cautious administration is not the same as bad administration, and mental patients are most likely to suffer as a result of excess zeal, rather than inefficiency or bad faith.

The requirements for making complaints are the same as for the Health Service Commissioner, save that they must be made in the first instance to a Member of Parliament, who will then decide whether to refer the matter on. Complainants are expected to consult their own Member first, but they can go elsewhere if he refuses to act. The report will go to the Member who referred the case, as well as to the complainant, the principal officer of the Department concerned, and the people involved in the action. If the complaint is upheld and has not and will not be remedied, the sanction is to report direct to Parliament.

5. *The Mental Health Act Commission*

The 1959 Act left mental patients in England and Wales without any independent body which was specifically committed to safeguarding their welfare and interests. None of the machinery explained in the previous section is adequate to fill the gap. Yet patients in Scotland have the benefit of the Mental Welfare Commission, which has a general duty to "exercise protective functions in respect of persons who may, by reason of mental disorder, be incapable of protecting their persons or their interests" (Mental Health (Scotland) Act 1960, s.4(1)). This covers patients both in and out of hospital, whether informal or compulsory. It includes a variety of functions, such as visiting patients, investigating their complaints, and even discharging them from compulsion. The Commission have championed many causes on behalf of patients, and anyone reading their publications (see 1972, 1975, 1981) must find it hard to understand why the Scots were thought to need such an informed and caring body while the English and Welsh were not.

The main advocates for a Mental Welfare Commission south of the border were the Royal College of Psychiatrists (1981). They undoubtedly hoped that the medical members might provide an informal means of reviewing questions of clinical judgment, by supplying general guidance and second opinions when asked. This might avoid the need for more specific restrictions and controls then being proposed by other bodies, such as MIND and the Butler Committee. These bodies tended to favour a patients' advocacy scheme (MIND) or a system of patients' friends (Butler Committee) rather than a new institution. New institutions are bound to be composed of representatives of various interest groups and can only proceed by securing at least a majority decision. Their jurisdiction is laid down by statute and they are often cautious about interpreting it too freely. Their level of activity is inevitably governed by the level of resources available to them. The experience of legal aid has shown that individuals acting on behalf of individuals, even if financed from public funds, are not subject to the same constraints. On the other hand, they may have far less real influence over the authorities involved.

The Government which produced the 1978 review of the Mental Health Act gave a cautious welcome to the combination of controls over certain treatments and patients' advocates or friends. The Government which sponsored the 1982 amendments preferred the approach of the Royal College. In the event, however, the controls over various forms of treatment were increased during the Bill's passage through Parliament. But the Government was by that time committed to the idea of a new Mental Health Act Commission. This has nothing like the scope of the Scottish equivalent, because it is almost exclusively concerned with the interests of detained patients in hospital. However, there is the possibility of extending its protective functions to informal patients in the future.

(a) *Constitution*

The Commission is set up as a special health authority under section 11 of the National Health Service Act 1977 (1983 Act, s.121(1)). The chairman and members are appointed by the Secretary of State, for varying periods of up to four years (Mental Health Act Commission Regulations 1983, reg. 3). Members are eligible for reappointment, but they may also be removed at any time and for any reason (regs. 5 and 4). The disqualifications which apply to membership of any health authority also apply to the Commission (reg. 9; see the National Health Service (Regional and District Health Authorities: Membership and Procedure) Regulations 1983, regs. 7 and 8). Otherwise, there are no qualifications laid down and no maximum or minimum limits on numbers. Initially, the Commission has around 90 members, drawn from medicine, nursing, psychology, social work and the law, and lay people. The combined professional interests heavily outweigh the lay and legal members, and the clinical professions may just be in a majority. There is no formal safeguard of the Commission's independence, but it will probably prove just as independent as most part-time quasi-autonomous institutions.

The Commission may establish its own committees and they may establish sub-committees (reg. 7(3) and (4)). The day-to-day functions are delegated to three regional panels, having offices in London, Nottingham and Liverpool. But there must always be at least one meeting of the whole Commission every year (reg. 8(3)). The Secretary of State appoints a central policy committee, which has power to co-opt members other than those he appoints (reg. 7(1)). Initially, he appointed no lawyers. This committee has the strategic task of drawing up proposals for the code of practice and drafting the Commission's biennial report, along with any other jobs which the Commission decides to give it (reg.7(2)).

(b) *Functions*

The Commission has six statutory functions under the 1983 Act and the Mental Health Act Commission (Establishment and

Constitution) Order 1983. The first is to appoint the independent doctors and other people whose certificates will be needed before certain types of treatment can be given (s.121(2)(*a*) and reg. 3(2)(*a*)). These need not be members of the Commission, and it is expected that the independent doctors probably will not be. The other non-medical people, who are required to certify that the patient has given an informed consent to psychosurgery or the surgical implantation of hormones, are more likely to be members of the Commission itself. Secondly, the Commission will receive reports from the RMO about all treatment which is carried out on detained patients under section 57, and all treatment which is carried out without consent but with a second opinion under section 58. Generally, these reports will arrive when a detained patient comes up for renewal, or when the RMO has to report to the Secretary of State about a restricted patient. But the Commission can require a report at any time, and the RMO has no obligation to report on the treatment of informal patients under section 57 unless the Commission asks. The Commission can cancel the certificates authorising these treatments, by notifying the RMO. This will usually, but not invariably, prevent the treatment taking place (s.121(2)(*b*) and reg. 3(2)(*b*)).

Thirdly, the Commission has a general protective function over all detained patients. It must "keep under review the exercise of the powers and the discharge of the duties conferred or imposed by this Act so far as relating to the detention of patients or to patients liable to be detained . . . "(ss.120(1), 121(2)(*b*) and reg. 3(2)(*c*)). This covers the admission and detention process, so that the Commission can scrutinise admission documents and consider whether they are happy with the way in which, for example, medical recommendations are being completed. They might also look at practice in relation to renewal of detention, leave of absence and discharge. But unlike the Scottish Mental Welfare Commission, they have no power to discharge patients and will not wish to trespass on the functions of the mental health review tribunals. They can certainly consider how patients are detained in the hospital, and the Government expects them to take a close interest in such issues as seclusion and the management of particularly difficult patients. They can also look at other issues relating to the treatment of detained patients, provided that some power or duty contained in the Act is involved. This obviously covers their treatment under sections 57 and 58, the emergencies in which those procedures are excluded, and all treatment given without consent under section 63. An adventurous view would include all treatment given to detained patients of any sort, but the cautious might suggest that if the patient has consented to something which is not covered by sections 57 or 58, no power or duty in the Act is involved. This is a good example of the sort of jurisdictional problem which bodies of this nature often experience. Clearly, however, the Commission will often be involved with matters of clinical judgment, and they are not required to leave these to the medical members alone.

Allied to this general supervisory function are two specific duties. The Commission must arrange to visit and interview in private detained patients in both hospitals and mental nursing homes (s.120(1)(*a*)). It is left to them to decide whether they will see all patients automatically and how often to visit. This will certainly be governed as much by the level of resources allocated to them as by the perceived need. There are around 7000 detained patients in approximately 300 hospitals, but the Commission hopes to visit each monthly and the special hospitals more often than that. Secondly, the Commission must arrange to investigate complaints. If the complaint relates to something which happened while the patient was detained in a hospital or mental nursing home, it must come from the patient himself, and the Commission need only investigate if they consider that it has not been properly dealt with by the hospital management. In NHS hospitals, they will therefore be able to insist that the patient first goes through the usual internal complaints machinery. This procedure does not apply in special hospitals or mental nursing homes, but the Commission can still require the patient to take the matter up with the DHSS or hospital administrator. However, the Commission could decide to investigate even though the internal machinery had not been used, perhaps where there was good reason to think that it would not produce results. These limitations do not apply to the duty to investigate other complaints about the use of the Act's powers and duties. These may be made by anyone and without pursuing other avenues first (s.120(1)(*b*)). However, the Commission need never pursue an investigation which they do not consider "appropriate" and their general arrangements can excluded specified types of case (s.120(2)).

Their investigatory powers are more limited than those of a formal inquiry. They may visit and interview and a doctor may examine in private any patient detained in a mental nursing home and they may also inspect the records relating to the detention and treatment of any patient who is or has been detained in a mental nursing home (s.120(4)). Similar facilities will be accorded to them as members of a health authority in respect of patients detained in NHS hospitals and it would be surprising if the DHSS denied them access to patients in special hospitals. But they cannot insist on people helping them or providing them with documents in the way that the ombudsmen can. Nor have they any specific sanction other than the threat of publicity. They will obviously inform the parties of the results of any investigation, and if the second type of complaint comes from a Member of Parliament, they must report to him (s.120(3)).

The Secretary of State does have power, after due consultation, to extend these supervisory and investigatory functions to the "care and treatment, or any aspect of the care and treatment" of informal patients in hospitals and mental nursing homes (s.124(4) and (5)). Curiously, this is wider than the exact wording of their powers in relation to detained patients, and perhaps an indication of what those powers were meant to mean. No doubt it is more important, and more practicable, to concentrate on detained patients, who are only about 5 per cent of the whole. But they already have the protection afforded by the mechanism of their detention and nearly three-quarters of them are mentally ill. The truly vulnerable patients in mental hospitals are the severely handicapped or psycho-geriatric cases. They are rarely "sectioned," because this is not needed to secure their co-operation, but they are totally dependent upon the hospital and its staff for their survival and comfort.

There may, however, be some scope for helping them through the code of practice. The Commission's fourth task is to make proposals to the Secretary of State about what should go into the code (reg. 3(2)(*d*)). It is his task to draw it up, and other bodies will be consulted, no doubt the Royal Colleges of Psychiatry and of Nursing, as well as the mental health charities and others. The code must be laid before Parliament, which can reject it by passing a resolution within 40 days. The object of the code is to give guidance to doctors, managers and staff of hospitals, and approved social workers, on the admission of patients to hospital; and to doctors and other professionals on the medical treatment of patients suffering from mental disorder. The former is not limited to detained patients and could cover guidelines for distinguishing informal and compulsory cases. The latter is not even limited to hospital patients but it does only cover medical treatment. In particular, the code is expected to identify treatments which give rise to such concern that they "should not be given" without both informed consent and a second opinion, even though this has not been made a legal requirement (s.118).

The Commission's fifth task is to review the special hospitals' censorship of their patients' mail, which has already been discussed. Finally, they must publish a report on their activities every second year, which must be laid before Parliament (s.121(10)). There can be nothing to stop them publishing reports at other times, just as other health authorities do, but these do not have to be placed before Parliament and may be less likely to produce results. Whether the Commission as a whole produce results will depend partly on how enthusiastically they approach their task, but also on their ability to gain the trust and confidence of hospitals and their staff. It is a delicate tight-rope to walk.

7 Leaving Hospital

Many patients cease to be liable to be detained when their current period of detention lapses and is not replaced or renewed. These may remain in hospital as informal patients. But there are many other ways in which the patient's detention may cease, or he may leave hospital, which are not quite the same thing. These are all discussed in this chapter, apart from the powers of mental health review tribunals, which appear in the next. Subject to section 5 of the Act (see Chapter 1), of course, informal patients may leave when they like.

1. *Leave of Absence*

The responsible medical officer can grant leave of absence to any compulsory patient (s.17(1)), but if the patient is restricted, the permission of the Home Secretary is also required (s.41(3)(c)(i); see Sched. 1, Pt. II). Leave can be given for a special occasion (such as a wedding), or for a definite period (such as a weekend), or indefinitely. It can be extended without bringing the patient back to hospital (s.17(2)). But it can also be revoked at any time if the RMO thinks this necessary in the interests of the patient's own health or safety or for the protection of other people. Notice of revocation and recall must be in writing and addressed either to the patient or to the person in charge of him (s.17(4)). The Home Secretary can himself recall a restricted patient from leave (Sched. 1, Pt. II). Leave can be subject to whatever conditions the RMO thinks necessary in the patient's own interests or to protect other people (s.17(1)). These can include staying in another hospital, living with a particular person, or attending a clinic for treatment. The patient is still liable to detention and can be obliged to accept medical treatment, subject to the usual safeguards. The RMO can also direct that the patient remains in the custody of a member of the hospital staff or of some other person authorised in writing (s.17(3)). The effect of this is that the patient can be recaptured the moment he escapes, instead of if and when he fails to return to hospital.

Most patients cannot be kept on a string indefinitely by giving them leave. They cannot be recalled once the power to detain them has lapsed (s.17(5)), although a long-term admission could be renewed while the patient was on leave, provided that the RMO had been able to examine him. However, the power to detail an unrestricted patient lapses automatically once he has been on six months' continuous leave. The six months' limit does not apply to restricted patients, who can be recalled by the Home Secretary (though not after six months by the RMO) at any time (Sched. 1, Pt. II). Nor does it apply to an unrestricted patient who has in the meantime returned to hospital, or been transferred to another, or, most importantly, is absent without leave at the end of those six months (s.17(5)). Patients who are on leave can apply to a mental health review tribunal just as if they were still in hospital. Tribunals also have power to recommend that unrestricted patients be given leave, although they cannot order it.

The Butler Committee on Mentally Abnormal Offenders (1975) were enthusiastic about leave of absence as a way of providing some compulsory after-care. For an unrestricted patient, the only other possibility is a transfer to guardianship, which gives no power to impose treatment or to recall to hospital. For a restricted patient, a conditional discharge does give a power of recall, but no power to impose treatment. But of course there are problems. In 1979, Ronald Sailes committed a particularly brutal murder while on leave from Broadmoor, where he had spent 15 years as a restricted patient and remained for another year under an ordinary hospital order after the restrictions expired. The subsequent Review of Leave Arrangements for Special Hospital Patients (DHSS, 1981b) recommended prior consultation with all the disciplines involved with the patient inside hospital and with the agencies outside it. The Home Office always informs the local police when a restricted patient is given leave, but the hospital should do this if (like Sailes) an unrestricted patient has previously been restricted or has been convicted of a serious sexual or violent offence, unless there are special circumstances. Otherwise, the police should not be told without a special reason to do so. But, unless the leave is very short, the local social services and probation departments, and of course the patient's general practitioner, should be given enough information to enable them to do their jobs. Other bodies, such as voluntary organisations, should not be given information without the patient's consent, unless there are special reasons.

These guidelines apply to all special hospital patients, whether or not they are restricted. By that stage, the legal label is often irrelevant to whether they can safely be allowed out. The far more serious problem is that the conditions and regime inside the hospital do little to prepare the patient for independence outside it. The Review recommended that much more attention should be devoted to this. But it is generally agreed that transfer to the more open conditions of an ordinary NHS hospital is a valuable intermediate step. At the other end of the scale, however, there are some patients who are given leave and recalled for the odd weekend simply to evade the six month rule. It is obviously not "necessary in the interests of their own health or safety or for the protection of other persons" for most of these to go on receiving treatment in a hospital. They should therefore be discharged.

2. *Transfers*

(a) *To other hospitals in England and Wales*

A patient detained in an ordinary NHS hospital can be transferred at any time without formality to another hospital, or other accommodation, under the same management (s.19(3)). Even if the patient is restricted, there is no need for the Home Secretary's consent. A patient detained in a special hospital can be transferred to another special hospital at any time by direction of the Secretary of State (s.123(1)). This does not apply to patients remanded to hospital by a court or on an interim hospital order.

A patient detained in an ordinary NHS hospital can be transferred into another hospital under different management, with just a little more formality (s.19(1)(*a*) and Mental Health (Hospital, Guardianship and Consent to Treatment) Regulations 1983, reg. 7(2)). Form 24 must be signed by the authorised officer of the managers of the first hospital, who must be satisfied that the patient can be admitted to the new hospital within 28 days. The form allows the patient to be taken there within that time, by an officer of the managers of either hospital, or by someone else authorised by the receiving hospital (reg. 9(1)(*a*)). Restricted patients can be transferred in just the same way as unrestricted, provided that the Home Secretary agrees (s.43(3)(*c*)(ii) and Sched. 1, Pt. II).

This procedure can also be used to transfer patients into the special hospitals. Any compulsory patient originally admitted to an ordinary hospital can be transferred into a special hospital if he meets the criteria and a bed is available (see Chapter 1). Some of their patients do not meet the criteria, but have found their way there because they are too difficult for an ordinary hospital to handle. Once there, it can be difficult to obtain a transfer back into an ordinary hospital. Transfers out of special hospitals are directed by the Secretary of State (s.125(2)). Once again, this does not apply to patients remanded there by a court or under an interim hospital order. The same regulations as to transport do apply (reg. 9(2)).

These procedures also apply to patients detained in mental nursing homes. But if they are maintained there by contract with a health authority, the authority (by an authorised officer) can authorise the transfer (reg. 7(4)).

After a patient has been transferred, the authority to detain him is simply amended as if he had been admitted to the new hospital on the date of his original admission (s.19(2)(*a*)).

(b) *To other parts of the United Kingdom and islands*

Any compulsory patient in England and Wales can be transferred to hospital in Scotland or Northern Ireland, provided that this is in his interests and the necessary arrangements have been made (ss.80 and 81). Once again, the only exceptions are patients remanded to hospital by a court or on an interim hospital order. Patients under guardianship here can be transferred to guardianship elsewhere in the same way. The transfer of unrestricted patients is authorised by the Secretary of State, and of restricted patients by the Home Secretary, Similarly, the Secretary of State for Scotland can transfer compulsory patients from Scotland (Mental Health (Scotland) Act 1960, s.73), the Department of Health and Social Services for Northern Ireland can transfer unrestricted patients, and the Secretary of State for Northern Ireland can transfer restricted patients (1983 Act, s.82). Similar powers exist between England and Wales and the Channel Islands or Isle of Man (1983 Act, ss.83 to 85 and local legislation), and between Scotland and Northern Ireland (1960 Act, ss.77 and 79) or the islands (1960 Act, s.81 and local legislation).

The general effect of a transfer is that the patient is treated as if he had been newly admitted under the equivalent law in the receiving country on the date when he arrives there. This is bound to alter the period for which he is liable to be detained. But a patient admitted for assessment here is treated as a short term admission in the receiving country and vice versa. Similarly, a restriction order or direction must end whenever it would have ended if he had remained in the original country. A person who was qualified to act as the patient's nearest relative in Scotland or England, but who is not qualified under the law of the receiving country, can continue to act. But a court order replacing the nearest relative is treated as if it had been made by a court in the receiving country, for such purposes as amendment and revocation. A hospital receiving a patient transferred here must record the admission date on Form 32 and must tell the nearest relative as soon as possible (reg. 11). The RMO must decide which of the four forms of mental disorder applies and record this on Form 33. If a patient is transferred out of England and Wales, the old application, order or direction ceases to have effect when he reaches the new place (s.91(1)).

(c) *Abroad*

The Home Secretary has power to transfer foreign patients out of the country, although he very rarely uses it. The patient must be neither a British citizen nor a Commonwealth citizen with a right of abode under section 2(1)(*b*) of the Immigration Act 1971. He must be receiving hospital in-patient treatment for mental illness. And he must be detained, either under a civil admission for treatment or under a hospital order, which includes a restriction order and a transfer direction (s.86(1)). Patients detained only for assessment, or remanded to hospital by a court or under an interim hospital order, cannot be transferred under this section. This section also applies to patients detained in Northern Ireland and there is an equivalent in the Mental Health (Scotland) Act 1960 for those detained in Scotland.

It must appear to the Home Secretary that proper arrangements have been made, not only for the transfer, but also for the patient's treatment and care in the country where he is going, and also that it is in the patient's own interests for him to go (s.86(2)). In theory, the patient could be sent to any country outside the United Kingdom or islands, but only his own country is likely to accept him. The Home Secretary authorises the transfer by warrant. He may also direct how the patient is to travel to his destination. This can be under escort or in some other form of custody, but obviously the Home Secretary can only insist on this until their arrival in the receiving country.

However, these transfers must now be approved by a mental health review tribunal (s.86(3)). This was suggested by what is now the Commission for Racial Equality. Obviously, the dangers of misinterpretation are particularly great where there are cultural differences and some independent safeguard is certainly desirable. But the tribunal's role will be quite different from their usual task of deciding whether the patient should be discharged. There is no provision for it in their new rules and it may be some time before it becomes clear how it will work. The DHSS (1978) expected that the tribunal would "form an opinion on the adequacy of information as to facilities in the receiving country," but that the Home Secretary would still have to make sure that the arrangements had been made.

A patient who is subject to a restriction order when he is transferred abroad will remain so subject, in case he returns to this country before it expires (s.91(2)).

(d) *Into guardianship*

Guardianship could also provide a form of statutory after-care for unrestricted patients, although the Butler Committee (1975) thought that leave of absence was preferable. Any unrestricted patient can be transferred into the guardianship of the local social services authority or a private individual approved by them (s.19(1)(a) and reg. 7(3)). The transfer is authorised by the hospital managers on part I of Form 25 and confirmed by the authority on part II. It may also be authorised by a health authority which is maintaining the patient in a mental nursing home (reg. 7(4)). The local authority must specify the date on which the transfer will take place and the consent of any private guardian must be obtained. Guardianship is discussed further in Chapter 9. It has suffered from a general lack of enthusiasm for compulsory powers in the community, as well as considerable confusion about what it entails. It might become a little more popular, now that some of that confusion has been dispelled, and mental health review tribunals have been given power to recommend that patients be transferred into it.

3. *Absconders and Escapers*

Theoretically, there is no difference between the escape of a dangerous psychopath from Broadmoor and the failure of a harmless schizophrenic to return from a shopping expedition, although the response in practice will be quite different. It is a crime punishable with up to two years' imprisonment to "induce or knowingly assist" any compulsory patient to absent himself without leave or to escape from legal custody, or knowingly to harbour one who has escaped, or to give him help in order to prevent or hinder his recapture (s.128). It can also be a conspiracy to commit a common law public nuisance, for example to bring in such things as rope, hacksaw, glass cutters and other tools to help a "homicidal lunatic" escape from Broadmoor (*R. v. Soul* (1980) 70 Cr. App. R. 295). The Act itself makes elaborate provision for the recapture of compulsory patients. None of this applies, of course, to informal patients.

(a) *Escaping from legal custody*

A person is in legal custody if he is required or authorised by or under the Act to be conveyed to any place, or to be kept in custody, or to be detained in a place of safety (s.137(1)). This usually applies to people on the move or those who have not yet been admitted to hospital. Those who take or detain such people have all the "powers, authorities, protection and privileges" of a constable for the purpose (s.137(2)). But this does not mean that they can do what they like. Even constables can only use such force as is reasonably necessary to achieve their lawful object.

A person who escapes from legal custody can be retaken by the person from whom he escaped, or by any police officer, or by any approved social worker. If he has already been compulsorily admitted to a hospital (and escapes, for example, when being escorted back from leave of absence), he can also be retaken by someone on the staff of, or authorised by, that hospital (s.138(1)). If he is being taken to or from a hospital under any of the Act's transfer powers or under any of the powers relating to people concerned in criminal proceedings or transferred from prison, or if he is being taken to or detained in a place of safety pending admission to hospital under those latter powers, he can also be retaken by someone on the staff of, or authorised by, the hospital to which he is eventually going as well as from the one from which he may be coming (s.138(4)). (This does not apply to transfers to and from the islands, or to patients remanded to hospital by a court, or those under interim hospital orders, or civil and Immigration Act detainees being returned to prison).

There are important time limits to some of these powers. A patient who escapes from or on the way to a "place of safety" under sections 135 or 136 can only be retaken within 72 hours of his escape or his arrival at the place of safety, whichever expires earlier (s.138(3)). A patient escaping on the way to hospital under civil powers of commitment can only be retaken if he can be got to hospital within the 14 days which begin on the date of the second medical examination. If it is only an emergency application, he must arrive within 24 hours of the medical examination or the time when the application was signed, whichever is the earlier (s.6(1)). A patient escaping before he gets to hospital under criminal powers can be retaken at any time (s.138(5)). But a patient who has already been admitted to a hospital can only be retaken within the same time limits as one who goes absent without leave (s.138(2)).

(b) *Going absent without leave*

A patient is absent without leave if he absconds from a hospital to which he has been compulsorily admitted, or from the place where he is required by his guardian to live, or fails to return at the expiry of or recall from leave of absence, or breaks a residence condition in his leave of absence. He may be taken into custody and returned to hospital by any police officer, any approved social worker, or by anyone on the staff of or authorised by, that hospital (s.18(1)). If he is living in another hospital as a condition of leave of absence, he can also be retaken by someone on the staff of, or authorised by, that hospital (s.18(2)).

An in-patient detained for six or 72 hours under section 5, or a patient admitted for assessment for 72 hours or 28 days, can never be retaken once that time has gone by (s.18(5)). Patients admitted for treatment can only be recaptured within the 28 days which begin on the first day of absence without leave. If a patient is not taken in time, the authority to detain him ends automatically (s.18(4)). However, if he is found soon enough, it does not matter that his detention would normally have expired in the meantime. On his return, the hospital can detain him for up to seven days to allow the necessary examination and report renewing his detention to be made. If the detention is renewed, it is backdated (s.21).

The 28 day limit applies equally to ordinary hospital order patients, but restricted patients can be recaptured at any time (Sched. 1, Pt. II). The rule originated in the days of tight security in mental hospitals, when the patient's ability to remain at large for so long was considered a strong indication that his detention was unjustified. It is far from obvious why it should apply to criminal offenders who have been admitted to the open conditions of a modern hospital. As many as 9 per cent. of the male hospital order patients studied by Walker and McCabe (1973) achieved their "discharge by operation of law" simply by walking out and staying away for four weeks. The Butler Committee (1975) recommended that the rule should no longer apply to hospital order patients, but they have not in fact been excluded.

(c) *Hospital remands and interim hospital orders*

Patients remanded to hospital or on interim hospital orders, who abscond from the hospital or on the way to or from it, may be arrested without warrant by any policeman and must then be brought before the court which made the remand or order as soon as possible (ss.35(10), 36(8) and 38(7)). The court can then end the remand or order and deal with the patient in another way. There is no time limit on these recaptures. Other people can presumably act under the usual procedures, where these apply.

(d) *Escaping from England and Wales*

A patient who would be subject to recapture under section 138 or 18 if he were still in England and Wales can be retaken and returned from any other part of the United Kingdom, Channel Islands or Isle of Man. Those who can do this include the national equivalents of an English constable and the Scottish and Northern Irish equivalents of an approved social worker (s.88). There are also powers to recapture in England and Wales patients escaping from Northern Ireland (s.87), the islands (s.89), or Scotland (Mental Health (Scotland) Act 1960, s.83). Criminal patients who escape to other countries may be extradited if this is provided for by treaty between that country and the United Kingdom. Restricted patients who escape to the Republic of Ireland can be extradited if an arrest warrant under section 72 of the Criminal Justice Act 1967 is obtained.

4. *Subsequent Court Orders*

A short period of detention in custody under the sentence or order of a United Kingdom court (including a committal or remand) has no effect upon a pre-existing civil admission for treatment or hospital order. If the patient's detention would normally have expired while he was in custody, it does not do so until the day of his discharge (s.22(2)). He is then treated as if he had gone absent without leave on that day, so that he can be taken back to hospital and the hospital has the usual week in which to complete the formalities for renewal (s.21(1) and (2)). They are then backdated (s.21(3)). The same would apply if he returned to hospital of his own accord.

But if the patient is detained for more than six months (or for successive periods totalling more than six months) a civil admission or ordinary hospital order automatically ceases to have effect (s.22(1)). A restriction order, however, carries on regardless. But a fresh hospital or guardianship order cancels any previous hospital admission or guardianship, including a restriction order (s.40(5)). Section 22 applies, however, if that second order is quashed on appeal.

5. *Discharge*

(a) *By the patient's nearest relative*

The nearest relative can discharge a patient admitted for treatment or for assessment under civil powers (s.23(2)), but not under any type of hospital order (Sched. 1). He must serve his order on the managers and may use Form 34 if he wishes (reg.15(1)). He is entitled to instruct an independent doctor to visit the patient at any reasonable time, examine him in private and inspect the records relating to his detention and treatment, in order to advise on a possible discharge. This could be wise because the nearest relative must always give the hospital at least 72 hours' prior notice of his intention. During this time, the RMO can report to the managers on Form 36 (reg. 15(3)) that the patient, if discharged, "would be likely to act in a manner dangerous to other persons or to himself." This prevents the nearest relative from discharging him, not only at once, but for the next six months (s.25(1)). If the patient is detained for treatment, the relative must be told. He can then apply to a mental health review tribunal within 28 days. The tribunal will have to allow the discharge if they are satisfied that the patient is not dangerous. If the patient is detained for assessment, there is nothing the relative can do, except wait for it to expire and object to any admission for treatment. A relative can be replaced if he proposes to discharge the patient without due regard for the patient's welfare or the interests of the public (s.29(3)(*d*)). This will not be necessary where the RMO can bar discharge, but it may occasionally be useful for patients under guardianship, where the RMO has no such power.

(b) *By the hospital, RMO or health authorities*

The hospital can discharge any patient admitted for treatment or for assessment at any time (s.23(2)(*a*)). This includes an ordinary hospital order patient (Sched. 1), but not one remanded to hospital or under an interim hospital order. A restricted patient can only be discharged with the consent of the Home Secretary (s.41(3)(*c*)(iii)). Technically, a discharge can be ordered either by the RMO or by the hospital managers, but the managers cannot usually be expected to disregard the advice of their consultants. Nevertheless, this was seen as an extra safeguard, particularly in the days when patients admitted for assessment could not be discharged by their relatives. The power can be exercised by any three or more members of the managing authority, or of a committee to which this function has been delegated (s.23(4)). Hospitals are advised to make known the names of those who can be approached. The RMO has no power to prevent the managers acting, even if he thinks the patient is dangerous. Patients in mental nursing homes may also be discharged by the registration authority, or by any health authority maintaining them there (s.23(3)). The inspecting officer of the registration authority may visit the patient at all reasonable times, interview him in private and inspect the documents authorising his detention. A doctor instructed by any of these authorities may do all those things and also examine the patient and his medical records (s.24(3) and (4)). Technically, a discharge is by order in writing (s.23(1)), but there is no form laid down in the regulations.

The Act does not expressly state when a patient must or may be set free. It contains nothing to prevent a discharge even though the statutory grounds for detention still exist. Equally, it contains nothing to insist on discharge the moment that they do not. Hospitals may well wonder where they stand if they release a patient who promptly does harm to himself or to others. There is one case under the old law in which the hospital was held legally liable, but it is of doubtful authority today. *Holgate* v. *Lancashire Mental Hospitals Board* [1937] 4 All E. R. 294 concerned a mental defective with a serious criminal record who had been ordered to be detained during His Majesty's pleasure. He was transferred from a special hospital to an ordinary institution. The institution released him for a short period on licence to stay with his brother, but took no steps to ensure that the brother would supervise him constantly. He visited the plaintiff and attacked her. The hospital authorities and doctors concerned were found to have failed in their duty of care towards people whom they could foresee might be injured if care were not taken. Damages totalling £4,208 were awarded.

However, even if we suppose that the ordinary principles of the law of negligence do apply, the hospital or doctor is only liable if they have failed to exercise the care that a reasonable hospital or doctor would take in all the circumstances, to prevent the harm which they should have foreseen might result if they did not. By no means all mental patients are likely to do harm. And if the judgments are made in accordance with a reasonable body of medical opinion, even if not with the majority view on every point, then they will have acted as a reasonable hospital or doctor would act.

But it is also probable that the ordinary principles do not apply. The power given to the hospital or doctor under the Act is more in the nature of an administrative discretion than an operational function. There is discretion to admit or release, which must be distinguished from the actual handling of the patient during that process. Civil liability only lies in respect of the former if the act or omission is outside the limits of the discretion delegated by Parliament (*Anns* v. *Merton London Borough Council* [1978] A.C. 728; see also the analysis by Lord Diplock in *Home Office* v. *Dorset Yacht Co.* [1970] A.C. 1004, where he expressly reserved his opinion as to whether the *Holgate* case was correct). There could be no question of liability for failure to control someone else if the statute itself did not give the power to impose some control. But the Mental Health Act does not give this power solely, or even primarily, in the interests of individual members of the public. It is given also in the interests of the patient, or of other patients, or of the community at large, with a view to the cure and rehabilitation of as many patients as possible. Hence the hospital or doctor could only be liable if they had ignored the instructions of Parliament or reached a decision which no reasonable doctor or hospital could have reached in the circumstances.

Clearly, it cannot be outside the limits of their discretion to release a patient who no longer fulfills the statutory criteria for detention. Indeed, it is more likely to be outside those limits if they do not release him. Thus a patient who is no longer suffering from one of the four forms of disorder needed for long term detention should be discharged from that detention, even if he is still "dangerous." Similarly, if he is still suffering, he should nevertheless be discharged if the other criteria do not apply. The only difficulty is whether to use the criteria for renewing his detention (see page 122), which include a "treatability" requirement, or those for discharge by a mental health review tribunal (see page 270), which do not. Even if there is still a statutory case for keeping the patient in hospital, there is clearly discretion to discharge him if, on balance, this seems the right thing to do.

(c) *By the Home Secretary*

The Home Secretary's consent is needed before the hospital or RMO can themselves discharge a restricted patient. But the Home Secretary also has his own powers of release (s.42(2)). These are more frequently used, because he can choose between an absolute and a conditional discharge. Now that restrictions tend to be imposed only in the most serious cases, these decisions are taken extremely seriously and a high proportion are considered personally by a Minister.

There has always been felt to be a clear division of responsibility between the hospital and the Home Secretary. The RMO would decide whether, on medical grounds, the patient was fit to leave. The Home Secretary would then decide whether it was safe to let him go. This would only be allowed when it was clear that no undue risk was involved, having regard to all the circumstances, including the patient's response to treatment, the prognosis, and the "safeguards which the arrangements proposed offer against recurrence of anti-social behaviour" (Aarvold Report, 1972). Fear of public opinion, as well as fear for the public themselves, led to a very cautious policy. Some patients, particularly those found guilty of manslaughter as a result of diminished responsibility while suffering from a specific and limited mental illness, might leave hospital quite soon. Others might remain a great deal longer than they would have remained under ordinary hospital orders, or than they would have stayed in prison, although obviously direct comparisons cannot be made. They may certainly stay in hospital longer than the patients transferred from prison, whose restrictions must end when the imprisonment would have ended (Home Office, 1982).

The system has generally been very effective in protecting the public (see Walker and McCabe, 1973). But no system can guarantee complete success unless patients are kept in hospital for ever, and there has always been much public concern about those (approximately one a year) who commit murder following their discharge. Graham Young, for example, committed murder and other offences by poisoning shortly after he had been released from Broadmoor, where he had been sent because of very similar offences committed when a boy. The resulting Aarvold Report (1972) recommended further safeguards in a minority of cases which were thought to require "special care in assessment." These are referred to an independent Advisory Board on Restricted Patients, consisting of two lawyers, two psychiatrists, a Chief Probation Officer and a Director of Social Services. They advise on about 50 proposals a year for the discharge or transfer of patients, generally from special hospitals, where the risk is particularly great or the prognosis particularly difficult or there are other special circumstances. The Board has no statutory basis. In *R. v. Secretary of State for the Home Department, ex parte Powell,* December 21, 1978 (see Gostin and Rassaby, 1980), the Divisional Court decided that it was not amenable to judicial review and need not observe the rules of natural justice. The Board's task is to advise specifically on the risks to the public if the patient should be released.

However, this must now be seen in the light of the decision of the European Court of Human Rights in the case of *X.* v. *United Kingdom,* applic. no. 6998/75, (1981) 4 E.H.R.R. 181 (page 178 above). Under the European Convention, a patient cannot be detained as a "person of unsound mind" unless he has a true and persisting mental disorder of a kind or degree which warrants his compulsory confinement. If he has not, he can no longer be detained in a hospital, no matter how likely he is to misbehave again if set at large. This point was accepted by Lawton L.J. in *Kynaston* v. *Secretary of State for Home Affairs* (1981) 73 Cr. App.R. 281 (page 177 above). Given the very broad definitions of the mental disorders involved, and of the medical treatment for which detention must be appropriate, this approach is hardly likely to open the floodgates. The Act itself has not been amended to require the Home Secretary to consider whether the criteria for detention still exist. Nevertheless, it seems clear that he should do so, whenever he receives the annual report from the RMO or a specific proposal for discharge from that officer.

The other result of *X.* v. *United Kingdom* was, of course, that restricted patients may now be discharged by mental health review tribunals. Why then does a government department, headed by a politician responsible to Parliament, retain the power of discharge? There are two good reasons. First, a patient may well become fit for discharge some time before his next right to apply to a tribunal comes round. Secondly, the tribunal can only discharge him if the criteria for detention no longer exist, whereas the Home Secretary has a much broader discretion. He could grant a discharge where there was still some mental disorder and it was difficult to determine whether hospital treatment was still appropriate. The Home Secretary may also find it much easier than a tribunal to make the necessary arrangements for a conditional discharge.

A conditional discharge has two consequences. Until the restrictions end or the patient is granted an absolute discharge, he remains liable to be recalled to hospital (s.42(3)). The Home Secretary issues a warrant and the patient can then be taken into custody and back to hospital as if he had gone absent without leave on the warrant date (s.42(4)). He can be recalled to a different hospital from the one in which he was originally detained, but not to some other establishment. At the time of the Butler Report (1975) there was concern about what should be done with a conditionally discharged patient whose conduct was worrying, but whose medical condition was not suitable for hospital. The report agreed that it would be a grave impairment of liberty to provide for recall to prison on mere suspicion, but suggested that the hospitals should be more willing to agree to recall. However, although no criteria for recall are laid down in the Act, the logic of *X. v. United Kingdom* is again quite clear. Patients must not be readmitted unless the grounds for detention exist. In any event, the case must now be referred to a tribunal, which would have to discharge if the grounds were not there.

The main purpose of conditional discharge, however, is to provide for compulsory supervision. This will normally be arranged by the hospital, but the choice of supervisor lies with the Home Office. The Butler Report considered the relative advantages of probation officers and local authority social workers. The latter have access to a wider range of community care facilities and may have more experience of mental disorder. The former have more experience of offenders and may have a "more controlling attitude". Where the need to safeguard the public is particularly important, the reports favour a probation officer, but all stress the need for the greatest possible exchange of information and co-operation with the hospital. The Home Secretary can vary the conditions at any time, whether imposed by a tribunal or by himself (s.73(4) and (5); the power to vary his own conditions is implicit rather than explicit). In due course, he may grant an absolute discharge. Technically, what he should do is to lift the restrictions under section 42(1), which then has the effect of an absolute discharge from hospital by virtue of section 42(5). This means that he ought to lift the restrictions when he is satisfied that they are no longer necessary to protect the public from serious harm. The patient may also apply to a tribunal for the conditions to be varied or the restrictions lifted altogether. But unless the tribunal grants an absolute discharge, the Home Secretary will still be in effective control of the conditions and how they operate.

However, conditionally discharged patients are excluded from the power to impose treatment without consent (s.56(1)*c*)). Attendance for treatment could be a condition, but refusal to accept it would have to be dealt with on the merits of recall rather than by direct action. And the power of recall can no longer be used simply as a sanction for breach of the conditions. Thus the 1983 Act may revolutionise the practice of conditional discharge, but whether this will be to patients' benefit or detriment remains to be seen.

6. *Habeas Corpus*

An important constitutional remedy for all who consider themselves illegally detained is the ancient writ of habeas corpus. Application is made to the Divisional Court of the Queen's Bench Division of the High Court, or, if it is not sitting, to any High Court judge, at his home if necessary. This should be done by or with the consent of the prisoner, but if he is incapable, a relative or friend can proceed on his behalf. If the evidence shows a prima facie case of illegal detention, the court will issue the writ. This requires the gaoler to produce the body or show lawful justification for holding it. The court, however, is concerned with whether there is legal power to detain the prisoner. It is a complex question, depending upon the precise terms of the particular power which is being claimed, how far the court can go in investigating the truth of the facts alleged by the gaoler or the merits of his case. There are at least three possible levels of intervention.

At the top is the case where the existence of the power to detain depends upon the prior existence of some fact. The best-known example is the power to detain an "illegal entrant" under the Immigration Act 1971. In *R.* v. *Secretary of State for Home Department, ex parte Khawaja* [1983] 2 W.L.R. 321, the House of Lords decided that the court could investigate whether the applicant was indeed an illegal entrant, rather than whether the immigration officer had reasonable grounds for thinking him one. The hospital's power to detain a mental patient does not depend upon prior facts in this way, but upon the existence of orders from a court, warrants or directions from the Home Secretary, or applications, recommendations and renewal reports from those authorised to make them under Part II of the 1983 Act. If no such document existed or if the document itself were bad on its face, then the court would have to order the patient's release. But what if the document itself were apparently good, but had been completed in circumstances which are not allowed under the Act?

If the document emanates from a criminal court, there is some doubt about whether the High Court can go behind it at all, but they can certainly do so in civil cases (for, as Lord Scarman pointed out in the *Khawaja* case, this was the whole point of the Habeas Corpus Act of 1816).The obvious example is some technical breach of the "sectioning" procedure. The various provisions differ slightly. Some simply say, for example, that the doctors must examine the patient either together or with no more than five days between the days on which their examinations took place, or that an approved social worker must interview the patient. Others say that the application shall not be made, for example, if the applicant has not seen the patient within the prescribed time, or a social worker applicant has not consulted the nearest relative. But it has always been assumed that such defects render the detention unlawful, so that the hospital must release the patient if they come to light. *A fortiori,* the court whose task it is to safeguard the citizen should be prepared to do so, although they might decide that some requirements were mandatory (so that detention without them is unlawful) and others were simply directory (so that it is not necessarily so). Unfortunately, there is at least one case under the 1959 Act which suggests that the court is not even prepared to do this. The complaint in *R.* v. *Governor of Broadmoor, ex parte Argles*, June 28, 1974 (see Gostin, 1977) was that the social worker had not consulted the patient's nearest relative, although this was allegedly quite practicable. The court did apparently investigate, but eventually refused the application. Melford Stevenson J. is reported to have said that the detention for treatment was lawful because the documents were properly completed, even though there might be a "terrible hinterland which demonstrates that it should not have been done."

It is submitted that this decision is plainly wrong, at least if it suggests that defects in the procedure laid down by the Act cannot invalidate documents which appear to be properly completed. The court has every power to investigate the validity of the detention to that extent. The more difficult problem is whether they can investigate whether the substantive grounds for making the application were made out. This is where the second level of investigation comes in. If detention is only allowed where certain facts exist, the court can look into those facts. But if detention is allowed where certain people think that certain facts exist, the court can only look into whether those people have exercised their powers lawfully, fairly and reasonably. The matter is not beyond doubt, but civil detention under the Mental Health Act is probably allowed where the doctors and applicant *think* that certain facts exist, even if it later turns out that they do not. An illustration can be provided from the most celebrated habeas corpus case under the old law. In *R.* v. *Board of Control, ex parte Rutty* [1956] 2 Q.B. 109 (see also *R.* v. *Rampton Institution Board of Control, ex parte Barker* [1957] Crim. L.R. 402; *Re Sage* [1958] Crim. L.R. 258), the applicant was a borderline "feeble-minded" patient who had been compulsorily admitted to an institution on the ground that she had been "found neglected." This was curious, as at the time she was living and working in a hospital under the care of the county council. The court held that there was no evidence that she was "neglected" and ordered her release. As a result, it seems that over 3,000 other patients in mental deficiency institutions had to be released.

However, it is clear that if there had been some evidence upon which the authorities could reasonably have concluded that she was neglected, the court would not have interfered. But at least they would have been applying the well-known principles of judicial review of administrative discretion, set out in *Associated Provincial Picture Houses Ltd.* v. *Wednesbury Corporation* [1948]

1 K.B. 223 (page 28 above). Logically, the court should be just as prepared to do this in habeas corpus cases as it is in applications for judicial review leading to other remedies. Most of the substantive decisions made by people other than courts under the Mental Health Act should be amenable to this sort of challenge. It should certainly apply to mental health review tribunals (as we shall see in the next chapter) but it cannot be used as an extra avenue of appeal against the decisions of the Crown Court (see for example, *Ex parte Corke* [1954] 1 W.L.R. 899; *R. v. Featherstone* (1953) 37 Cr. App. R. 146).

Of course, there are some powers in the Mental Health Act which are given in extremely general terms, without specific grounds expressed. The best example is the Home Secretary's power to recall a conditionally discharged restricted patient. The case of *X v. United Kingdom* (page 178 above) began with an attempt by such a patient to get habeas corpus. This was unsuccessful, because the Home Secretary had done just what the Act allowed him to do. For that reason, the European Court held that habeas corpus was not enough. Nowadays, the court might just accept the argument (page 239 above) that the Home Secretary can only recall if he thinks that the criteria for detention exist, and at least apply the *Wednesbury* principle to his decision. For most mental patients whose detention is procedurally correct, however, the remedy of habeas corpus will be of little use.

8 Mental Health Review Tribunals

Mental health review tribunals were the main safeguard devised by the Percy Commission (1957) for long term compulsory patients when they recommended the abolition of judicial commitment. The right to apply has now been given to almost all types of patient, including those admitted for short periods of assessment, or on restriction orders, or transferred from prison. Under Article 5(4) of the European Convention on Human Rights, everyone deprived of his liberty by arrest or detention is entitled to take proceedings "by which the lawfulness of his detention shall be decided speedily by a court and his release ordered if the detention is not lawful." In *X*. v. *United Kingdom*, applic. no. 6998/75, (1981) 4 E.H.R.R. 181 (page 178 above), the European Court of Human Rights decided that all people who were detained because they were "of unsound mind," even those originally admitted from the criminal courts, were entitled to a periodic judicial consideration of the merits of their continued detention. Habeas corpus proceedings were not enough, because they could not provide a full assessment of the merits. Where the initial admission is not from a court, Article 5(4) obviously applies straightaway, although the European Court thought that habeas corpus might be a sufficient safeguard for a brief period of detention in an emergency.

Mental health review tribunals can count as a court for this purpose. In fact, they have many advantages over traditional courts of law. Their membership can be tailored to the particular problem and their more flexible and informal procedures to the peculiarities of the subject matter. They are not stuck in the adversarial model of British court procedure and can adopt elements of the inquisitorial approach. This is most important in mental health cases, where it is vital that the tribunal should not be too overawed by the hospital evidence, but also that the experience should not have an adverse effect on the patient's health and treatment. The difficulty lies in deciding how far it is possible to go in balancing these considerations against the traditional requirements of natural justice.

1. *Applications and References*

(a) *The right to apply*

Patients admitted for assessment can apply within the 14 days beginning on the day of their admission (s.66(1)(*a*) and (2)(*a*)). Emergency admissions are not excluded, but obviously there will be no need to proceed if the admission is not converted into a full admission for assessment within the first 72 hours. Patients admitted for treatment, or transferred from guardianship, or received into guardianship can apply during the first six months (s.66(1)(*b*), (*c*), (*e*) and (2)(*b*), (*c*), (*e*)). This now includes patients under the age of 16, who were unable to apply under the 1959 Act. Patients placed under guardianship by a court can also apply during the first six months (s.69(1)(*b*)(i)). But for reasons explained in Chapter 5, neither hospital order nor restriction order patients can do so. However, patients found unfit to plead or not guilty by reason of insanity and admitted under section 5(1) of the Criminal Procedure (Insanity) Act 1964 can apply in their first six months, and so can patients transferred from prison by the Home Secretary (with or without restrictions), patients transferred from other parts of the United Kingdom, and patients who become ordinary hospital order patients when their restriction orders come to an end (s.69(2)).

However, ordinary hospital order patients, along with those admitted for treatment and those under guardianship, can apply once within each period for which their detention (or guardianship) is renewed (s.66(1)(*f*) and (2)(*f*)). This means once during their second six months and in every year after that. By halving these periods, the 1983 Act has effectively doubled these patients' opportunities to apply. Patients transferred from prison without restrictions are just the same as ordinary hospital order patients. The detention of restricted patients of all types does not have to be renewed, but they have now been given the right to apply within the equivalent periods (ss. 70 and 79). Conditionally discharged restricted patients, who have not been recalled to hospital, may apply within the second 12 months after their discharge, and in every two year period after that (s.75(2)). If they are recalled, they are treated as if a new order or transfer had been made on that date, and so can apply during the second six months and in every year after that. But there is also an automatic review after each recall (see below).

Any patient whose disorder is reclassified under section 16 may apply within 28 days of being informed of this (s.66(1)(*d*) and (2)(*d*)). He is only likely to want to do this if he has been reclassified upwards, from psychopathic disorder or mental impairment to mental illness or severe mental impairment, because this will deprive him of the wider treatability test at his next renewal. If he has been reclassified downwards, he might want to argue that the treatability test is not fulfilled. But even if he shows this, the tribunal does not have to discharge him (see below).

The patient's nearest relative can also apply within 28 days of being told that the patient's disorder has been reclassified, but the use of "or" in section 66(1)(*i*) suggests that they cannot both do so. In any event, the nearest relative of a patient admitted for treatment would be much better advised to make use of his power to discharge the patient (he cannot, of course, do this with a hospital order patient). If the RMO then blocks the discharge by issuing a report that the patient would be likely to act "in a manner dangerous to other persons or to himself" if released, the relative can apply to a tribunal within 28 days (s.66(1)(*g*)) and (2)(*d*)). The tribunal will then have to discharge the patient if they are satisfied that he is not dangerous. This is a more stringent test than the one which usually applies, so the patient will be better off if his relative can be persuaded to take the initiative in this way (see Gostin and Rassaby, 1980). The relative does not have the right to apply to a tribunal if he is prevented from discharging a patient admitted for assessment, no doubt because the admission will have lapsed before a hearing can be arranged. But he does have the right to apply in the other cases where he cannot himself discharge the patient. After a hospital order, he may apply during the second six months and in every year after that (s.69(1)(*a*)). This now applies to restriction orders as well as to ordinary hospital orders. After a guardianship order, he may apply at any time during the first 12 months and in every year after that (s.69(1)(*b*)(ii)). Lastly, after an order taking away his right to act as a nearest relative, he may apply during the first 12 months and in every year after that (s.66(1)(*h*) and (2)(*g*)).

(b) *Automatic reviews*

A large number of patients never exercise their right to apply. In 1979, for example, there were approximately 6000 residents in mental hospitals detained under long-term powers. Around half of these should have been entitled to a hearing during the year, but only 790 cases were dealt with by tribunals (a typical figure in recent years). Some patients may be incapable of applying, some may not appreciate their right to do so, others may not want to upset themselves or the hospital staff, and others may be frightened of doing this. The introduction of automatic reviews, however infrequent, is an important step.

For long-term patients, the purpose is not to expel them from their homes and unless the news of the hearing is broken to them very carefully they can become extremely agitated and distressed. But experience of references to clear the backlog before the 1983 Act came into force revealed that in some hospitals almost all the compulsory patients could be discharged, some by the hospital before the hearing. There is no doubt that a tribunal can concentrate the mind.

The hospital managers must refer to a tribunal any patient admitted for treatment under civil powers (including one transferred from guardianship) who has not exercised his right to apply within his first six months (s.68(1)). They must do this the moment the six months have expired, unless there is then pending a reference by the Social Services Secretary (see below), or an application by the nearest relative, or an application by the patient as a result of his reclassification. They must still make the reference even though the patient has exercised his right to apply on renewal. He could then withdraw that, so that it will not be lost, but patients should probably be advised to wait until the hospital reference has been determined before making their own applications. The hospital managers must refer the case if the patient did apply during the first six months but withdrew the application before it was heard (s.68(5)). None of this applies to hospital order patients or transferred prisoners. But if a patient admitted under the Criminal Procedure (Insanity) Act 1964 does not apply within the first six months, the Home Secretary must refer his case to a tribunal, and again a withdrawn application is ignored (s.71(5) and (6)).

The hospital managers must also refer any patient admitted for treatment, including an ordinary hospital order patient, if his detention is renewed and three years have gone by since his case was last considered by a tribunal (for any reason). If the patient is under 16, he must be referred if only one year has gone by since his last review (s.68(2)). It seems clear from this wording that the managers must refer the case, not when the one or three years have gone by, but when the detention is next renewed. Similarly, the Home Secretary must refer the case of any restricted patient who is still in hospital and whose case has not been considered for the past three years (s.71(2)). This includes restriction order patients, prisoners transferred with restrictions, and patients admitted under the Criminal Procedure (Insanity) Act 1964 (s.79(1)). It does not include restricted patients who have been conditionally discharged. Many restricted patients, however, will need little encouragement to make the fullest possible use of their own rights of application.

Finally, if a patient who has been conditionally discharged by the Home Secretary or by a tribunal is recalled to hospital, the Home Secretary must refer his case to a tribunal within one month of the day on which he arrives back (s.75(1)(*a*)). This is the answer to the precise problem raised by the case of *X* v. *United Kingdom*, applic. no. 6998/75, (1981) 4 E.H.R.R. 181. Tribunal hearings take place, at best, between five and eight weeks after the tribunal gets the case. A review within about three months of the recall probably counts as "speedy" for the purposes of Article 5(4), although it may not seem like it at the time.

(c) *Discretionary references*

The Social Services Secretary can refer the case of any patient detained under Part II of the Act (or subject to guardianship) to a tribunal at any time (s.67(1)). This must include ordinary hospital order patients, to whom most of the provisions of Part II apply without modification and who are certainly detained under them rather than the court order once the first renewal has taken place. The equivalent provision in the 1959 Act was not thought to apply to restricted patients, whose detention does not have to be renewed at all. However, the Home Secretary has power to refer the case of any restricted patient to a tribunal at any time (s.71(1)). This includes a restricted patient who has been conditionally discharged from hospital.

A request for a reference may be useful if the patient's own rights have been lost on a technicality, although this may be less common now that withdrawing an application does not prejudice his right to try again. But sometimes the situation may change quickly and the next right to apply may be some time away. The DHSS found its power of reference very helpful in ensuring that large numbers of patients whose cases had not been heard for three years did not all have to be referred the moment the 1983 Act came into force. This meant, of course, that their cases were heard under the old rather than the new law. Apart from these, however, the power has been very little used.

(d) *Withdrawal, consolidation and postponement*

There is no right to apply to a tribunal apart from those expressly provided in the Act and only one applicaton can be made during each of the specified periods (s.77(1) and (2)). But any applicant can now apply in writing to the tribunal at any time for permission to withdraw his application (Mental Health Review Tribunal Rules 1983, r.19). If that permission is granted, the application can be ignored and the applicant can try again later (s.77(1)). References cannot be withdrawn.

If there is more than one application pending in respect of the same patient, the tribunal can consider both of them together (r.18). This again does not apply when an application is pending at the same time as a reference. However, provided that the conditions were right, there might be circumstances in which the tribunal would think it appropriate to postpone an application to a future date.

References cannot be postponed, but the tribunal may put off the consideration of an application if an application or reference in respect of the same patient has recently been determined (r.9). It cannot be put off for longer than six months from that earlier determination or the date when the current period of detention expires, whichever is the earlier. The power does not apply at all if the previous determination was before a break or change in the authority for the patient's detention or guardianship. For this purpose, a break or change happens if (but only if) a patient turns into a patient detained for treatment under civil powers or an ordinary hospital order (whether on admission or transfer from prison or guardianship or the ending of restrictions) or when a patient is received into guardianship. So a previous hearing during an admission for assessment will not prejudice the patient's right to an immediate hearing of his application after he is admitted for treatment. Similarly, a patient who has recently been considered as a restricted patient (where the tribunal's powers are more limited) will be entitled to an immediate hearing of his application as an unrestricted patient. Again, the power to postpone does not apply to an unrestricted patient's application following the renewal of his detention or guardianship for the second six months, unless the earlier application or reference was made more than three months after the initial admission or reception. This means that a patient who applies early in his detention will be entitled to prompt consideration of an application early in his first renewal period. But a patient who puts it off or who does not apply at all and so has to be referred to the tribunal may find that the tribunal postpones his own renewal application. This should be to his benefit. Lastly, there is no power to postpone applications following reclassification, or by a nearest relative who has been barred from discharging the patient himself.

The tribunal cannot postpone consideration in this way unless it is satisfied, after making appropriate inquiries of the applicant and the patient, that it would be in the patient's interests. It must state both its reasons and the period of postponement in writing and send a copy to the applicant, the patient, the responsible authority, the Home Office (for restricted patients) and anyone else who has already been notified of the application. Seven days before the period of postponement ends, the tribunal must start the ball rolling again, unless by that time the application has been withdrawn. If there is by then a new application or reference, the two can be dealt with together.

Clearly then, anyone advising a patient or relative whether to apply should give careful consideration to timing, bearing in mind both the automatic references to which the patient is entitled and the tribunal's powers of postponement.

2. *Information, Advice and Representation*

It is obviously important that both patients and relatives should be aware of their rights. Hospital managers now have a statutory duty to do their best to ensure that the patient understands his. This includes giving him the information both orally and in writing and (unless the patient asks them not to) sending a copy to his nearest relative (s.132). It does not include doing their best to ensure that the relative understands his own position. It has always been DHSS policy to provide leaflets, but in the past patients have often not been properly informed (see Greenland, 1970). Hospitals vary in their attitudes towards tribunals. Some enthusiastic doctors see an application as a helpful step in encouraging the patient to take responsibility for himself. Some even see it as a way of sharing or relieving their own responsibility. But others fear that knowing his rights will unsettle the patient and interfere with treatment. Some may see the tribunal as a threat to their professional judgment, although there is no jurisdiction over questions of treatment. Rather more fear that the hearing will drive a wedge between them and the patient. Unfortunately, however, the fact of compulsion has already created that wedge. The doctor-patient relationship can never be quite what it would be in an ordinary case. There can certainly be no justification for keeping a patient in ignorance of the rights which Parliament intended that he should have. Hospitals are now taking a more positive view and the leaflets available from the DHSS, the tribunal, and from voluntary organisations such as MIND, are far more attractive than they were.

Patients also have access to a great deal more outside help than used to be the case. It has always been possible for an independent doctor instructed by or on behalf of the patient or applicant to visit an unrestricted patient in hospital and examine him in private. This may now include an inspection of any records relating to his detention and treatment (s.76). This is to advise on an application, but there is an equivalent right to obtain advice on a hospital or DHSS reference (ss.68(3) and 67(2)). Restricted patients do not have these rights. In practice, it is unlikely that access would be denied, but this does mean that the authorities have some control over the choice of doctor.

It is also possible for the patient to have someone to represent him at the tribunal, as long as this is not another compulsory patient or even an informal patient at the same hospital. The representative must notify the tribunal of his authorisation and his address. He will then be sent all the documents and notices which would normally go to his client and can take the steps that his client could take. But unless the tribunal directs otherwise, the patient can take someone else along to the hearing, in addition to any representative. If the patient does not want to conduct his own case and has not authorised anyone else to do so, the tribunal can now appoint someone to act as his authorised representative (r.10). This should prove particularly helpful in references concerning severely disabled patients who are unable to do anything for themselves. Most, however, are quite capable of instructing someone to represent them. These rules apply equally to any other "party" to the proceedings. A "party" means the applicant, the patient, the responsible authority (usually the hospital) and any other person who is notified under rules 7 or 31 (see pages 263 and 260 below) or who is added as a party by the tribunal (r.2(1)). Unless added by the tribunal, the Home Secretary is not a party to the proceedings concerning restricted patients but is involved in other ways.

However, the financial help available for both doctors and advocates used to be very limited. The tribunal can pay travelling, subsistence and loss of earnings allowances to anyone who attends as a witness or representative of the applicant (apart from a barrister or solicitor). This also applies to the applicant and to the patient if he is not the applicant, although the patient will rarely have far to come (s.78(7)). But these expenses do not cover any fee for the representative or for an expert witness, nor any expenditure on preparatory work before coming to the hearing. This is still the position if the patient or applicant is represented by someone other than a practising lawyer.

Since 1972, however, it has been possible for lawyers to give legal advice and assistance under the so-called "green form" scheme (Legal Aid Act 1974, ss.1 to 4; the principal regulations are the Legal Advice and Assistance Regulations 1980). The green form enables the solicitor to operate the means test himself, rather than using the more cumbersome machinery of legal aid. The financial eligibility limits are usually updated in April each year. In 1983–84, the limit of disposable income was £99.00 a week, but contributions were payable on a sliding scale for incomes of £47.00 a week or more. People who are directly or indirectly in receipt of supplementary benefit or family income supplement, however, are automatically eligible and do not have to pay contributions. The great majority of long term detained patients depend upon supplementary benefit or hospital pocket money and will certainly qualify. But advice and assistance is only available to people with less than, in 1983–84, £700 of disposable capital. This could exclude some patients with particular types of savings, although not every asset is regarded as disposable.

If the client qualifies, the solicitor may give him certain kinds of help without seeking the approval of the Law Society's area committee. This covers advising him on how the law applies to his particular circumstances and on any steps which he might take as a result. It generally includes helping him to take those steps or taking them for him. But the solicitor cannot begin or conduct any proceedings on behalf of a client, although he can help the client to do so for himself and can negotiate a settlement. All these steps must not exceed a fixed limit in cost (currently being raised to £50.00). If it looks as though the necessary steps are going to cost more, the solicitor must seek approval from the Law Society, although this must be given if the help is "reasonable" and the cost "fair and reasonable." Practice in area committees used to be very variable, but in 1979 MIND prepared a detailed submission on the tasks involved in helping a patient with a tribunal application (see Gostin and Rassaby, 1980). These will obviously involve a meeting with the patient, which will necessitate a trip to the hospital unless the patient is given leave of absence. It may be necessary to visit the patient's family and it will almost always be essential to investigate the placements and other facilities available for when the patient leaves hospital. This may need an independent social worker's report if the social circumstances report in the hospital statement (see below) is inadequate. Sometimes, it may require negotiations with local authorities or other bodies who could provide accommodation. Above all, however, an independent psychiatrist's report will almost always be indicated, at least in long term cases.

This list gives a very good idea of the preparatory work involved in a tribunal application and the response of area committees was apparently favourable. Nevertheless, solicitors were still not allowed to represent patients at the actual hearing. Some were prepared to do so at their own expense. These, of necessity, were a select and dedicated band who had usually acquired some expertise in this difficult and sensitive work. Since December 1, 1982, however, solicitors have been able to seek approval to extend the assistance given under the green form scheme to "assistance by way of representation" at the hearing (see Legal Advice and Assistance (Amendment) (No. 3) Regulations 1983). In other types of case, these extensions are only granted if the area committee considers that the client has reasonable grounds for bringing proceedings, but this was not thought right in cases where the liberty of the subject is in issue. In principle, he must always be reasonable in availing himself of a right which Parliament has provided for his protection (and which is guaranteed by the European Convention on Human Rights) regardless of whether he is likely to succeed. Both the Lord Chancellor's Department and the DHSS have accepted that approval should be automatic. Nevertheless, the regulation 17(3) does allow the committee to refuse if it appears unreasonable that it should be granted in all the circumstances of the case.

The area committee can always set a limit on the costs to be incurred and prior approval must be sought for expert opinions and evidence or for any other unusual or unusually large expenditure. Approval for an independent psychiatrist's report should be almost automatic, except perhaps for patients detained for assessment, when there will rarely be time to obtain one. For reasons which will appear later, the role of the medical member on the tribunal is not an adequate substitute for a doctor instructed on the patient's behalf. Approval for independent social workers' reports may be a little more difficult to get, for the tribunal can always call for more evidence from the social services authority. It can also be difficult to balance the advantages of getting these reports against the disadvantage of having to wait for them.

Legal representation can have its own disadvantages. The "assistance by way of representation" scheme was preferred to ordinary legal aid, because it is quicker and less complicated. Speed is obviously of the essence where a client is deprived of both his liberty and his right to object to most forms of medical intervention. Any delay should be caused by his needs and not those of his representative. Unfortunately, representative-induced delays are common in all types of tribunal and may increase as legal representation increases, not only because of the other demands upon the lawyer's time but also because he is more likely to call for independent reports. A lawyer may also be relatively inexperienced in the legal and practical issues involved, as well as in communicating with mental patients. Few lawyers have had much to do with mental health until very recently. Quite apart from the financial problem, tribunal hearings have been very few and far between outside the special hospitals. Even now, detained patients are widely distributed and experience may not be easy to obtain. It would be disastrous if lawyers began to import a court-room style of advocacy into these hitherto informal hearings, which depend so much upon an understanding of the personalities involved. The hospital and RMO do not at present employ advocates (although the hospital is allowed representation under the rules) because there is no need for them to do so. If ever they felt such a need, the major advantage of a tribunal would be lost. For all these reasons, Bell (1969; 1970) advocated a skilled non-legal representation service for these (and some other) tribunals. Even now, a non-lawyer may be just as helpful, but there remains the problem of finance.

Some tribunals may even regret the spread of representation, feeling that they can themselves provide the patient with all the help he needs. Members have certainly developed considerable skill in communicating with patients. They also have ample power to seek any further information they need. In practice, however, they have not always used this energetically, even to the extent of chasing up alternatives to hospital care. They would certainly not seek an independent doctor's report. The other great advantage of a representative is that he can be shown all the evidence and documents, even if there are grounds for withholding some from the patient. He can also remain throughout the hearing, even though the patient (or anyone else) is excluded. The rules give an authorised representative both of these rights, but only if he is either a barrister or a solicitor, or a registered medical practitioner, or some other person authorised by the patient or applicant whom the tribunal considers to be suitable because of his experience or professional qualification (rr. 12(3) and 21(4)).

The point of this is that the tribunal must be able to trust the representative not to disclose to the patient the information which the tribunal has decided should be withheld from him (see below). Professionally, this is obviously ethical because the rules insist upon it. But the representative must beware of colluding too closely with the tribunal to achieve a result which may be in his client's best interests but contrary to his instructions. In principle, it is for the doctors, social workers and other professionals to devote themselves to the patient's best interests. A representative must obviously advise his client where he thinks the client's bests interests lie, but in the end it is his instructions that he must follow. He is the only person who can do this.

3. *The Tribunal*

There is a tribunal for each of the 14 regional health authority regions in England and one for Wales (s.65). Each panel has three types of member: (a) legal members appointed by the Lord Chancellor, who have such legal experience as he considers suitable; normally these are senior practitioners, but some academics have been appointed; (b) medical members appointed by the Lord Chancellor after consultation with the DHSS; these are usually consultant psychiatrists, but other doctors with psychiatric experience, including community physicians, may be appointed; and (c) lay members, also appointed by the Lord Chancellor after consultation with the DHSS, who have "such experience in administration, such knowledge of social services or such other qualifications or experience as the Lord Chancellor considers suitable" (1983 Act, Sched. 2). Lay members are very diverse. Some are magistrates or members of local or health authorities or similar public figures, who then supply the responsible layman's view. Others have relevant professional experience, for example in social or community work, which they can bring to the task. The suggestion that there should always be a social worker on the tribunal has, however, not been adopted.

The regional chairman of the tribunal is a lawyer. Technically, it is his job to nominate the members for a particular hearing or class of hearings (Sched. 2 and r.8). At any time up to the hearing he may exercise the tribunal's powers on preliminary and incidental matters (under rules 6, 7, 9, 10, 12, 13, 14(1), 15, 17, 19, 20, 26 and 28; see r.5). These include the power to give whatever directions it thinks fit to secure a "speedy and just determination," subject to the Rules (r.13). These functions can be delegated to another member appointed to act when he is unable to do so (s.78(6)). In practice, the chairman may give general instructions to the tribunal clerks on some matters. There are regional tribunal offices in London, Liverpool and Nottingham, each handling several tribunal regions, and one in Cardiff for Wales. Generally, they are staffed by a small number of full time civil servants. These are totally independent of the hospital authorities and accountable to the regional chairmen. The regional chairmen may also organise conferences and training for their members, but there has not been much of this in the past. Generally, members have been initiated by sitting in on one or two tribunals before taking part. In this way they have no doubt learned to follow the practice in their region. But until the 1983 Act members did not sit at all frequently outside the special hospitals and contact between them was very limited. Contact between members of different regions was totally non-existent, although the regional chairmen met from time to time. They differed widely in their views about the conduct of tribunals and very different practices emerged in different places. This made it hard for patients and their representatives to predict how their particular case would be conducted. A committee was formed to review the procedures in 1977 and published a discussion paper in 1978. But the task of producing some uniformity and predictability has not proved easy to reconcile with the wide divergence of view on some crucial issues. Everyone would gain from a greater emphasis on training for new members and regular opportunities for members of all types to meet and learn from one another.

For any one case, a tribunal is made up of at least one member from each of the three groups and the lawyer presides. This is not because he is the most important, but because he should be able to conduct the hearing in a fair and judicial manner and advise on any question of law which may arise. But there are no decisions which, under the rules, are reserved for him. Each member is entitled to an equal voice on questions of law, procedure and substance. In practice, Fennell (1979) found that the lawyer was usually the most powerful member, but the doctor's opinions and character are crucial because of his peculiar role (see below). However, this pattern could change a little in cases concerning restricted patients. The 1983 Act gave tribunals the power to release them, when previously there had only been power to make recommendations to the Home Secretary. The government feared that neither the courts nor the public would have confidence in the ordinary membership. The special hospital doctors feared that they might have to modify their treatment to ensure that their patients were not discharged prematurely. There was no evidence that tribunals had acted at all irresponsibly in the past or would do so in the future, but there could be problems if other people even began to think that they might. Hence for restricted patients, the presiding legal member must be specially approved for the purpose (s.78(4) and r.8(3)). Some circuit judges and recorders have been appointed to do this, but there is nothing to stop them sitting on other cases as well and everything to be said for their doing so. There is all the difference in the world between trying a criminal case in the Crown Court and making an assessment of the patient's current mental state and treatment needs. There is also much to be said for appointing a legal member with more diverse experience to serve as a fourth in these cases, but the judge must preside.

Any member is disqualified from sitting if he is a member or officer of the "responsible authority" (r.8(2)). This means the hospital managers (see page 23 above) or the local social services authority which is responsible for a patient in guardianship (r. 2(1)). If the patient is in a mental nursing home, also disqualified are members or officers of the health authority with which it is registered and of any authority which maintains the patient there. Finally, the member must not have a close knowledge of or connection with the patient, or have recently treated him in a professional medical capacity. This may seem obvious, but psychiatry is a very small profession. It will be almost impossible to ensure that the medical member and the RMO do not know one another, and often they will be quite well acquainted, but it must not appear to the patient or applicant that the tribunal is anything other than completely independent of those who are at present responsible for him.

4. *The Preliminaries*

The preliminary procedure in applications by patients detained for assessment is shorter and simpler than that in other applications and references of all types. But they all have essentially the same rules about withholding information from the patient.

(a) *Assessment cases*

Time is short and little is expected from either the patient or the hospital before the hearing. The patient must apply in writing, but he can get someone else (perhaps a social worker or a nurse) to do this for him. There is no prescribed form, although the tribunal or the hospital managers will supply a suitable one if asked. The application must indicate that it is an assessment case, and if possible it should give the patient's name, the hospital address, the name, address and relationship of the nearest relative, and the name and address of anyone authorised by the patient to represent him, but that is all. It is hard to see how the tribunal could proceed at all without the second two items of information, but it can ask the hospital to fill in any gaps as best it can. The application must be sent to the offices of the tribunal serving the area where the hospital is (r.30). It would obviously be sensible to send it by first class post and as soon as possible after the patient is admitted. The hospital ought to be able to supply the appropriate address.

The tribunal will then arrange a hearing for no more than seven days after it has received the application, and notify the patient, the hospital managers, the nearest relative (if this is practicable), and anyone else whom it thinks should be heard (r. 31). An obvious candidate would be the approved social worker who "sectioned" the patient, for the tribunal certainly ought to hear why he did so. If the patient has a representative, notices and other material which would normally go to the patient will be sent to him instead and he may take any step which the patient would otherwise have been able to take in the proceedings (r.10(4)). When the hospital gets notice of the hearing, or earlier if asked (a telephone call would be sensible), it must supply the tribunal with copies of the admission documents. These are the application for admission to hospital and the medical recommendations supporting it (r.2(1)). Often, the tribunal will have little more than this to go on, and these are not very revealing. But the hospital must also supply as much of the information and reports required in long term cases as can reasonably be provided in the time available (r.32).

(b) *Long term cases*

The procedure for all other types of application is only a little more complicated. The method of applying is the same (r.3). If possible, the application must give the patient's name, his address (which must include the hospital address, or for a conditionally discharged patient the address of the hospital where he was last detained, or the name and address of the patient's private guardian), the section under which the patient is detained, and the name and address of any representative (or whether he intends to authorise one). A nearest relative applicant must also give his name, address and relationship to the patient. Again, the tribunal can ask the responsible authority or (for restricted patients) the Home Office to fill any gaps. Once it gets the application, the tribunal must notify the responsible authority, the patient (if he is not the applicant), and the Home Office (if the patient is restricted). This must be done even if the application is postponed and this is where the procedure begins again at the end of the postponement, whatever the point it had reached before (r.4). The same people must be told of any type of reference, but obviously if it has been made by the responsible authority this will take the form of a request for their statement.

Within three weeks at the latest, the responsible authority must send a "rule 6 statement" to the tribunal, and also to the Home Office if the patient is restricted (r. 6(1)). This must contain some basic facts listed in Part A of Schedule 1 to the Rules. These are the patient's full name and age; the date of his admission to the present hospital (or reception into guardianship); the name of any health authority maintaining him in a mental nursing home; details of the original authority for the detention or guardianship (including the section and Act involved) and of any later renewals or changes; the legal category of disorder from which the patient is recorded as suffering (except for patients detained under the Criminal Procedure (Insanity) Act 1964, to whom these are irrelevant); the name of the responsible medical officer and the length of time the patient has been under his care; the name and period of involvement of any other doctor who is or has recently been largely concerned in the patient's treatment; the dates, decisions and reasons of any previous tribunal hearings (but not of recommendations relating to restricted patients under the old law); details of any Court of Protection proceedings and receivership; the name and address of the nearest relative or person acting as such; the name and address of any other person who takes a close interest in the patient; and details of any leave of absence given to the patient during the past two years, its duration and where the patient lived.

The authority must also supply an up-to-date medical report on the patient's medical history and present condition, specially prepared for the tribunal (Part B of Sched. 1). Regrettably, in some hospitals this may be the patient's best chance of a thorough consultation with his RMO, although the report could be prepared by another doctor. The authority must also supply a social circumstances report, as far as this is practicable. This should cover the patient's home and family circumstances, including the attitude of the nearest relative, the opportunities for employment and occupation and the housing facilities which would be available if the patient were discharged, the availability of community support and medical facilities, and the patient's financial circumstances. The social circumstances report is a vital factor in any tribunal decision. But Greenland (1970), who has made the most comprehensive study of tribunal operation to date, found that many hospital statements (except those from Broadmoor) were defective or incomplete in this respect.

Reports from a hospital social worker can be very different from those prepared by a fieldworker from the patient's home area, often a long way away. The hospital social worker should know the patient and regard him as the primary client. The patient's rehabilitation will be his main task and he will go to considerable lengths to investigate what might be available outside hospital. But if he is not employed by the social services authority for the patient's home area, he will not have the same access to its facilities as a local fieldworker would have. The fieldworker may have this access, but unless the patient is already his client, he is much less likely to see the patient's rehabilitation as his priority. He may be more involved with the family. This is where a good representative who is prepared to do a certain amount of investigation can be so helpful.

Finally, the hospital statement should, if practicable, give their views on the suitability of the patient for discharge, and any other observations which they wish to make. If the patient is restricted, the Home Office must supply a supplementary statement containing any further information it has. This should arrive no later than three weeks after it received the hospital's statement (r.6(2)). The Home Office is solely responsible for statements on conditionally discharged patients, which must arrive within six weeks (r.6(3)). They must state the patient's full name and age; the history of his present liability to detention (including details of the offence(s) and dates of the original order or transfer direction and of the discharge); the legal category of mental disorder (again not applicable to cases under the 1964 Act); the name and address and period of care of any doctor responsible for the care and supervision of the patient in the community; and the name and address and period of care of any social worker or probation officer responsible for his care and supervision in the community (Part C, Sched. 1). If practicable, they should supply an up-to-date medical report if there is a doctor responsible for him, an up-to-date progress report from any supervisor, and a report on his home circumstances. The Home Office may also give its views on his suitability for discharge and any other observations it may wish to make (Part D, Sched. 1).

Once these statements have been received, the tribunal must notify the nearest relative (unless he is the applicant), the private guardian of a patient under guardianship, the registration authority of a private nursing home where the patient is liable to be detained, any health authority which is maintaining him in a private nursing home, the Court of Protection if the patient's affairs are under its control, and any other person whom the tribunal thinks should be given an opportunity of being heard (r.7). At this point, it ought also to be possible to fix the time and place of the actual hearing. 14 days' notice of this must be given to the applicant, the patient, the responsible authority, the Home Office (if the patient is restricted), and anyone else who is notified of the proceedings (r.20). For these last, the two notices can obviously be combined. The 14 days can be reduced by agreement with all concerned, but it is unlikely that the hearing will take place less than five or six weeks after the application, and for restricted patients the wait is bound to be longer.

(c) *Disclosing and withholding information*

The normal principle of natural justice is that a person is entitled to know the case against him and that no information should be available to the tribunal which is not also available to him. However, mental health review tribunal procedure has always been designed on the assumption that full disclosure may be harmful to the very people whom the proceedings are trying to help. Hence the hospital and Home Office can indicate that some or all of their statements, or the information supplied in assessment cases, should be withheld because its disclosure would "adversely affect the health or welfare of the patient or others" (rr.6(4) and 32(2)). They must give their reasons for thinking this, and in long term cases the information withheld will be sent in a separate document. The rest of the information will be sent to the patient and applicant automatically, but this will be kept back from them both (rr.6(5) and 32(3)).

However, the tribunal's normal duty is to send a copy of every relevant document it receives to the applicant, the patient, the responsible authority and (if the patient is restricted) the Home Office (r.12(1)). If the tribunal receives any documents, including these statements, which have not been copied to the applicant or patient, it *must* consider whether disclosure would adversely affect the health or welfare of the patient or others. If satisfied that it would, it must record in writing its decision not to disclose (r.12(2)). Otherwise, the document must be revealed. This decision is one which can be made by the regional clairman before the hearing (r.5). But he may find it difficult to do so without seeing the patient, unless the hospital's reasons are obviously bad.

Withholding information is one of the most controversial aspects of tribunal procedure. Hospital practice varies greatly. Some doctors believe that it is risky even to tell the patient what they think is wrong with him, whereas others believe that it is wrong not to do so. Some believe that candour can only help their relationship with the patient, whereas others believe that it can hinder. The criterion, however, is not whether it will damage the doctor-patient relationship, but whether it will damage the health or welfare of the patient or others. Some information may lower the hospital or its staff in the esteem of the patient or applicant, but that cannot damage the welfare of others unless it is likely to provoke the patient to violence. In practice, there is liittle evidence that disclosure is damaging. Tribunals which have adopted a reasonably open posture in the past have experienced few difficulties, although restricted patients may cause rather more. The biggest problem is often that caused by the views of the patient's family. They often wish to give these in confidence, because they do not want the patient to know that they feel unable to cope with him at home. Social workers who interview them for the social circumstances report can promise that there will be no automatic disclosure, but the last word will lie with the tribunal.

But if the tribunal is minded not to disclose any document to a patient or applicant, it must nevertheless disclose it to a representative, provided that he falls within one of the "qualified" categories whom they can trust (r.12(3)). This information must not be disclosed to the client (directly or indirectly) or to anyone else without the tribunal's permission, nor can it be used for any other purpose than the present proceedings. This is an important reason for having a representative. A patient may indeed be further disturbed by such information, but it should never be forgotten that the whole purpose of the proceedings is to decide whether he is indeed as ill as the authorities think he is. It is even possible that he is not ill at all.

These same rules apply to any further information sought by the tribunal itself. This it may do before or during any hearing (again, the regional chairman may do this beforehand) and direct how and by whom it is to be supplied (r.15).

5. *The Hearing*

There must always be a hearing. Under the old rules, the tribunal could determine cases informally, by collecting information in whatever way it wanted. But in practice there was always some sort of hearing (Greenland, 1970) and this is now required.

Before the hearing (often, but not always, on the same day), the medical member of the tribunal must examine the patient and do whatever else he thinks necessary to form an opinion on the patient's mental condition. To do this, he may see the patient in private, look at and copy all his medical records (r.11). The original purpose of this was to give the tribunal its own objective medical opinion, so that an independent report on behalf of the patient would rarely be needed. This can be so, but those familiar with the British adversarial tradition can see at least two objections. A doctor who is to play a part in deciding whether the patient is fit for release will obviously approach his examination in a different way from a doctor whose responsibility is to the patient himself. Rightly or wrongly, the proceedings can easily turn into a sort of case conference (Fennell, 1977), in which the RMO and the tribunal engage in discussion about the best solution, usually in the patient's absence. Some medical members are quite inventive in suggesting ways forward which are quite outside the tribunal's formal powers. This may often benefit the patient, but it is not conducive to the objective examination of the medical issues. There is the odd patient who is not mentally ill at all and many more who are a risk neither to other people nor to themselves. A report on the patient's behalf can help the tribunal to spot these. The other problem with the medical member's role is one of natural justice. He gives his opinion in confidence to the tribunal and there is no formal opportunity for either the patient or the hospital to learn what it is and to challenge it. In some places, it is the practice for him to give the other members his views before the hearing starts. This has the advantage that his opinion will usually emerge during the hearing and points of disagreement can be explored. It has the disadvantage that the members all approach the case with the same preconceived ideas. In some places, therefore, his report is postponed to the decision-making stage. But then none of the parties have any chance of knowing what it is. There is no obvious solution, for it would be foolish not to have a medical member and equally foolish not to make use of his skills. These are particularly important when the patient is unrepresented, or in an assessment case where there has been no time to get an independent report. The difficulties can best be overcome if everyone involved is sensitive to them.

The hearing itself will almost always take place at the hospital (unless the patient is under guardianship or conditionally discharged). In the past tribunals were often convened for just one case, except in the special hospitals. But it has been estimated that hearings will multiply by five under the 1983 Act (DHSS and others, 1981). The tribunal must sit in private, unless the patient asks for it to be in public and the tribunal is satisfied that this would not be contrary to his interests. Only he has the right to ask for a public hearing. If the tribunal refuses or reverts to privacy during the hearing, it must record its reasons in writing and explain them to the patient (r.21(1) and (2)). However, there may not be much difference between a private and a public hearing. When sitting in private, the tribunal may admit anyone it likes, on such terms as it thinks appropriate (r.21(3)). Whether sitting in private or public, it can exclude anyone from all or part of the proceedings for whatever reason it likes. But if it decides to exclude the applicant or the patient or their representatives or a representative of the responsible authority, it must again record its reasons in writing and explain them to the person excluded. It cannot exclude a "qualified" representative of the applicant or patient (r.21(4)) or a member of the Council on Tribunals (r.21(6)). Again, whether sitting in private or public, information about the proceedings and the names of anyone involved cannot be made public unless the tribunal so directs (r.21(5)).

At the beginning of the hearing, the presiding member must explain how the tribunal intends to proceed (r.22(3)). It is also good practice to introduce the members of the tribunal and the other people present, to explain their functions, and to stress that the tribunal is independent of the hospital and all its works. The tribunal may conduct the hearing in whatever manner it thinks most suitable, bearing in mind the health and interests of the patient. As far as it is appropriate, it must try to avoid formality (r.22(1)). It is certainly common for tribunals to address patients by their given names and sometimes to allow them to smoke. It is not common for patients to address members of the tribunal by their given names. Informality can be a great benefit in all kinds of tribunal, but particularly here where there are advantages in questioning people directly, rather than listening to advocates doing so. But informality can be unpredictable and can lose sight of the basic principles of a fair and open hearing of both sides of the case.

Thus the applicant, patient, responsible authority and anyone else notified of the proceedings may appear at the hearing and take such part as the tribunal thinks proper. So may anyone else with the tribunal's permission. In particular, the tribunal *must* hear and take evidence from the applicant, the patient, and the responsible authority who may hear each other's evidence, put questions to each other, call witnesses and put questions to any witness or other person appearing before the tribunal (r. 21(4)). This rule is subject to the tribunal's power to exclude even these people for some or all of the time, provided that it records and explains its reasons. Nevertheless, it clearly expects that the two "sides" will be there for most of the time and have much the same rights as parties to an ordinary dispute. The tribunal has power to subpoena witnesses to appeal or produce documents and to hear evidence on oath, but this is hardly ever necessary. It is not bound by the usual rules of evidence, in that it can admit things which would not be admissible in a court of law, but it cannot force someone to disclose things which he could not be forced to disclose in court (r.14). In practice, medical judgments are often based on hearsay evidence from interested parties and the tribunal should be prepared to submit this to critical examination. Once all the evidence has been given, the applicant and patient must be given another opportunity to address the tribunal (r.22(5)).

At any time before the proceedings end, however, the tribunal (or one of its members) may interview the patient. It must do so if he asks, and it must do so without anyone else being present if he asks for this (r.22(2)). In practice, he will usually give evidence at the hearing and the tribunal can ask the representative of the responsible authority to leave while he does so, but this rule guarantees him a private hearing if he wants one. There can be no serious objections to this. The doctor does not have a close personal interest in the outcome, such as would make this unfair to him, but there is a very real risk that the patient will be intimidated by the presence of one who has so much power over him. Tribunals may therefore find it appropriate to take the initiative and ask the patient whether he would like a private word.

The tribunal may ask the patient to leave while others are giving evidence, but it must explain why. It has been very common practice to hear his family in his absence, because they are often reluctant to speak freely and he may be prejudiced if they do not, or upset if he hears what they have to say. Practice with regard to the patient's doctor and other staff has varied. Some have assumed that doctor and patient will be present throughout, some have assumed that they will be seen separately, and some have seen them both together but then offered each a private word. Up to a point, the tribunal can go on doing any of these things, but the expectation is that all stay unless excluded.

However, it is clear that the tribunal must hear from both sides. In the past, some tribunals have found it possible to hear a case without ever taking evidence from the RMO or any other person who is responsible for the patient's care in hospital. It is difficult to understand how they can possibly examine the issues properly in such circumstances. They can, of course, call for whom they wish.

The rule does not require them to hear the parties in any particular order. Some tribunals like the hospital to begin, partly because they think that in practice the burden of proof should lie on that side, and partly so that the patient will know the case he has to meet. Others believe that the patient wants his "day in court" and will not understand the proper method of proceeding by examination and cross-examination if he is not allowed to go first. Technically, the burden of proof is on the patient or applicant, and he who speaks last (r.22(5)) usually speaks first.

The tribunal can adjourn the hearing at any time to obtain further information or for any other purpose. It can give directions to ensure that it is heard again promptly. But unless it adjourns to a fixed date, it must give at least 14 days' notice of the resumed hearing (or less if everyone agrees). The applicant, patient or responsible authority is entitled to insist that the hearing be resumed, provided that the tribunal is satisfied that this would be in the patient's interests (r.16). Tribunals have always had these inquisitorial powers and this has been the predominant model in the past. But with increasing representation, it may be less likely to be so in the future.

6. *The Issues*

The tribunal is not concerned with whether the admission procedures were properly carried out. Nor is it directly concerned with how the patient is being treated in hospital. Its task is to decide whether he should be detained there any longer (or remain subject to compulsion in the community). Its powers to discharge an unrestricted patient are more flexible than its powers to discharge a restriction order patient and quite different from its role in relation to patients transferred from prison. If it does not discharge an unrestricted patient, it may recommend that he be given leave of absence, or transferred to another hospital or into guardianship. If it does not discharge any patient, it may decide that he is suffering from a different legal category of disorder. Other than this, it has no jurisdiction over the patient's present treatment and care.

(a) *Unrestricted patients*

The tribunal's criteria are not identical to those for the original admission or the renewal of detention, but the general effect is that it must discharge a patient if the grounds for detaining him do not exist. Thus if the patient is detained for assessment, it must discharge him if it finds (a) that he is not mentally disordered at all, *or* (b) that his disorder is not of a nature or degree to warrant his detention in hospital for assessment (or for assessment followed by medical treatment) for at least a limited period, *or* (c) that his detention is not justified in the interests of his own health or safety or with a view to the protection of other persons (s.72(1)(*a*)). These conditions are in the negative. Strictly speaking, the hospital does not have to prove that the grounds exist and it is up to the patient to prove that they do not. The tribunal need only be satisfied on the balance of probabilities, but we all know how difficult it is to prove a negative. It is particularly difficult to prove that you are either sane or safe once the label "patient" has been officially attached to you. However, some tribunals have in practice been prepared to place the burden of proof on the hospital and they may continue to do so. In assessment cases, it should be possible to scrutinise the evidence upon which that initial judgment was made. The incident or behaviour which led to the detention should be fresh in everyone's minds and the issue will not be unduly clouded by what has since happened in hospital. Misinterpretation of events by family, neighbours, social workers, doctors and other hospital staff is not unknown. The quality of the evidence on which their judgments were made can be assessed. These hearings should give an unrivalled opportunity to clarify matters before the patient embarks upon his career.

If the patient is detained for treatment, under civil powers or under an ordinary hospital order, he must be discharged if (a) he is not suffering from mental illness, psychopathic disorder, severe mental impairment or mental impairment, *or* (b) his disorder is not of a nature or degree which makes it appropriate for him to be liable to be detained in a hospital for medical treatment, *or* (c) it is not necessary for the health or safety of the patient or for the protection of other persons that he should receive such treatment. If the nearest relative is applying because the RMO has prevented him from discharging the patient, the tribunal must also grant a discharge if it is satisfied that, if released, the patient would not be likely to act in a manner dangerous to other persons or to himself (s.72(1)(*b*)). All these matters have been discussed in Chapter 2. The test of whether someone is *dangerous* is obviously much narrower than the test of whether he should be in hospital for his own sake or that of others. The tribunal is only obliged to apply the stricter test if the patient's nearest relative has already tried to discharge him. The relative has no power to do this in hospital order cases, and so the wider test will always apply to them. In civil cases, however, the patient will stand a better chance of being discharged if his relative first tries to do so and then applies to the tribunal.

However, the tribunal does not have to discharge patients who are "untreatable." This is strange, because a psychopathic or non-severely impaired patient will have to be discharged by the hospital at his next renewal date if hospital treatment is unlikely to make him better or at least prevent his getting worse. An untreatable mentally ill or severely impaired patient will have to be discharged on renewal unless he is unable to fend for himself in the community (see page 122). It is odd that the tribunal may sanction a detention which the hospital could not.

But the tribunal does have a complete discretion to discharge *any* unrestricted patient, short-term or long-term, even though it is not satisfied that he is entitled to a mandatory discharge. In exercising this discretion in a long-term case, it must take treatability into account. In any case, it must have regard to the likelihood of medical treatment alleviating or preventing a deterioration of the patient's condition. If the patient is suffering from mental illness or severe mental impairment, it must also have regard to the likelihood of his being able to care for himself, to obtain the care he needs or to guard himself against serious exploitation, if discharged (s.72(2)). This is a clear hint that tribunals ought to discharge patients if the hospital will not be able to keep them at their next renewal.

In practice, the issue does not usually turn on whether the patient is indeed mentally disordered. In long-term cases, it is difficult to reassess the original judgment that he was so on admission. It is certainly possible to discuss whether he is so any longer. But the definitions of the various conditions are either so vague, or in the case of the most common category of "mental illness" non-existent, that the non-medical members will find it hard to disagree if the medical member and the other doctors are agreed. Nevertheless, it is open to them to question the definition of mental illness which is being employed, remembering that the Act's original progenitors expected this to be a serious illness akin to what used to be called insanity. It is open to them to scrutinise the evidence upon which diagnosis is based. If the patient is not now suffering from the required form of mental disorder, he must be discharged, no matter how much of a nuisance he may be to those outside or how much more comfortable and well cared for he would be in hospital.

The same is true even when he is still disordered, if that disorder is no longer of a type or severity to warrant (or make appropriate) his treatment in hospital. The disorder may be such that everyone would much prefer it if he could be kept out of harm's way. But that is not the same as to "make it appropriate that he should be detained in hospital for medical treatment." It can scarcely be appropriate to keep him in hospital for treatment if he is not receiving any treatment there, still less if he is out on leave and not receiving any in the community either. Nor can it be appropriate to keep him there for that purpose if there is no medical treatment which is suitable to his case. That is why tribunals keep discharging people like Dawn Clarke (page 184 and Mrs. Y. (page 63), even though they are an unmitigated nuisance to everyone around them.

However, the tribunal will often be concerned with whether the patient still needs medical treatment in the conventional sense. There will be discussion about his medication. The non-medical members can ask the doctors to justify their opinions and to explain the advantages and disadvantages of the various drugs involved. Even if medication is clearly needed, it may be possible to arrange for the patient to receive long-acting injections given in an out-patient clinic or by a community nurse. It may be perfectly possible for the patient to go on being treated in hospital, but on an informal rather than compulsory basis. The question then changes to whether the patient will be prepared to co-operate with these plans, because there is no way of forcing him to do so once he has been discharged, save by "sectioning" him once again. Tribunals have certainly been known to grant a patient's discharge after accepting his assurances of co-operation, but with the clear threat that compulsion will be re-imposed if he actually tries to assert the rights which his discharge theoretically gives. The practice may be difficult to justify, but it can benefit the patient's morale and make some improvement in his legal status.

The other issue which often arises is how the patient is going to cope in the outside world, if he intends to leave the hospital rather than to remain as an informal patient. Strictly speaking, this is irrelevant if his condition is not bad enough to make hospital treatment appropriate. But the Act defines "medical treatment" to include nursing and also "care, habilitation and rehabilitation under medical supervision." Most patients who are still disordered will need some sort of care, although not always under medical supervision. The question of whether hospital treatment is appropriate will often depend upon the alternative. The tribunal will be keenly interest in where the patient might live, whether he could get a job, how else he might occupy his time, and what support would be available from social services, family and community.

But what about the patients who have been detained because of their behaviour to other people? The tribunal is bound to be concerned with the risks of this happening again. Here also, this is irrelevant if his mental condition is not such as to make hospital treatment appropriate. The tribunal may find that there is no longer any mental disorder which it is appropriate to treat, even within the very wide definition given in the Act. The patient should be discharged, even if he is likely to offend again, for the problem is then one for the penal system rather than the hospital. The law now accepts the doctors' view that they cannot be expected to provide indefinite preventive detention if what they can provide is not suitable for the patient. The patient is also entitled to expect this, for unless his offence was very serious (in which case a restriction order is more likely) he would otherwise have received a non-custodial or determinate sentence.

However, the patient may still be to some extent either mentally ill or psychopathic. It is not difficult for a tribunal to conclude that an offender who has no gross symptons of mental illness has still a pathological tendency to abnormally aggressive or seriously irresponsible behaviour. This question, along with the question of whether he needs to be detained in the interests of other persons, depends upon his ability to resist the influences which triggered his earlier anti-social conduct. Unfortunately, hospital treatment, particularly in a secure unit, makes it difficult to assess this. The tribunal has no control over the social skills training and general rehabilitative effort made in hospital. All it can do is to subject its predictions of future behaviour to critical scrutiny and remember that this is an area in which the inter-relationship of mental condition and social situation is particularly important.

Tribunals are often faced with the problem that the patient cannot be discharged unless the hospital has at least been trying to prepare him for it. The worse the hospital, the worse the patient's chances before the tribunal are likely to be. Tribunals will therefore find their new powers in the 1983 Act particularly useful. First, they may direct the patient's discharge on a future specified date, rather than straightaway (s.72(3)). This applies to any discharge under section 72(1), presumably whether it is mandatory or discretionary. Logically, however, the tribunal should not delay a discharge to which the patient is immediately entitled. He might only be entitled to a discharge once the necessary arrangements have been made, and a short delay could be proper to enable this to be done. In discretionary cases, a longer period might be appropriate, perhaps where the doctors predict that the patient will be ready in two or three months' time.

If the tribunal does not discharge the patient under section 72(1), it may recommend that he be granted leave of absence, or transferred to another hospital, or into guardianship, with a view to facilitating his discharge on a future date (s.72(3)(*a*)). Tribunals have wanted the power to do this for some time, but there is no obligation on the medical of social services to comply. No doubt they will do their best to do so. The tribunal must set a time limit, at the end of which it will reconsider the case if its recommendations have not borne fruit (s.72(3)(*b*); r.24(4)). The hearing may be reconvened with 14 days' notice, or less if all agree (r.25(2)). By that time, the tribunal may feel that a discharge is preferable to keeping the patient in hospital any longer.

There are many other suggestions which tribunals often want to make, particularly about the rehabilitative effort within the hospital. Some medical members take these up during their discussions with the hospital representatives. There is nothing to stop the tribunal making its views clear, both during the hearing and when it comes to give written reasons for whatever it decides.

(b) *Restriction order patients*

The tribunal must discharge a restriction order patient if it finds (a) that he is not suffering mental illness, psychopathic disorder, severe mental impairment or mental impairment; *or* (b) that his disorder is not of a nature or degree which makes it appropriate for him to be liable to be detained in a hospital for medical treatment; *or* (c) that it is not necessary for the health or safety of the patient or for the protection of other persons that he should receive such treatment (s.73(1) and (2)). These are exactly the same as the criteria for the mandatory discharge of unrestricted patients and raise exactly the same issues. But tribunals may be a little sceptical if a person has recently been sent to hospital as a psychopath after committing a very serious offence and then claims (or is thought) to be no such thing. Similarly, the second criterion is not whether hospital treatment will do him some good, but whether it is appropriate for him to be detained there for medical treatment, defined in the very wide sense to include nursing and care, habilitation and rehabilitation under medical supervision (s.145(1)). Can it be appropriate to detain a patient for these purposes simply because he has already committed at least one serious offence and may do so again? The gulf between pure preventive detention and some sort of medical care and treatment may be very narrow, but it is nonetheless deep. If detention in hospital is not appropriate, the patient must be discharged, no matter how dangerous he may be. However, if it is still appropriate, the tribunal is not concerned with whether it is necessary to protect the public from *serious* harm. Unlike the Home Secretary, it has no power to lift the restrictions while leaving the patient to be detained as an ordinary hospital order patient.

However, it does have power to choose between an absolute and a conditional discharge, provided that it is satisfied that the criteria for a mandatory discharge are met. It must grant an absolute discharge if satisfied that it is not appropriate for the patient to remain liable to recall to hospital for further treatment (s.73(1)). Otherwise, it must discharge him upon conditions (s.73(2)). Apart from the power of recall, it can decide what the conditions should be. The Act lays down no limits, but the obvious candidates are residence, supervision and medical treatment. The tribunal can insist that he attends for treatment, although the treatment cannot be forced upon him by doctors and nurses outside the hospital should he refuse it (s.56(1)). It could also decide on what he can or cannot do, in the way of going to public houses or other provoking places. The discharge may be deferred until the necessary arrangements have been made (s.73(7)). The tribunal can then make another decision without a further hearing (r.25(1)). But if the case is deferred so long that there has been another reference or application in the meantime, the second one supersedes the first (s.73(7)).

The effect of a tribunal's conditional discharge is just the same as a Home Secretary's. He can recall the patient at any time, in theory immediately after an unwelcome decision by a tribunal. In practice, this is unlikely to happen. Unless the criteria for detention exist, the patient would have to be released when his case is referred to a tribunal within a month of recall. However, the Home Secretary can also vary the tribunal's conditions (s.73(4) and (5)). Recall apart, there is no sanction for breach of the conditions. If, for example, an alcoholic is discharged on condition that he does not drink (not usually the wisest thing to do), the mere fact that he has a lapse will not invariably justify a recall.

Patients who have been conditionally discharged by a tribunal or by the Home Secretary may apply to the tribunal for the area where they live. The tribunal can then vary the conditions or even impose new ones. Alternatively, they can lift the restrictions altogether (s.75(3)). This has the same effect as an absolute discharge. Both mean that the patient is no longer subject to any form of compulsion (s.73(3)).

If a restriction order patient does not qualify for mandatory discharge, the tribunal has no discretion to release him. Tribunals may find it easier to decide that he no longer needs to be in hospital, given their power to impose conditions and ensure that he is liable to instant recall. Nevertheless, the lack of discretion is unfortunate and even surprising, given the exalted membership of tribunals in these cases. The patient may be so much better that he does not need to be in a special hospital, even though some transitional care in a local hospital may be appropriate before he is discharged into the community. The formal power to recommend leave of absence or transfer does not apply to restricted patients (because it can only apply to those who do not qualify for a mandatory discharge under section 72(1)). Tribunals used to give detailed advice to the Home Secretary under the old law, when they had no power to discharge patients themselves. This advice was most valuable to the Home Office in building up a picture of the patient's progress. Although it was confidential, it could also help the patient to make that progress through the hospital system. The tribunal can still make its views thoroughly clear when giving its reasons for refusing a discharge. These will be sent to the Home Office, and some parts can be withheld from the patient (r.24(1) and (2)). Presumably tribunals could also make informal comments to the Home Office if they wished. Certainly, unless tribunals are prepared to contribute towards the Home Office understanding of individual patients in this way, hearings will usually be less useful to patients than they were in the old days. The cases in which the tribunal can be satisfied of the grounds for a mandatory discharge will be relatively few and far between, particularly in the early days of a patient's detention.

(c) *Prisoners transferred with restrictions*

If the patient has been transferred from prison under section 47 or 48, together with a restriction direction under section 49, the task of the tribunal is to decide whether or not he ought to remain in hospital. The task of the Home Secretary is then to decide whether to transfer him back to prison, or in some cases to leave him in hospital, or in others to release him into the community.

After hearing the case, the tribunal must notify the Home Secretary whether the patient would be entitled to an absolute or conditional discharge if he were a restriction order patient. If he is entitled to a conditional discharge, it may recommend that he should stay in hospital if he is not released, rather than be returned to prison (s.74(1)). If the patient was transferred under section 48 (which relates to remand, civil and Immigration Act prisoners), the Home Secretary must transfer him back to prison, unless he is only entitled to a conditional discharge and the tribunal has recommended that he should be allowed to stay in hospital (s.74(4)). In other cases, the Home Secretary can decide to allow the discharge. The tribunal will do this in the usual way, if it is notified by the Home Office within 90 days of giving its views (s.74(3)). If nothing is heard from the Home Office within that time, the hospital must transfer the patient back to prison, unless the tribunal has recommended that he is entitled to a conditional discharge but should be allowed to stay in hospital instead (s.74(3)).

However, even if the patient is not entitled to either sort of discharge, the tribunal can notify the Home Secretary that he no longer requires treatment in hospital for mental disorder or that no effective treatment can be given for his disorder in the hospital where he is. The Home Secretary may then decide to transfer the patient back to prison; alternatively, if the patient was under sentence, he can exercise any power of releasing on licence or under supervision which would have applied from prison (ss.50(1), 51(3), and 53(2)). There is no power to do this if the patient was originally remanded by a magistrates' court (*cf.* s.52). But even if there is no effective treatment for these patients, the Home Secretary could decide to leave them in hospital for the time being.

(d) *Guardianship patients*

If the patient is subject to guardianship, whether under a court order or civil powers, the tribunal has always a discretion to discharge him. It must do so if it finds (a) that he is not then suffering from mental illness, psychopathic disorder, severe mental impairment or mental impairment, *or* (b) that it is not necessary in the interests of the welfare of the patient, or for the protection of other persons, that he should remain under such guardianship (s.72(4)). These applications are almost unheard of, as guardianship is generally used for handicapped people who are unlikely to improve. There could, however, be some interesting discussion of whether their handicap is any longer associated with abnormally aggressive or seriously irresponsible behaviour so as to fall within the new definition of "mental impairment."

(e) *Reclassification*

If the tribunal does not discharge the patient, it may decide that he is suffering from a different legal category of disorder from that recorded in his admission application, order or direction (s.72(5)). This will be amended accordingly, with exactly the same effect as a reclassification by the RMO (see page 123). For an unrestricted patient, it will determine which "treatability" test is to be applied at his next renewal. For a restricted patient, it will have no effect other than administrative tidiness.

7. *The Decision and After*

The tribunal may reach a majority decision, and where a tribunal with equal numbers is equally divided, the presiding member has a second or casting vote. It must always record its reasons in writing, and where it is satisfied that the grounds for a mandatory discharge are made out, it must explain its reasons for thinking so (r.23). Giving reasons for one's decision is not the same as stating the legal ground upon which it was made, and tribunals will have to be a great deal more explicit than some have been in the past. There should, however, be no need to produce a lengthy judgment. Some tribunals may be more inclined to go into detail about the reasons why they are *not* prepared to discharge the patient at present, in the hope that this will stir the authorities to more positive action.

The decision, with reasons, must be communicated in writing to the applicant, the patient (if he is not the applicant), the responsible authority, the Home Secretary (if the patient is restricted), and to anyone else whom the tribunal directs. This must be done within seven days in long term cases, or three days in assessment cases (rr.24(1) and 33)). The decision may also be announced orally by the president at the end of the hearing if it wishes and this could be most appropriate in assessment cases. This has been a common practice in some tribunals, unless the staff have already taken the patient back to the ward because of his mental state. Even if the patient does not get the reasons at the time, he is now entitled to a written explanation in most cases. However, if the tribunal considers that full disclosure would adversely affect his health or interests or those of others, it may communicate its decision to him in whatever way it thinks appropriate, and when giving its decision to the others, may do so on whatever condition it thinks appropriate about disclosing it to the patient. But it can never keep anything from his "qualified" representative, although it may prevent him from telling all to his client (r. 24(2)).

There are two ways of challenging the proceedings in a mental health review tribunal, but neither of them gives a right of appeal against the merits of the decision as such. The first is to apply to the High Court for judicial review under Order 53 of the Rules of the Supreme Court. This requires the leave of a High Court judge and must usually be done within three months of the tribunal's decision. The object would be to quash the decision on the ground that the tribunal had erred on a point of law or procedure. The first would arise if it had exceeded its powers, or made an error of law which appeared on the face of the record, or had reached a decision on the merits which no reasonable tribunal could possibly have reached, taking the relevant considerations into account and excluding the irrelevant. The second would arise if it had broken the statutory rules of procedure or the common law rules of natural justice. Normally, of course, if a tribunal does something which is allowed by its rules, this cannot be a breach of the rules of natural justice unless the tribunal's rules exceed what is allowed by the parent statute. This is unlikely in mental health cases, because section 78(1) of the 1983 Act gives the Lord Chancellor a great deal of latitude over such matters as the disclosure of documents and the exclusion of people from the hearing. The rules of natural justice are themselves flexible according to the subject-matter, but the courts could be expected to take a strict view of what was required where the liberty of the subject is in issue, were it not for what the Act itself allows. However, the new rules do require the tribunal to record and sometimes explain at almost every point when it departs from what would normally be expected. The High Court can certainly examine whether the stated reason is sufficient, either in the light of the ground permitted in the rules or for the proper exercise of a discretion. If something has gone wrong, the appropriate remedy would be certiorari, to quash the decision and get the tribunal to take it again in a proper manner. But this and all the remedies available on judicial review are themselves within the discretion of the court.

The second possibility is to get the tribunal to state a case for the determination by the High Court of any point of law arising before it (s.78(8)). It could do this on its own initiative, but in practice it will be asked to do so by one of the parties. The parties for this purpose are the applicant and any of the bodies initially notified of the application or reference (R.S.C. Ord. 94, r.11(3)). This would enable, for example, the Home Office to take the case of a restricted patient to the High Court if they felt that the tribunal had applied the wrong test (perhaps on the knotty question of what makes detention in hospital for medical treatment appropriate). A written request to the tribunal to state a case must be made within 21 days after its decision is communicated (r.11(1)). If the tribunal then refuses to state a case, or fails to do so within 21 days (r.11(2)), the party concerned then has 14 days in which to apply under Order 56 to the High Court for an order compelling it to do so. Unlike an application for judicial review, the tribunal and other parties must be notified of such an application. But the High Court would probably be looking for a prima facie case on much the same sorts of points. If the High Court does order the tribunal to state a case, the tribunal is entitled to appear and be heard in the proceedings (R.S.C. Ord. 94, r.11(4)). If the High Court thinks that the tribunal's decision on the question of law raised by the case was wrong, it can give any direction that the tribunal ought to have given under Mental Health Act (r.11(5)).

This procedure has two advantages over judicial review. It compels the tribunal to give a much fuller account of the problem as it sees it than may have appeared in the reasons for its decision. And it allows the High Court to discharge the patient if the tribunal should have done so. On the other hand, unless the tribunal can be persuaded to state a case in a very short time, it will be touch and go whether there will be any effective result until the patient's next right to a tribunal comes round.

8. *Commentary*

Tribunals have tended to operate more like a case conference or "patient's welfare assessment panel" (Fennell, 1977) than like a court. This is how they have seen themselves (Peay, 1981 and 1982). The issue has been whether the patient is yet ready for a change and if so how to find the best placement for him now. They have been encouraged to do this by several things. Under the old law, they were asked to advise the Home Office without fixed criteria when dealing with restricted patients. For others, the criteria were (and are) so vague on crucial points that it was not difficult to replace them with something which sounded more sensible and straightforward. Tribunals were bound to rely heavily on their medical member. Even if he disagreed with the RMO on some points of diagnosis, management or prognosis, they would share the same basic methods and approach. These methods could include a ready acceptance of statements made in medical records or by other interested parties, such as members of the patient's family. The informal method of determining cases by a series of interviews was more conducive to discussing the present and the future than to examining the evidence upon which the earlier judgments had been made. They were usually dealing with patients who had been in hospital for some time and to whom the various labels had already been firmly attached. They were interested in getting some "feel" for his current mental state and in assessing his needs along with those of his family and the public. The normal model of adjudication, based upon the application of fixed rules to proven facts, simply did not apply.

But how far should it be expected to apply? These cases will always be more like child custody disputes than running-down actions. They will always centre round what sort of a person the patient is and on how he can be expected to behave in the future. They will usually involve picking the best out of a meagre range of options available for him. But there *are* legal criteria and it is important that they be taken seriously. Many of today's judgments are based upon what is said to have happened in the past and it is important that the evidence for this should be carefully scrutinised. Provided that both these things are done, the tribunal's efforts to get to know and understand the people involved through direct communication can only be helpful. Informality is important for this purpose, but also to reduce the stresses upon those patients who are in fact unable to cope with them.

Several of the recent developments may help tribunals to achieve this. Legal representation may focus minds upon the proper legal issues. But its more likely effect is to induce a greater scepticism about the truth of some of the assumptions made in the past, a more careful scrutiny of the facts, and an independent medical assessment. The participation of judges in cases concerning restricted patients may reduce informality and have an unsettling effect upon some of the patients. It may lead to a greater concentration upon the offence for its own sake than on what it reveals about the future. But it may also lead to a more rigorous testing of the evidence on both sides. Above all, however, the involvement of tribunals in assessment cases may prove little short of revolutionary. They provide so much more scope for discussing whether the patient is indeed mentally disordered, whether it is bad enough for him to be in hospital, and what the alternatives might be. In these cases, the burden of proof ought to be placed on the authorities to justify their action. If they cannot do so, there should be some way of "wiping the slate clean" for the patient. But these cases may have a considerable effect upon hospital admission practices, which have been so variable in the past. They may also influence how tribunals are prepared to see the long-term cases. Of course the professionals involved are hoping to find the best solution for the patient. The tribunal's task is something rather different.

9 Community Care

1. *The Legal Issues*

Ever since the report of the Percy Commission in 1957, it has been official policy to provide for as many mentally disordered people as possible outside hospital. This is good for the hospitals, who can then concentrate on their proper role of providing specialist medical services and continuous nursing care for people who require them. It is also good for the patients, if they can be helped to live as normal and as independent a life as possible in the least restrictive environment. It is even good for the rest of us, and only partly because community services are generally cheaper than those in hospitals. These things are true of all forms of mental disorder, but particularly of mental handicap. Here the hospitals are still providing residential care for large numbers of people who do not need their specialist services. In 1948, the NHS inherited those local authority institutions which had been set up during the early part of the century, when it was official policy to segregate the "unfit" from society. Hence, in practice, the development of community care means two rather different things. One is to speed up the transfer into the community of patients who are at present in hospital unnecessarily, estimated in 1981 at around 15,000 of the mentally handicapped and 5,000 of the mentally ill (DHSS, 1981a). The other is the provision of services which will enhance the quality of life of those who are still in the community, and of their families, both as an end in itself and so that they are less likely to have to go into hospital. Unless equal priority is given to each of these aims, "community care" can so easily mean "no care at all" and an increasing and eventually intolerable burden on patients' families. There is a great deal being done to encourage community care at present, but it is almost entirely directed towards transferring existing patients out of hospital. Eventually, however, the services generated in this way could do much to improve the lives of others.

The legal problems involved are very different from those of hospital care. This is mainly because few community services are provided on an overtly compulsory basis. But that can easily blind us to the very real issues which do exist. These are of two different kinds. They can largely be illustrated by the admirable objectives of the United Nations Declaration on the Rights of Mentally Retarded Persons (1971). Unlike the European Convention on Human Rights, this has no immediate implications for the law of this country and can aim far higher. The European Convention has only limited relevance in this area. The aim of the United Nations Declaration is to recognise the dignity and worth of all human beings and to promote their integration as far as possible in normal life.

To this end, it declares that a mentally handicapped person is entitled to certain services. Thus he "has a right to proper medical care and physical therapy and to such education, training, rehabilitation and guidance as will enable him to develop his ability and maximum potential" (Art. 2). He also has the right to "economic security and a decent standard of living" and to "perform productive work or to engage in any other meaningful occupation to the fullest extent of his capabilities" (Art. 3). Wherever possible, he "should live with his own family or with foster parents and participate in different forms of community life. The family with which he lives should receive assistance. If care in an institution becomes necessary, it should be provided in surroundings and other circumstances as close as possible to those of normal life" (Art. 4). Direct financial support is of course the responsibility of national government through the social security and supplementary benefit systems which are outside the scope of this book. But the Declaration also expects that appropriate accommodation, education, training and occupation will be provided for mentally handicapped people who need them. One purpose of this chapter is to discuss the legal basis for such services in this country and whether a mentally disordered individual has any real right to receive them.

The other set of issues relates to the first of the rights declared by the United Nations. The mentally handicapped person "has, to the maximum degree of feasibility, the same rights as other human beings" (Art. 1). But he also has the right to a "qualified guardian when this is required to protect his personal well-being and interests" (Art. 5) and to "protection from exploitation, abuse and degrading treatment" (Art. 6). The ordinary rights of other human beings, in English law at least, are based on the right of self-determination. We can do as we please, provided that we do not cause certain kinds of harm to our fellow men. But how can we protect the mentally disordered person against exploitation, without at the same time taking away at least some of his right to self-determination? This problem arises whether he is living in hospital, in residential accommodation, with his family, or independently. But it is particularly relevant to the administration of residential accommodation and to the institution of guardianship under the Mental Health Act, both of which are discussed in this chapter.

2. *Governmental Responsibilities*

Most of the legal responsibility for providing community services rests with local social services authorities, although some are the province of local education authorities or central government, and the role of the health authorities and their resources is increasing. The legislation itself dates mainly from the establishment of the welfare state after the Second World War, but this is misleading because much of it had only limited application to the mentally disordered until the 1959 Act was passed. In other areas of health care, a clear distinction had been drawn between the medical functions of hospitals and the welfare functions of local authorities. Mental hospitals, however, continued to provide residential care for many patients. They still do so today, but since the 1959 Act this is no longer a matter of law. That Act adopted the Percy Commission's principle that "no-one should be excluded from benefiting from any of the general social services simply because his need arises from mental disorder rather than from some other cause." The clear division between health and social services was extended to mental disorder. In practice, however, local authorities were very slow to develop their services on anything like the scale needed to transfer patients into the community. Recent initiatives have therefore concentrated on finding ways to use health service resources to fund developments.

The main legal provisions overlap considerably. Section 29 of the National Assistance Act 1948 deals with the responsibilities of social services authorities towards the welfare of disabled people, the blind, deaf or dumb or those who are substantially or permanently handicapped by illness, injury or congenital deformity, and people suffering from mental disorder of any kind. These duties are extended by the Chronically Sick and Disabled Persons Act 1970. Paragraph 2 of Schedule 8 to the National Health Service Act 1977 (replacing similar powers dating back to the same Act of 1946) deals with the responsibilities of local social services authorities in the prevention of illness, the care of people suffering from illness, and the after-care of those who have been suffering. "Illness" includes any form of mental disorder within the meaning of the Mental Health Act. Under section 3(2)(*e*) of the same Act, health authorities must also provide facilities for prevention, care and after-care, if these are considered appropriate as part of the health service. Some authorities have been most enterprising in developing their own rehabilitation and after-care facilities for mental patients.

The Mental Health Act 1983 has taken this dual responsibility a little further in respect of one particular group. These are people who are detained for treatment under civil powers, or under a hospital order, or under a transfer from prison, and then "cease to be detained and leave hospital" (s.117(1)). This might include patients who remain informally in hospital for a short time after their detention ends. It might also include restricted patients who are conditionally discharged, for although they remain liable to recall, they are not for the time being detained. It certainly includes restricted patients who are discharged absolutely. For these patients, it is the duty of the district health authority and the local social services authority to provide, in co-operation with relevant voluntary agencies, "after-care services" until both authorities are satisfied that the person concerned no longer needs them (s.117(2)). The authorities on whom this responsibility rests are those covering the area where the person concerned "is resident" or to which he is sent on discharge by the hospital in which he was detained (s.117(3)). These duties were inserted at the insistence of members of the House of Lords when the 1982 amendments were passed. The Government argued that the authorities' existing duties were quite sufficient to cover the matter and that this added nothing new.

In one way, the Government were probably right. Local authority powers under both the 1948 and 1977 Acts are conditional on ministerial approval, but they can be converted into positive duties by a directive. General approval for the provision of certain services, and directions that some of them must be provided, have been given in two circulars (DHSS Local Authority Circulars 13/74 and 19/74 respectively; and WO 46/74 and 100/74 for Wales). Local authorities who want to provide services apparently within the scope of the legislation but outside that of the circulars must seek specific approval. Reference will therefore be made to the circulars, rather than to these two particular provisions, when dealing with the specific services below. However, they do make two general points. First, because the powers in relation to mental disorder are part of the powers to help the sick and disabled generally, authorities need not hesitate to provide a particular service because of doubts about the precise definition of mental disorder. The examples given are hostels for alcoholics, drug dependants, or homeless inadequates, the first two of whom are now excluded from the definition of mental disorder unless there is some other sign of it. Secondly, the overlap between the various powers means that authorities can expand existing services to meet whichever happens to be the wider.

Now that resources are so limited, however, a more relevant question is what can be done if the authorities fail to make adequate provision. The Secretary of State has power under all of these Acts to step into the shoes of a local or health authority if he finds that they have not been carrying out these functions properly, or at all (Mental Health Act 1983, s.124; National Health Service Act 1977, s.85; and National Assistance Act 1948, s.36). These days it is rather more likely that he will take action against authorities who spend more than their target than against those who spend less, but the threat can produce results. But is there any legal action that the individual can take? The answer, as we have already seen in Chapter 1 (pages 26 to 29), is very often "no". The courts will not intervene where Parliament has provided another remedy, at least unless that remedy has first been tried (see *Wyatt* v. *Hillingdon London Borough Council* (1978) 76 L.G.R. 727). Some judges clearly believe that ministerial default powers are the only appropriate remedy where what is really at issue is the level of taxation and public expenditure. Others (including Lord Denning in *R.* v. *Secretary of State for Social Services ex parte Hincks*, April 1980, unreported, and in *Meade* v. *Haringey London Borough Council* [1979] 1 W.L.R. 637) believe that this reasoning does not apply where the authorities have acted *ultra vires*. It may be possible to draw a distinction between the decision about the level of services to be provided and the decision about whether to allocate some of those services to this particular individual. If the individual is clearly a member of a defined class of people for whom the law insists that something be done, the courts might be more prepared to say that the authorities must at least behave reasonably in considering his case and what to do for him. This applies particularly to those former compulsory patients for whom "after-care" of some sort must be provided under section 117 of the 1983 Act. The authorities might find themselves in difficulties if they did nothing at all, or even if what they did provide was so manifestly inadequate or inappropriate to his needs that no reasonable authority could have reached that decision. The same would apply if they took irrelevant considerations, including irrational objections from some quarters, into account. Lack of funds is not always the real reason why something has not been done which ought to have been done.

However, lack of funds is very frequently the reason. Thus the current moves to extend the ways in which health service resources can be used to provide social services in the community are particularly important. Section 28A of the 1977 Act allows district health authorities (and special health authorities for the London post-graduate teaching hospitals) to make payments to local social service authorities for any of their social services apart from the provision of sheltered employment, to district councils towards the meals and recreation provided for old people, to education authorities for the education of disabled people, and to housing authorities and other public bodies providing housing accommodation (the references to education and housing are to be added by the Health and Social Services and Social Security Adjudications Act 1983). Either the health authorities or any of the local authorities can make these payments to voluntary organisations providing the same services. These payments can only be made if they are recommended by a joint consultative committee set up under section 22 of the Act and in accordance with the directions given by the Secretary of State.

The current guidance on care in the community and joint finance

(DHSS Circular HC(83)6; LAC(83)5) describes how these powers are to be used in order to transfer patients out of hospital and encourage the development of community services. Health authorities are allowed to use their ordinary funds to finance any individual patient who is moved out of hospital into the community, for as long as this is necessary. This in effect allows them to finance places in community facilities. If the patient then moves out, his place can be filled either with another hospital patient or with someone who would otherwise have to go into hospital almost at once. This is independent of the funds available for jointly financed projects, although the power to spend these funds is also derived from section 28A. Joint finance is essentially a pump-priming arrangement, under which health service money can be used for a short time to help schemes get under way. Grants can be made to meet the whole capital cost, although they should not usually be more than two-thirds. Grants towards running costs can usually only meet them in full for three years, then tapering to nothing over the next 10 years. But where the project is to get patients out of hospital, these can in special circumstances be extended to 10 years of the full cost and 13 years in all. This is primarily because extra money may be needed to get the scheme going before the savings in ordinary health service expenditure become apparent. Once this has happened, funds going to the health and social services from central government will be adjusted accordingly. The Government is also making money available for pilot projects to encourage this development.

In the long run, the facilities developed in this way, and the shift of funds from health to local authorities, may also help people who are currently living in the community to go on doing so. But that is not the main aim of the present policy and there is always a risk that these potential patients will find themselves without the help that they need. Further, as Carson (1982b) points out, the transfer of resources does not automatically produce a better service, even for patients who have been in hospital. The crucial question is the type and quality of the care provided, rather than which authority should be responsible and who should pay for it.

3. *Residential Accommodation*

Local social services authorities can provide residential accommodation under three different powers. The first is paragraph

2(1)(*a*) of Schedule 8 to the 1977 Act. Circular 19/74 defines this accommodation very broadly as "residential homes, hostels, group houses, minimum support facilities or other appropriate accommodation," whether actually owned or managed by the authority or not. There is a positive duty to provide this for people ordinarily resident in their area and for people actually in the area who have no settled residence. More commonly, however, accommodation is provided under Part III of the 1948 Act. Section 21(1)(*a*) allows this for people "who by reason of age, infirmity or any other circumstances are in need of care and attention which is not otherwise available to them." This again is a positive duty for people ordinarily resident in their area or who are in urgent need. Authorities can accommodate people from other areas in their homes, or arrange for people from their own area to be accommodated in homes managed by another authority (s.21(4)) or by a voluntary organisation or a registered person (s.26). Section 29 of the same Act allows them to provide hostels for disabled people undertaking training or employment, and holiday homes, and to assist with finding suitable supportive lodgings, to employ wardens on warden-assisted housing schemes run by housing authorities, or to provide warden services for occupiers of private housing. All these can also be arranged with other authorities, or with voluntary organisations, "or otherwise" (circular 13/74).

Unlike the health authorities, however, social services authorities can charge for their services. Part III accommodation must be paid for (1948 Act, s.22; Health and Social Services and Social Security Adjudications Act 1983, Pt. VII). The amount levied is means-tested and residents living on supplementary benefit have their accommodation paid for and receive a small amount of pocket money for themselves. Local authorities have power to make whatever charges they think reasonable for their services under the 1977 Act or under section 29 of the 1948 Act (Health and Social Services and Social Security Adjudications Act 1983, s.17). But they do not have to do this, and they cannot charge more than it is reasonably practicable for the person to pay.

If a child is mentally disordered, he may be taken into care in any of the usual ways, provided of course that the grounds exist. His parents will usually have to contribute towards the cost of this, except when they are receiving supplementary benefit or family income supplement (Child Care Act 1980, ss.45 and 46). But the local authority is also allowed to accommodate a mentally disordered child who is being cared for under paragraph 2 of Schedule 8 to the 1977 Act in any community home, even though he is not technically in care (Mental Health Act 1959, s.9). This means that the normal contributions procedure does not apply, although the authority will be able to make a charge under section 17 of the Health and Social Services and Social Security Adjudications Act 1983.

Schedule 4 of that Act will replace the old system for the registration of residential care homes provided by voluntary organisations or by private individuals or concerns. This will be required for "any establishment which provides or is intended to provide, whether for reward or not, residential accommodation with both board and personal care for persons in need of personal care by reason of old age, disablement, past or present dependence on alcohol or drugs or past or present mental disorder" (para. 1(1)). Homes catering for fewer than four people are exempt (para. 1(4)) and so are a long list of places controlled under different legislation (para. 1(5)). These are, basically, hospitals, children's homes, schools, colleges and universities, and "any establishment managed or provided by a government department or local authority or by any authority or body constituted by an Act of Parliament or incorporated by Royal Charter." Mental nursing homes are also excluded, if that is their sole purpose, but dual registration will be necessary for homes which have some residents and some patients, and the Schedule introduces the option of dual registration for homes which may sometimes have both (para. 6).

Both the manager and the person in control of the home must be registered with the local social services authority for the area where the home is (paras. 4, 5 and 2). The authority must lay down a maximum number of residents and can make other conditions regulating the age, sex or category of people who can be accommodated there. These can be varied or added to from time to time (para. 7). The authority can refuse registration if the applicant or any other person concerned in carrying on the home is unfit to be so; or if the premises are unfit, because of their situation, construction, state of repair, accommodation, staffing or equipment; or if the way in which it is intended to carry on the home is such as not to provide the services or facilities reasonably required (para. 11).

In fact, the Secretary of State makes regulations about the facilities and service to be provided, the numbers and qualifications of staff to be employed and to be on duty, the records to be kept, the notices to be given about residents, events such as deaths, and the absences of staff, the information to be supplied by applicants for registration, and the form of the local authorities' registers (para. 19; there may be new regulations when the Act comes into force). Homes can be inspected at any time on behalf of either the Secretary of State or the registration authority and the regulations also provide for how often this must be done (para. 20).

Registration can be cancelled if the annual fee is not paid, or if the authority could have refused registration, or if the conditions are not complied with, or if the registered person is convicted of an offence under the Schedule or regulations in respect of this or any other home, or anyone is convicted of an offence in respect of this home (para. 12). Under the urgent procedure for cancellation, or for varying the conditions or adding a new one, the registration authority can apply *ex parte* to a single magistrate. He can make the order if it appears to him that there will be a serious risk to the life, health or well-being of the residents. The application must be supported by a written statement of the authority's reasons and the order itself must also be in writing. The authority must then service notice of the order and its terms, together with a copy of the supporting statement, on any registered person as soon as possible (para. 13). Otherwise, the normal procedure for refusing registration, or granting it subject to conditions which have not been agreed, or varying conditions, or cancelling registration, involves serving notices on the people concerned and allowing them to make representations to the authority (paras. 14 and 15). There is a right of appeal, against the decisions of the single magistrate or the registration authority, to the new registered homes tribunal established under the same Schedule (para. 17).

All of this is obviously aimed at securing reasonable standards in homes which cater for people who may not be able to insist on such standards for themselves. But the quality of life for residents in all types of home, public or private, is crucially affected by how far the home is prepared to go in allowing them to live their own lives and take their own decisions. There are two aspects to this. The home's own rules may restrict the residents' rights to choose how and where they spend their time. Homes are quite entitled to offer their accommodation on these terms, take it or leave it, despite the fact that their residents have nowhere else to go. More creditably, homes are only too well aware of their common law duty to take reasonable care of their residents. Rules may well be devised in order to avoid claims for personal injuries brought, for example, by an elderly resident who falls downstairs because there was no one to accompany him. However, homes have nothing to fear if they have taken reasonable precautions, or if a resident has chosen to take a risk of which he is perfectly well aware. The other aspect is more likely to arise in homes for mentally handicapped adults or for the elderly mentally infirm. Staff in these homes may be tempted to take decisions for their residents even though the law gives them no power to do so. We have already seen that people are entitled to make their own choices about such things as medical and dental treatment, provided that they are capable of understanding in very broad terms what is involved. We shall see in the next chapter that the same applies to such things as how their pocket money is to be spent. The mere fact that a person lives in residential care does not remove his right to self-determination in such matters, any more than the fact that he lives in hospital.

Some local authorities are becoming particularly conscious of how important this is, not only for the quality of life in their homes, but also in promoting the future independence of residents who could go further. They are developing codes of conduct which recognise the right of any resident to take those personal decisions which he is capable of understanding in very simple terms, even if his decision may not be the best. They are also trying to devise patterns of care which give residents as much freedom of action as possible, consistent with taking reasonable care for their safety. However, it should not be forgotten that the procedure under the National Assistance Acts (pages 128 to 133 above) can be used for admitting some residents compulsorily, little though anyone involved may like this.

4. *Education and Training*

Since 1971, it has been impossible for a local education authority (LEA) to declare any child ineducable. Every child, no matter how handicapped, became the responsibility of the education authorities, rather than the health or social services. LEAs must provide sufficient schools for all the pupils in their area (Education Act 1944, s.8(1)). This includes all children of compulsory school age, but also senior pupils up to the age of 19 who want to continue their education (ss.8(2)(*b*) and 114(1)). This is particularly important for mentally handicapped young people, who are often just beginning to make real progress around the age of 16. A successful campaign was launched on their behalf during 1980 to ensure that LEAs recognised their responsibilities. During this, there was a real possibility of the Secretary of State invoking his powers under section 68 or 99 of the 1944 Act. Section 68 allows him to intervene if an LEA has behaved unreasonably, while section 99 allows him to step in where they are in default. LEAs also have power, but no duty, to provide schools for children below compulsory school age, which is again particularly valuable for those with learning difficulties (Education Act 1980, s.24).

In providing schools, LEAs must have regard to the need for securing that special educational provision is made for pupils who have special educational needs (s.8(2)(*c*)). Generally, however, these children should be educated in ordinary schools (Education Act 1981, s.2(2)). But this is only a duty if it is compatible with giving a particular child the special education which he needs, with the efficient education of his school mates, and with the efficient use of resources (s.2(3)). Otherwise, he must be educated in a special school, unless the LEA are satisfied that even this would be "inappropriate." In that case, after consultation with his parents, they may arrange for all or part of his education to be provided in some other way. (s.3).

The procedure for identifying children with special educational needs, and deciding how best to provide for those needs, is also laid down in the 1981 Act (see Hannon, 1982). LEAs have first to make an assessment of whether a child for whom they are responsible has such needs. They are responsible for all the children in their own schools, or whom they maintain in school, and for any other child who is drawn to their attention and is at least two years old but not over compulsory school age (s.4). Parents can ask the LEA to assess any child for whom the LEA are responsible and they must do so unless they think this unreasonable (s.9(1)). LEAs can also assess the needs of a child under the age of two, provided that the parents agree, and they must do so if the parents ask (s.6). But even if they do decide that he has special needs, they do not have the same duty to provide for them as they have for children over the age of two. Nevertheless, early identification is most important and will usually take place during the developmental assessments provided by the district health authority. If a health authority think that a child under five probably has special needs, they must tell the parents about this, and also about any voluntary organisation which may be able to help. After giving the parents an opportunity of discussing things, the authority must notify the LEA (s.10). But children may also be drawn to their attention by other people and in other ways.

Even if the LEA are responsible, they need only make an assessment if they think that the child either has or probably has special needs (s.5(1)). This means one of three things: (a) that he has significantly greater difficulty in learning than the majority of children of his age; or (b) that he has a disability which prevents or hinders him from using the educational facilities generally provided for children of his age in the local schools; or (c) that he is under the age of five and likely to fall within either of these categories, or to do so unless special provision is made for him now (s.1(2)). Parents must be involved in this assessment, but they also have a duty to co-operate with any medical, psychological, educational or other examination required (s.5(3) and Sched. 1). The LEA will decide whether the child has special educational needs, and if so, whether they are called upon to determine what special educational provision should be made for him. If they decide that they are not called upon to do this (which they could do even if he had special needs), the parents can appeal to the Secretary of State for Education and Science (s.5(6)). But all he can do is ask the LEA to think again (s.5(8)). Only if what they decide is manifestly unreasonable, or in some way defaults on their legal obligations, can he use his powers under section 68 or 99 of the 1944 Act. He is usually most reluctant to do this.

He has much more control once the LEA do decide that they should determine what special educational provision should be made for the child. Then they must set about making and maintaining a statement of his needs and the provision to be made. This process must again involve the parents (s.7) and afterwards they can appeal to an education appeal committee (s.8). In ordinary school allocation cases, the committee's decision is binding, but in these cases, the committee can only either confirm what the LEA has decided or send the case back for them to think again. But the parents can then appeal against the final outcome to the Secretary of State, who can either confirm, amend or scrap the statement altogether. The parents can also ask for the reassessment of a "statemented" child who has not been assessed for the last six months, and the LEA must comply unless they think this inappropriate (s.9(2)). The statement itself must always be reviewed if there is a reassessment and within 12 months of its making or last review (Sched. 1).

While a statement exists for a child for whom the LEA are responsible, the LEA *must* provide the education specified in it, unless the parents have made suitable arrangements for themselves (s.7(2)). Parents have the usual duty to ensure that children of compulsory school age receive efficient full-time education suitable to their age, ability, aptitude and any special educational needs they may have (1944 Act, s.36). If they do not send such a child to school or make proper alternative provision, the usual enforcement procedures can be invoked (ss.37 to 40). But if the parents and LEA disagree about the school to be named in a school attendance order, the matter can be resolved by reference to the Secretary of State (1981 Act, ss.15 and 16). This is not an option available to other parents. Similarly, parents cannot withdraw their child from a special school without the LEA's agreement, but they can then refer the matter to the Secretary of State (s.11(2)). This all means that the Secretary of State has, in effect, the final word about what the child's statement should contain. Unfortunately, he does not have so much control over whether the statement should be made at all. Some parents may be fighting to have proper provision made for their child in an ordinary school, while others may be fighting to get him into a special school. The armour at their disposal will vary according to the stage at which the LEA says "no". That cannot be right.

Once the LEA's responsibilities are over, the local social services authority should assume the task of continuing training for those suffering from mental disorder of any type. It is their duty under Schedule 8 to the 1977 Act to provide adult training centres and other facilities for this purpose (circular 19/74).

5. *Other Services*

Assisting disabled people of all kinds to find work is primarily the responsibility of the Department of Employment's agencies, under the Disabled Persons (Employment) Act 1944. The definition of disablement includes those whose mental disorder substantially handicaps them from obtaining or keeping a job, or doing work on their own account, of a kind which apart from their disability they would be suited to doing. Under section 3 of the Disabled Persons (Employment) Act 1958, however, local social services authorities have the power (and the duty for people living in their area) to provide sheltered employment for the disabled, either themselves or through voluntary organisations. This duty has obviously not resulted in a place in a sheltered workshop for every unemployed mentally disordered person who would like one.

Social services authorities also have power, under both the 1977 Act and section 29 of the 1948 Act, to provide occupational, social, cultural and recreational facilities, at day centres and elsewhere. They may make payments for work undertaken and also provide meals. They may provide home helps and laundry services under paragraph 3 of schedule 8 to the 1977 Act. District councils have, of course, power to provide meals and recreation for old people (rather than for the mentally disordered as such) under Part II of Schedule 9 to the Health and Social Services and Social Security Adjudications Act 1983. This can be done through voluntary organisations, and meals are often provided in the old person's own home. But day services for elderly and psychiatric patients are also provided on a large scale by the health authorities in day treatment units.

A wide variety of other services can be provided to help people living independently or with their families. The support and advice of social workers can be given under both the 1977 Act and section 29 of the 1948 Act. Under the former, this is comprehensively described as "social work and related services to help in the identification, diagnosis, assessment and social treatment of mental disorder and to provide social work support and other domiciliary and care services to people living in their own homes or elsewhere" (circular 19/74). Social workers are the main protection provided by society against the exploitation and abuse of mental patients living in the community. Those approved under the Mental Health Act have powers to enter private premises, and to apply for warrants to remove patients to a place of safety, which are designed to help them carry out this essential function (see Chapter 4).

More commonly, however, their unhappy task is to act as gate-keepers and rationers of the scarce facilities which exist. A great many things can and should be provided for disabled people under section 2 of the Chronically Sick and Disabled Persons Act 1970. These include home adaptations, televisions, telephones in the home, as well as holidays, and cultural and recreational facilities outside it. Once again, this is a duty towards people who are ordinarily resident in the area and for whom they are necessary. Section 1 of that Act also obliges social services authorities to discover how many people in their area are covered by section 29 of the 1948 Act and to ensure that they are adequately informed of the service available. The first of these objects is secured by keeping registers of disabled people (circular 13/74). The mentally disordered have just as much right as any other person falling within that definition to be included upon those registers.

6. *Guardianship*

Guardianship was originally intended as the community care equivalent of compulsory admission for treatment or an ordinary hospital order. The grounds and procedures are still remarkably similar and in theory patients can readily be transferred from hospital to guardianship and vice versa. In practice, this does not happen. Long term civil commitment was used more than 2,000 times in 1978, but there were only 138 cases of guardianship. The Royal College of Psychiatrists, the British Association of Social Workers, MIND, and also the Butler Committee on Mentally Abnormal Offenders all thought that it should be used more often. Quite unintentionally, the 1959 Act had led to a deep divide between possible compulsion in hospital and almost complete freedom outside it. Unfortunately, they disagreed about the purposes for which compulsion should be available in the community. The DHSS could see all the arguments against it. The effect of guardianship has therefore been reduced and clarified.

Only time will tell whether it has become any more useful or the authorities any more willing to take it on.

(a) *The grounds*

In both civil and criminal cases, the patient must be at least 16 years old (Mental Health Act 1983, ss.7(1) and 37(2)(*a*)(ii)). There are plenty of other ways of ensuring that a child below that age receives the care or control which he needs, and these have already been discussed in Chapter 3. The purpose of guardianship is to provide a more limited form of control for people over that age. The patient must be suffering from mental illness, psychopathic disorder, severe mental impairment or mental impairment, of a nature or degree which warrants his reception into guardianship under the Act (ss.7(2)(*a*) and 37(2)(*a*)). There is no need for the disorder to be "treatable," because the object is not medical treatment as such. But a handicapped person does have to fall within the definition of "impairment" discussed in Chapter 2. This means that guardianship cannot be used to help handicapped people unless their impaired intelligence and social functioning is also associated with abnormally aggressive or seriously irresponsible conduct on their part (s.1(2)). Guardianship might have provided a valuable method of protecting, rather than undermining, the rights of mentally handicapped adults, but the opportunity of developing it as such has been lost.

The second criterion in a civil case is that "it is necessary in the interests of the welfare of the patient or for the protection of other persons that the patient should be so received" (s.7(2)(*b*)). The reference to welfare clearly indicates that the institution is meant to help the patient and improve his general quality of life. The alternative of protecting other people is unlikely to arise very often, because the guardian's powers are not very effective in doing this. For a court guardianship order, there is no reference to the patient's welfare or the protection of other people, but the court must consider it the most suitable method of dealing with the case, in all the circumstances (s.37(2)(*b*)). The choices available to courts dealing with mentally disordered offenders have already been canvassed in Chapter 5. But as hospitals become ever more reluctant to accept handicapped and inadequate offenders, guardianship could provide a useful alternative if only courts and social services authorities could be persuaded to adopt it.

(b) *The procedures*

Courts can make guardianship orders for the same offences and with the same sort of medical evidence as is required for an ordinary hospital order. In civil cases, the application for reception may be made either by an approved social worker (on Form 18) or by the patient's nearest relative (on Form 17)(s.11(1)). As with an application for admission to hospital for treatment, the social worker must if possible consult the nearest relative and cannot apply if the relative objects (s.11(4)). But he could then ask the county court to replace the nearest relative on the ground that the objection was unreasonable (s.29(3)(c)). The details appear in Chapter 3. The obvious assumption is that guardianship is neither necessary nor appropriate if the patient is being cared for by a nearest relative who is acting responsibly. This is questionable. The application must be founded on the recommendations of two doctors (s.7(3)). Forms 19 and 20 require them to give a clinical description of the patient's mental condition and to explain why he cannot appropriately be cared for without powers of guardianship. The implication is that guardianship is something to be avoided unless the patient will not accept care without it. The rules about the medical examinations, the doctors' qualifications and relationships with one another and with the other people involved are the same as those for compulsory admission to hospital. There is obviously no problem about a possible connection with the admitting hospital, but neither doctor may be or be related to the proposed guardian (s.12(7)). The details appear in Chapter 3. There is nothing to prevent the applicant proposing himself as guardian, but neither the nearest relative nor an approved social worker is at all likely to do so.

The application is always addressed to the local social services authority and must reach them within 14 days of the second medical examination (s.8(2)). If the proposed guardian is a private individual, the application must state that he is willing to act, but is ineffective unless accepted on his behalf by the local social services authority for the area where he, not the patient, lives (s.7(5)). Otherwise, the proposed guardian may be any social services authority, not necessarily the one for the area where the patient lives. But the application has no effect unless it is accepted by the authority proposed as guardian (s.8(1)). Most authorities are unlikely to accept responsibility for patients to whom they owe no legal duty to provide care. Similarly, a court cannot make a guardianship order unless satisfied that the proposed guardian is willing to act (s.37(6)). If he is a private individual, he must be approved by a local social services authority (s.37(1)). Guardianship is effective the moment the order is made or the application accepted.

(c) *The effect*

The 1959 Act gave the guardian the powers which a father has over a child under the age of 14. Some people thought that this reduced the patient to the status of such a child, so that he could never marry or make contracts. Others thought that it simply prevented him from doing these things without his guardian's consent. No one knew whether the guardian had any power over the patient's property. In any case, it was much too vague. But because it was so wide, it was generally used to provide a substitute parent for a mentally handicapped person living in the community. Even then, it was not thought necessary unless he seemed reluctant to accept the authority of those who were looking after him. No one seems to have considered whether it might actually be illegal to exercise control over the affairs of a handicapped adult without obtaining some statutory power to do so.

The British Association of Social Workers (1977) wanted to develop guardianship along the lines originally intended by the Percy Commission, as a full-scale alternative to hospital care. The Butler Committee (1975) and MIND (Gostin, 1977) were particularly concerned about the compulsory supervision of unrestricted patients after their discharge from hospital. Guardianship could certainly be used for this, but the Butler Committee thought that leave of absence was preferable. This is controlled by hospital doctors, and includes both the power to impose treatment and a right of recall. Guardianship is controlled by local authority social workers and gives no right of recall. Nor does it any longer give the power to impose treatment. It is very doubtful whether it should.

Undoubtedly, many hospital patients could be discharged if there were a way of ensuring that they accepted long-acting injections from a clinic or visiting nurse. But these drugs do have undesirable side-effects and other consequences if used for long periods. It is much easier for the Mental Health Act Commission to control and monitor their compulsory use inside hospitals.

The DHSS (1978) were sympathetic to the argument that compulsion outside hospital should be kept to a minimum. They were clearly suspicious of the ability of social workers to handle it properly, and of the lack of any effective sanctions for patients who refused to co-operate. The precise ways in which patients might be given protection against abuse and exploitation by those around them were not explored. Instead, they opted for the approach which limited guardianship to the "essential powers" needed to secure the patient's co-operation with his community care.

The guardian now has three powers over the patient, to the exclusion of any other person who might have them: (a) to require the patient to reside at a place specified by the guardian or by the local social services authority; (b) to require the patient to attend at places and times similarly specified for the purpose of medical treatment, occupation, education or training; and (c) to require access to the patient to be given, at any place where the patient is residing, to any doctor, approved social worker or other person similarly specified (ss.8(2) and 40(2)). The guardian can therefore insist that the patient attends a clinic for treatment, or receives a visit from a doctor or a nurse. But should the patient refuse the treatment, the Act gives no power to force it upon him (see s.56(1)). There is no sanction for disobeying the guardian's commands, but a patient who absconds from the place where his guardian requires him to live can be recaptured in the same way as a hospital patient who goes absent without leave (see page 232). In their current mood, the courts might threaten to punish him for contempt of a guardianship order, but this is not even a possibility in civil cases. In practice, the lack of sanctions is probably not a problem, for most people are prepared to obey those who have a clear right to command them.

The guardian also has duties, laid down in the Mental Health (Hospital, Guardianship and Consent to Treatment) Regulations 1983. A private guardian is in fact under the control of the responsible local social services authority, for he must comply with their directions when exercising his powers and duties. He must appoint a doctor as the patient's "nominated medical attendant" and notify the name and address to the authority. He must notify his own and the patient's address to the authority straightaway, and any permanent change in either address beforehand or within seven days. But if he moves into a different local authority area, he must give all these particulars to the new authority and also tell the old one what has happened. He must also furnish the responsible authority with whatever reports or other information about the patient they require, and tell them as soon as possible if the guardianship comes to an end (reg. 12).

Whoever is the guardian, the responsible local social services authority must arrange for the patient to be visited at regular intervals. This must be at least every three months, and at least one visit annually must be by an approved doctor (reg. 13). The Mental Welfare Commission for Scotland (1970) were enthusiastic about guardianship, perhaps because of the long-standing Scottish tradition of boarding-out handicapped people on remote crofts and farms. They point out that the statutory powers ensure that someone keeps an eye on patients who may well need support and protection from outside. Compulsory supervision in the community should not be regarded with as much disfavour as detention and treatment in hospital.

If a private guardian dies or resigns (by written notice to the authority) the authority automatically take over for the time being, but could transfer the patient into the guardianship of another individual (s.10(1)). The authority, or someone authorised by them, may also exercise the functions of a private guardian while he is incapacitated in some way (s.10(2)). A private guardian may also be replaced by order of the county court, on the application of an approved social worker, if he has performed his functions negligently or in a manner contrary to the patient's interests (s.10(3)).

The patient can be transferred from one guardian to another on the authority of his existing guardian (Form 26), provided that this is confirmed by the incoming responsible social services authority, who must specify a date, and agreed by any proposed new private guardian (reg. 8(2)). The form of the patient's disorder may be reclassified on Form 23, by his nominated medical attendant if he is in private guardianship, or by the responsible medical officer if the guardian is a local authority (s.16(5)). The responsible medical officer means the medical officer authorised by the authority to act, either generally or in any particular case or for any particular purpose (s.34(1)). Now that the medical officer of health has disappeared, authorities will have to look outside their own employees, but will probably still turn to community physicians. Reclassification will have no legal effect, because there is no distinction between the different forms of disorder for the purposes of guardianship (unlike hospital admission, where the "treatability" test applies differently between the major and minor disorders), but it will preserve the accuracy of the documents.

From all this it is clear that the role of a private guardian is modelled on that of foster parents, although the local authority does not have quite the same degree of control and the patient's family is more powerful than it is when a child is in compulsory care. Boarding patients out is not as common here as it used to be in Scotland and there is likely to be little scope for private guardianship in its new form. Local authorities may, however, be more willing to use it themselves.

(d) *Duration and termination*

Like hospital admission for treatment, guardianship lasts initially for six months, but may be renewed for a further six months and then for a year at a time (s.20(1)). The RMO or nominated medical attendant must examine the patient within the last two months of the period, and report to the guardian and to the responsible social services authority on Form 31 if the grounds for guardianship still exist. This automatically renews it, unless the authority decides to discharge the patient (s.20(6), (7) and (8)). The patient can be discharged at any time by the RMO, by the responsible local social services authority, or in civil cases but not in court orders (section 40(4) and Sched. 1, Pt. I) by his nearest relative (who may use Form 35 and must serve the order on the authority)(s.23(2)(*b*). The RMO cannot prevent the nearest relative from discharging the patient, but an application could be made to the county court to replace the relative on the ground that he was proposing to discharge, or had discharged, the patient without due regard to the patient's welfare or the interests of the public (page 86 above). Interestingly, the private guardian or the nominated medical attendant of a patient with a private guardian cannot discharge the patient. The powers of mental health review tribunals to do so are discussed in Chapter 8. Transfer from guardianship to hospital and from hospital to guardianship are discussed in Chapters 4 and 7 respectively.

7. Commentary

English law still cuts a pretty poor figure on both sets of issues outlined at the beginning of this chapter. In theory, the welfare state has accepted the "ideology of entitlement" (Gostin, 1983a). The courts, however, have largely abandoned the enforcement of that ideology to the politicians. They, as we know, have found it hard to persuade themselves or their constituents of the public good involved in developing community services for the mentally disordered. The public good in keeping them out of sight is so much more obvious. Significantly, the most progress has been made in education. Here the law is much more explicit and is allied to a century-long tradition of universal provision. The hospital services are also allied to such a tradition, although they would now prefer others to take it on. There is not, and never has been, any tradition of universal provision in the social services. The current enthusiasm for community care may indicate a political change of heart. But it is just as likely to indicate a desire to transfer responsibility from one service to another, without any corresponding increase in what is available.

We may have done a little better on the issue of safeguarding people's ordinary rights. Local authorities are very much more conscious of the status of residents in their homes than they used to be. The best local authority practice can often be ahead of that in the private sector on issues such as this. The "essential powers" approach to guardianship may have two advantages. Local authorities could become much more willing to take it on, even though they will have to arrange regular visits. These in themselves should assist in guarding patients against exploitation and abuse. And the patients themselves will lose far fewer of their ordinary rights than they used to do. This is very much to the good, if only we could be sure that other people were not in fact invading those rights every day. This will almost always be with the best of intentions and by people who are doing a wonderful job in caring for mentally handicapped and elderly people. The law is too often seen by such people as a means of taking rights away from their charges. It is also, however, a means of ensuring that they themselves do not do so. Guardianship has never been designed with this problem in mind and we must now turn to whether there are other ways of safeguarding the ordinary legal rights of mental patients.

10 Ordinary Legal Rights

Many ordinary legal rights can be affected by a person's mental disorder and there is certainly no room in this book to discuss them all (see Venables, 1975). Two principles stand out. First, in most cases, the decision turns on the individual's capacity to perform the particular function in question. It does not depend upon whether or not he is in hospital, or whether he is an informal or a compulsory patient. Nor does it usually turn on his capacity to perform the function well or wisely, but on whether he can understand in broad terms what he is doing and the effects of doing it. Secondly, however, there are circumstances in which a person may be denied the right to make his own decisions, either in general or in a particular case. But this can only happen where there is a legal power to control him. It must not happen simply because, for example, the parents of a mentally handicapped adult believe that they can spend his money for his benefit more wisely than he can.

The underlying philosophy suggested by the United Nations Declaration on the Rights of Mentally Retarded Persons (1971) expects them to enjoy the same rights as other people, to the maximum degree of feasibility (Art. 1). But if they are unable to exercise those rights in a meaningful way, or it becomes necessary to restrict or deny them, there should be legal safeguards against every form of abuse. "This procedure must be based on the evaluation of the social capability of the mentally retarded person by qualified experts and must be subject to periodic review and to the right of appeal to higher authorities" (Art. 7). The European Declaration of Human Rights is not so precise, but it does insist that "in the determination of his civil rights and obligations or of any criminal charge against him, everyone is entitled to a fair and public hearing within a reasonable time by an independent and impartial tribunal established by law" (Art. 6(1)). Other Articles of the Convention are relevant to the right to vote and to family relationships.

1. *Public Law*

(a) *Standing and voting in elections*

At common law, "persons of unsound mind" and "idiots" can neither vote nor stand in elections. But these terms probably depend upon the usual test of legal capacity: at the time of voting, can the individual understand in broad terms what he is doing and the effects of doing it? If the person is on the register and turns up to vote, the question is one of fact for the officer presiding at the polling station. People are in practice asked only their name and address and whether they have already voted in the election. If they can answer, they are allowed to vote and the result is unlikely to be challenged.

However it can be difficult for a patient to obtain registration or get to the polling station. To be registered, a person must be resident in the constituency or ward on the qualifying date. A person who enters hospital after that date may be on the register, but he will only be able to cast his vote if he can leave hospital to go to the polls or qualifies for a postal vote. He will only qualify for a postal vote if he has since become resident in a constituency other than the one where he is registered. These rules will obviously make it very difficult for a compulsory patient to vote, even if he is registered in his home constituency. And if he is already in hospital on the qualifying date, he may or may not still be regarded as resident at his home. This is a complex question, depending on such factors as the length of absence, his intention to return, and any legal restraint on his return home. Some compulsory patients may be entitled to register (provided that some-one remembers to put them on the form or they remember to check) whereas others may not. But if a compulsory patient cannot be treated as resident at home, he cannot be treated as resident at the hospital where he is detained (Representation of the People Act 1983, s.7(1)).

Similarly, an informal patient may still be resident at his home address. He may even be resident at the hospital, provided that it is not one which is "maintained wholly or mainly for the reception and treatment of persons suffering from any form of mental disorder" (s.7(2)). Patients in such hospitals used to be entirely disenfranchised, whereas those in general hospitals were not. The

Scottish Mental Welfare Commission had long been campaigning for a change in the law, and reforms were supported by the Speaker's Conferences on Electoral Law in 1968 and 1973. The rule was probably also a breach of Article 3 of Protocol No. 1 to the European Convention on Human Rights. This binds the contracting countries to "hold free elections at reasonable intervals by secret ballot, under conditions which will ensure the free expression of the opinion of the people in the choice of the legislature." This has been said to imply the recognition of universal suffrage, although certain limited groups may be disqualified (*X.* v. *Federal Republic of Germany*, applic. no. 2728/66, (1967) 10 Y.B. E.Comm. H.R. 336). The Commission has also said that the restrictions should not be arbitrary (*W.X.Y.Z.* v. *Belgium*, applic. nos. 6573/74 and 6746/74, (1975) 2 D.R.E.Comm. H.R. 110). A disqualification which depends upon a person's address, rather than his capacity to vote, is clearly arbitrary. Nevertheless, the greatest impetus to reform probably came when two county court judges decided that people who were not suffering from mental disorder, but who lived in the hospital because they had nowhere else to go, were not "patients" and might therefore be registered as resident at the hospital (*Wild and Others* v. *Registration Officer for the Borough of Warrington*, Warrington County Court, June 15, 1976; *Smith and Others* v. *Jackson*, Blackburn County Court, September 16, 1981). The results of local, if not national, elections in constituencies where there were large mental hospitals might well have been affected. Hence a different procedure has been devised for registering people who are voluntary patients in these hospitals (Representation of the People Act 1983, s.7(2) to (9)).

During the 12 months before a qualifying date, the patient may make a declaration, provided that he can do so without assistance (unless this is required because of blindness or some other physical incapacity). This must state that on the date of the declaration, and on the next qualifying date, unless the two are the same, he is or will be a "voluntary mental patient" at a "mental hospital." It must give the address of the hospital, but also the United Kingdom address where the patient would be resident if he were not in hospital, or, if he cannot give such an address, any address (apart from a mental hospital) in the United Kingdom where he has at some time resided. It must also state that he is a Commonwealth or Irish Republic citizen, whether he has reached the age of 18, and if he has not, his date of birth. It must confirm that it has been made without help and be attested in the prescribed way. Once this is sent to the registration officer, the patient is entitled to be registered as resident at the address *outside* the hospital. Hence if he gives more than one, the declaration is void. But if the patient applies, he is entitled to a postal vote, so that there will be no problem about getting to the polling station. The declaration is effective for both national and local elections, but it cannot be made specially for the purpose of local elections unless the patient is a peer (who is only entitled to vote in local elections).

Curiously, therefore, residents in mental hospitals may have to pass a rather more stringent capacity test than most, but they are then given rather more help in recording their votes than are many other people who are away from home. Hospitals are also more likely be aware of their patients' rights than are the people in charge of residential homes for mentally disordered people in the community. It would be interesting to know how many of them think to register their residents or take them to the polling station.

It is to be hoped that no legally incapable candidate would ever be elected, but a sitting member might later become so. It cannot be a breach of Parliamentary privilege for him to be compulsorily admitted to hospital, as there is now a statutory procedure for vacating the seat of any Member of Parliament who has been compulsorily detained because of mental illness for more than six months (Mental Health Act 1983, s.141). (The detention of peers was to be tested by habeas corpus in 1983, but the patient was discharged before the hearing).

(b) *Serving on juries*

Apart from standing and voting in elections, the main badge of citizenship is the right and duty to serve on a jury. But a large number of mentally disordered people are ineligible to do so (Juries Act 1974, s.1 and Sched. 1, Group D). They fall into three categories. One is any person who is at present under guardianship. Another is any person who has been determined by a judge to be incapable of managing his property and affairs. But the main category is very wide. It covers anyone who suffers or has suffered from mental illness, psychopathic disorder, mental handicap or severe mental handicap and because of that is either resident in a hospital "or other similar institution" or "regularly attends for treatment by a medical practitioner." The definition of ordinary and severe mental handicap for this purpose is the same as the definition of ordinary or severe mental impairment under the Mental Health Act (page 53 above), but without the reference to abnormally aggressive or seriously irresponsible conduct. Significant or severe impairment of intellectual and social functioning is enough. Of course, if a broad view of "mental illness" is taken, an anxious or depressed person who regularly takes medication prescribed by a doctor is ineligible to serve. A psychopath who has been discharged from Broadmoor and is at present receiving no medical treatment can do so, unless disqualified on other grounds.

(c) *Driving*

An applicant for a driving licence must disclose any prescribed disability, as must a licence holder if he acquires one or it gets worse (Road Traffic Act 1972, ss.87 and 87A). The prescribed disabilities used to cover both detained and informal hospital patients and those whose property was in the hands of a receiver, neither of which has any necessary connection with driving ability. Now the only mental disabilities are severe mental handicap, as a result of which the patient is under guardianship or receiving local authority care, and epilepsy, unless the patient has been free from attacks for two years or has had attacks only while asleep for the past three years, and his driving is not likely to be a source of danger (Motor Vehicle (Driving Licence) Regulations 1981, as amended). On learning of such a disability, the Department must refuse or revoke a licence.

2. *Sexual and Family Relationships*

Article 8 of the European Convention on Human Rights secures for everyone the right to respect for his private and family life, his home and his correspondence. The only exceptions allowed are those which are necessary in a democratic society in the interests of national security, public safety or the economic well-being of the country, for the prevention of disorder or crime, for the protection of health or morals, or for the protection of the rights and freedoms of others. On the other hand, the United Nations

Declaration on the Rights of Mentally Retarded Persons (1971) recognises the person's right to live with his own family. But it says nothing about his right to develop sexual and family relationships for himself. The whole subject is still regarded as extremely delicate. There are obvious risks of degradation and exploitation, against which some people may need protection. But that protection need not be given at the cost of denying to mentally handicapped people the opportunity to form warm and satisfying relationships. English law is more liberal on the subject than many people seem to realise.

(a) *Sexual offences against mentally disordered people*

All the usual offences which protect people against sexual aggression or the exploitation of youth apply equally to mentally disordered people (although the difficulties of proof are even more formidable than usual). They are also protected against exploitation by the people who ought to be looking after them. It is an offence for a man on the staff of, or employed in, or who is one of the managers of a hospital or mental nursing home to have extra-marital sexual intercourse with a woman who is at present receiving treatment for mental disorder in that hospital or home; it is also an offence for him to have such intercourse on the premises with a woman who is receiving treatment there as an out-patient; and it is an offence for a man to have such intercourse with a mentally disordered woman who is under his guardianship, or otherwise in his custody or care under the Mental Health Act, or under arrangements made under the National Health Service Act 1977, Part III of the National Assistance Act 1948, or as a resident in a residential care home under the Health and Social Services and Social Security Adjudications Act 1983 (Mental Health Act 1959, s.128). The maximum penalty is two years' imprisonment, but it is not an offence if the man did not know and had no reason to suspect the woman to be a mentally disordered patient, and the consent of the Director of Public Prosecutions is required for any proceedings.

This offence applies to people suffering from any form of mental disorder, but otherwise the only people who are protected from, or denied the benefit of, extra-marital sexual intercourse are the severely mentally handicapped. It is an offence for a man to have such intercourse with any woman who suffers from "a state of arrested or incomplete development of mind which includes severe impairment of intelligence and social functioning," unless he did not know and had no reason to suspect her to be so (Sexual Offences Act 1956, ss.7 and 45). The man involved may find it difficult to determine whether the woman is "severely" rather than only "significantly" handicapped. So may the authorities. But the definition could include some women who are capable of giving an effective consent to intercourse and would not be harmed by it. Hence the Criminal Law Revision Committee (1980b) have tentatively suggested replacing section 7 with a civil procedure for prohibiting a particular man from having intercourse with a particular woman. The nearest relative, Mental Health Act guardian, an approved social worker or manager of services being used by the woman might apply to the county court on the ground either of risk of harm or of her incapacity to consent. This would remove any general deterrent, particularly to intercourse with promiscuous women, and the risk of pregnancy might increase. But the idea of giving county courts some paternal jurisdiction over severely handicapped people could be extended to other fields, including the vexed questions of contraception and abortion (discussed in Chapter 6). It has far-reaching implications which would be better discussed as a whole than in isolation.

Ironically, of course, the man himself is also likely to be handicapped. It is wrong that he should run a greater risk of prosecution than does the woman if neither has been in any way exploiting the other. No doubt the authorities will bear these things in mind. Severely handicapped men are protected against, or denied the benefit of, homosexual acts in the same circumstances as the two offences against women described above (Sexual Offences Act 1967, s.1(3) and (4)).

(b) *Marriage*

The capacity to marry is not the same as the capacity to have extra-marital sexual relations. English law takes a relaxed view of the qualifications for matrimony, although it seeks to preserve the idea that it is a voluntary union. There are two grounds on which marriage of a mentally disordered person might be annulled. The first is that he did not give a valid consent to it, because of "unsoundness of mind" (Matrimonial Causes Act 1973, s.12(c)).

This only applies if at the time of the ceremony the bride or groom could not understand the nature of the contract being entered and appreciate its basic responsibilities. As marriage is a relatively simple and well-known concept, few people who can actually get through the ceremony are likely to be incapable under this test. An elderly and confused person might even be able to get married but unable to make a new will on the same day (*In the Estate of Park, Park* v. *Park* [1954] P. 112). The second ground is that, although able to give a valid consent, the bride or groom was suffering (whether continously or intermittently) from mental disorder within the meaning of the Mental Health Act, but this must be "of such a kind or to such an extent as to be unfitted for marriage" (s.12(*d*)). In *Bennett* v. *Bennett* [1969] 1 W.L.R. 430, Ormrod J. decided that it was not enough that the wife was difficult to live with because of her disorder and should probably not have got married. She had to be incapable of living in the married state and carrying out the ordinary duties and obligations of marriage, and this she was not.

In that case, it was the mentally disordered person's spouse who wished to have the marriage annulled. But the mentally disordered person himself might equally well wish to do so, particularly if he had been tricked or exploited in some way. However, although either party may apply to the court, these grounds render the marriage voidable, rather than void. They do not invalidate it completely and automatically. They simply allow the court to annul it, if asked to do so by either party while they are both alive. Even after a decree, it is treated as if it had existed up till that time (s.16). This means that any children of the marriage are automatically legitimate, but it also has less desirable effects. Marriage automatically revokes a previous will, unless that will provides that this is not to happen when the testator marries a particular person (Wills Act 1937, s.18). Even if the testator was so disordered as to be incapable of consenting to the marriage, his surviving spouse will be entitled to claim his estate under rules of intestacy (*Re Roberts, Roberts* v. *Roberts* [1978] 1 W.L.R. 653).

There is obviously a danger that "old and lonely people not fully in control of all their mental faculties are particularly susceptible to the attentions of fortune hunters" (Law Commission, 1982). There are two possible solutions. If the person is unable to make a new will for himself, the Court of Protection may now agree to make one for him (see below and *Re Davey* (*deceased*) [1980] 1 W.L.R. 164, for an example of a will made by the court in just these circumstances). The alternative is to petition for nullity. This will not revive the earlier will, but it will remove the automatic right of the spouse to a share in the intestacy or under any will which was made after the marriage (Wills Act 1837, s.18A). If the mentally disordered person is unable to petition for himself, once again the Court of Protection may do it for him (see below). At present, a petition on either of these grounds must be brought within three years of the marriage (Matrimonial Causes Act 1973, s.13(2)). The Law Commission (1980 and 1982) have been troubled that these marriages may only be discovered some time afterwards and that it may take still more time to get the proceedings under way. Hence they suggest that the court should have power to extend the limit, if this seems just, and this is provided for in the Matrimonial and Family Proceedings Bill 1983–84.

None of this will solve the problem of the person who dies before anything is done. In view of all this, it might be thought better to prevent the marriage taking place at all. Anyone can enter a caveat with a superintendant registrar against the issue of a certificate or licence for the marriage of a named person (Marriage Act 1949, s.29). The registrar cannot then issue the certificate or licence until he has looked into the matter and satisfied himself that the caveat ought not to obstruct it. If in doubt, he can refer it to the Registrar-General, or if he refuses the certificate or licence, the person named can appeal to the Registrar-General. A frivolous caveat can result in costs and damages for the named person. Even if the Registrar-General refuses the certificate or licence, the matter could be taken to the High Court by way of judicial review. The question would then arise of the principles to be applied in dealing with caveats.

Fairly obviously, the purpose is to prevent marriages which would otherwise be void. It cannot be intended to obstruct the freedom of adults to marry whom they wish. But marriages which might be voidable on either of the above grounds fall between these two extremes. The general reason for making a marriage voidable rather than void is to allow the parties themselves to decide whether they wish to continue it or not. If they are happy, the state does not interfere. Logically, therefore, the registrar should not deny a certificate for the marriage of a mentally disordered person any more than he should deny one to a person who cannot consummate the marriage. He certainly should not deny one simply because some doctor believes that his patient ought not to get married. But this logic rather breaks down at the point where the person is actually incapable of consenting to the marriage, for to carry out such a ceremony knowing this fact would be contrary to the long-standing tradition of the "voluntary union." With hindsight, it is a great shame that marriages without consent, which were void at common law, became voidable if contracted on or after August 1, 1971. Although the matter has never been tested, the registrar probably could refuse to carry out the marriage of an incapable person, but not one which simply *might* be voidable because of mental disorder.

Indeed, the law now goes out of its way to help the marriage of patients who are detained under any of the long term powers in the Mental Health Act. Under the Marriage Act 1983, they may be married at the hospital (s.1 and Sched. 1).

(c) *Divorce*

An existing marriage may break down because of one spouse's mental disorder. The fact that he is not to blame is no longer an obstacle to divorce or other forms of relief. A divorce can be granted after they have lived apart for five years, unless this would cause the respondent grave financial or other hardship and it would be wrong to grant it (Matrimonial Causes Act 1973, ss.1(2)(e) and 5). People living in hospital or long term care are unlikely to suffer grave hardship simply because they are no longer married. A divorce can also be granted after only two years' separation, provided that the respondent consents (s.1(2)(d)). In *Mason* v. *Mason* [1972] Fam. 302, Sir George Baker P. decided that the test of capacity to agree to a divorce was the same as that to agree to a marriage. The respondent must be able to understand its nature, effect and consequences, and to express his consent. He can do this even if he is not otherwise capable of managing his property and affairs and is therefore represented by the Official Solicitor and subject to the jurisdiction of the Court of Protection. The judge considered, however, that consent had to be the expression of the state of mind of one of the parties to the marriage, so that the Official Solicitor could not give it on his behalf. He did not decide whether the Court of Protection might be able to do so, as part of its power to conduct proceedings. But the Court could always file a petition on the patient's behalf, so the point is academic.

An immediate divorce may be obtained if the respondent has behaved in such a way that the petitioner cannot reasonably be expected to live with him (s.1(2)(*b*); see also Domestic Proceedings and Magistrates Courts Act 1978, s.1(*c*)). The test is whether a "right-thinking person would come to the conclusion that *this* husband has behaved in such a way that *this* wife cannot reasonably be expected to live with him, taking into account the whole of the circumstances and the characters and personalities of the parties" (*Livingstone-Stallard* v. *Livingstone-Stallard* [1974] Fam. 47; approved in *O'Neill* v. *O'Neill* [1975] 1 W.L.R. 1118), not whether the behaviour itself is unreasonable or blameworthy. A spouse may reasonably be expected to be more tolerant of behaviour which is the result of illness than of the deliberate, malicious or merely thoughtless behaviour of a normal person (*Richards* v. *Richards* [1972] 1 W.L.R. 1073). But conduct which has a serious effect upon the petitioner will certainly be enough (*Williams* v. *Williams* [1964] A.C.698; *Katz* v. *Katz* [1972] 1 W.L.R. 955). It may even be both completely blameless and largely negative in character. In *Thurlow* v. *Thurlow* [1976] Fam. 32, the wife suffered from a severe neurological disorder leading to a gradual mental and physical deterioration at an early age. She eventually became bedridden, unable to walk or stand unaided, or to feed and dress herself. She had displayed some temper, thrown things at her mother-in-law, burned things, and had a tendency to wander. Her husband coped with her at home for as long as he could, until his own health was affected and she had to go into hospital, where she would require indefinite care. The husband was granted his decree. Rees J. expressly disagreed with the result in *Smith* v. *Smith* [1973] 118 S.J. 184, where the husband failed to get a decree after caring for his wife for many years while she degenerated into a cabbage-like existence as a result of pre-senile dementia. Ironically, he would have been able to do so had he put her into hospital five years earlier instead of looking after her at home for as long as possible. Once it is clear that the marriage has broken down irretrievably and that the respondent will not be prejudiced, the courts are likely to be sympathetic to petitioners who now want to be free. But they must still have evidence of something which can be called "behaviour" and which the petitioner cannot reasonably be expected to bear any longer.

In cases such as these, the question of blame is irrelevant to the financial and property adjustments which will be made. The court will do what it can to ensure that each party suffers as little as possible from the breakdown of the marriage. Fault-based grounds such as desertion (s.1(2)(*c*)) are therefore very little used. To found a divorce, desertion must last for at least two years, and this normally requires an intention to desert. But if a person who has deserted his spouse later becomes incapable of retaining the necessary intent, he remains in desertion for this purpose provided that the court thinks that he would have done so had he been capable (s.2(4)). Desertion is a useful ground for obtaining financial relief from a magistrates' court the moment a spouse walks out (1978 Act, s.1(*d*)), but only if he has the necessary intention. But relief can be obtained if he fails to make reasonable financial provision for his spouse or children (s.1(*a*) and (*b*)). In practice, of course, he is unlikely to have the resources to do so.

(d) *Children*

Undoubtedly, the relationships of mentally disordered people with their children are the most vulnerable to outside intervention by the agencies of the state. This is because the welfare of the child is the first and paramount consideration in any court proceedings where his legal custody or upbringing is in issue (Guardianship of Minors Act 1971, s.1). If parents split up, this usually means that the mother gets custody, particularly of young children. But should mental disorder affect her capacity to love and care for them, she may lose them to the father or to the local authority. Courts hearing custody cases can commit a child to care whenever there are exceptional circumstances making it impracticable or undesirable for him to be in the care of either party or any other individual. The same principles apply if a child is made a ward of court, perhaps by a local authority which is trying to protect the child in circumstances not covered by their statutory powers.

A local authority may receive a child into "voluntary" care if the parents are prevented from looking after him for a variety of reasons, including mental "disease or infirmity." Once the child is in care, the authority may assume the parent's rights by passing a resolution, which the parent may challenge in court. One of the grounds for this is that the parent suffers from some permanent disability rendering him incapable of caring for the child (Child Care Act 1980, s.3(1)(*b*)(ii)). This will cover some mentally handicapped parents, who may well lose their child permanently if they agree to his going into care. The resolution does not deprive them of their right to object to an adoption application, but the court could dispense with their consent on the ground that they were incapable of giving it or were withholding it unreasonably. Another ground for passing a resolution is that the parent, while not permanently incapable, suffers from some mental disorder within the meaning of the Mental Health Act which renders him unfit to have the care of the child (s.3(2)(*b*)(iii)). This is not limited to people who are compulsorily detained, or even admitted to hospital. Nor is there any question of blame-worthy or culpable conduct towards the child. Psychiatrists are very troubled when patients run the risk of losing their children if they have to put them in care during a bad patch or when they go into hospital. The social workers' dilemma is that it is irrelevant to the child's well-being that his parent cannot be blamed for what happened. By the time that the parent is well enough to look after him again, things may have changed. The social workers' legal duty is to give first consideration to the need to safeguard and promote the welfare of the child throughout his childhood (s.18(1)). It is no easy task to distinguish those parents who will be able to cater for the child's needs in a "good enough" way before too long from those who will not. Hasty judgments and inadequate attempts at rehabilitation can destroy a family for ever. But social workers (or psychiatrists) have little hope of making lasting improvements in the parenting capacities of some pathological personalities. Leaving matters for too long in the vague hope that things will get better can destroy the child's chances of finding emotional security elsewhere.

More difficult still are the cases where the child has not been placed in care and the authority has to decide whether to take care proceedings on the ground that the parent's condition is having an adverse affect upon the child's own health or development

(Children and Young Persons Act 1969, s.1(2)(*a*)). Although social workers rarely look at it in this way, there is often a choice between removing the child and removing one of the adults from the household. A further problem, which is receiving some attention at present, is whether proceedings can or should be taken to remove a new-born baby, particularly from a severely handicapped mother. There is no mechanism for removing parental rights before a child is born. Even at birth, care proceedings cannot be taken on the ground of parental unfitness or incapability, but only on present neglect or ill-treatment, unless another child in the same household has been neglected or ill-treated in the past, or an adult in the same household has been convicted of an offence against a child (s.1(2)(*b*) and (*bb*)). The only other possibility is to make the child a ward of court.

This raises some very serious issues indeed. The right of any handicapped person to normal family relationships must be respected to the greatest possible extent. But so must the right of any child to a minimum standard of physical and emotional care. We have already seen in Chapter 5 that mentally handicapped adults should not be sterilised, given contraceptive injections, or abortions, without their consent, unless this is necessary to save their lives or prevent a serious deterioration in their health, or can be termed treatment for the mental disorder of a detained patient. In practice, the issue may be blurred by the ease with which the patient's co-operation may be obtained. But that is not an acceptable solution to a problem which the 1983 Act has inadvertently made worse.

3. *Managing and Leaving Money*

(a) *Making a will*

As with every other juristic act, a person's capacity to make a will depends upon the extent of his understanding of the particular transaction concerned. The test is the same, but it can lead to different conclusions between transactions of different complexity (so that a rich man's will may be a more difficult affair than his marriage). According to the classic statement, "He ought to be capable of making his will with an understanding of the nature of the business in which he is engaged, a recollection of the property he means to dispose of, of the persons who are the objects of his bounty, and the manner in which it is to be distributed between them . . . ," but only in simple terms — he does not have to be a lawyer (*Banks* v. *Goodfellow* (1870) L.R. 5 Q.B. 549). Provided that he has this capacity, the testator does not have to weigh these various factors wisely. He can make whatever dispositions he chooses, however foolish, cruel or improvident (although if he fails to make reasonable financial provision for certain members of his family and dependants, they may apply for the court to order such provision from the estate, under the Inheritance (Provision for Family and Dependants) Act 1975). Despite this, it is often the curiosity of the will itself which prompts the dispute.

Testators rarely fall into the easy category of the permanently, totally and completely incapable. Even here, it may be possible, although very difficult, to prove that the will was made in a "lucid interval." If the testator has recovered enough, and for long enough, to have the required capacity, he need not have recovered completely and may relapse again quite quickly (*Ex parte Holyland* (1805) 11 Ves. Jun. 10; *Cartwright* v. *Cartwright* (1793) 1 Phill. Ecc. 90; *Banks* v. *Goodfellow*, above). Alternatively, a testator may have delusions about some things, but not about others. Thus, "a degree or form of unsoundness which neither disturbs the exercise of the faculties necessary for such an act, nor is capable of influencing the result ought not to take away the power of making a will . . . " (*Banks* v. *Goodfellow*, above). If so, it will all depend on whether his particular delusional system has influenced the provisions in the will. Above all, however, mere eccentricity, whether in previous life-style or in the contents of the will, is not the same as incapacity. But capricious, harsh and unreasonable views could amount to delusions (*Boughton* v. *Knight* (1873) L.R. 3 P.&D. 64). Similarly, confusion and forgetfulness are not enough, if the testator was able to concentrate at the time when he made the will, but of course they could be if they induced him to make it (*Benyon* v. *Benyon* (1844) 2 L.T. 477; *Singh* v. *Armirchand* [1948] A.C. 161).

If the testator does have capacity to make a will, he can do so even if he is otherwise incapable of managing his property and affairs. The Court of Protection has no power to stop him. This is because of the general principle, dating back as far as the Statute *De Praerogativa Regis* in Edward II's time, that the court only has jurisdiction over the patient's estate while he is alive (*e.g. Re Bennett* [1913] 2 Ch. 318). However, the Administration of Justice Act 1969 made an exception to that rule. Provided that the Court has reason to believe that the patient is incapable of making a valid will for himself, it can now make a statutory will for him (Mental Health Act 1983, s.96(i)(*e*) and (4)(*b*)). This can do anything that the patient could have done if he were not mentally disordered. It will then have the same effect (at least for property which is governed by the law in England and Wales) as if the patient had made it and was capable of doing so (s.97).

The Court may not wish to use this power very often, for it is difficult to guess what the patient would have wanted. The only guidance given is in the Court's general power to do whatever is "necessary or expedient" for the maintenance or other benefit of the patient or members of his family, for providing for other people or purposes for which the patient might be expected to provide, or otherwise for administering his affairs (s.95(1)). The Court may also bear in mind that some members of the patient's family will be able to apply under the Inheritance (Provision for Family and Dependants) Act 1975 if they are disinherited. However, a good example of the case for making a will occurred in *Re Davey* (*deceased*) [1981] 1 W.L.R. 164. An elderly spinster with quite a large estate moved into a nursing home in June. In July, she made a will dividing her property between a large number of relations. In September she was married to a middle-aged employee at the nursing home. This automatically revoked the will. The marriage came to light in December during the process of placing her affairs under the jurisdiction of the Court of Protection. Her receiver, at the instance of the Court, immediately applied for a statutory will in the same terms as the one which she herself made in July. The Court granted this without giving notice to her husband or to the proposed beneficiaries. She died six days after it was executed. The husband's appeal was dismissed. In all the circumstances, this had been the best possible way of providing for a full investigation and a just result in the end, for the husband could always apply for reasonable provision under the 1975 Act while the other beneficiaries could not.

(b) *Making, getting and keeping contracts*

A patient's capacity to make contracts is governed by much the same principles as his capacity to make a will (see *Boughton* v. *Knight* (1873) L.R. 3 P.&D. 64). It all depends upon whether he was capable of understanding the nature of the contract involved. Even a person who is generally incapable may have contracted in a lucid interval, or the particular transaction may be one which he is quite capable of understanding, or his particular delusional system may have nothing to do with the transaction in question. Hence, the incapability may affect all transactions at all times, or only some or at some times (Law Commission, 1976). Once again, the test is understanding, not wisdom.

However, the effects of incapacity are quite different. The law has had to balance two conflicting policy considerations. One is the need to protect those who cannot protect themselves. But another is that the other party should not be prejudiced by an incapacity which he had no reason to believe was there. By the end of the nineteenth century, the courts had decided that the first consideration could not outweigh the second. Therefore, the general rule is that a mentally incapable person is bound by a contract he has made, unless he can prove that the other person knew of his incapacity (*Imperial Loan Co.* v. *Stone* [1892] 1 Q.B. 599). However, the circumstances may be such that any reasonable man would have realised that the patient was incapable (*York Glass Co.* v. *Jubb* (1925) 134 L.T. 36). This may apply particularly to severely handicapped people. But apart from these very obvious cases, the other person does not seem to have any duty to make inquiries.

The only exception to this general rule relates to "necessaries." Section 3(2) of the Sale of Goods Act 1979 provides that if necessaries are supplied to a mentally incompetent person, he must pay a reasonable price for them. Necessaries means goods which are suitable to his condition in life and to his actual requirements at the time. The object of this rule seems to be that people should not be deterred from supplying the needs of mentally incapable people by fear of not being paid (Law Commission, 1976). But it also protects the incapable patient, who need only pay a reasonable price, rather than the inflated one which may have been agreed. Similar principles apply to the supply of services which are "necessaries,"such as accommodation and medical attention (see *Re Rhodes* [1890] 44 Ch. D. 94), and also the money to buy such things (*Re Beavan* [1912] 1 Ch. 196).

There is another important difference between contracts and wills. Once a person's affairs have been taken over by the Court of Protection, he cannot deal with them in a way which is inconsistent with the Court's powers of control (*Re Walker* [1905] 1 Ch. 160; *Re Marshall* [1920] 1 Ch. 284). Even if he happens to have the capacity to make the contract in question, it seems that he cannot do so. Indeed, logically, the contract should be quite void, even if the other party did not know of the Court's jurisdiction. But the rule about necessaries should remain.

All of these rules assume that the other person is only too happy to deal with the mentally disordered person. But of course, this might not be so, particularly if he fears that the person is incapable and may therefore be able to avoid the contract. Even if there is no risk of incapacity, people may be very reluctant to supply services, housing, accommodation, finance, and employment to a mentally disordered person. There is no legislation such as the Race Relations Act 1976 or the Sex Discrimination Act 1975 to protect the mentally disordered against discrimination in these matters. People are free to choose to supply or not to supply, whether they are doing so for a good reason or for pure prejudice. A good illustration is the case of *O'Brien* v. *Prudential Assurance Co. Ltd.* [1979] I.R.L.R. 140. Mr. O'Brien had a long history of mental illness, possibly schizophrenia, but had not been receiving treatment for some years. He deliberately gave false information about this in order to obtain a job with the company, no doubt fearing that he would not get it if they knew. Events proved him right, for they dismissed him when they found out about it, without seeking a psychiatric opinion about his present condition. In fact, there was no evidence of present schizophrenia and he was suitable for the work he was doing. His claim for unfair dismissal was rejected by an industrial tribunal and the employment appeal tribunal. The falsification of his history provided a good reason for the company to dismiss him, even though he was fit to do the job.

Of course, mental disorder which affects an employee's capability to do his job can also be a good reason for dismissal, but only if in all the circumstances the employer was reasonable in treating it as such (Employment Protection (Consolidation) Act 1978, s.57(2)). Employers are also expected to go about making the decision in a fair and reasonable way (s.57(3)). Unless the case is exceptional, they should consult the employee and also take steps to discover the true medical position (*East Lindsey District Council* v. *Daubney* [1977] I.L.R. 566). This must be particularly important in cases of mental illness, where laymen are so apt to leap to unjustified conclusions. But the principles to be applied are just the same as they are with any physical illness (see Clarke, 1981). They only apply to employees who are entitled to the protection of the law of unfair dismissal. Otherwise, an employer is entitled to dismiss for whatever reason he likes, provided that he does so in accordance with the contract of employment.

4. *The Incapable Patient*

Most of the people who suffer from mental disorder within the meaning of the Mental Health Act are quite capable of looking after their own property and affairs, whether or not they are in hospital. The law now assumes this until the contrary is proved and there is no category of patient whose affairs are automatically taken out of his hands. Generally, a person must be allowed to manage for himself, unless he is placed under the jurisdiction of the Court of Protection. This is all very well in theory, but in practice it can cause difficulties both for the mentally disordered person and for the people looking after him. Once again, there are several conflicting policy considerations. The mentally disordered person must be protected against the risk of exploitation and abuse. But there must be adequate procedural safeguards against the unjustified removal of his right to look after his own affairs. This is reflected in both the United Nations Declaration on the Rights of Mentally Retarded Persons, and in Article 6 of the European Declaration of Human Rights (page 308 above). But both of these can lead to procedures which are, "it is said, inevitably cumbersome, time-consuming and expensive" (Law Commission, 1976). This means that there is a great temptation to ignore them. Many children of mentally infirm parents would be horrified to learn that they cannot strictly decide to give up a tenancy or sell the furniture. Finally, therefore, the protective mechanism should not take a sledge-hammer to crack a nut. It should provide essential protection while interfering as little as possible in the person's ordinary rights and freedoms (Gostin, 1983b). The machinery of the Court of Protection can be criticised for fulfilling none of these objectives adequately, although this is obviously not the fault of the Court itself. Before considering it, therefore, we shall look at what can be done without invoking it.

(a) *Statutory powers*

Several types of income can by statute be paid to someone other than the person who is entitled to them, if that person is incapable of managing his property and affairs. The most important of these are social security and supplementary benefits. The DHSS have power to appoint a suitable person to receive both of these on behalf of a person who is "unable to act" (Supplementary Benefit (Claims and Payments) Regulations 1981, reg.26; Social Security (Claims and Payments) Regulations 1979, reg.28). Patients living with their families or independently are, of course, entitled to the full rate of benefit appropriate to their circumstances. Patients who have to spend any length of time in hospital or residential accommodation will usually only receive money for their personal expenses, once their accommodation and any dependants have been taken care of. The hospital management have power to pay pocket money to in-patients in hospitals which are wholly or mainly used for the treatment of people suffering from mental disorder, if they would otherwise be without resources for personal expenses (Mental Health Act 1983, s.122). In fact, the hospitals take responsibility for most patients admitted before November 17, 1975 and the supplementary benefit authorities for patients admitted thereafter. The amount will be the same, but supplementary benefit is a right whereas hospital pocket money is not.

Social security benefits, supplementary benefit and hospital pocket money can all be reduced if the doctor responsible for the patient's treatment considers that, because of the patient's medical condition, the full amount cannot be used by or on behalf of the patient for his personal comfort or enjoyment. Means-tested benefits will, of course, be reduced if the patient has other resources, including both outside earnings and "reward payments" for therapeutic or rehabilitative work inside the hospital.

There are two important points to note. First, the patient is entitled to have and to spend his own money unless he is incapable of doing so. That right can only be taken away if he cannot manage his property and affairs, and his personal allowance is usually all the property and affairs that he has. Many quite severely disabled patients should be able, with a little help, to decide whether to spend this on sweets, cigarettes or other transient comforts, or to save for new clothes, a radio, cassette player or the like. Secondly, if the patient is indeed incapable, the money must still be spent for his personal benefit. Hence there are practical problems about pooling some of it to buy such things as mini-buses for excursions, because of the difficulty of proving individual benefit in proportion to contributions and of reimbursement should the patient be discharged. Nor should the money be spent on general improvements and amenities inside a hospital which it is clearly the responsibility of the NHS to supply. There is obviously a potential conflict of interest where hospital authorities are appointed to receive their patients' benefits. Certainly, hospitals have found it difficult to spend their patients' money within the limits of the law and large balances have accumulated. Tentative proposals to allow a form of pooling by means of subscriptions to patients' clubs were made (DHSS letter, 1981) but received much criticism. Revised guidance on the use of patients' money is expected shortly, but the main problem may well be that hard-pressed nursing staff have little time to consider how best a small sum might to used to enhance each patient's quality of life. It seems most unlikely that the money could not in fact be used in this way.

There is a similar power for salaries, pensions and other work-related periodical payments made from funds administered by government departments. The department must have medical evidence of the recipient's incapacity. They can then pay all or part of the money to the institution or person caring for him to be applied for his benefit. Any remainder may go to or for the benefit of his family or other people for whom he might be expected to provide, or to reimburse people who have helped to pay his debts or to maintain him and his dependants (Mental Health Act 1983, s.142). Armed forces' pay and pensions are dealt with under the Royal Warrant. There are similar powers for Members of Parliaments' pensions (Parliamentary and Other Pensions Act 1972), those of Church of England clergymen (Clergy Pensions Measure 1961, s.36), and of some local authority employees (Local Government Act 1972, s.118), but the last is only up to

£1500 (Local Government (Application of Salary due to Mentally Disordered Persons) (Limits) Regulations 1983), and in the last two the Court of Protection must be informed.

In all of these cases, there is at least some risk of the patient being deprived of the right to control what little he has without any effective safeguard. But the awareness of all concerned of the limits of what they can do may be a better protection than control from an authority which is remote from the patient and from those who are looking after him.

(b) *Trusts and powers of attorney*

Trustees of a will or a settlement may have discretionary powers to apply the income or capital for the benefit of an incapable person. There is obviously a great deal to be said for providing for mentally handicapped people in this way, for it allows the giver to decide what can be done. Professional advice will be needed in drawing up the settlement, for it must avoid giving the person an income which is bound to require the attentions of the Court of Protection. Even so, the Court may sometimes have to inquire how the trustees are exercising their discretion. With a certain amount of care, property can also be left in such a way as to provide an incapable person with a home, but without jeopardising his claim to means-tested benefits. This will usually involve leaving a house to a charity, which can then use it as a small group home. Such a scheme has recently been started by MENCAP.

But what if a person would like to appoint his own agent to manage his affairs in case he becomes incapable of doing so for himself? No doubt many people would like to put their affairs in the hands of a trusted friend or adviser before their faculties fail. They would probably be very surprised to learn that they cannot do so. Any agency, even if given by deed in a power of attorney, is automatically revoked when the person giving it becomes incapable of contracting. It is not always easy to know when this has happened, because capacity can vary from time to time and from transaction to transaction. For as long as the agent remains in ignorance of the incapacity, he is probably safe. This is certainly true when he acts under a power of attorney (Powers of Attorney Act 1971, s.5(1)). Similarly, the transaction itself will usually be valid if the third party with whom it is made does not know of the incapacity. This again is certainly true where he deals with an agent who has power of attorney (s.5(2)). It is also true of any contract which is within the scope of the agent's apparent authority (*Drew* v. *Nunn* (1879) 4 Q.B.D. 661). Other transactions however, may be invalid even if the third party did not know of the incapacity. And in that case, the agent will be liable to the third party for breach of warranty of authority (*Yonge* v. *Toynbee* [1910] 1 K.B. 215). This is so even if the agent did not know about the incapacity, although in that case he should be able to claim reimbursement from his principal. The moment that the agent knows of the incapacity, however, he acts at his peril, except where he contracts for "necessaries" for the patient (Law Commission, 1976).

The Law Commission (1983) have recently made proposals for an enduring power of attorney which can continue in force during a person's incapacity. This would often be cheaper, quicker, more convenient and more in line with the patient's own wishes, than calling in the Court of Protection to appoint a receiver or otherwise manage the estate. But these considerations have to be balanced against the need to protect the interests of someone who by definition is incapable of protecting them for himself. The mechanism proposed is notification of the relatives. This would be secured by a requirement of registration with the Court, which would be bound to register the power unless a valid objection were received from the donor or his relatives. Unless registered, the power would be suspended during the donor's incapacity. The Court would have several supervisory powers after registration, but would not be expected to use these unless given a good reason to do so. Any provision for automatic checks would obviously defeat the whole object of the exercise. These proposals would only relate to powers which the donor expressly intended to continue during his incapacity and various other formalities are suggested. If implemented, there is good reason to believe that they would be welcomed and used by a large number of people, particularly the elderly.

(c) *Otherwise*

Where a person has property and affairs which cannot be dealt with in the ways outlined earlier, the only way of acquiring the right to act on his behalf is to apply to the Court of Protection. The

Court itself makes one or two exceptions (P.N. 1). If a relative or friend, acting on the advice of the patient's doctor, thinks that in all the circumstances it would be in the patient's best interests (bearing in mind the distress that such knowledge would cause) to give up the tenancy of a rented home, the Court will make no objection if this is done and the furniture sold or put into safe keeping. The same would probably apply to the surrender of items on hire purchase, although it would be advisable to check with the Court first. Where the patient's needs are otherwise provided for, and the sole property consists of small savings (such as national savings certificates) the Court may not insist on application for an order if the pass books or other documents are held in safe custody. But of course the money cannot be used without the Court's order. Assurance companies have discretion to deal with very small amounts of policy money as they see fit.

5. *The Court of Protection*

The Court has a long history as it stems from the power (and duty) of the monarch to look after the property of lunatics and idiots, which was recognised even before the Statute *De Praerogativa Regis* of Edward II. The King delegated this function to the Lord Chancellor, and later to other judges. Patients had to be found of unsound mind by inquisition, and then their affairs would be managed by a committee. Nineteenth century legislation gave power to the Master or Judge in Lunacy to deal with the estate of people who were medically certified to be of unsound mind, by appointing a receiver. This is essentially the jurisdiction which is now exercised by the Court of Protection. It is an office of the Supreme Court (Mental Health Act 1983, s.93(2)), but it is more concerned with providing a service than with arbitrating disputes over legal rights and responsibilities. Its functions may be carried out by judges nominated by the Lord Chancellor. He nominates those in the Chancery Division of the High Court, because they deal mainly with property matters, but it is not part of the High Court. But almost all functions can be, and are, carried out by the Master, Deputy Master, and assistant Masters or other officers nominated by the Lord Chancellor (ss.93(2),(3) and (4)). They are assisted by the Lord Chancellor's Visitors (ss.102 and 103). There are panels of legal, medical and general Visitors, who visit patients and investigate either their capacities or any aspect of the Court's functions in respect of them. All Visitors may interview patients in private and medical Visitors may examine them and their records. Reports˙ to the Court are confidential unless the Court allows disclosure. Visits are now to be made by general Visitors unless legal or medical expertise is essential. The Master may also visit patients for the same purpose and interview them in private (s.103(7)). A person aggrieved by the decision of a master (and this includes the patient) can appeal to a judge and thereafter to the Court of Appeal. The Court's powers and procedure are governed by Part VII of the Mental Health Act 1983 and by the Court of Protection Rules 1982 (see Heywood and Massey, 1978; Compton and Whiteman, 1976).

(a) *Procedure*

Proceedings are normally started by originating application (r.5). This can be made by anyone. Usually, the patient's nearest or any relative applies, but a friend or social worker or even a creditor or debtor could do so. In the last resort, the Court can direct one of its own officers or the Official Solicitor to apply. If the patient's property is worth no more than £5,000, the Court can make a summary order without any application, directing one of its officers or some other suitable person to deal with it in a particular way (r.6). The Court can also do this even if there has been an application, or if the property is worth more than £5,000, if it is not necessary to appoint a receiver for the patient. If the patient's estate is large or complicated, or something needs to be done which will require a solicitor anyway (such as selling a house), the applicant should instruct a solicitor. But if the estate is small or relatively straightforward, application can be made directly through the Court's personal application branch.

The Court supplies the necessary forms. Apart from the application itself, there must be a medical certificate from a doctor that the patient is incapable, by reason of mental disorder, of managing and administering his property and affairs. Unlike a compulsory admission to hospital, only one certificate is required and the doctor need have no particular expertise in mental disorder. There is no statutory form for the certificate and inexperienced doctors will have very little guidance on what the statutory criterion involves. Clearly, some of them will take a much broader view of incapacity than do others. The other document required is an affidavit of family and property (if the patient's income is no more than £500 a year or his capital no more than £5,000, a certificate may be used instead of a sworn affidavit). This sets out particulars of his relatives, property and affairs and of the circumstances giving rise to the application (r.38).

The patient must normally be served with notice of the application or proposed summary order, but not with a copy of the actual application. But the Court can dispense with service if satisfied that the patient is incapable of understanding the notice (which is scarcely drafted to encourage understanding), or if it would injure his health, or indeed for any other reason (r.28). The Court can then ask one of the Lord Chancellor's medical Visitors to visit the patient and report on his condition and welfare. But there is no guarantee that the Court will do this. It cannot be right that the patient may be deprived of his right to administer his own affairs without even being told that this is under consideration. In the *Winterwerp Case*, applic. no. 6301/73 (1979) 2 E.H.R.R. 387, the European Court of Human Rights held that Article 6(1) of the Convention (page 308 above) applied to decisions as to a person's capacity to deal with his own property. And a fair hearing under that Article clearly involves an opportunity of being heard, either in person or through a representative. So it seems that the present English law is in breach of the Convention on this point.

If the patient is given notice, he then has seven days or until the hearing date (whichever is the later) in which to write to the Court. He may object to the whole proceedings on the ground that he is not incapable and some medical support for this is important. Alternatively, he may simply wish to object to or make comments on what is proposed and to make his own suggestions, but he may find this hard to do if he is not given a full statement of what has been asked for. The Court may try to take his wishes into account. But the rules do not give the patient a right to be heard in person if he wants. If the Court is satisfied that the patient is incapable, it will usually make the order applied for. If it has any doubt, it may ask a medical Visitor to examine the patient and report confidentially on his condition. If he reports that the patient is incapable, a new hearing date will be set for the application to be reconsidered if there are any further objections.

The Court can make any relative or anyone else who seems interested in the application a respondent to it, and any relative who is closer than the applicant should certainly be informed. Unlike the patient, these people will have full party status in the proceedings. Disputes may arise about what is best, although basically the Court is interested in what should be done for the patient and the proceedings ought not to be contentious.

(b) *Grounds*

The Court's jurisdiction only arises "where, after considering the medical evidence (it) is satisfied that a person is incapable, by reason of mental disorder, of managing and administering his property and affairs" (1983 Act, s.94(2)). It may make interim orders pending the determination of that question, if there is reason to believe that the person may be incapable and it is necessary to act immediately (s.98). But the fact that some other Court has decided that the person is incapable, for example, for the purpose of appointing someone to act as his next friend in a nullity suit, does not automatically mean that he is subject to the Court of Protection (*Re S. (F.G.) (mental health patient)* [1973] 1 W.L.R. 178).

The criterion for intervention is both wide and vague. It covers any form of mental disorder, including "arrested or incomplete development of mind" and "any other disorder or disability of mind" which are not sufficient for long-term compulsory admission to hospital. It is not clear what is meant by an incapacity to manage one's property and affairs, but it is clear that a patient may be unable to do this despite the fact that he is able to carry out many individual transactions. This means that the Court's intervention can prevent his doing things that he would otherwise be able to do. There is no specific provision in the procedure for an assessment of his social competence, such as is contemplated by the United Nations Declaration on the Rights of Mentally Retarded Persons (above page 308). It is also unfortunate that the procedure places most of the burden on the patient. Once a medical certificate has been produced, it is up to him to raise doubts about whether he is indeed incapable.

(c) *Effect*

Once the patient is subject to the Court's jurisdiction, it has exclusive control over all his property and all his affairs. Its guidance must be sought whenever anything not provided for in an existing order or direction needs to be done (*Re W.(E.E.M.)* [1971] Ch. 123). Its general function is to "do or secure the doing of all such things as appear necessary or expedient" for the maintenance or other benefit of the patient or his family, for providing for other people or purposes for which he might be expected to provide, or for otherwise administering his affairs (s.95(1)). Without prejudice to that general proposition, the Court may do a long list of things for that purpose: control and manage any property of the patient; sell, dispose or deal with it; acquire property for him; make settlements or give it away to members of his family or other people or purposes for which he might be expected to provide if he were not mentally disordered; make a will (see page 323 above); carry on his profession, trade or business through any suitable person; dissolve a partnership; carry out a contract entered into by the patient; conduct legal proceedings in his name or on his behalf; reimburse those who have paid his debts or supported him or his family or provided for other purposes for which he might be expected to provide; and exercise any power (including a power to consent) vested in him, either for himself or as a trustee or guardian, or otherwise (s.96(1)). The Court's first concern is always for the maintenance and other requirements of the patient, and it has a wide discretion about whether and to what extent to discharge his debts and other obligations, although it must have regard to the interests of creditors, who are no longer entitled to enforce their rights in the normal way (s.95(2)). The Court has no jurisdiction over the management and care of the patient's person and so is not concerned with his admission to or discharge from hospital, his medical treatment, or other aspects of caring for him. But the dividing line is not always easy to draw, for arrangements for his accommodation (for example, in a private nursing home) which will involve expenditure are clearly within the Court's jurisdiction. And its powers to conduct legal proceedings can be used for purposes such as divorce, with obvious personal consequences. The Court will want to know if the patient is contemplating marriage. One object of this will be to enable it to make a statutory will if need be. But it might want to direct the entry of a caveat in the hope of stopping the wedding (see Gostin, 1983b). Whether this would succeed is more doubtful (page 316 above), but the possibility illustrates how all-embracing the Court's powers can be.

It may deal with a particular case by a simple order authorising and directing whatever is necessary to be done. However, the normal method of protecting the patient's estate and using it for his benefit is to appoint a receiver under section 99. The receiver will usually, but not inevitably, be the person who applied to the Court. The Court prefers a close, but not too elderly, relative. If there is no suitable relative, it is not normal practice to appoint a solicitor (because the solicitor dealing with the case is an independent protection for the patient), but an accountant or estate agent (in the old sense) may be appropriate. A friend could be appointed, or the local Director of Social Services, if he could be persuaded to take it on. Where there is no other suitable person, or there is a dispute within the family, the Official Solicitor may be appointed.

The order appointing the receiver will be in very precise terms, setting out what he must and what he may do. He will have to return to Court for specific authority to do anything else. The order will probably give him authority to receive the patient's income and direct how it is to be spent for the maintenance of the patient and his family. It may deal with carrying on or closing down a business, the retention or surrender of insurance policies, savings certificates and other investments, the upkeep or surrender of the patient's home, furniture and the like. The sale of a house is normally dealt with in a separate order. A receiver is usually required to give security for the proper performance of his duties, as is the administrator of a dead person's estate. This is normally done through an insurance company's fidelity guarantee bond, the premium being allowable out of the patient's estate. He will be required to render precise accounts to the Court, normally annually at first, but if he is a professional man he may be allowed remuneration out of the estate. He may of course be removed or replaced by the Court if appropriate, or he might ask to be discharged because of ill-health or other commitments.

(d) *An endless burden?*

The Court's functions usually come to an end when the patient dies. If he recovers, a specific finding that he is now capable of managing his own affairs, together with the discharge of any receiver and release of any funds held by the Court, is required. There is no automatic review of whether the Court's intervention is any longer necessary. Gostin (1983b) suggests that many of the 23,000 patients under the Court's control might be able to take care of their own affairs, but each year there are only around 60 applications for discharge of receivership, most of which apparently succeed. The receiver is under no obligation even to visit the patient, let alone to report regularly to the Court on how he is getting on. The Court itself will not initiate a review unless asked. Gostin suggests that there should be an annual review, and that orders should have to be renewed in much the same way that compulsory admission for treatment is renewed. This would inevitably mean more work, but it would remove one of the major criticisms—that the Court is too remote from its patients and out of touch with what is happening to them, despite the large measure of control which it has over their lives.

He also criticises the breadth of that control, which he contrasts with the now much more restricted scope of guardianship under the Act. Undoubtedly, patients and their families feel that their attempts to do the right thing do not always produce the right results. Matters are taken out of their hands by a slow and complicated machine which is not always able to adapt to changing needs. No doubt the Court is doing its very best within the limits of the statutory framework and the resources available to it. But unfortunately, families try to avoid it if they possibly can, and in this way it may be letting down the very people whom it is there to help. One of the greatest disincentives of all is that the Court charges fees for its services, at the beginning of the proceedings, for many specific transactions, and annually, although there is exemption from the first and last if the patient's clear annual income is less than £1,000 a year (some, but not all, state benefits are excluded from this calculation). These come out of the patient's property, in addition to any fees charged by the receiver or the solicitor. There is a small additional fee for personal applications. In a welfare state, it may be difficult to justify charging for a service which a patient needs but may not want, although by definition he will have some means to pay for it. But the Court's whole approach dates from an earlier age.

6. *Legal Liability towards Mental Patients and Restrictions on their Access to the Courts*

Everything has so far been discussed on the assumption that legal liability for acts and omissions concerning mental patients can be decided on the same principles as legal liability concerning anyone else. However, this is not entirely true. One of the most controversial provisions in the Mental Health Act 1983 provides certain individuals with an added defence against legal liability when dealing with certain types of patient. It also contains restrictions on the free access to the courts in such cases, and may therefore be a breach of Article 6(1) of the European Convention on Human Rights (page 308 above). Before looking at these two points, however, it is necessary to take a brief look at what the position would be if they did not exist.

(a) *Ordinary civil and criminal liability*

A great many things that can happen to patients are obviously capable of resulting in civil or criminal liability, principally for assault, battery and false imprisonment. It is a nice question whether doctors recommending compulsory admission to hospital could be responsible at all for an imprisonment which is the result of the applicant's decision to follow their recommendations, or whether the applicant could be responsible for the imprisonment which followed the hospital's decision to admit the patient (see *Harnett* v. *Bond* [1925] A.C. 669). But the hospital could obviously be liable for the subsequent detention and the staff for acts of treatment or restraint which involve the application of force to the patient's person. There will usually be no question of legal liability, however, because the Mental Health Act itself, or occasionally other legislation, or other principles of the common law, provide lawful authority for what has happened and a perfectly good defence to any civil or criminal action which might be brought.

We have seen (mainly in Chapter 6) that there are undoubtedly limits to what can be done, some clear and some not so clear, and lawful authority will provide no defence to people who exceed those limits. It is also clear that everyone involved in the process of compulsory admission, or in the treatment of any kind of hospital patient, owes the patient a duty of care (see *Harnett* v. *Fisher* [1927] A.C. 573). Thus a recommending doctor or an approved social worker could be liable for negligence if he failed to take the care that a reasonable professional person would take in his position. This could sometimes cut both ways. The possibility of liability for failing to section a patient who clearly could and should have been sectioned cannot be entirely ruled out (for hospitals have sometimes been held liable for serious failure to supervise a suicidal patient, even though the injury is self-inflicted; see *Selfe* v. *Ilford and District Hospital Management Committee* (1970) 114 S.J. 935; but in *Hyde* v. *Tameside Area Health Authority* [1981] C.L.Y.B. 1854 Lord Denning M.R. said that the policy of the law should be to discourage such actions). Normally, however, there is no liability for failing to act as a "good Samaritan" towards people who are not already under your care. There could certainly be liability for failing to take reasonable care when deciding to section a patient (see *Buxton* v. *Jayne* [1960] 1 W.L.R. 783, but also [1962] C.L.Y. 1167). Doctors, nurses and other staff working in hospital or in the community can obviously be liable for failing to take reasonable care in their actions and decisions.

There are also three criminal offences specifically designed to protect mental patients. That relating to sexual exploitation by staff of patients in their care has already been mentioned (page 313 above). A similar offence covers ill-treatment or wilful neglect. This may be committed by anyone on the staff of, or employed in, or who is one of the managers of, a hospital or mental nursing home, towards people who are receiving treatment for mental disorder as in-patients there, or towards people who are receiving treatment there as out-patients, but the second only applies to neglect or ill-treatment on the premises of which the hospital or home forms part ((s.127(1)). A similar offence may be committed by any individual towards a patient in his guardianship under the Act or "otherwise in his custody or care (whether by virtue of any legal or moral obligation or otherwise)" (s.127(2)). The maximum penalty if these are tried on indictment is imprisonment for two years, or an unlimited fine, or both (s.127(3)). But proceedings cannot be taken without the consent of the Director of Public Prosecutions (s.127(4)).

The other offences relate to falsifying documents. It is an offence wilfully to make a false entry or statement in any document required or authorised to be made for the purposes of the Act, or to use such an entry or statement with intent to deceive knowing it to be false (s.126(4)). It is also an offence to have any such document in your custody or control without lawful authority or excuse, knowing or believing it to be false (s.126(1)), or without lawful authority or excuse to make or have in your custody or control any document which so closely resembles one made under the Act as to be calculated to deceive (s.126(2)). The penalties are the same as for the other offences, and the consent of the Director of Public Prosecutions will usually, but not invariably, be required under section 139(2) (see below).

Local social services authorities can prosecute for offences under section 126 and 127 (s.130), as well as for the offences of helping compulsory patients to escape (s.128; page 231 above), and of obstructing inspection, visiting, interviewing, examining, or any other function authorised under the Act (s.129).

(b) *Section 139: the substantive defence*

Under section 139(1) of the 1983 Act, "No person shall be liable, whether on the ground of want of jurisdiction or on any other ground, to any civil or criminal proceedings to which he would have been liable apart from this section in respect of any act purporting to be done in pursuance of this Act or any regulations or rules made under this Act, or in, or in pursuance of anything done in, the discharge of functions conferred by any other enactment on the authority having jurisdiction under Part VII of this Act, unless the act was done in bad faith or without reasonable care." (Part VII of the Act deals with the functions of the Court of Protection.)

But what is an "act purporting to be done in pursuance of" the mental health legislation? It clearly covers any action where the defendant can point to the particular provision under which he thought he was acting. The earlier versions of this section were designed to protect the people involved in the compulsory commitment procedures and it was in this context that the Percy Commission (1957) recommended that it should be retained. But it was given a much broader interpretation by the House of Lords in *Pountney* v. *Griffiths* [1976] A.C. 314. A nurse at Broadmoor was charged with common assault upon a patient who had been transferred there under what was section 71 of the 1959 Act, after being sentenced to detention during Her Majesty's Pleasure for murder. The incident had taken place at the end of visiting time, when the nurse alleged that he had merely touched the patient's shoulder, whereas the patient alleged that he had been punched. Whatever the truth of the matter, the magistrates must have believed that the nurse had over-stepped his powers, for they convicted him. Nevertheless, the conviction was set aside on the ground that his act was one "purporting to be done in pursuance of" the legislation and that the necessary leave to begin proceedings (see below) had not been obtained.

It was argued in support of the conviction that the section was only concerned with the functions expressly provided for in the legislation, and not with the day-to-day work of hospital staff. But their lordships decided that the Act did provide for the patient's detention and treatment, and that necessarily involved the exercise of control and discipline. Suitable arrangements for visiting by family and friends were obviously part of a patient's treatment. These inevitably involved ushering him back to the ward when visiting time ended. Hence the nurse was entitled to the Act's protection, although obviously, if the necessary leave had been obtained, he might still have been convicted if he had acted in bad faith or without reasonable care.

Whether or not one agrees with this interpretation (see White, 1975; Gostin, 1977; Howlett, 1979 and many others), it has obvious problems. It is easy to tell when a recommending doctor or applicant social worker is purporting to act under the Mental Health Act. Now that the Act also deals with the medical treatment of compulsory patients, it will be easier to tell when the hospital doctors are purporting to do so. But the House of Lords had only the nurse's word that he was trying to usher the patient back to the ward. He might, just possibly, have committed a totally unprovoked act of aggression which had nothing to do with his duties. Section 139 certainly does not apply to that. Drawing the line cannot be easy, particularly on the preliminary application for leave.

Generally, of course, an act purporting to be done in pursuance of the legislation will be committed against the patient himself. But the section applies just as much to proceedings brought by other people, or to prosecutions for acts against other people, for example, if it were alleged that a nurse had assaulted the patient's family while trying to separate them at the end of visiting time. For the most part, however, the section will not apply to acts in respect of informal patients. It might be said that informal admission is an act in pursuance of section 131(1) of the Act (page 5 above). But this is very far-fetched, as the law would be just the same if that section did not exist. Hence, it was held in the Crown Court in the case of *R.* v. *Moonsami Runighian* [1977] Crim. L.R. 361 that leave was not required for proceedings against those who assaulted informal patients. However, the section might apply to any proceedings relating to the treatment of an informal patient under section 57 (above page 209) by psycho-surgery or the surgical implantation of hormones. And of course it also applies to patients under guardianship or in the jurisdiction of the Court of Protection, insofar as the act relates to those powers.

The section does not apply to the offence of ill-treatment or neglect under section 127 of the Act (s.139(3)), but otherwise it applies to both civil and criminal proceedings. The DHSS (1978) suggestion that criminal proceedings should be excluded met with opposition from hospital staff who felt that their job was difficult enough already. However, it does now relate mainly to proceedings against individuals. Actions against the Secretary of State or any health authority are excluded (s.139(4)), although actions against local authorities are not. Thus the actions brought against the Home Secretary, DHSS, and health authorities by Kynaston (page 177 above) and Ashingdane (page 26 above) would no longer be caught. This means that it is very unlikely to arise in any claim for judicial review of administrative action. But in any event it has never been argued that a claim for judicial review amounts to "liability to civil proceedings" for this purpose. Nor has there ever been any suggestion that this includes action for habeas corpus. It is one thing to protect people against punishment or having to pay damages, but quite another thing to deny remedies to quash illegal action. However, it would not be possible to get round the protection given to individuals by suing their employing health authority or the DHSS. Employers' vicarious liability cannot arise if the employee has a good defence (*I.C.I.* v. *Shatwell* [1965] A.C. 656).

But how much protection does section 139(1) in fact give? People who are acting within their lawful powers will not be liable at all and the section gives no protection against negligence. But it does give protection to people who have made an honest and reasonable mistake about the extent of their powers. If the Act is so clear that even a layman could not have misconstrued it, then he will still be liable, but if it could reasonably be thought to mean what he thought it did, then he will be protected (see *Richardson* v. *L.C.C* [1957] 1 W.L.R. 751). This will be particularly useful for staff in their day-to-day dealings with detained patients, where the precise extent of their powers of control and discipline is so difficult to define. Two lawyer members of the Butler Committee on Mentally Abnormal Offenders (1975) thought that the whole section needed reconsideration, but particularly the protection given against mistakes of law. As Gostin (1975) points out, one of the reasons why the powers of hospital staff are so unclear is that they cannot be tested in the courts. No one disputes that they have a difficult and sometimes dangerous job to do. But even in special hospitals, it is hardly more difficult or dangerous than that of the police or prison officers, who have no equivalent protection.

(c) *Section 139: the procedural bar*

The main criticism of the equivalent section in the 1959 Act was against the procedural barrier which it raised. All proceedings required the leave of a High Court judge and this could only be given where he was satisfied that there was "substantial ground" for the contention that the proposed defendant had acted in bad faith or without reasonable care. This meant, in effect, that the plaintiff or prosecution had to have a proven case on paper before they could even begin. For example, Mrs. Carter could not persuade the judge that her version of how she had been admitted to hospital under section 136 of the Act was more credible than the police version, even though if she was right they must have acted outside their powers (*Carter* v. *Metropolitan Police Commissioner* [1975] 1 W.L.R. 507, page 138 above). Mrs. Buxton, on the other hand, was given leave to bring proceedings against the mental welfare officer who had removed her to hospital under his power in the Lunacy Act 1890 (page 73 above), but mainly because he made the mistake of not stating in his affidavit whether he had any grounds for thinking her to be of unsound mind, or what those grounds were (*Buxton* v. *Jayne* [1960] 1 W.L.R. 783). Once the action was tried, it could not be shown that he had acted without reasonable care and the case was lost (see [1962] C.L.Y. 1167).

The leave of a High Court judge is no longer required for criminal proceedings in respect of acts covered by the section. Instead, the prosecution must be brought by or with the consent of the Director of Public Prosecutions. The leave of a High Court judge is still needed for any civil proceedings, even if the amount claimed is within the jurisdiction of the county court (s.139(2)). But neither the Director of Public Prosecutions nor the High Court judge has to be satisfied that there is substantial ground for the contention of bad faith or lack of reasonable care. They are given no guidance at all on the principles to be applied. No doubt the Director of Public Prosecutions will consider all the usual factors, including the substantive protection afforded by section 139(1)). But will the High Court judge want to be satisfied that the proposed plaintiff has a case on the balance of probabilities or simply that he has a prima facie case if what *he* says is right? Mrs. Carter would still fail on the first test, but would succeed on the second.

Even if the second test is adopted, plaintiffs will still be at a disadvantage compared with other litigants. They will have to go first to a High Court judge whatever the size of their claim (see R.S.C. Ord. 32, r.9). They will have to verify the case by affidavit, whereas most other litigants do not have to prove anything until the hearing. They will run the risk that the judge considers their case bad on the facts, whereas other defendants can only escape by alleging that there is no cause of action in law. It is difficult to know whether these things amount to a denial of the plaintiff's right to have his rights determined by a fair and public hearing within a reasonable time by an independent and impartial hearing as required by Article 6(1) of the European Convention. But it could easily be a discrimination against him in the enjoyment of that right, contrary to Article 14. If restricted and unrestricted hospital order patients must enjoy the same rights of application to mental health review tribunals (page 171 above), why should not mental patients and others enjoy the same rights of access to the courts?

In any event, there is no objective justification for the section, even in its new and attenuated form. In *Pountney* v. *Griffiths* (page 341 above), Lord Simon of Glaisdale observed that "patients under the Mental Health Act 1959 may generally be inherently likely to harass those concerned with them by groundless charges and litigation, and may therefore have to suffer modification of the general right of access to the courts. But they are, on the other hand, a class of citizen which experience has shown to be peculiarly vulnerable." But only a minority of patients, even of those compulsorily detained, are suffering from disorders which make it at all likely that they will harass other people with groundless accusations. Rather more of them are suffering from disorders which make it likely that they will not complain at all, even if they have every reason to do so. There is no evidence that the floodgates would open if section 139 were entirely repealed. There is very much more evidence, from a series of reports and investigations, that mental patients are in a peculiarly powerless position which merits, if anything, extra safeguards rather than the removal of those available to everyone else.

(d) *The conduct of litigation*

There is another way in which some mental patients may be denied the usual access to the courts, although in general this is to their benefit rather than their detriment. Actions cannot be brought or defended in the courts by "patients" unless they are represented by a "next friend" (if the patient is the plaintiff, petitioner or applicant) or by a guardian ad litem (if he is the defendant or respondent). A patient for this purpose is someone who is incapable of managing or administering his property and affairs. This is a matter for the court in which the litigation is taking place, and which will also approve the appointment. The Official Solicitor often acts for these patients, but any suitable person may do so. Although the criterion is the same, the patient is not necessarily under the jurisdiction of the Court of Protection (*Re S.(F.G.)* (*mental health patient*) [1973] 1 W.L.R. 178). If he were, that Court would have exclusive control over any litigation in which he was involved. The guardian's role is to conduct the action in the interests of the patient, and he may be able to secure a benefit for the patient which the patient could not secure for himself. Nevertheless, the patient is denied the right to conduct the action in the way that he would have wished to do. For that reason, appointments should be confined to people who are genuinely unable to act for themselves, even with legal representation.

In one respect, however, the law is kind to people who may not be able to recognise their own interests. People under a disability are exempt from the normal rules requiring that actions be brought within a certain time of the cause of action arising. In general, time only begins to run from when the patient ceases to be under a disability (Limitation Act 1980, s.28). People under disability include not only those who are incapable of managing their property and affairs, but also those subject to detention or guardianship under the Mental Health Act, and even those informal in-patients whose treatment immediately follows a period of detention (s.38(2) to (4)). This tenderness contrasts very oddly with the barriers placed in their way by section 139 of the 1983 Act.

Bibliography of References and Further Reading

Aarvold, Sir C. (1972) *Report on the Review of Procedures for the Discharge and Supervision of Psychiatric Patients subject to Special Restrictions* Cmnd. 5191 (London: H.M.S.O.).

Anderson, E.W. (1962) "The Official Concept of Psychopathic Personality in England" in Kranze, H. (ed.), *Psychopathalogie Heute* (Stuttgart: Georg Thieme Verlag).

Anderson, E.W. and Trethowan, W.H. (1979) *Psychiatry* (4th ed., 1979, London: Baillière Tindall).

Armond, A.D. (1982) "Violence in the Semi-secure Ward of a Psychiatric Hospital" 22 *Med. Sci. & L.* 203.

Ashworth, A. and Shapland, J. (1980) "Psychopaths in the Criminal Process" [1980] *Crim. L. Rev.* 628.

Ball, A.G. (1967) "Why is section 29 misused?" [1967] *Brit. Hosp. J. and Social Service Review* 1639.

Barton, R. and Haider, I. (1966) "Unnecessary Compulsory Admissions to Psychiatric Hospital" 6 *Med. Sci. & L.* 147.

Bean, P. (1979) "The Mental Health Act 1959: Rethinking an old problem" 6 *Brit. J. Law & Soc.* 99.

Bean, P. (1980) *Compulsory Admissions to Mental Hospitals* (Chichester: Wiley).

Beardmore, V. (1981) *Conscientious Objectors at Work—Mental Hospital Nurses—A Case Study* (London: Social Audit).

Beebe, M., Ellis, D. and Evans, P. (1973) "Research Report on Statutory Work under the Mental Health Act 1959: Experience in the London Borough of Camden" 5 *The Human Context* 377.

Bell, K. (1969) *Tribunals in the Social Services* (London: Routledge & Kegan Paul).

Bell, K. (1970) "Mental Health Review Tribunals: A Question of Balance" 16 *Case Conference* 385.

Bloch, S. and Chodoff, P. (eds.) (1981) *Psychiatric Ethics* (Oxford: Oxford University Press).

Bluglass, R. (1979) "The Psychiatric Court Report" 19 *Med. Sci. & L.* 121.

Boehringer, G.H. and McCabe, S. (1973) *The Hospital Order in London Magistrates' Courts* (Oxford: Blackwell).

Bott, E. (1971) *Family and Social Network: Roles, Norms and*

External Relationships in Ordinary Urban Families (2nd ed., 1971, London: Tavistock).

Bottoms, A.E. and Brownsword, R. (1982) "The Dangerousness Debate after the Floud Report" 22 *Brit. J. Criminol.* 229.

Bowden, P. (1978) "Men remanded into custody for medical report: the selection for treatment" 133 *Brit. J. Psych.* 320.

Bowden, P. (1978) "Men remanded into custody for medical report: the outcome of the treatment recommendations" 133 *Brit. J. Psych.* 332.

Bowden, P. (1981) "What Happens to Patients Released from Special Hospitals?" 138 *Brit. J. Psych.* 340.

Boynton, Sir J. (1980) *Report of the Review of Rampton Hospital* Cmnd. 8073 (London: H.M.S.O.).

Brandon, D. (1981) *Voices of Experience: Consumer Perspectives of Psychiatric Treatment* (London: MIND).

Brazier, M.R. (1979) "Informed Consent to Surgery" 19 *Med. Sci. & L.* 49.

Brazier, M.R. (1980) "Prison Doctors and their Involuntary Patients" [1982] *Public Law* 282.

British Association of Social Workers (1977) *Mental Health Crisis Services—A New Philosophy* (Birmingham: British Association of Social Workers).

Bute, S. (1979) "Guidelines for Coping with Violence by Clients" 11 *Social Work Today* No. 15.

Butler, Lord (1974) *Interim Report of the Committee on Mentally Abnormal Offenders* Cmnd. 5698 (London: H.M.S.O.).

Butler, Lord (1975) *Report of the Committee on Mentally Abnormal Offenders* Cmnd. 6244 (London: H.M.S.O.).

Carson, D. (1982a) "Detention of the Mentally Disordered" 146 *Loc. Gov. Rev.* 887.

Carson, D. (1982b) "Comment on 'Care in the Community: A Consultative Document on Moving Resources for Care in England' " [1982] *J.S.W.L.* 42.

Carson, D. (1983) "Mental Processes: The Mental Health Act 1983" [1983] *J.S.W.L.* 195.

C.C.E.T.S.W. (1983) Paper 19.1, *Assessment and training of social workers to be considered for approval under the Mental Health (Amendment) Act 1982—Guidance for Local Authorities* (London: Central Council for Education and Training in Social Work).

C.C.E.T.S.W. (1983) Paper 19.2, *Regulations for the assessment of social workers who are to be considered for approval under mental health legislation* (London: Central Council for Education and Training in Social Work).

Chief Medical Officer (1966) *Annual Report of the Chief Medical Officer—on the State of the Public Health* (London: H.M.S.O.).

Clare, A.W. (1978a) "In Defence of Compulsory Psychiatric Intervention" [1978] 1 *Lancet* 1197.

Clare, A.W. (1978b) "Therapeutic and Ethical Aspects of Electro-Convulsive Therapy: A British Perspective" 1 *Int. J. Law & Psych.* 237.

Clare, A.W. (1980) *Psychiatry in Dissent: Controversial Issues in Thought and Practice* (2nd ed., London: Tavistock).

Clarke, A. (1981) "Sickness and the Law of Unfair Dismissal" [1981] *J.S.W.L.* 215.

Clarke, C.S.C. (1979) "The COHSE report on the management of violent patients: Counsel's opinion" *Bulletin of the Royal College of Psychiatrists*, February 21, 1979.

Clerk, J.F. and Lindsell, W.H.B. (1982) *Torts* (15th ed., ed. by R.W.M. Dias, London: Sweet and Maxwell).

Cocozza, J.J. and Steadman, H.L. (1976) "The Failure of Psychiatric Predictions of Dangerousness: Clear and Convincing Evidence" 29 *Rutgers Law Rev.* 1084.

Cohen, D. (1981) *Broadmoor* (London: Psychology News Press).

COHSE (Confederation of Health Service Employers) (1977) *The Management of Violent or Potentially Violent Patients* (Banstead: COHSE).

Committee on Mental Health Review Tribunal Procedures (1978) *The Procedures of the Mental Health Review Tribunals: A Discussion Paper by the Committee on Mental Health Review Tribunal Procedures* (London: DHSS).

Compton, H.F. and Whiteman, R.T. (1976) *Receivership under the Mental Health Act 1959* (5th ed., London: Oyez).

Cooke, J.A. (1969) "Mental Health Review Tribunals" 113 *Sol. Jo.* 843.

Cooper, D.G. (1967) *Psychiatry and Anti-Psychiatry* (London: Tavistock).

Council of Europe (1950) *Convention for the Protection of Human Rights and Fundamental Freedoms* (Strasbourg: Council of Europe).

Court of Protection, P.N.I, *Mental Patients Possessed of Property* (London: Court of Protection).

Craft, A. and M. (1981) "Sexuality and Mental Handicap: A Review" 139 *Brit. J. Psych.* 494.

Criminal Law Revision Committee (1980a), 14th Report, *Offences against the Person* Cmnd. 7844 (London: H.M.S.O.).

Criminal Law Revision Committee (1980b) *Working Paper on Sexual Offences* (London: H.M.S.O.).

Curran, D., Partridge, M.A. and Storey, P.B. (1980) *Psychological Medicine: An Introduction to Psychiatry* (9th ed., Edinburgh: Churchill, Livingstone).

Curran, W.J. and Harding, T.W. (1978). *The law and mental health: harmonizing objectives: a comparative survey of existing legislation together with guidelines for its assessment and alternative approaches to its improvement* (Geneva: W.H.O.).

Davies, Sir M. (1973) *Report of the Committee on Hospital Complaints Procedure* (London: H.M.S.O.).

Dawson, H. (1972) "Reasons for Compulsory Admission" in Wing, J.K. and Hailey, A.M. (eds.) *Evaluating a Community Psychiatric Service: The Camberwell Register, 1964–1971* (London: Oxford University Press).

Dell, S. (1980) "The Transfer of Special Hospital Patients to the N.H.S." 136 *Brit. J. Psych.* 222.

Dell, S. (1982) "Diminished Responsibility Reconsidered" [1982] *Crim. L. Rev.* 809.

Dell, S. and Smith, A. (1983) "Changes in the Sentencing of Diminished Responsibility Homicides" 142 *Brit. J. Psych.* 20.

Department of Education and Science (1980) *Special Needs in Education* Cmnd. 7996 (London: H.M.S.O.).

DHSS (1971) *Better Services for the Mentally Handicapped* Cmnd. 4683 (London: H.M.S.O.).

DHSS (1972) *Census of Mentally Handicapped Patients in Hospital in England and Wales at the end of 1970* Statistical and Research Report Series No. 3 (London: H.M.S.O.).

DHSS (1975) *Censuses of: A. Patients in Mental Illness Hospitals and Units in England and Wales at the end of 1971, B. Mental Illness Day Patients in England and Wales at April 1972* Statistical and Research Report Series No. 10 (London: H.M.S.O.).

DHSS (1975) *Better Services for the Mentally Ill* Cmnd. 6233 (London: H.M.S.O.).

DHSS (1976) *A Review of the Mental Health Act 1959* (London: H.M.S.O.).

DHSS (1980) *Guidelines on the Seclusion of Patients at Broadmoor Special Hospital* Hansard, House of Commons, vol. 977 Written Answers, cols. 257–259 (London: H.M.S.O.).

DHSS (1981a) *Care in the Community: A Consultative Document on Moving Resources for Care in England* (London: DHSS).

DHSS (1981b) *Review of Leave Arrangements for Special Hospital Patients* (London: DHSS).

DHSS (1983) *In-patient Statistics from the Mental Health Enquiry for England 1978* Statistical and Research Report Series No. 24 (London: H.M.S.O.).

DHSS Circular HC(76)11, *The Management of Violent or Potentially Violent, Hospital Patients* (London: DHSS).

DHSS Circular HC(81)5, *Health Services Management: Health Service Complaints Procedure* (London: DHSS).

DHSS Circular HC(81)8, LAC(81)4, *Health Service Management: Registration and Inspection of Private Nursing Homes and Mental Nursing Homes (Including Hospitals)* (London: DHSS).

DHSS Circular HC(83)6, LAC(83)5, *Health Service Development: Care in the Community and Joint Finance* (London: DHSS).

DHSS Circular HM(66)15, *Methods of Dealing with Complaints by Patients* (London: DHSS).

DHSS Circular HSC(15)18 (1974), *The Mental Health Act 1959: Approval of Medical Practitioners under Section 28(2) and the Exercise by Officers of Functions under the Act* (London: DHSS).

DHSS, Local Authority Circular 13/74, *Section 195 of the Local Government Act 1972: Sections 21 and 29 of the National Assistance Act 1948: Replacement of Schemes by Arrangements* (London: DHSS).

DHSS, Local Authority Circular 19/74, *Services for the Mentally Disordered provided under Section 12 of the Health Services and Public Health Act 1968: Replacement of Schemes by Arrangements in Consequence of Section 195 of the Local Government Act 1972* (London: DHSS).

DHSS, Local Authority Circular LAC(83)7, *Mental Health*

(Amendment) Act 1982: Mental Health Act 1983: Approved Social Workers (London: DHSS).

DHSS letter (1981) *Patients' Money: Accumulation of Balances in Long Stay Hospitals* January 29, 1981 (London: DHSS).

DHSS, Home Office, Welsh Office, Lord Chancellor's Department (1978) *Review of the Mental Health Act 1959* Cmnd. 7320 (London: H.M.S.O.).

DHSS, Home Office, Welsh Office, Lord Chancellor's Department (1981) *Reform of Mental Health Legislation* Cmnd. 8405 (London: H.M.S.O.).

DHSS, Scottish Home and Health Department, Welsh Office (1983) *Report on Operation of Procedure for Independent Review of Complaints involving the Clinical Judgment of Hospital Doctors and Dentists* (London: DHSS).

Donovan, W.M. and O'Brien, K.P. (1981) "Psychiatric Court Reports—Too Many or Too Few?" 21 *Med. Sci. and L.* 153.

Durrant, P. (1979) "Theory and practice in a mental health admission" 10 *Social Work Today* No. 42.

Emery, D. (1961) *Report of the Working Party on the Special Hospitals* (London: H.M.S.O.).

Ennis, B.J. (1972) *Prisoners of Psychiatry: Mental Patients, Psychiatrists and the Law* (New York: Harcourt, Brace Jovanovich).

Ennis, B.J. and Emery, R.D. (1978) *The Rights of Mental Patients* (New York: Avon).

Ennis, B.J. and Litwack, T.R. (1974) "Psychiatry and the Presumption of Expertise: Flipping Coins in the Courtroom" 62 *Calif. L. Rev.* 693.

Faulk, M. (1979) "Mentally Disordered Offenders in an Interim Regional Medium Secure Unit" [1979] *Crim. L. Rev.* 686.

Fennell, P.W.H. (1977) "The Mental Health Review Tribunal: A Question of Imbalance" 4 *Brit. J. Law & Soc.* 186.

Fennell, P.W.H. (1979) *Justice, Discretion and the Therapeutic State* M. Phil. Thesis, University of Kent at Canterbury.

Finch, J. (1979) "Legislating the Mental Norms" 42 *Mod. L. Rev.* 438.

Fingarette, H. (1972) *The Meaning of Criminal Insanity* (London: University of California Press).

Fisher, Sir H.A.P. (1977) *Report of an Inquiry into circumstances leading to the trial of three persons on charges arising out of the death of Maxwell Confait and the fire at 27 Doggett Road, London SE6*, Session 1977–78, H.C. 90 (London: H.M.S.O.).

Flew, A.G.N. (1973) *Crime or Disease?* (London: Macmillan).

Floud, J. and Young, W. (1981) *Dangerousness and Criminal Justice* (London: Heinemann).

Fottrell, E. (1980) "A Study of Violent Behaviour Among Patients in Psychiatric Hospitals" 136 *Brit. J. Psych.* 216.

Fottrell, E., Bewley, T. and Squizzoni, M. (1978) "A Study of Aggressive and Violent Behaviour among a group of Psychiatric In-Patients" 18 *Med. Sci. & L.* 66.

Foucault, M. (1967) *Madness and Civilisation: A History of Insanity in the Age of Reason* (trs. R. Howard) (London: Tavistock).

Foulkes, D. (1970) "Consent to Medical Treatment" 120 *New L. J.* 194.

Freeman, M.D.A. (1980) "The Rights of Children in the International Year of the Child" 33 *Current Legal Problems* 1.

Gibbens, T., Soothill, W. and Pope, P. (1977) *Medical Remands in Criminal Court* (London: Oxford University Press).

Glancy, J. (1974) *Revised Report of the Working-Party on Security in NHS Psychiatric Hospitals* (London: DHSS).

Goffman, E. (1961) *Asylums: Essays on the Social Situation of Mental Patients and Other Inmates* (New York: Doubleday).

Goffman, E. (1968) *Stigma: Notes on the Management of Spoiled Identity* (Harmondsworth: Penguin).

Goldstein, J. (1975) "For Harold Lasswell: Some Reflections on Human Dignity, Entrapment, Informed Consent and the Plea Bargain" 84 *Yale L. J.* 683.

Gostin, L.O. (1975) *A Human Condition: The Mental Health Act from 1959 to 1975: Observations, analysis and proposals for reform* (Vol. 1) (London: MIND).

Gostin, L.O. (1977) *A Human Condition: The law relating to mentally abnormal offenders: Observations, analysis and proposals for reform* (Vol. 2) (London: MIND).

Gostin, L.O. (1978) *The Great Debate: MIND's comments on the White Paper on the Review of the Mental Health Act 1959* (London: MIND).

Gostin, L.O. (1979) "The Merger of Incompetency and Certification: The Illustration of Unauthorised Medical Contact in the Psychiatric Context" 2 *Int. J. Law & Psych.* 127.

Gostin, L.O. (1982) "Psychosurgery: A Hazardous and Unestablished Treatment? A Case for the Importation of American Legal Safeguards to Great Britain" [1982] *J.S.W.L.* 83.

Gostin, L.O. (1982) "Human Rights, Judicial Review and the Mentally Disordered Offender" [1982] *Crim. L. Rev.* 779.

Gostin, L.O. (1983a) "The ideology of entitlement: the application of contemporary legal approaches to psychiatry" in Bean, P. (ed.) *Mental Illness: Changes and Trends* (Chichester: Wiley).

Gostin, L.O. (1983b) *The Court of Protection—a legal and policy analysis of the guardianship of the estate* (London: MIND).

Gostin, L.O. and Rassaby, E. (1980) *Representing the Mentally Ill and Mentally Handicapped* (Sunbury, Middlesex: Quartermaine House (for National Association for Mental Health and Legal Action Group)).

Greenland, C. (1970) *Mental Illness and Civil Liberty* Occasional Papers in Social Administration, No. 38 (London: Bell).

Gove, W.R. and Fain, T. (1977) "A Comparison of Voluntary and Committed Psychiatric Patients" 34 *Arch. Gen. Psychiatry* 699.

Grey, M. (1979) "Forcing Old People to Leave Their Homes: The Principle" [1979] *Community Care* March 8, p.19.

Grünhüt, M. (1963) *Probation and Mental Treatment* (London: Tavistock).

Gudjohnson, G.H. and Gunn, J. (1982) "The Competence and Reliability of a Witness in a Criminal Court: A Case Report" 141 *Brit. J. Psych.* 624.

Gunn, J. (1979) "The Law and the Mentally Abnormal Offender in England and Wales" 2 *Int. J. Law and Psych.* 199.

Guze, S., Goodwin, D. and Crane, J. (1969) "Criminality and Psychiatric Disorder" 20 *Archives of General Psychiatry* 583.

Hamilton, J.R. (1981) "Diminished Responsibility" 138 *Brit. J. Psych.* 434.

Hannon, V. (1982) "The Education Act 1981: New Rights and Duties in Special Education" [1982] *J.S.W.L.* 275.

Harlow, C. (1974) "Self Defence: Public Right or Private Privilege" [1974] *Crim. L. Rev.* 528.

Harvey, C. (1979) "Forcing Old People to Leave Their Homes: The Practice" [1979] *Community Care*, March 8, p.20.

Hepworth, D. (1982) "The Influence of the Concept of 'Danger' on the Assessment of 'Danger to Self or Others' " 22 *Med. Sci. and L.* 245.

Heywood, N.A. and Massey, A. (1978) *Court of Protection Practice* (10th ed., by Taylor, E.R.) 2nd Supplement to 10th Edn. (1982) (London: Stevens).

Higgins, J. (1981) "Four years' experience of an interim secure unit" 282 *Brit. Med. J.* 889.

Hoenig, J. (1983) "The Concept of Schizophrenia: Kraepelin–Bleuler–Schneider" 142 *Brit. J. Psych.* 547.

Hoggett, B. (1984) "Legal Aspects of Secure Provision" in Gostin, L.O. (ed.) *A Review of Secure Provision for Mentally Ill and Handicapped People in England and Wales* (London: Tavistock, forthcoming).

Home Office (1978) *Judges' Rules and Administrative Directions to the Police* Home Office Circular No. 89/1978 (London: H.M.S.O.).

Home Office (1982) *Statistics of Mentally Disordered Offenders made subject to Restrictions, England and Wales, 1981* Statistical Bulletin 19/82 (London: Home Office).

Home Office (1983) *Draft Codes of Practice for the Treatment, Questioning and Identification of Persons Suspected of Crime: Revised draft* (London: Home Office).

Home Office (1983) *Criminal Statistics England and Wales 1982* Cmnd. 9048 (London: H.M.S.O.).

Home Office (1983) *Report on the Work of the Prison Department 1982* Cmnd. 9057 (London: H.M.S.O.).

Home Office Circular 26/83, *Prosecution Policy* together with memorandum *Criteria for Prosecution* (London: Home Office).

Howlett, M.V. (1979) "Mental Patients and the Right to Litigate" [1978–79] *J.S.W.L.* 337.

Hudson, B. (1982) *Social Work with Psychiatric Patients* (London: Macmillan).

Hunt, D.G. and Reed, M.E. (1970) "Statutory Wills for Mentally Disordered Persons" 34 *Conveyancer* 150.

Hunt, L. (1978) "Conflict, Pressure and the Psychiatric Emergency" 10 *Social Work Today* No. 42.

Ingleby, D. (ed.) (1981) *Critical Psychiatry: The Politics of Mental Health* (Harmondsworth: Penguin).

Ingram, I.M., Timbury, G.C. and Mowbray, R.M. (1981) *Notes on Psychiatry* (5th ed., Edinburgh: Churchill Livingstone).

Jacob, J. (1976) "The Right of the Mental Patient to his Psychosis" 39 *Med. L. Rev.* 17.

Jay, P. (1979) *Report of the Committee of Enquiry into Mental Handicap Nursing and Care* Cmnd. 7468 (London: H.M.S.O.).

Jones, K. (1972) *A History of the Mental Health Services* (London: Routledge & Kegan Paul).

Jones, K. (1980) "The Limitations of the Legal Approach to Mental Health" 3 *Int. J. Law & Psych.* 1.

Jones, K. (1982) "Scull's Dilemma" 141 *Brit. J. Psych.* 221.

Jordan, B. (1981) *Review* of Bean (1980), [1981] *J.S.W.L.* 383.

Kelleher, M.J. and Copeland, J.R.M. (1972) "Compulsory Psychiatric Admission by the Police: A Study of the Use of Section 136" 12 *Med. Sci. & L.* 220.

Kenny, A. (1983) "The Expert in Court" 99 *L.Q.R.* 197.

Kenny, D.J. (1981) *The Law relating to Mentally Disordered Persons* M. Phil. Thesis, University of Nottingham.

Kent, D.A. (1972) "Police Admissions to Two English Mental Hospitals" 48 *Acta Psychiatrica Scandinavica* 78.

Kidd, H.B. (1963) "Misuse of Section 29" [1963] 1 *Lancet* 997.

King, M. (ed.) (1981) *Childhood, Welfare and Justice* (London: Batsford).

Kittrie, N.N. (1971) *The Right to be Different* (Baltimore: Johns Hopkins Press).

Kloss, D.M. (1965) "Consent to Medical Treatment" 5 *Med. Sci. & L.* 89.

Laing, R.D. (1959) *The Divided Self* (London: Tavistock).

Laing, R.D. and Esterson, A. (1971) *Sanity, Madness and the Family* (2nd ed., London: Tavistock).

Lanham, D. (1974) "Arresting the Insane" [1974] *Crim. L. Rev.* 515.

Law Commission (1976) Working Paper No. 69 *The Incapacitated Principal* (London: H.M.S.O.).

Law Commission (1980) Working Paper No. 76 *Time Restrictions on Presentation of Divorce and Nullity Petitions* (London: H.M.S.O.).

Law Commission (1982) *Time Restrictions on Presentation of Divorce and Nullity Petitions* Law Com. No. 116, HC 513 (London: H.M.S.O.).

Law Commission (1983) *The Incapacitated Principal* Law Com. No. 122, Cmnd. 8977 (London: H.M.S.O.).

Lawson, A.R. Le Vay (1966) *The Recognition of Mental Illness in London: A Study of the Social Processes determining Compulsory Admission to an Observation Unit in a London Hospital* Maudsley Monograph No. 15 (London: Oxford University Press).

Leigh, D., Pare, C.M.B. and Marks, J. (1982) *Concise Encyclopedia of Psychiatry* (London: M.T.P. Press).

Le Mesurier, A.A. (1949) "The Duly Authorised Officer" (1947–1950) 1 *Brit. J. Psych. Social Work* 45.

Lewis, P. (1980) *Psychiatric Probation Orders: Roles and Expectations of Probation Officers and Psychiatrists* (Cambridge: University of Cambridge Institute of Criminology).

Loder, M. (1981) *The Mind Benders: The Use of Drugs in Psychiatry* (London: MIND).

MacDermott, J. (1981) *Report of the Northern Ireland Review Committee on Mental Health Legislation* (Belfast: H.M.S.O.).

MacMillan, H.P. (1926) *Report of the Royal Commission on Lunacy and Mental Disorders 1924–1926* Cmd. 2700 (London: H.M.S.O.).

Masterson, G., Hewlands, C.A. and Timbury, C. (1980) "The Validity of Emergency Recommendations for Compulsory Psychiatric Care" 25 *Scot. Med. J.* 299.

Meacher, M. (ed.) (1979) *New Methods of Mental Health Care* (Oxford: Pergamon).

Mental Welfare Commission for Scotland (1970) *No Folks of their Own* (Edinburgh: H.M.S.O.).

Mental Welfare Commission for Scotland (1972) *A Duty to Care* (Edinburgh: H.M.S.O.).

Mental Welfare Commission for Scotland (1975) *No Place to Go* (Edinburgh: H.M.S.O.).

Mental Welfare Commission for Scotland (1981) *Does the patient come first? An account of the work of the Commission between 1975 and 1980* (Edinburgh: H.M.S.O.).

Merrison, Sir A. (1979) *Report of the Royal Commission on the National Health Service* Cmnd. 7615 (London: H.M.S.O.).

Milner, N. (1981) "Models of Rationality and Mental Health Rights" 4 *Int. J. Law & Psych.* 35.

Mittler, P.J. (1979) *People not Patients: Problems and Policies in Mental Handicap* (London: Methven).

Monahan, J. (1977) "John Stuart Mill on the Liberty of the

Mentally Ill: A Historical Note" 134 *American J. of Psych.* 1428.

Morris, G.H. (1978) *The Insanity Defense: A Blueprint for Legislative Reform* (Farnborough: Lexington).

Morris, P. (1969) *Put Away: a Sociological Study of Institutions for the Mentally Retarded* (London: Routledge & Kegan Paul).

Mill, J.S. (1859) *On Liberty* (reprinted as *Three Essays: On Liberty, Representative Government, The Subjection of Women*) (London: Oxford University Press (1975)).

Miller, D.W. (1975) "The Mentally Disordered Patient in Hospital" 125 *New L.J.* 884.

Muchlinski, P.T. (1980) "Mental Patients' Rights and the European Human Rights Convention" 5 *Human Rights Rev.* 90.

N.C.C.L. (1973) *The Rights of the Mentally Abnormal Offender: The National Council for Civil Liberties' Evidence to the Butler Committee* (London: N.C.C.L.).

Noble, P. (1981) "Mental Health Services and Legislation. A Historical Review" 21 *Med. Sci & L.* 16.

Norman, A.J. (1980) *Rights and Risk: A Discussion Document on Civil Liberty in Old Age* (London: National Corporation for the Care of Old People).

Olsen, M. (ed.) (1976) *Differential Approaches in Social Work with the Mentally Disordered* (Birmingham: British Association of Social Workers).

Oram, E.V. (1972) "The Case for More Informal Admissions" 2(19) *Social Work Today* 21.

Orr, H.H. (1978) "The Imprisonment of the Mentally Disordered Offender" 133 *Brit. J. Psych.* 191.

Parker, E. and Tennent, G. (1979) "The 1959 Mental Health Act and Mentally Abnormal Offenders: A Comparative Study" 19 *Med. Sci. & L.* 29.

Payne, C., McCabe, S. and Walker, N.D. (1974) "Predicting Offender Patients' Reconvictions" 125 *Brit. J. Psych.* 60.

Peay, J. (1981) "Mental Health Review Tribunals: just or efficacious safeguards?" 5 *Law and Human Behaviour* 161.

Peay, J. (1982) "Mental Health Review Tribunals and the Mental Health (Amendment) Act" [1982] *Crim. L. Rev.* 794.

Percy, Lord (1957) *Report of the Royal Commission on the Law relating to Mental Illness and Mental Deficiency 1954–1957* Cmd. 169 (London: H.M.S.O.).

Prichard, J.C. (1835) *Treatise on Insanity and other Disorders affecting the Mind.*

Prins, H.A. (1975) "A Danger to Themselves and Others (Social Workers and Potentially Dangerous Clients)" 5 *Brit. J. Social Work* 297.

Prins, H.A. (1980) *Offenders, Deviants or Patients? An Introduction to the Study of Socio-Forensic Problems* (London: Tavistock).

Prins, H.A. (1981) "Dangerous People or Dangerous Situations? Some Implications for Assessment and Management" 21 *Med. Sci. & L.* 125.

Radnor, Lord (1908) *Report of the Royal Commission on the Care and Control of the Feeble-Minded 1904–1908* Cd. 4202 (London: H.M.S.O.).

Robb, E. (1967) *Sans Everything—A Case to Answer* (presented on behalf of AEGIS) (London: Nelson).

Robertson, G. (1981) "Informed Consent to Medical Treatment" 97 *L.Q.R.* 102.

Rollin, H.R. (1969) *The Mentally Abnormal Offender and the Law* (Oxford: Pergamon).

Rosenhan, D.C. (1973) "On Being Sane in Insane Places" 179 *Science* 250.

Roy, R.G. (1966) "A Brief Study of Night Calls" 13 *Case Conference* 97.

Roy, R.G. (1968) "Problems of Compulsory Admissions" [1968] 1 *Lancet* 83.

Royal College of Psychiatrists (1977) "Memorandum on the use of Electro-Convulsive Therapy" 131 *Brit. J. Psych.* 261.

Royal College of Psychiatrists (1980) *Isolation of Patients in Protected Rooms during Psychiatric Treatment* (Approved by Council, June).

Royal College of Psychiatrists (1981) *Mental Health Commissions—The Recommendations of the Royal College of Psychiatrists* (Approved by Council, June 16).

Royal College of Psychiatrists, Royal College of Nursing, British Psychological Society (1980) *Behaviour Modification: Report of a Joint Working Party to Formulate Ethical Guidelines for the Conduct of Programmes of Behaviour Modification in the National Health Service: A Consultative Document with Suggested Guidelines* (London: H.M.S.O.).

Russell-Davies, D. (1979) "Compulsion under Part IV of the Mental Health Act 1959" 2 *Int. J. Law & Psych.* 169.

Ryan, J. (1980) *The Politics of Mental Handicap* (Harmondsworth: Penguin).

Samuels, A. (1983) "Can a Minor (Under 16) Consent to a Medical Operation" 13 *Family Law* 30.

Scheff, T.J. (ed.) (1975) *Labelling Madness* (Englewood Cliffs M.J.: Prentice Hall).

Scull, A.T. (1979) *Museums of Madness: The Social Organisation of Insanity in Nineteenth Century England* (London: Allen Lane).

Scull, A.T. (ed.) (1981) *Madhouses, Mad-doctors and Madmen: The Social History of Psychiatry in the Victorian Era* (London: Athlons Press).

Sedgwick, P. (1982) *Psychopolitics* (London: Pluto Press).

Seebohm, F. (1968) *Report of the Committee on Local Authority and Allied Personal Social Services* Cmnd. 3703 (London: H.M.S.O.).

Sharpe, R.J. (1976) *The Law of Habeas Corpus* (London: Oxford University Press).

Sims, A.C.P. and Symonds, R.L. (1975) "Psychiatric Referrals from the Police" 127 *Brit. J. Psych.* 171.

Skegg, P.D.G. (1973) "Consent to Medical Procedures on Minors" 36 *M.L.R.* 370.

Skegg, P.D.G. (1974) "A Justification for Medical Procedures Performed without Consent" 90 *L.Q.R.* 512.

Soothill, K.L., Harding, T.W., Adserballe, H., Bernheim, J., Erne, S., Mogdi, S., Panpreecha, C. and Reinhold, F. (1981) "Compulsory Admissions to Mental Hospitals in Six Countries" 4 *Int. J. Law & Psych.* 327.

Soothill, K.L., Way, C.K. and Gibbens, T.C.M. (1980) "Subsequent Dangerousness among Compulsory Hospital Patients" 20 *Brit. J. Criminol.* 289.

Speaker's Conference on Electoral Law (1968) *Final Report of the Conference on Electoral Law: Letter dated 9th February 1968 from Mr. Speaker to the Prime Minister* Cmnd. 3550 (London: H.M.S.O.).

Speaker's Conference on Electoral Law (1973) *Letter dated 25th October 1973 from Mr. Speaker to the Prime Minister* Cmnd. 5469 (London: H.M.S.O.).

Spencer, S. (1977) "The Right of a Mental Patient to his Psychosis" 40 *Mod. L. Rev.* 748.

Steadman, H.J. (1979) "Attempting to Protect Patients' Rights under a Medical Model" 2 *Int. J. Law & Psych.* 185.

Steadman, H.J. and Cocozza, J.J. (1974) *Careers of the Criminally Insane: Excessive Social Control of Deviance* (Lexington, Neb.: D.C. Heath).

Stephen, Sir J.F. (1950) *Digest of the Criminal Law* (9th ed. by Sturge, J.F.) (1st ed. 1877) London: Sweet and Maxwell).

Szasz, T.S. (1961) *The Myth of Mental Illness: Foundations of a Theory of Personal Conduct* (New York: Harper & Row).

Szasz, T.S. (1963) *Law, Liberty and Psychiatry* (New York: Macmillan).

Szasz, T.S. (1970) *Ideology and Insanity: Essays on the Psychiatric Dehumanisation of Man* (New York: Doubleday).

Tennent, G. and Treves-Brown, C. (1980) "A Survey of Psychiatric Hospital Reports on Potential Special Hospital Patients" 20 *Med. Sci. & L.* 104.

Thomas, D.A. (1979) *Principles of Sentencing* (2nd ed., London: Heinemann).

Trick, K.L.K. and Tennant, J.G. (1982) *Forensic Psychiatry: An Introductory Text* (London: Pitman).

United Nations (1971) *Declaration on the Rights of Mentally Retarded Persons* General Assembly Resolution 2865 (XXVI) of December 20, 1971.

Venables, H.D.S. (1975) *A Guide to the Law affecting Mental Patients* (London: Butterworths).

Walker, N.D. (1973) *Crime and Insanity in England: Vol. 1: The Historical Perspective* (Edinburgh: Edinburgh University Press).

Walker, N.D. (1978) "Dangerous People" 1 *Int. J. Law & Psych.* 37.

Walker, N.D. (1981) "Butler v. The C.L.R.C. and Others" [1981] *Crim. L. Rev.* 596.

Walker, N.D. and McCabe, S. (1973) *Crime and Insanity in England: Vol. 2: New Solutions and New Problems* (Edinburgh: Edinburgh University Press).

Walshe-Brennan, K.S. (1978) "Classification Inconsistencies in Defining the Criminally Mentally Abnormal" 18 *Med. Sci. & L.* 283.

Warnock, M. (1978) *Report of the Committee of Enquiry into the*

Education of Handicapped Children and Young People Cmnd. 7212 (London: H.M.S.O.).

Webb, D. (1976) "Wise after the Event: Some Comments on 'A Danger to Themselves and Others' " 6 *Brit. J. Social Work* 91.

Weisstub, D.N. (ed.) *Law and Psychiatry: Proceedings of an International Symposium Held at the Clarke Institute of Psychiatry, Toronto, Canada, February 1977* (Oxford: Pergamon).

White, R.J. (1975) "Mental Patients' Rights to Institute Criminal Proceedings" 119 *Sol. Jo.* 788.

Whitehead, J.A. and Ahmad, M. (1970) "Chance, Mental Illness and Crime" [1970] 1 *Lancet* 135.

Williams, G.L. (1983) *Textbook of Criminal Law* (2nd ed., London: Stevens).

Willis, J. (1980) *Lecture Notes on Psychiatry* (5th ed., Oxford: Blackwell).

Wing, J.K. (1978) *Reasoning about Madness* (Oxford: Oxford University Press).

Wing, J.K. and Olsen, R. (1979) *Community Care for the Mentally Disabled* (London: Oxford University Press).

Wood, Sir J. (1982) "The Impact of Legal Modes of Thought upon the Practice of Psychiatry" 140 *Brit. J. Psych.* 551.

Woolf, G.P. (1966) " 'The Back Door' (Discharge by Operation of the Law after Twenty-eight Days' Absence)" 6 *Brit. J. Criminol.* 59.

Wootton, B. (assisted by Seal, V.G. and Chambers, R.) (1959) *Social Science and Social Pathology* (London: Allen and Unwin).

Wootton, B. (1960) "Diminished Responsibility—A Layman's View" 76 *L.Q.R.* 224.

Wootton, B. (1980) "Psychiatry, Ethics and the Criminal Law" 136 *Brit. J. Psych.* 525.

World Health Organisation (1978) *Mental Disorders: Glossary and Guide to their Classification in Accordance with the Ninth Revision of the International Classification of Diseases* (Geneva: W.H.O.).

Younghusband, E.L. (1959) *Report of the Working Party on Social Workers in the Local Authority Health and Welfare Services* (London: H.M.S.O.).

Index